Four Paws
Five Directions

A GUIDE TO CHINESE MEDICINE
FOR CATS AND DOGS

Cheryl Schwartz, DVM

CELESTIAL ARTS • *Berkeley, California*

Dedication

This book is dedicated to Cheer Barbour and all the animals who have shown me humor,
humility, integrity and fortitude. It is also a salute to all the healers
and veterinarians before me who have used Traditional Chinese Medicine
to better animals' lives.

Acknowledgments

I wish to thank Drs. Alyce Tarcher, Sally Savitz, Lana Sandahl and Paul Pitchford for
their support and assistance in preparing the text, as well as Nancy O'Brien
and Judith Kaufman for their wonderful photos and illustrations.
A special thanks goes to my editors, Veronica and Victoria Randall, for their
patience, and to my friend John Gruntfest for keeping the office going
while I've been working on this, forever.

Celestial Arts Publishing
P.O. Box 7123
Berkeley, California 94707
www.tenspeed.com

Distributed in Australia by Simon and Schuster Australia, in Canada by Ten speed Press Canada, in New Zealand by Southern Publishers Group, in South Africa by Real Books, and in the United Kingdom and Europe by Airlift Book Company

Cover design: Greene Design
Interior design and typesetting: Star Type, Berkeley

Library of Congress Cataloging-in-Publication Data

Schwartz, Cheryl (Cheryl M.)
    Four paws, five directions : a guide to Chinese medicine for cats
and dogs / Cheryl Schwartz.
        p.   cm.
    Includes bibliographical references and index.
    ISBN-13: 978-0-89087-790-6
    ISBN-10: 0-89087-790-4
    1. Dogs—Diseases.   2. Cats—Diseases.   3. Alternative veterinary
medicine.   4. Medicine, Chinese.   I. Title.
SF991.S323   1996
636.7 0890951—dc20   96-15931
                                                              CIP

First Printing, 1996
Printed in the United States of America

9 10 11 12 13 / 09 08 07 06 05

Table of Contents

List of Plates

Meridians

Lungs. . . . . a
Large Intestine. . . . . b
Stomach. c
Spleen/Pancreas. . . . . d
Heart . . . . e
Small Intestine . . . . f
Urinary Bladder. . . . . g
Kidney. . . . . h
Pericardium i
Triple Heater . . . . j
Gall Bladder . . . . k
Liver l
Conception Vessel . . . . m
Governing Vessel . . . . m

Acupressure Points

Eyes . . . . n
Cold/Sinus . . . . n, o
Ears . . . . o, p
Teeth & Gums . . . . p
Lungs. p, q
Heart . . . . q
Liver & Gall Bladder . . . . q, r
Spleen/Pancreas/Stomach . . . . r, s, t
Kidneys & Urinary Bladder. . . . . t, u
Urinary Bladder. . . . . u
Large Intestine. . . . . u, v
Bones & Muscles . . . . v, w
Skin x
Immune System & Glands x

Introduction

WELCOME TO THE WORLD OF TRADITIONAL CHINESE MEDICINE. Those of you who are trained in, or who use Western medicine, please leave your shoes at the door and enter a different, though logical, way of thinking. In Traditional Chinese Medicine you will use your powers of sight, smell, hearing and touch to their utmost advantage in order to aid your four-legged friend or client.

This system relies on thousands of years of experience, hundreds of thousands of medical practitioners and millions of patients. Traditional Chinese Medicine (TCM), includes **acupuncture, herbal medicine, acupressure, food therapies, meditation** and **exercises.** We will look at all of these modalities except meditation and exercises, as these may be hard to teach your animal friend.

Acupuncture was used on animals as long as 3,500 years ago, when, legend has it, an elephant was treated for a stomach disorder similar to bloating. Since then, acupuncture and other forms of TCM have been used to treat a variety of problems, including pain, arthritis, heart, lung, kidney, digestive, hormonal, allergic, reproductive and mental illness. In fact, TCM can be used to treat almost any imbalance except those requiring surgery. Why, you might ask, is it important to know about these ancient healing arts, when we have such a technologically advanced system of Western medicine in this country? For the simple reason that Western medicine can deal effectively with acute, traumatic illness, but is limited in its approach to the chronic problems.

A more rounded and holistic approach, TCM recognizes patterns of disease and imbalances that Western medicine does not. If an imbalance can be recognized, it can also be treated. Additionally, because Traditional Chinese Medicine encompasses a broad framework of interactions, it can pick up an imbalance *before* it becomes a disease. Thus, it can be used as a *preventative therapy* to help keep an individual healthy.

When I graduated from veterinary school in 1978, I knew I would need a great deal of experience in order to utilize the vast amount of information I had studied. After two years of practice, however, I found that most of my treatments consisted of prescribing *anti*biotics and *anti*-inflammatories. In fact, all of my treatments seemed *anti*something. I also noticed that I would see some animals once every year or two for general health checks, and a small group of animals on a very consistent, frequent basis. The frequently seen animals would come in first for an ear infection, which cleared with antibiotics. Then a month later, the same animal would have an eye infection or a vomiting or diarrhea problem. Each of these conditions was treated as a separate entity and each cleared with the appropriate medication. No connection was acknowledged between the ear condition, the eye condition and the general health of the animal. This seemed incongruous to me, because prior to vet school, I was taught that "the thigh bone connected to the hip bone, the hip bone connected to the back bone, etc." How then could one animal have a series of problems that were *un*connected if they all lived in the same body? With the Western approach, one looks at the most specific, minute part of an individual, and loses sight of the individual as a whole. As questions arose more and more in my mind, I began to feel somewhat limited by the Western approach, and began to think it was time to look at some other approaches.

In 1979, I became involved with a group of veterinarians who founded the International Veterinary Acupuncture Society in 1974. In 1981, another group was formed, the American Holistic Veterinary Medical Association. Having experienced the limitations of Western approaches, the practitioners in these groups began to investigate applications of TCM with animals as part of the holistic approach. After fifteen years of practice using Traditional Chinese Medicine with animals, I would like to share with you what my patients have taught me.

Part 1
THE THEORY

CHAPTER ONE # The Five Elements

In ancient China, before there was modern technology, doctors relied upon their sense of sight, smell, taste, hearing and touch to diagnose and treat illness. A practice of medicine evolved as an extension of contemporary lifestyle in the third and fourth centuries B.C. Doctors used careful observation to formulate associations between the physical lay of the land and the inner workings of the body.

As they studied the world around them, practitioners discerned connections between major forces in nature and specific internal organ systems. They studied the seasons, how they merged into one another, and how each phase of a plant's or animal's life changed by growing, flourishing and dying. They looked at the earth with its soil, the mountains with their metal ore, the rivers with their water, the trees with their wood, and the fire that could inflame them all. They thought about what must take place within the body to help it live and function. They observed the muscles and skin that held the body intact, the chest that inspired the breath, the lower abdomen that moved the urine, the upper abdomen that helped the digestion and the beating heart that pumped and warmed the blood.

Seeing similarities between the natural elements and the body, these early physicians developed a concept of health care that encompassed both systems. This doctrine became known as the **Five Element Theory**. The five elements are **earth, metal, water, wood** and **fire**. Each **element** is linked to an **organ system**.

Earth is linked to the **digestion**. It is comprised of the **spleen/pancreas** and the **stomach**. Metal is linked to **respiration** and **elimination**. It is comprised of the **lungs** and **large intestine**. **Water** is linked to the **plumbing**. It

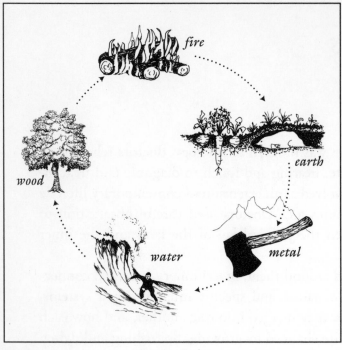

Creation Cycle

is comprised of the **kidneys** and **urinary bladder**. **Wood** is linked to the tree of **toxic processing**. It is comprised of the **liver** and **gall bladder**. **Fire** is linked to the **circulation** of blood, hormones and food. It is comprised of the **heart, small intestine** and their assistants.

Peculiar as this may sound to the modern Western mind, this early form of medicine gave birth to a complex system of checks and balances that explained health and disease. With over 4,000 years of experience, the Five Element Theory continues to be practiced throughout the world today. Treatment of illness using acupuncture and herbs depends upon understanding the five elements and how they interact.

The Five Element Theory is also known as the **Five Phases Theory**. Practitioners understood that the elements themselves did not represent static objects. Mountains and rivers changed constantly with time, as did the other elements in a continuous cycle of birth, life and death. It is the "process of change" that underlies the Five Element Theory, rather than the element substances themselves.

The similarities between the rhythm of events taking place in the physical world and those taking place in the physical body resembled a circle. This circular rhythm became known as the **Creation Cycle**. Poetically, the Chinese say that **fire** burned, creating the **earth** (soil). The earth gave rise to mountains which contain **metal** ores. The metal separated, making way for the **water**. The water flowed and nourished the **wood** of the trees. And the trees, vulnerable to burning, kindled the **fire**.

The relationship between the elements helps us to use TCM in the diagnosis and treatment of health problems. As I mentioned earlier, each element is related to a specific organ system. So, if there is a problem with the earth element of the stomach, this problem will ultimately affect the metal element that follows it in the Creation Cycle. The metal element contains the large intestine. The stomach and the large intestine are both part of the digestive system. I'm sure each of us has experienced incidents of vomiting or diarrhea. A Western physician might recommend a drug that slows down the digestive tract. A doctor practicing TCM might use acupuncture or herbs to strengthen the stomach.

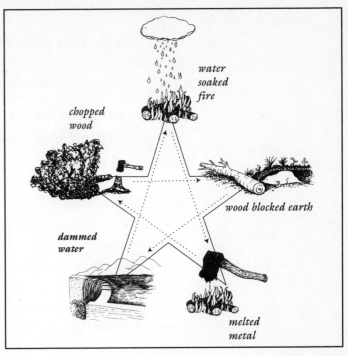

Control Cycle

In order to maintain this harmonious circular rhythm, TCM employs checks and balances to keep the elements in their correct places. This is called the **Control Cycle**. This concept forms a star shape. Using the five elements, it is easy to see how fire melts metal. Metal axes chop wood. As the wooden tree falls, it blocks the earth. As the earth's soil builds up, it dams water. As the water floods, it douses the fire.

If there is a problem with the water element of the kidneys, it can flood the rest of the body with fluid. This fluid can build up in the chest so that the heart can no longer pump the blood and fluid efficiently, causing congestive heart failure. Here we see the Control Cycle at work. Remember that the water element of the kidneys keeps the fire element of the heart in check. Western medicine might treat this with a drug that helps eliminate water from the body, thus decreasing the load on the heart. TCM might treat with acupuncture or herbs to balance the work between the heart and the kidney by strengthening the heart and regulating the kidneys.

THE FIVE ELEMENTS AND
THEIR YIN / YANG PARTNERS

In addition to seeing how the elements are interwoven through cycles, each element is comprised of a pair of internal organs. One organ is solid and dense, like the liver, while its partner is hollow or forms a pocket, like the gall bladder. The denser, more solid organ is known as the **yin** partner. The tubular or pocket-type organ is known as the **yang** partner. The proper interaction of the partners facilitates how well the element works as part of the whole. In other words, a faulty connection between the partners can be the first symptom of a problem that will occur later on. For example, let's look at the metal element of the lung and large intestine. The lung is the yin partner and the large intestine is the yang partner. If your animal develops a hacking, dry cough, TCM might regard this as an imbalance in the lungs that has created a dryness. Because of the coupling between the lung and large intestine, if this same dryness is not treated, it can eventually cause constipation, which is a dryness in the large intestine.

The following are the yin and yang partners of the elements:

ELEMENT	YIN	YANG
Earth	Spleen / Pancreas	Stomach
Metal	Lung	Large Intestine
Water	Kidney	Urinary Bladder
Wood	Liver	Gall Bladder
Fire	Heart / Pericardium	Small Intestine / Triple Heater

Each yin and yang organ will be discussed in detail later in this section.

It is necessary here to address a major difference between Western and Eastern thinking. In the West, we usually see things as having a cause and effect. Our thinking is very linear: If A happens, B follows. There is health. There is disease. In Eastern thought, however, things are more circular. Eastern medicine talks about balance and imbalance. Tipping the scales in any direction can affect imbalances. The healthy state is a constant flux of circumstances. Illness can develop if the balance is disturbed for any length of time. Therefore, health is maintained by recognizing an imbalance before it becomes a disease. Then the imbalance can be corrected to re-establish the harmonious interactions.

THE FIVE ELEMENTS AND THEIR RELATIONSHIPS

In order to recognize the imbalances, each organ is assigned an intricate set of affiliations. Each organ is related to a time of the day when it functions optimally and a season of the year when it is most vulnerable to the environment. If a problem occurs during those hours or during that season, it may alert a TCM practitioner to an imbalance occurring in that organ system. If the imbalance can be recognized and treated early, serious future problems may be averted. Additionally, each organ is related to specific emotions, colors, sense organs, body parts and foods.

The following table was amassed from information I gathered from one of the International Veterinary Acupuncture Society's founding members, Dr. Grady Young.

THE FIVE ELEMENTS AND THEIR RELATIONSHIPS

ELEMENT / ORGANS	Sound	Emotion	Climate	Season	Time	Odor
Fire / Heart & Small Intestine, Pericardium & Triple Heater	laugh	joy	heat	summer	11 a.m. to 3 p.m. to 7 p.m. to 11 p.m.	scorched
Earth / Spleen-Pancreas & Stomach	song	sympathy	humid	late summer	7 a.m. to 11 a.m.	sickly sweet
Metal / Lung & Large Intestine	weeping	grief	dry	autumn	3 a.m. to 7 a.m.	rotten
Water / Kidney & Urinary Bladder	groaning	fear	cold	winter	3 p.m. to 7 p.m.	putrid
Wood / Liver & Gall Bladder	shout	anger	windy	spring	11 p.m. to 3 a.m.	rancid

Although this may be very interesting, right now you are probably thinking, "How does this relate to my animal friend?" Well, for example, the liver in TCM is associated with the **wood** element, the season of **spring**, the emotion **anger**, the sound of **shouting**, the flavor **sour**, the odor **rancid**, the color **green**, the direction **east**, the sense organ the **eye**, the body part of **tendons** and **ligaments**, the time 1:00 a.m. to 3:00 a.m., and the foods **wheat, peach** and **chicken**. So, if you have a dog with **itchy red eyes**, especially in the springtime, who **barks loudly** and **lunges** at the mailman **angrily**, who craves your **chicken** dinner and bowl of **pasta** or your **sour ball candy**, who has a

Element	Food	Color	Direction	Body Opening	Secretion	Body Part
Fire	millet mutton plum	red	south	ears (hearing)	perspiration	palate, tongue
Earth	rice, millet beef, apricot scallion	yellow	center	mouth	saliva	muscles
Metal	rice, onions chestnut horsemeat	white	west	nose	mucous	skin
Water	barley beans peas, leeks pork	blue black	north	ears (w / fire element)	saliva	bone, marrow, teeth genitals, (w / liver element) urethra
Wood	wheat chicken peach	green	east	eyes	tears	tendons, ligaments nails, genitals

rancid skin odor, who wakes up every night to scratch at 1:00 a.m., and who wants to wear your **green** T-shirts, you may have a dog with a potential **liver** problem.

Seriously, though, each of our animals displays peculiarities that are heightened by organ imbalances in the TCM system. For example, if an individual animal vomits after breakfast, but not after dinner, by referring to the chart you will see that this weakness or imbalance may be associated with the earth element of the spleen/pancreas or stomach. If she vomits late at night, however, the weakness may be with the liver or gall bladder and the wood element. These peculiar symptoms can send a signal to a TCM practitioner to address a problem occurring within an organ system at a much earlier time than irregularities can be picked up in blood scans or radiographs. Remember, illness can be averted if the system can be re-balanced early on. This is why part of a TCM examination includes the taking of a detailed history which encompasses information that fits into the Five Element Theory.

THE FIVE CONSTITUTIONS

From aspects of these relationships, composite pictures of certain **constitutional types** and their usual imbalances emerge which correspond to the specific elements.

Summer is an example of the element FIRE.

◆ The Fire Constitution

Summer is a Toy Poodle who is the happiest little dog you've ever seen, except when her person is not around. Then she is anxious, hyperactive, barking hysterically, driving herself into tantrum fits until she can barely breathe. Her heart races, she overheats easily and is unable to take the sun for long periods. She also tends to dream excessively, talking and paddling in her sleep so that she appears restless. When her person finally returns, Summer pees nervously because she is so overjoyed.

Summer is an example of the element **fire** which is related to the **heart** and the circulatory system. As indicated earlier, the heart is coupled, or paired, with the **small intestine**, which is also considered a "fire organ." If you think about it, the small intestine is the place where the digestive enzymes are activated or "fired up" to help break down the food.

◆ The Earth Constitution

Kiwi is a Chocolate Labrador Retriever who tends to be overweight. She is a great tracking dog, always willing to please, very obedient, and extremely sensitive to her person's moods. She sometimes poops out easily however, having low stamina. In fact, there are days when she prefers to be a couch potato. She

tends to be a worrier and when Kiwi is stressed out, she may either vomit or have diarrhea. She likes to "sleep in" in the morning and sometimes seems grumpy when she awakens. Her energy and appetite pick up as the day goes on. Whenever she can, she sneaks a lick of her person's ice cream cone or cookie.

Kiwi is an example of the element **earth**. As indicated in the chart, the earth element is related to the **spleen/pancreas** and the **stomach**. In Traditional Chinese Medicine the spleen encompasses much more than our Western definition which involves only the production of blood and immune cells. The spleen is coupled with the pancreas in TCM and is involved with sugar metabolism and the breakdown of food in general, in addition to its blood-forming abilities.

Kiwi is an example of the element EARTH.

◆ The Metal Constitution

Rose is a Siamese Cross who has a continually runny nose. As a kitten, she developed an upper respiratory infection which took her a long time to get over. In fact, her breathing has never been quite the same since her recovery. She snores and snuffles on a regular basis. Her sinuses always sound congested and she has a hard time sniffing out her food unless her person adds highly fragrant garlic. During the fall, her susceptibility to pollen allergies has her sneezing and wheezing. Her veterinarian has told her that she might develop asthma as she gets older. She's especially uncomfortable in the early hours of the morning, about 4:00 a.m., when she struggles to breathe deeply. Her skin flakes and her coat is dry. She has a tendency to be constipated. Since the death of her littermate, she's been very aloof and sad, seemingly unable to get over her grief.

Rose is an example of the element METAL.

Rose is an example of the **metal** element which is related to the **lung** and **large intestine**.

◆ The Water Constitution

Teddy is a Domestic Shorthair who is terrified of strangers, noises, moving objects, in fact, just about everything. The vacuum cleaner is a monster from outer space and he shrieks and hides in the closet when he hears it coming. As he rises from a prone position, he seems to grunt and groan until he gets moving. He is constantly thirsty and likes to drink from the toilet bowl or bathtub. Teddy loves stealing his person's salted pretzels, and he craves salty dry cat food instead of canned food. Teddy has a history of bladder infections. His urinary problems seem to start in the winter with the onset of cold weather.

Teddy is an example of the element WATER.

Teddy is an example of the **water** element which is related to the **kidney** and **urinary bladder**.

◆ The Wood Constitution

Dixby is a Terrier Cross with a bad temper. Leering and barking at the mailman and lunging for other dogs while he's on the leash are favorite activities. (Even better would be lunging for them when he is not on the leash, but his person has gotten wise to that one.) Dixby picks fights and bullies other dogs into submission. His bark sounds loud and ferocious and he can be moody and possessive over food. Though small in stature, pound for pound, Dixby is a powerful little dog. He has an ear discharge with an unpleasant odor. He paws and scratches his eyes, which get red and irritated and leak a greenish mucous. Although his person feeds him hypo-allergenic food, Dixby's skin also has a very strong smell and he frequently gets hot spots and flea allergies. He's almost always on medication for his eyes, ears or skin problems. Bathing helps, but the doggy odor returns quickly. Dixby's stools occasionally have mucous or blood in them.

Dixby is an example of the **wood** element which is related to the **liver** and **gall bladder**.

Dixby is an example of the element WOOD.

These composites of elemental constitutions can give you an idea of the **pure personality** of each element. In life, however, one rarely sees pure pictures involving only one element, as everything is interconnected and effects everything else. As an individual develops, the interactions between the elements gets a little more complex, especially in humans. Fortunately, animals tend to embody strong elemental preferences making it easier to see where an imbalance may be occurring. Each element will be discussed along with its corresponding imbalances, disease patterns and treatments.

THE DAILY CIRCADIAN RHYTHM CLOCK

Even though our circulation is always at work, pumping blood, lymph, fluids ans oxygen through our bodies, each organ system in TCM is assigned a specific time of day when it functions optimally. The flow also conducts a vital and animated force that emanates from the physical, spiritual and emotional body. The Chinese call this **qi** (pronounced "chi"). The qi directs and coordinates this flow of energies and is the mainstay of one's life force. Each individual inherits qi from his ancestors which is then reinforced by environmental conditions.

Qi cannot be touched or seen, but it is inherently present in all functions of our body. The concept of qi will be discussed in more detail later.

Ancient Traditional Chinese Medicine practitioners first mapped the flow of qi within the body thousands of years ago. Today, we take for granted that our circulation is always pumping. But what TCM discovered was that during certain times of the day or night, the energy flow had more focus in a certain part of the body. This focus followed a path through the body that mimicked the way the organs related to each other. From these discoveries followed a circadian clock and meridian system.

CIRCADIAN BODY CLOCK

3:00 a.m.	–	5:00 a.m. lung
5:00 a.m.	–	7:00 a.m. large intestine
7:00 a.m.	–	9:00 a.m. stomach
9:00 a.m.	–	11:00 a.m. spleen/pancreas
11:00 a.m.	–	1:00 p.m. heart
1:00 p.m.	–	3:00 p.m. small intestine

3:00 p.m.	–	5:00 p.m. urinary bladder
5:00 p.m.	–	7:00 p.m. kidney
7:00 p.m.	–	9:00 p.m. pericardium
9:00 p.m.	–	11:00 p.m. triple heater
11:00 p.m.	–	1:00 a.m. gall bladder
1:00 a.m.	–	3:00 a.m. liver

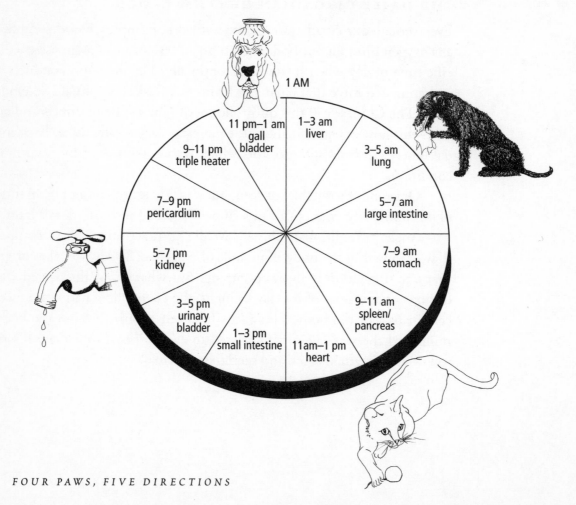

CHAPTER TWO # The Meridians

We have seen how energy flows and moves through the body in its own circadian rhythm as well as how the elements relate to specific organs. Now we need to take a look at how these systems connect. And to do this, I will introduce the concept of **meridians**.

Understanding meridians is essential because it is through the meridian system that the treatment methods of acupuncture and acupressure evolved. Without an understanding of the meridians, the Five Element Theory cannot be applied to the practice of acupuncture or herbal medicine.

A meridian is a channel of energy that courses beneath the skin's surface. Each meridian pathway follows aspects of the circulatory, lymphatic, muscular and nervous systems. The meridians form a network of vessels that connect all parts of the body. Qi flows within each meridian or vessel, directing the blood and other body fluids that keep us alive.

Each pathway has on/off ramps that exit to the skin's surface. Each exit point has a very small diameter (0.1cm–5cm) and yet is an area of greatly increased electrical conductivity compared to the surrounding skin areas. With an increased number of nerve and small circulatory endings, these highly reactive punctate skin areas are called **acupuncture points.**[1]

If one were to connect the dots of the acupuncture points on the body's surface, one could follow the pathway of each of the twelve major meridians. The meridians are like major power lines running through the body, and the acupuncture points are the relay switches to access the energy.[2] Since each meridian is associated with an internal organ, the acupuncture points offer us *surface access* to the internal organ systems.

For example, let's say that your cat, Twink, has a skin sore on her leg.

One of the first thoughts that a TCM doctor would have is, "Where is this skin sore and what meridian does it involve?" If the skin sore is on the outside, or lateral, aspect of the leg, let's say at the hip, the energy vessel, or meridian, that is involved belongs to the gall bladder. So, in addition to treating the hot spot, its location directs the doctor to look beneath the surface for the cause of the problem.

If there is a problem along the meridian, it may relate to the organ that the pathway serves or to something along its body path. Visualize an inner-city highway system with entrance and exit ramps, merging roads and connecting surface streets. If there is a flood blocking an exit ramp, the streets that are served by this ramp are inaccessible. This, in turn, affects the houses on those streets and the people who live in them. Also, the traffic may be backed up on the highway waiting for the ramp to re-open, creating a traffic jam. Well, it's just like this in your cat's body. If there is some kind of blockage happening at her hip, the pathways of energy leading to that hip get "backed up." The pathways leaving the hip may have a decreased energy flow. This may make her back stiff or painful in front of the hip, and her hind legs weak below the hip.

In continuing the flow of energy from one meridian to the next as seen in the circadian clock, we see that each meridian joins with another until all aspects of the body are connected. As each meridian is associated with an organ system, this is how all the organs are joined and how everything circulates. Keeping the flow open and regular assures us of a state of balance and health.

LOCATIONS OF MERIDIANS

Now let's look at where the merdians are located in the body. Beginning in the torso, there are three **yin meridians** that begin in the chest and travel along the inside of the forelimbs. These are the **lung**, **pericardium** and **heart**. At the paws, each yin meridian meets its yang partner, and travels up along the outside of the arm to the face and head. These are the **large intestine, triple heater** and **small intestine.**

In the head and face area, the yang meridians meet other yang pathways. These **yang meridians** are the **gall bladder, urinary bladder** and **stomach.** This set of meridians travels downward from the head through the body, to the outer side of the hind legs and down to the hind toes. Here, they meet their **yin** partners, the **liver, kidney** and **spleen/pancreas.** These three yin meridians travel back up the inside of the leg towards the chest area to eventually meet the **lung, pericardium** and **heart,** and begin the cycle again.

With this overview in mind, let's look at each meridian and follow its path through the body.

◆ The Lung Meridian

The lung meridian naturally begins in the chest area. Its pathway comes toward the surface in the space where the forelimb attaches to the chest area, near the underarm and in the pectoral muscles. The lung meridian runs downward on the inside or medial aspect of the limb to end up at the tip of the dewclaw. There are 11 acupuncture points along the lung meridian.

◆ The Large Intestine Meridian

The large intestine meridian begins on the inside, or medial side, of the second toe (which is the first regular-sized toe of your cat or dog). It runs upward along the front of the forelimb, across the shoulder to end up just below and on the side of the nostril. There is an internal branch of the meridian that connects with the large intestine organ itself, but the major pathway is as shown here. If your animal friend has diarrhea, it is not uncommon to treat forelimb acupuncture points to regulate the intestine. There are 20 acupuncture points along the large intestine meridian.

◆ The Stomach Meridian

From the side of the nose, we cross to just below the middle of the eye, just above the cheek bone. The stomach meridian begins here and travels downward along the face, around and up the jaw, then down along the underside or abdominal surface of the body. After sending a branch to the stomach, the meridian continues to travel down along the front of the knee (stifle) to the tip of the third toe on the hind leg. There are 45 acupuncture points along the stomach meridian.

◆ The Spleen/Pancreas Meridian

On the back paw, the stomach meridian hooks up with its yin partner, the spleen/pancreas. In humans, this meridian runs along the line between the red and white skin of the foot, along the first toe. Most of our small animal friends have only four hind toes. Their big toe is not present, or it is stunted and equivalent to the hind dewclaw. There is no demarcation of red and white skin. So, although there is controversy over where the spleen/pancreas meridian begins, I have found through experience that the pathway begins on the lower portion of the inside aspect of the second toe. It runs along the side of the second toe until it meets the ankle where it becomes more topsided. When it reaches the space in front of the Achilles tendon, it follows along the inside of the limb, up through the groin area, along the abdomen and upwards toward the chest. It ends in the sixth rib space. In the abdomen, it sends a branch to its organs, the spleen and pancreas. There are 21 acupuncture points along the spleen/pancreas meridian.

◆ The Heart Meridian

The heart meridian meets the spleen meridian in the chest area, and travels toward the underarm or axillary area. It travels downward along the inside back portion of the front leg to the inside tip of the fifth (outside) toe. There are 9 acupuncture points along the heart meridian.

◆ The Small Intestine Meridian

Just across the foreleg's fifth toe from the end of the heart meridian, the small intestine meridian begins. As the yang partner of the heart, the small intestine meridian runs upward along the outside aspect of the front leg, just on the other side of the limb from the heart meridian's path. The small intestine meridian then jogs around the inside of the elbow, and returns to the outside of the upper arm and shoulder to the face, to end up at the ear. An internal branch connects with the small intestine. There are 19 acupuncture points along the small intestine meridian.

◆ The Urinary Bladder Meridian

At the base of the ear, it's just a short distance to the eye where the small intestine meets the urinary bladder meridian. Beginning at the inside margin of the eye, the pathway follows very closely along the midline of the face, past the bridge of the nose, up over the forehead and cranium, and then downward along the back of the head to the neck. At the neck, the urinary bladder meridian actually branches into a double meridian which runs parallel to the spine, the inner branch lying approximately ½ inch from the spine midline and the outer branch lying about 1 inch from the spine midline. These parallel meridians run the length of the spine to the sacrum, one of which sends a branch to the urinary bladder along the way. The double meridian runs around the hind end of the animal, down the backside of the leg to the back of the knee, where they meet. The single branch bladder meridian runs down the middle of the back of the lower leg from the stifle and around the outside of the ankle, to end at the tip of the fifth toe.[3] The urinary bladder meridian has 67 acupuncture points.

◆ The Kidney Meridian

At the hind paw, the urinary bladder meridian meets its yin partner the kidney. The pathway begins just under the main pad of the paw. This point can be accessed at the tip of the triangle of the main foot pad. The kidney meridian runs upward along the inside of the hind leg and up towards the chest, to end just in front of the first rib. In the lower abdomen, an internal branch of the meridian joins the kidney. The kidney meridian has 27 points.

◆ The Pericardium Meridian

When the kidney meridian ends up in the chest, it meets with the pericardium meridian. The pericardium is the thin filmy membrane that surrounds and protects the heart. In TCM, the pericardium not only physically protects the heart by absorbing the early onset of disease, but it also protects the mental and spiritual aspects of the heart. The heart houses the spirit of the body known as the **shen,** from which happiness and well being arise. Mental disillusionment and emotional disorders in Traditional Chinese Medicine are affiliated with the heart spirit and the pericardium. The pericardium meridian is used to treat depression, anxiety and disorientation. In this capacity, it is said to "protect the heart spirit."

The pericardium meridian begins in the chest where the kidney meridian leaves off. It emerges next to the upper chest nipple and runs along the middle of the inside of the front leg, through the large pad at the wrist (accessory carpal pad), to end at the tip of the third toe. The pericardium meridian has 9 points.

◆ The Triple Heater Meridian

A concept unique to Traditional Chinese Medicine is that of a **triple heater** meridian. It is a function in the body *without* a specific organ alignment. As its name implies, it describes temperature regulation in the body. An animal's body, as well as our own, is comprised of three separate compartments: one encompasses the head to just below the chest at the diaphragm; another includes the diaphragm to just below the umbilicus (navel); and a third comprises the umbilicus to the lower part of the body. Each compartment needs a regulator, or traffic director to help it communicate with its neighbor. Think of the triple heater as "middle management" in charge of regulating the metabolism.

Both the triple heater and the pericardium are considered part of the fire element. Therefore, the fire element contains the heart, the small intestine, the pericardium and the triple heater.

The triple heater meets up with the pericardium meridian on the fourth toe of the front paw. Here it travels upward along the front side of the fore-limb, around the outside of the elbow, up to the shoulder, ending just above the outside (lateral) border of the eye. From the shoulder an internal branch enters the chest area and goes through the diaphragm to hook up with the other compartments.[4] There are 23 points on the triple heater meridian.

◆ The Gall Bladder Meridian

The gall bladder meridian begins at the outside margin of the eye, very close to where the triple heater meridian ends. The gall bladder meridian traverses the side and top of the head, like a cloche hat, touching the ears, and passing at the back of the head to the nape of the neck. It then travels downward, across and under the shoulder, along the sides of the body, and along the outside flanks to the hip area. Here the gall bladder meridian circles the hip and runs down the outside of the leg, passing the knee, ending up at the tip of the fourth toe on the hind paw. An internal branch from the head area goes through the chest and abdomen to reach the gall bladder. The gall bladder meridian has 44 acupuncture points.

◆ The Liver Meridian

The liver meridian meets the gall bladder meridian at the foot. In humans, the liver meridian is found between the big and second toes. Since most of our cats and dogs either don't have a big toe, or have a vestigial toe or dew-claw, the beginning of the liver meridian, like that of the spleen/pancreas meridian, is hazy. I usually find the liver meridian running along the upper side portion of the inside of the second toe. In comparison to the spleen meridian which also runs along the inside of this toe, the liver meridian is more topside (or dorsal), but still travels along the side of the toe. The liver meridian travels upward until it reaches the ankle where it runs along the inside of the hind leg, closely paralleling the spleen and kidney meridians. The liver meridian runs upward through the groin area, encompassing parts of the genitalia, along the abdomen and ends up in the diaphragm area. It sends a branch to the liver before leaving the abdomen. At the diaphragm it meets the lung to start the energy flow again. The liver meridian has 14 points.

This completes one cycle of energy or qi flow through the body. The cycle covers a 24-hour period.

There are two "extra" meridians that do not have their own two-hour time span that will play a part in the treatment of your animals. Each runs along the midline, one along the back midline, one along the abdominal midline.

◆ The Governing & Conception Vessel Meridians

The meridian running along the back midline is called the **governing vessel**. The governing vessel meridian is the most yang of all the yang meridians. As it runs over the anatomical areas in the body, the yang aspect of that organ can be reached through the governing vessel meridian. At several places along the governing vessel meridian, branches from the yang meridians will actually come up and meet it.

The meridian running along the abdominal midline is called the **conception vessel**. The conception vessel is the most yin of the meridians. There are places on the conception vessel meridian where the yin meridians coalesce and the yin aspects of the organs can be reached.

Aside from the last two extra meridians, which run along the back and abdominal midlines, each meridian is paired and runs along each side of the body. There is the large intestine meridian on the right side *and* the large intestine meridian on the left side.

Additionally, each organ system has a maximal energy focus through its meridian every two hours. This energy flow is related to the circadian clock, discussed earlier. I understand how complicated this must sound, but it is necessary to introduce these concepts in order to understand how to treat your animal. Acupuncture, acupressure and herbal medicine are all integrally related to the meridians and their elements.

When I explain these concepts to veterinarians for the first time, I remind them that TCM evolved over many many centuries as part of intense observation of the natural world. As I have said before (and will doubtless say again), TCM correlates the outside world with its corresponding microcosm occurring inside the body.

What follows is an example of a day in the life of the meridian system. Although greatly simplified, this little scenario illustrates how everything we've discussed thus far is connected and related. If you can keep this in mind as you continue to read, Traditional Chinese Medicine will always make sense.

3 am–5 am Lung

Let's say we are awakened at 3:00 a.m. with a dry cough. It hurts our lungs to cough, and patting or holding the chest seems to make us feel better. We may lie awake for a while trying to regulate our breathing.

At about 6:00 a.m., we are ready to begin the day. After rising, we have our daily bowel movement. The large intestine has announced itself in a normal fashion.

5 am–7 am Large Intestine

7 am–9 am Stomach

After our morning ablutions, it's now about 7:00 a.m. and we are ready for breakfast. Our stomachs are empty from the night before and it's time to nourish the body. By 9:00 a.m., we are beginning to digest our first meal, including the breakdown of

proteins, fats and carbohydrates. Our metabolism, which is overseen by our spleen/pancreas, begins to transform and assimilate the foods from our breakfast into workable energy.

9 am–11 am
Spleen / Pancreas

By 11:00 a.m., the foods we've eaten have been transformed into qi (energy). We are now ready to pump up our circulation. Some exercise may be appropriate to help move the blood from the heart, especially since it's almost time to eat again.

11 am–1 pm Heart

At 1:00 p.m. its time for lunch, after which our digestive enzymes fire up again, this time regulated by the small intestine.

1 pm–3 pm Small Intestine

Later in the afternoon, about 3:00 p.m., we need to take a urinary bladder break. When we get up from our desks, we remember to stretch out the spine, recalling its association with the urinary bladder meridian. By 5:00 p.m. it's almost time to leave work, and our lower back feels weak as we stand up. As we stretch our back and legs, a small grunt escapes from our mouths. We may need to rub our back just below the rib cage to increase circulation to the kidneys. Although the events of the day's work have made us agitated and tense, visualizing a free flowing stream may help douse the mental fire and help us face the afternoon commute traffic.

3 pm–7 pm
Urinary Bladder & Kidney

7 pm–9 pm
Pericardium

By 7:00 p.m. we are just getting home and finally beginning to calm down, when a phone call from the boss reminds us about tomorrow's deadline. Our heart starts racing in anticipation of more stress, and we have to make a conscious effort to calm down. It's time for the pericardium to protect the heart.

At 9:00 p.m. we are starting to feel tired, but we remember that we have promised to get together with a friend before bedtime. Our body temperature may be dropping a little from using so much energy to digest the day's events, but we call on our triple heater to warm us up, if only for a short time.

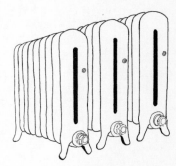

9 pm–11 pm
Triple Heater

11 pm–1 am
Gall Bladder

By 11:00 p.m. we're back home and ready to go to sleep. But the worry and aggravation of the day's events have given us a headache, especially around the temple area of the gall bladder meridian. If only someone could rub just behind the neck and the sides of the forehead, we would feel much better.

By 1:00 a.m. we are restless and frustrated because we can't fall asleep. We feel pain just under the rib cage and a bitter taste rises in the mouth, like bile in the liver.

Endnotes

1. Liu, Ky, C.C. Gunn, T. Matsumoto. Reported by Y-C Hwang. *Veterinary Acupuncture, Anatomy and Classification of Acupoints, Problems in Veterinary Medicine*. A. Schoen, ed. (Philadelphia, PA: J. B. Lippincott Co., Vol. 4, No. 1, March 1992), 12.

2, 3, 4. Dr. Kuan Hin. *Chinese Massage and Acupressure*. (New York: Bergh Publishing, Inc., 1991), 95, 90, 91.

CHAPTER THREE

The Eight Principles

Along with the Five Element Theory which works with the meridians, there is a system in Traditional Chinese Medicine that was developed as an outgrowth of the concepts of yin and yang called the Eight Principles. This system is based upon the **quality, quantity** and **location** of a problem.[1]

The Eight Principles include the categories and concepts of:

- ◆ **Yin and Yang**
- ◆ **Interior and Exterior**
- ◆ **Cold and Hot**
- ◆ **Deficiency and Excess**

The quality of the system refers to whether the disease pattern or its response has yin or yang or cold or hot tendencies. The quantity refers to the deficiency or excess aspect of the condition, and the location depends upon interior or exterior aspects. Each will be discussed in detail a little later.

In addition to the Eight Principles, other aspects of the external environment are taken into account as these, too, can affect the individual. These are known as the **pathologic external factors.** They can become "pathological" and threatening to an individual if conditions are severe and the individual is in a vulnerable state.

The pathologic external factors are:

windy weather	humidity or dampness
summer heat	dryness

These classifications help to distinguish and describe an individual's imbalance. Each of the organs from the meridian system is vulnerable to environmental influences and each has propensities for involvment with the Eight Principles. Practitioners will usually use a combination of the Five Elements and Eight Principles to help with diagnosis and treatment of the patient.

Reading about TCM principles for the first time is a little like reading subtitles at a foreign movie — in a language you don't understand! Unusual and unfamiliar concepts are being introduced and you may feel very confused. Try to keep in mind that Traditional Chinese Medicine is merely a view of the body, whether human or animal, from a different perspective. Like learning anything new, a basic vocabulary is necessary in order to understand the concepts and utilize the tool's of Traditional Chinese Medicine.

YIN AND YANG

Almost everyone today is at least somewhat familiar with the terms yin and yang, which are the universal principles of the opposite aspects of life. These two principles are the two sides of every coin, the inseparable extremes of every relationship, object, action, concept or idea. There is no night without day; no heat without cold. We could never know happiness without having an experience of sadness; we could never appreciate the feeling of security, if we have never known fear; we would never feel full if we have never felt hungry. According to the Chinese, *everything* ultimately functions as a result of the dynamic interaction of these polar opposites.

From the medical perspective, the basis of health is the appropriate balance of yin and yang as they interact in the body. An imbalance of these two aspects is considered to be the cause of illness.

Yin is like water with a tendency to be cold and heavy. Yin moistens both the surface and the interior of the body, helping fluids to flow and cool us. Yin directs the restfulness of the body by providing balance during less active periods. Yin is said to live in the shaded parts of the universe, like the underside

Yin

of the body or the underside of a leaf. It is found at a deeper level within the body than its yang partner. Yin is affiliated more with substance, rather than with energy or function.

Yang

Yang is like fire with its heating and circulating capabilities. If the heat is too great, it can consume the yin of the body and cause fever, inflammation and dryness. Yang directs the active movements of the body, being the energetic force pushing and supporting its substance. Think of it as the horsepower of an engine. The engine itself is made up of yin components, but the power that is created to make it move is the yang energy. Therefore, yang is associated with wakefulness and activity. Circulating closer to the surface of the body than its yin partner, it tries to protect the inner yin substance. Yang is said to live in the sunshine and on the upper and outer parts of the body. For the animals this means the back and the outside surfaces of the limbs.

One thing to keep in mind is that yin and yang cannot exist independently of each other. In other words, nothing is either all yin or all yang. For example, in the body, an organ may be considered to be predominantly yang, such as the stomach, because it is so active in the digestion of food. Its soft, moist inner lining, however, is considered yin. In all aspects of the body both yin and yang are always present.

Cold is similar to yin, though not as encompassing. Cold is like glacial ice that moves imperceptibly. It is the water that contracts and stagnates inside of the body, causing sluggishness. Cold is like the winter in most places, or the damp, foggy summers of the San Francisco Bay area where I live. Cold individuals dislike cold weather. They tend to catch colds easily, have cooler extremities, and are sedentary and sleepy. They remain cool, calm and collected in most situations, sometimes to a fault. If they produce bodily discharges, they are thin, watery and clear. Cold individuals have a slow response to illness.

Cold

Hot is similar to yang, but not as pervasive. Hot is like a fuming volcano, active and intense. Hot individuals usually cannot tolerate much heat and summer can be excruciating for them. Hot individuals tend to be nervous, restless and agitated. They blow off steam frequently and have intense reactions to almost everything. When ill they develop high fevers and swollen glands. If they produce any discharges they tend to be thick and foul-smelling, and green, yellow, or brown in color. Unlike their cold partners, **hot** individuals tend to develop acute illnesses quickly and get over them quickly.

Hot

The principle of **exterior** has to do with the location of the condition. When we get a flu or upper respiratory condition, this mild virus attacks the outside or surface of the body. Exterior conditions are usually acute, of short duration and leave no long-lasting detrimental effects. If, however, the problem goes unchecked by the body's immune system, it can migrate to deeper levels of the body, becoming an interior condition.

Exterior

The principle of **interior** denotes that a problem is deep below the surface, affecting an internal organ. Interior usually indicates a serious problem. It can arise from an infection that began as an exterior condition which then overwhelmed the body. Interior conditions can also arise from hereditary problems. The Chinese also believe that strong emotions can wear the body down and cause an interior condition. Individuals suffering from severe grief, for example, can develop pneumonia. Unlike its exterior partner, interior problems can cause death.

Interior

Excess means too much of something. For example, too much heat can cause inflammation of the skin. Too much water can cause fluid buildup in the chest cavity or the belly. Excess can also refer to how an individual moves through and takes up space. An excess individual is forceful in voice and movement and can be large in frame, muscle, fat or attitude. An excess individual always wants more.

Excess

Deficiency means too little of something. For example, a deficiency of energy can cause fatigue or lethargy. A deficiency of red blood cells in the blood can cause anemia. Not enough water in the intestines can cause constipation or small, dry stool. Deficient individuals tend to be soft-spoken, somewhat hesitant, take up less space, and are often thin and even weak. A deficient individual may want more but lacks the wherewithall to attain it.

Deficiency

Although I have listed the categories separately, most individuals, animal and human, are made up of combinations of these principles.

Yin can be affiliated with **excess** or **deficiency**. As mentioned above, yin is usually associated with cold. Eloise is an overweight, lethargic Burmese cat. She doesn't drink much water, but she loves to eat! Rather than giving her energy, eating seems to make her more tired. The only thing that gets Eloise moving is a warm sunny day or a pet heater, because she tends to feel the cold. In fact, in the middle of the night, she may get so cold that she urinates in her bed, because she cannot warm and tighten her bladder sphincter muscles. She also tends to get watery discharges from her eyes and nose and often has soft stools. Everyone loves her because she's so sweet and calm, snuggling in the warmth of the nearest friendly lap. Eloise epitomizes a **yin excess** and **cold** condition.

If, however, Eloise were thinner, with a round, distended hanging belly, these same signs might be characterized as a **deficiency of yang** condition. Since everything is relative, a deficient yang individual might mimic an excess yin individual except in the underlying stature and constitution. What makes Eloise an **excess** constitution, in the first example, is her large frame *and* her exuberance in demanding attention. Here we see that a patient is considered in her entirety when assessing the Eight Principles.

Sally is an older cat who used to run wild when she was young. She lives in the Southwest where desert conditions make it hot and dry for much of the year. Eventually, Sally found a home with a loving family who adopted her. But recently, Sally has become very thirsty. She can't seem to get enough to drink. Her tongue and mouth are always dry. She has lost most of the moist protective coating on her tongue. Her skin feels dry, itchy and hot to the touch, especially when it is hot outside, and most often late in the afternoon. She has a cat door so that she can go out whenever she likes, but lately, she's feeling unsettled, and a little weak. If she goes outdoors, she always seeks shade. Loud noises bother her, and she gets irritable easily. Although she's thirsty, she hardly urinates, and wonders where all the fluid is going. It's even become difficult to have daily bowel movements. She just doesn't seem to have the energy to go. She's losing weight and although she used to enjoy sitting on her person's lap, lately she feels too hot and finds the contact annoying. Sally illustrates a **yin deficient** and **hot** condition.

Her general attitude of weakness indicates a deficient rather than excess constitution. All the signs of not enough fluid are present: increased thirst, dry mouth, no tongue coating, irritability and constipation. Her inability to tolerate warmth, either outside or on her person's lap, is a heat sign. These heat signs are coming to light not because she is a **hot** type constitution, but because she has relatively less water or yin. This makes her *appear* hot. If she were truly **hot** and **yang**, she might be more aggressive and loud. She would also have a yellow coating on her tongue (see tongue diagnosis on page 47).

Thus, individuals can show both sides of a condition. Eloise had too much (excess) water and yin, making her cold and sedate. Sally had too little (deficiency) water and yin, making her hot and restless.

Max is an enormous, unruly Rottweiller who is rather full of himself, with a swaggering gait and an assertive manner. His bark can be heard across the county. No one interferes with Max while he's eating and none of his dog friends will challenge him for a bone. He drinks a quart of water at a time and still wants more. He seems to be sensitive to hot weather and likes winter best.

During the past summer, Max got sick and ran a temperature of 105 degrees F. His glands were swollen and he was laid up for three days, though his recovery was quick. He has recently developed a yellow, foul-smelling discharge from his ear that is hot and painful to the touch. His eyes get very red and itchy, and when his ear or eyes bother him, he paces around and growls. Max illustrates a **yang excess** and **hot** condition.

PATHOLOGICAL ENVIRONMENTAL INFLUENCES

In addition to the Eight Principles, environmental influences are also used for diagnosis. Traditional Chinese Medicine asserts that certain weather conditions effect the body. In fact, these elements can cause conditions inside the body that resemble what's happening outside. These environmental influences are **wind, dampness, dryness** and **summer heat.**

All this may sound metaphysical, but talk to someone who suffers with arthritis. He will tell you that when it rains, the dampness goes right to his bones and makes them ache. Or talk to someone who lives in the desert about her dry, flaky skin. There is no doubt that our physical environment has an impact on the body.

The Chinese say that the wind can attack the body by entering through the back of the neck, just below the head. There is an acupuncture point at this place that has the name "Wind Pond." Have you ever sat with a fan or air conditioning duct blowing on the back of your head? After a while, your neck probably got stiff. In Traditional Chinese Medicine, it would have been deduced that the "wind" had entered your body, affecting the muscles, causing the stiff neck. I know a dog who likes to ride in the car with his head hanging out of the window. After an afternoon of this, not only does he have a stiff neck, but he also has very runny eyes. The wind has entered his body.

Wind can enter the layers of muscle and tendons and, eventually, the bones of susceptible individuals. The result is arthritis that changes joint locations and often worsens in wind, damp, heat or cold.

In addition to stiff muscles, the wind can also invade and overpower an individual's immune system. In TCM there is a circulating immune system that travels just below the surface of the body. It is called the **wei qi.** If the wind is stronger than an individual's wei qi, it can invade the body, making the individual sick, with an upper respiratory infection involving the nose, throat and eyes. For years, mothers have been telling children to wear scarves and keep their necks warm to avoid getting sick. Although animals do not usually wear scarves, long exposure to cold, windy weather, can certainly increase their chances of catching cold, especially if they have sparse coats.

The wind can also penetrate to a deeper level, and enter the central nervous system. The Chinese say the wind has entered the channels and meridian system — not just the wei qi. If you remember, the wood element of the liver and gall bladder is related to the wind. If an individual has a propensity for an imbalance in the liver, she is already sensitive to the wind. The internal predispositon can set up an "internal wind" that increases sensitivity to the external environment. The wind may then, in turn, affect the nervous system causing twitching, trembling and even convulsions.

Dampness is another environmental condition. As its name implies, dampness saturates one with moisture. Moisture is yin and heavy. Unlike the wind that tends to rise up and circulate, dampness sinks. As tissues get soggy with moisture, circulation can become sluggish, making the individual feel heavy and reluctant to move around. "Water on the knee" is an example of a damp type arthritis problem in humans, as is "stocking up" in horses.

The digestive tract is also effected by dampness. If you remember, part of the earth element, the spleen/pancreas, is susceptible to dampness. It is the spleen/pancreas' job to assimilate the foods we eat and turn them into useable energy. If there is too much fluid in the foods we eat, it can slow the process by diluting the digestive juices. Your dog's abdomen may sag, causing a pot-bellied appearance. Certain foods tend to exacerbate dampness in the body which may cause a loose, mushy stool. And an excessively humid climate may aggravate these conditions.

If moisture or dampness accumulates in one place, it's like a dammed river. Boggy places can develop in the body and can actually congeal and form nodules, lumps, lipomas and other types of tumors. The Chinese call this boggy substance "phlegm." Phlegm that becomes sticky, hot and stagnant is a chronic form of dampness. Other signs of phlegm may be mucous in the stool, in the throat or lungs, or chronic stiffness in the joints that doesn't go away when the weather becomes drier.

Dryness is another environmental factor that can cause illness. Animals and humans who live in arid climates tend to use up the fluids in the body more quickly than individuals living in more varied climates. Dryness is just the opposite of dampness. Here, there is not enough water to bathe and lubricate the internal and external body properly.

Dry, itchy skin eruptions along with an itchy anus and constant thirst are all manifestations of dryness. Lubrication for the joints and intestines can also be affected by dryness, as can the nose, throat and eyes. Eventually the lungs can become dry, causing a dry cough, asthma and many allergies.

You may remember that the metal element of the lungs and large intestine is sensitive to dryness. The stomach and the liver are also affected by too much dryness.

Technically speaking, the environmental influence of **summer heat** is also encountered. This refers to acute conditions that can cause vomiting, diarrhea, bleeding from the nose or rectum caused by severe forms of food poisoning, heat stroke and dysentery. Summer heat does not play a major role in TCM veterinary therapy as the Western treatment of fluids and medications are usually preferred.

Endnotes

1. Kaptchuk, Ted J., OMD. *The Web That Has No Weaver.* (New York: Congdon & Weed, 1983), 178–200.

CHAPTER FOUR

The Vital Essences

The Chinese have long believed that a combination of life force components make up the substance and functions of the body and mind. The substances provide the fluid, blood, energy and spirit that allow us to exist, either happily or unhappily.

The Taoists call these components the three "vital treasures." They are **jing,** meaning basic essence, **qi** meaning vitality or life force, and **shen,** meaning spirit and mind.[1]

Traditional Chinese Medicine divides the substance of the jing essence into blood and fluids. All together, we will call them the **vital essences of jing, blood, fluids, qi** and **shen.**

The vital essences are responsible for carrying out every manifestation of our lives. The balance of their abundance or deficiency directs the state of our health. The vital essences, encompassed by the basic understanding of yin and yang, are the integral tools of the Five Element Meridian System and the Eight Principles.

JING ESSENCE

Jing is the substinative essence we are born with. It is similar in Western understanding to the genes, DNA, and heredity. It is the basic material that resides in each cell and allows it to function. Derived from the kidney, according to Traditional Chinese Medicine, it is the underlying factor predisposing us to health. Jing has substance: blood and fluid, as well as function: qi. Jing is used up during a lifetime and is said to be depleted through sexual endeavors and stress.[2]

QI

Qi is vitality. It is not a palpable entity, but a function. I'm sure you've experienced meeting someone with very high energy and vitality. You can sense it but not actually touch it. I'm sure you are also familiar with an individual who lacks vitality. It can be tiring just to be around them.

Qi has three main components. The hereditary qi, which is from the jing; nutritive qi that is derived from the food we eat, under the auspices of the spleen and stomach; and cosmic qi that is from the air we breathe via the lungs.[3] There is also a specialized qi associated with the immune system, called **wei qi**. Wei qi is that part of the qi that circulates near the surface of the body and is affiliated with the lungs and the triple heater. As part of our protective immunity it is the first level that goes into battle when an infection tries to enter the body. If the circulating wei qi is weak, it can allow a pathogen to enter the body and we become ill.

When qi in general is weak, we feel tired, our appetite diminishes, our immunity suffers, and we are prone to frequent illness.

BLOOD

Qi and **blood** are very closely related. It is said that wherever the qi goes, the blood will follow. They are integrally connected like yin and yang: one cannot exist without the other.

Blood in Traditional Chinese Medicine is the same as we know it in Western medicine: the red fluid that spurts from a cut, and travels in our arteries and veins. It is also closely associated with the heart that pumps it through the body. In Traditional Chinese Medicine the heart is known as the "prince of circulation."

In TCM, blood is formed from the essence of the food that is digested and absorbed by the spleen and stomach. The Chinese believe that the spleen/pancreas plays two roles with the blood. First, it takes the substance from the food we eat and transforms it into useable energy (qi) and blood cells. Then it keeps the blood within the vessels, that is, it prevents hemorrhage. Remember that the spleen/pancreas is part of the earth element, which keeps everything in nature in its place, like tree roots, flowing rivers and mountains.

The blood essence derived from food is then mixed with the bone marrow, which is stored in the bones as part of the function of the kidney. The bone marrow is part of the system of inherited jing that the kidney oversees. Blood is then circulated and directed by the heart, or the prince of circulation.

The last organ related to the blood is the liver which acts as the "general," giving orders to all the body functions. It directs the blood that the heart is circulating, keeping it flowing and unclotted. The liver has a special role to play when the body is at rest. While asleep or when the body is lying still, the liver bathes the internal organs and tissues in blood using very little energy. Its like taking a relaxing, hot bath—our body is still functioning as it is being bathed in warm fluid, but its functioning is relaxed and passive. In the same way the liver allows the blood to be in a passive relaxed state while the body is at rest. Therefore, problems with the blood can be correlated to the heart, spleen/pancreas, kidney or liver.

Bast is a Saluki who came to see me because of severe allergic skin problems. This dog had a history of irregular and low red and white blood cell counts, and as her condition worsened she developed small hemorrhages under her skin that appeared as purple blotches. She was both restless and exhausted, trying to move around because of her discomfort, but being too weak to sustain much motion. She had lost her appetite and lost some weight. When I examined her, I found her pulse to be very rapid and weak, and her tongue slightly purplish. She felt very warm to the touch and there were hot, dry scabs on her skin. The muscle mass along her spine seemed shrunken and her abdomen sagged slightly, making this normally sleek breed of dog look somewhat potbellied.

Bast had multiple organ systems out of balance. From the viewpoint of Western medicine, her condition involved the immune system and was probably a form of hemolytic anemia, a condition in which the body attacks and destroys it's own red blood cells. From a TCM point of view, Bast's problem was with her blood and her qi. The spleen/pancreas could not keep the blood in their vessels, which produced the hemorrhages under the skin. The weak qi caused her lack of appetite and poor muscle tone. Her condition was recurring because of weakened hereditary kidney jing. The heart was not being properly bathed in blood because the spleen couldn't deliver it. This made her restless and uncomfortable. She was hot to the touch because there was not enough blood to bathe her tissues and skin.

I treated Bast with acupuncture, specific foods and herbs to strengthen the blood and the qi, the kidney, spleen/pancreas and heart.

FLUID

Fluid is like yin substance, and is one of the vital essences that maintain and balance health. Fluid, of course, includes aspects of the blood, but in addition, it covers the tears, saliva, joint fluid, lymph, urine and central nervous system fluids. Fluid bathes every cell and every cell constituent. Each tiny mitochondria, liposome and protein complex relies on fluid as its medium of energy. Since our body is made up of bioelectrical mechanisms, every function is guided by the movement of ions. The ions travel in a liquid medium. This medium is the fluid of the body in Traditional Chinese Medicine.

Whitey is an older cat with a great personality and diabetes. Although her insulin dosage was steadily increased over a period of time, Whitey was still very uncomfortable and became weaker and weaker in her hind legs. She had severe thirst and urinated more than ususal. When I examined her, she had very sticky, stringy saliva in the back of her mouth and on the sides of her tongue that stuck to the teeth, but the tongue itself appeared dry. Her eyes seemed dry, her coat appeared brittle and her skin was a bit flaky. I heard a sort of "gritty" sound when she changed position or stood up and her lungs had a dry, slightly harsh sound as she breathed.

Whitey had a problem with the fluids in her body and clearly several organ systems were involved. The lungs were dry, which explained the dry sounds, her increased thirst and her dry skin. The spleen/pancreas and stomach were also involved and accounted for the dry mouth. The involvement of the kidney caused the increased urination and the gritty sounds I heard around the spine and hind legs. But the underlying problem with Whitey was an imbalance in the fluid *essence*. I gave Whitey herbal and acupuncture treatments that generated and supported her fluids. Gradually her insulin requirements dropped to a low, steady level. Her hind legs strengthened and her thirst and urination normalized. Today she is leading a more normal life.

SHEN

Shen is a metaphysical or pscyological term. The shen is the spirit and the psyche of the body. It encompasses our emotional well being, our thoughts and our beliefs. "When the qi enters the heart meridian, some of it turns to Shen."[4] Shen helps guide our survival instincts, it allows us to express love, compassion and caring, and it keeps our heart spirit calm.

In order for an individual to be healthy, their physical, emotional, spritual and mental aspects need to be balanced. Emotions can and do effect the physical body. Our animal friends are no different. Too much anger or frustration can adversely affect the liver and cause pain in the rib cage, such as in the dog who is continually chained, who barks furiuosly at every passerby. Too much worrying or thinking, (remember the Chocolate Lab who was constantly worried about pleasing her human?) can adversely affect the spleen. Too much fear can adversely affect the kidneys, such as in the cat who is terrorized by any loud sound or sudden movement after too many incidents of children screaming and throwing things at her.

Shen is a vital essence that bathes both the spirit and the mind, which are inseparable.

Endnotes

1, 2, 4. Teeguarden, Ron. *Chinese Tonic Herbs.* (Tokyo & New York: Japan Publications, Inc., 1984), 73, 74, 75.

3. Dr. Kuan Hin. *Chinese Massage and Acupressure.* (New York: Bergh Publishing, Inc., 1991), 76.

Part 2
THE DIAGNOSIS

CHAPTER FIVE

The Diagnosis: What to Expect

You are probably used to taking your animal to a veterinary office and immediately placing her on the exam table. The doctor comes in, inserts a thermometer in the private space under her tail, listens to her chest sounds with a stethoscope, feels her abdomen then looks at the specific problem. All of this may take about ten minutes. Blood tests, radiographs, sonograms and specific laboratory tests may be advised. A prescription is made up and you go home with instructions for giving pills, cleaning the ears, applying eye medication, etc.

When you go to a veterinarian who practices Traditional Chinese Medicine, the scenario is a little different. Before placing the animal on the table, the veterinarian may first ask you some questions concerning your animal's history and behavior. Does the animal like to sit in the sun or does she prefer to find a cool, shady place. Does she like to lean against a firm surface, like the back of a couch or a wall, or does she like to be on a soft, non-supportive surface, like a pillow? When the animal drinks water, does she drink small amounts at a time or large amounts? What are her particular symptoms? During what season or what time of the day is the problem, symptom, or condition worse? What time of the year did it first occur?

Although these questions may seem odd at first, every one of them is meaningful and places the imbalances into the Five Element/Phase System or the Eight Principles of Traditional Chinese Medicine. You will remember that each element is related to an organ that is most active during a specific season and each has been assigned a two-hour time period during the course of each day.

Leaning against a hard surface may indicate that the animal has a deficient type constitution and needs support for the spine or abdominal muscles. Drinking large amounts of water all at once may indicate a propensity for overheating and an internal heat pattern in the Eight Principles. So, one of the first things you may expect when you visit a TCM practitioner is that it may take more time, and you need to prepare yourself for remembering details that might seem unimportant to Western practitioners.

An individual, animal or human, is made up of physical, mental and emotional aspects. Therefore, questions about living conditions, potential stress situations and behavioral tendencies may be addressed. Diet will also be discussed, as it applies to the concept of food therapies in TCM.

The TCM practitioner relies on all the senses: sight, smell, hearing, touch and, in some cases, taste to perform an exam. Although modern veterinarians who practice Traditional Chinese Medicine may require blood tests and other Western laboratory diagnostics, you can be sure that an enormous amount of information is first gleaned from the initial exam that takes place prior to any testing. What is important to remember is that every patient is viewed as a *whole* patient, not as a kidney, liver or ear patient.

THE TRADITIONAL CHINESE PHYSICAL EXAM

The exam has four parts, consisting of **observation, auscultation, palpation** and **olfaction.**

A practitioner will **observe** the animal's behavior in the exam room and during the examination, noticing how calm, restless or focused he is. The practitioner will then look at the animal's tongue, body shape, the coat and integrity of the skin. Finally the individual is observed for vitality by assessing the eyes, muscle tone and gait.

The **auscultation** part of the exam includes listening to the chest with a stethoscope, as in Western medicine. Also noted is the force and character of the breathing and, very importantly, the voice — which in this case may be a soft or loud bark or meow.

Palpation includes the usual feeling of the abdomen and limbs that

Western medical practitioners perform, but in addition, the TCM practitioner palpates, or feels, the pulse. This is a specialized process that I will discuss in detail a bit later. After assessing the pulse, certain acupuncture points are touched to locate any sensitivities. There are specific **diagnostic points** along the back, sides and abdomen that correspond to internal organs. Sensitivity at any of these points may indicate a problem occurring in the corresponding organ. If sensitivity is picked up early, a serious disease may be averted.

Olfaction includes checking the orifices, like the nose, eyes, mouth and ears for odors. The odors are assessed according to the Five Elements and Eight Principles.

Let's look at each part in more detail.

◆ Observation

Pepe, a Cocker Spaniel cross, entered the exam room very cautiously. He sniffed everything very carefully, and moved very slowly, slinking along the wall. When he finally settled down, he stationed himself under the chair where his person was sitting, peering fearfully through his person's legs. The first thing I noticed about Pepe was that he was timid and insecure. This observation had already given me a clue that part of Pepe's imbalance centered around a **deficiency of blood.** A sufficiency of blood in TCM terms gives an individual confidence. Since the heart and pericardium circulate the blood and are responsible for the spirit, or shen, that gives an individual a sense of well being, a deficiency of the heart blood can cause insecurity. If Pepe were under the chair shaking, and his person told me that he was frightened of loud noises, trucks and people, I would probably conclude that the kidney was involved, as the emotion associated with the kidney is fear.

The gait with which an animal moves is also observed and assessed as part of the examination. Is the step strong or weak? This can indicate the suppleness of the spine and limbs and the strength of the bones which are under the auspices of the kidney. Is there vitality in his movement? Vitality reflects an individual's heart blood circulation, kidney essence and qi, and spleen/

pancreas qi. The muscles should be supple and well-toned, indicating a balanced spleen/pancreas. The tendons should be flexible and strong. If they are not, the liver and gall bladder may be out of balance.

When the animal interacts with other animals or people, is he distracted easily or does he stay focused? The earth element of the spleen/pancreas and stomach is primarily responsible for the qi we get from food. The earth element "centers" an individual and allows for clear focus and attention to the world around us. If an animal is constantly distracted, both the qi and the spleen/pancreas may be involved.

The eyes should have a certain shine or brightness. When humans or animals are ill, the eyes lose their normal luster and appear dull. The eyes are the sense organ connected to the liver. Eye problems in general, and brightness in particular, may indicate how well the liver is functioning.

Just as in a Western medical exam, the coat is checked by the TCM practitioner for its luster. In TCM, the coat is a reflection of the blood and fluids of the body, and is also related to the metal elements of the lung and large intestine. Dry, brittle hair may indicate a respiratory weakness or a deficiency in the blood and fluids in the body. It may also predispose an individual to constipation. When I identify deficiency of blood, it does not necessarily indicate anemia, although extreme deficiency of blood will lead to anemia. Rather, this terminology, as discussed in the preceding section on blood, refers to the job the blood does in moistening and nourishing the tissues and organs of the body. When the blood is deficient, one of the first signs we often see is dry skin or hair.

Body type or constitution is also observed. A thin, hyperactive animal may have an imbalance between yin and yang. The more hyper the animal — the more yang. Too much yang, in fact, may make it hard to keep weight on the animal because he is burning it up so quickly. A heavy individual, on the other hand, may have a more yin type constitution and be more phlegmatic and slow-moving.

The other distinction that is made on a first TCM exam is that of a strong or weak constitution. These categories are not critiques of an individual, but observations to help the practitioner fit the patient into an overall diagnostic picture. If a strong individual falls ill, the illness is usually manifested by dramatic symptoms, such as a high fever, swollen glands and much pain, while a weak constitution type might get chills, milder pains and minimal swelling. The strong constitution type will usually recover more quickly, while those with a weak constitution might take longer to heal. It is important to distinguish between the constitutions in Chinese medicine because different herbs would be prescribed in each case, as well as different acupuncture techniques. A weaker constitution type would require milder herbs and acupuncture/acupressure treatment, while a stronger individual would respond better to a stronger regimen of herbs and acupuncture/acupressure technique. In a mild treatment, the number of points would probably be fewer and the depth of the needle or pressure more shallow. On the other hand, a strong treatment might require more needles or deeper or harder pressure.

OBSERVATION	ASSESSMENT
Behavioral & emotional aspects	Heart shen, yin, yang & blood
Emotions exhibited	Five Element association
Hair coat	Blood, fluid, lung health
Eye brightness	Liver health
Vitality & gait	Heart blood, kidney essence, spleen/ pancreas, stomach & kidney qi
Constitution	Strong or weak

◆ Tongue Diagnosis

The tongue is a visual gateway to the interior of the body. The whole body "lives" on the tongue, rather like a hologram. Different areas of the tongue itself correspond to specific internal organs. Abnormalities in the coating, texture, shape and color of the tongue give the TCM practitioner important information for piecing together the state of balance in the patient's body. Tongue diagnosis is part of the observation section of a TCM exam.

The vitality of the tongue reflects the entire body's circulation and is affiliated with the heart. The coating is a reflection of a healthy stomach whose fermentation products produce its color, texture and moisture. The texture of the tongue muscles show the qi of the spleen and blood of the heart. Cracks in the tongue suggest weakened qi or yin or deficiency of heart blood.

A thin white tongue coating is normal in healthy dogs. Cats have thicker tongue coatings than dogs. The coating changes with either the onset of an illness, like a cold, or a deep-seated, chronic, internal problem. Changes in tongue coatings can occur quickly. At the onset of an illness, there may be no change, but if a fever persists, fluids inside the body are used up, and the tongue coating can become dry, or turn yellow or dark in color. This is a heat sign. If no acute illness is present, and a tongue coating is yellow, dark brown or black, this is an indication of internal heat generated from the lungs, liver, stomach or kidney. Whichever organ is involved, if the coating is dark, it is usually a sign of a serious illness.

For some time I had been treating a poodle patient for a weak immune system and weak digestion. Her diagnosis centered around weak spleen qi. This had affected all the qi in her body and compromised her immune system. She felt better after acupuncture treatments and herb therapy. Unfortunately, she had to have a minor surgical procedure, requiring general anesthesia. Her recovery was slow, and several days after the procedure she was still lethargic. You may remember that the liver controls the spleen in the Five Element System, and the liver is also the main organ of detoxification from anesthesia. Since the dog had an inherently weakened spleen, the liver overpowered the spleen, and over-reacted to the anesthetic. The spleen was thereby weakened and unable to produce normal qi, so the dog had no energy and remained lethargic.

When she came in for treatment, I noticed that her tongue had a brownish-yellow coating in the area corresponding to the spleen. This indicated heat and depletion of fluids in that organ. Immediately after the first acupuncture treatment to strengthen the spleen, the tongue coating was normal!

As shown by this example, tongue coating can change quickly, so it is a true reflection of the "now state" of an individual's health.[1]

Tongue coatings may also be thick and white, which indicate an internal coldness in the body. I have seen thick, white, moist coatings on individual animals who have undergone radiation therapy. From the TCM point of view, radiation seems to produce an internal coldness in the body. This slows everything down, sometimes causing depression. If the coating is slimy or greasy, this is known as **phlegm.** Phlegm is stagnant water produced when the movement of fluid in the body is hampered. Pockets of heat can build up, and turn the thin water to a sticky pudding-like phlegm. Everyone is familiar with mucous. If you've ever gotten it on your fingers, and then spread your fingers apart, you know how sticky it is. Phlegm is like mucous, and it can occur not only in the nose, but also in the digestive tract and joints.

The shape and size of the tongue itself is a general reflection of the internal organs. Although tongue coatings can change rapidly, the tongue shape and structure change slowly over a long period of time. The tongue should comfortably fit into the mouth, not hang out or appear shriveled. A tongue that is too large and has teeth imprints on the sides, shows an imbalance in the spleen, which is sensitive to retaining dampness and moisture. A tongue that is shriveled indicates a severe deficiency of fluids in the body, especially of the kidney. It may also indicate an internal coldness that has caused the muscles of the tongue to conract.

The color of the tongue is also important to note. Normal tongues are pink. A darker red indicates an internal heat. If a tongue is pale, there is a deficiency of blood, and also an internal cold. If the tongue is purple, the liver is not functioning properly, because purple signals congestion and a lack of smoothly flowing circulation, which is one of the jobs of the liver.

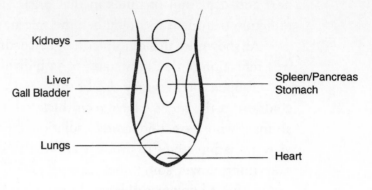

TONGUE MAP

THE TONGUE MAP

The Five Element Organ Systems are located in various positions on the tongue. Although there are variations regarding this **tongue map,** the most common is as follows: The central area houses the spleen/pancreas and stomach. The root of the tongue (at the very back, near the throat) houses the kidney and urinary bladder. The sides of the tongue reflect the liver and gall bladder. The very tip of the tongue corresponds to the Heart. Surrounding the heart in the frontal third portion of the tongue sits the lung.

Changes in the coating or tongue itself in any of these locations may indicate a problem with the interior organ it represents. Since the tongue reflects both the current state of an individual's health, as well as a long-term overview of his or her general well-being, one may also use tongue diagnosis to assess how a patient is responding to a treatment program. Tongue diagnosis is an invaluable tool for the TCM practitioner.

Try noticing your animal friend's tongue the next time she opens her mouth. The most informative reference I have found in the English language on tongue diagnosis is the book by Dr. Giovanni Maciocia, *Tongue Diagnosis in Chinese Medicine.*

This part of the exam focuses on the internal and external sounds made by the individual animal. Aside from breathing patterns, animals may whine or grunt and groan as they change positions. Each sound is associated with a particular element and organ system.[2]

spleen/pancreas–stomach	sing-song whining
lung–large intestine	weeping
kidney–urinary bladder	groaning
liver–gall bladder	shouting/intense barking
heart–small intestine	laughing

If an animal is continually grunting or groaning as he moves about, the kidney may be an underlying problem. Although cats and dogs do not usually laugh, they can appear very happy, even in the most difficult situations. This may be a very good character trait, but in TCM, if there is too much joy, this signals an imbalance in the heart or other fire meridians. It would seem unnatural, for example, to see an animal acting very happy after being caught in a fire or flood or other traumatic situation.

How the animal is breathing is a good indication of the status of the lung, liver, spleen/pancreas and kidney. The lungs, obviously, take in air with each breath. In TCM, the lungs are also responsible for extracting the moisture from the air and directing it downwards to be utilized by the body. It is the kidney's job to "rise up and grasp" the moisture that the lung is directing toward it. Since the kidney lives in the lower part of the body, it has to reach through the center of the body to the upper limits of the diaphragm where the lungs are. To do this effectively, the kidney is aided by the liver and spleen.

If an animal exhibits shallow breathing, there may be a problem with the qi of the lungs which cannot breathe in deeply enough. It may also indicate a weakness of the kidney, especially if the individual has a problem breathing out smoothly and evenly. If there is bloating or distension of the belly that hinders the breathing, the spleen or liver is most likely involved.

Loud breathing may indicate an excess or strong type constitution, while weak breathing, which hardly moves the rib cage, can indicate a deficient or weak type of constitution.

If the breathing is dry, the lung and kidney fluids are low. If the breathing is moist, thick, or wet-sounding, there is usually a problem with an internal coldness and accumulation of dampness which points to a problem with the spleen/pancreas. One can learn all this from observing and listening to the breath.

After listening to and assessing the qualities presented earlier, the next step in the TCM exam is taking the medical history of the dog or cat patient. At this point, questions regarding environmental and behavioral preferences are asked along with specific questions relating to each organ system. For example, does the animal like to "sleep in" in the morning, rather than go out for a walk? If the answer is yes, the spleen/pancreas which is most active in the morning, may be weak, causing heaviness upon rising. If the animal likes to sleep near an open window, or on the cold cement floor, she may be seeking the coolness due to an overheating situation. Is there an inherited problem or was the animal the runt of the litter? This reflects imbalances with the kidney jing or essence.

All of the information that is gathered is aimed at putting together the pieces of a puzzle — when the puzzle is complete, it will be a portrait of your animal companion. Each element of the puzzle, whether it is physical, mental or emotional, is an indispensible part of the total picture according to the principles of TCM.

PALPATION

The next element of the TCM exam focuses on the **pulse** and the **diagnostic points.** While Western medical practitioners check for the strength and rate of the pulse to assess circulation in general, Traditional Chinese Medicine sets

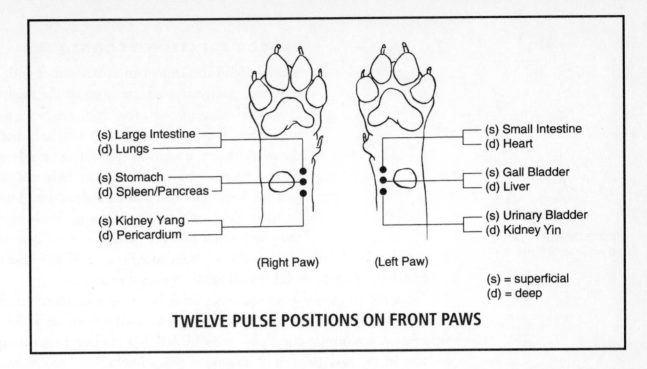

TWELVE PULSE POSITIONS ON FRONT PAWS

even greater store on **reading the pulses.** In humans, pulse diagnosis can be performed using the radial artery on the wrist, the carotid artery on the neck and the dorsal pedal artery on the foot and ankle. Today it is mostly taken from the radial artery of the wrist.[3]

The pulse is felt in three positions and two layers, each corresponding to an organ system and meridian. The more superficial, or surface layer, belongs to the yang organs, while the deeper layer belongs to the yin organs.[4] With three positions and two layers, all twelve meridians and organ systems are assessed. The graphic shows the pulse positions as they would appear on your animal friend's wrist/paw.

However, on small animals such as dogs and cats, it is usually impossible to palpate the pulse at the wrist. Instead, I palpate the femoral artery on the inside of the hind leg at the thigh, very close to the groin area, where the leg joins the body. The first position is closest to the groin, the third position is farthest away.

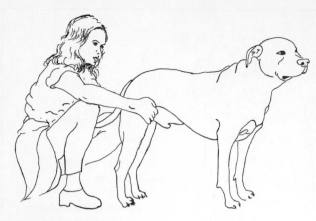

Finding the "pulse"
on your animal friend

PULSE PALPATION TECHNIQUE

Stand behind the animal and place your hands carefully and gently around the front of the thighs and up toward the groin area until you can feel a pulsating artery. There is a small triangular area between the muscles at the topmost part of the inside of the thigh where the pulse can be felt. This is a private area for most animals, and care should be taken to let them know what you are doing. With humans, the practitioner asks the patient to relax before feeling the pulse. With animals, I find it is better to relax myself, so I take some deep breaths and try to center myself before feeling the pulse.

There are seventeen pulse qualities described in the Chinese veterinary literature.[5] It is beyond the scope of this book to discuss them all. Pulse diagnosis takes enormous practice, patience and skill. My purpose here is to introduce you to the *concept* of pulse diagnosis and to help you become familiar with the most simple of the qualities.

The basic qualities that should be noted are **rate, rhythm, shape** and **force**.

The **rate** of the pulse falls into averages, with cats and small dogs having the quickest rate, and larger dogs having the slowest rate. When feeling the pulse rise and fall, it should feel similar to the way the heart beat feels. The pulse rate and the heart rate should be the same. A normal heart rate for a cat is between 120–140 beats per minute. Small dogs run around 100–120 beats per minute. Large dogs, 40–90 beats per minute. The practitioner will count how many heart beats fill a fifteen-second period and multiply the number by four to get a beat per minute figure.

A **fast** pulse may indicate an infection with fever if an acute condition is present. If the condition is not acute, a fast pulse either indicates a yang excess, meaning internal yang, or heat that is overriding the yin and its calming tendencies. The yang excess conditions may signal a problem with an overactive heart or liver, the two most likely culprits of increased yang. A fast pulse may also indicate pain. If there is too little yin, then it may signal a problem with the kidney or lung. One way to tell these conditions apart is to look at the tongue of this individual. If the tongue has a yellow or dark coating and the tongue itself is red *and* the pulse is rapid, this is probably a yang excess condition. If the tongue has no coating *and* the pulse is rapid, this is usually a problem with not enough yin to counter the yang. In the first case, there is too much heat, no matter what the status of the yin. In the second case, the pulse rate has increased because the yin is very weak, and even though the yang is normal, it is *relatively* higher than it should be. This is known as **false heat** or **deficiency fire.**

If the pulse is **slow,** it may indicate a cold and yin condition, such as sluggishness in the digestive system, or a weakened qi. This is just the opposite of the yang and hot individual. During cold weather conditions, there may not be enough warming or heating capacity, so it slows the body down. The practitioner would look at the tongue to see if it was pale in color or had a thick white coating, which would corroborate the cold diagnosis. If a pulse really has an excess yin quality, it might be difficult to find, as it is buried deep in the tissues. Overweight individuals often have this type of pulse.

The pulse should feel the same size in **diameter** on the right and left hind legs. The rhythm should feel smooth, rising and falling equally. The average diameter of the femoral artery, is:

Cat, small dog:	1/8 inch (#9 spaghetti, apple stem)
Medium dog:	1/4 inch (narrow end of chopstick)
Large dog:	3/8 – 1/2 inch (chopstick to drinking straw)

If, when you feel the pulse of the animal, it seems significantly smaller or greater than these examples, there may be a problem with the amount of blood circulating. A pulse that is very thin, or "thread-like" has a blood or fluid deficiency. If it feels very large, there may be an overactive heart or liver imbalance.

After feeling the diameter, see if you can get an idea about the **shape**. Wide, flat and soft pulses may indicate a spleen problem with too much moisture. Narrow, but forceful pulses may indicate stagnation in the liver, giving a taut edge. If the pulse feels like knots in a clothesline, a heart problem may be present.

The **force** of the pulse is next to be observed. A strong pulse means that you barely put your fingers to the skin, and you can feel the pulse pounding. If it is too forceful it is an indication of too much yang. If it is weak and mushy, this is a problem with weak qi.

In any of these cases, it is important to get a general idea of the pulse of the individual and use it as one of the puzzle pieces in the patterns of Traditional Chinese Medicine.

THE DIAGNOSTIC POINTS

One of the most useful tools of the TCM exam in veterinary medicine, is the palpation of the **diagnostic points.** These points are situated along the back, sides and abdomen of your animal.[7] Each point is associated with an internal organ system or meridian.

The points that run alongside the spine can be found in depressions in the long muscle groups that parallel the vertebrae. They begin between the shoulder blades and end in the sacral area. They are part of the urinary bladder meridian that runs the entire length of the spine. Sensitivity at any of these points may indicate a problem occurring within the associated organ. The points along the spine can also correspond to local back and muscle problems.

The diagnostic points along the spine are called **association points.** There are twelve pairs of association points found along the spine.

In addition to the association points, there are points that are more specific to each internal organ itself, and do not usually indicate local muscle problems. These points are called **alarm points.** They are found on different meridians and are located along the abdomen and side areas. All points, excluding those on the abdominal midline, are paired.

The acupoints that make up the association and alarm points together make up the diagnostic points. As the name implies, diagnostic points are used to check the balance of an organ. As part of the palpation phase of the exam, the practitioner will assess the sensitivity of these points by using fingertip pressure. If an animal is sensitive at a specific point, she will turn around and let the practitioner know. If a point is sensitive, the animal may snap or growl. The skin around the point may begin to ripple or twitch when touched. If the point is sensitive and there is a weakness, merely touching this point can make the animal sink to her knees. This usually indicates a milder type of problem.

Diagnostic points are useful because, as in other forms of Traditional Chinese Medicine, early recognition of an imbalance may avoid a serious disease process from developing. Additionally, they can alert the practitioner to look for abnormalities in the organs which may require further testing.

In a review of 175 cases that I've seen in my clinic, there has been a strong correlation between sensitivity at diagnostic points and irregularities in blood tests.[6] In cases where the points were sensitive and the blood tests were abnormal, treating these points either with acupuncture or acupressure often restored a normal blood value. In other cases, where the points were sensitive, the animal was uncomfortable, but the blood tests were normal, the points were treated until the sensitivity vanished, and hopefully, the potential problem was cleared.

To test the diagnostic points, stand behind the animal and place your index fingers on either side of the spine at the points indicated on the charts on pages 59–64. Apply light to moderate pressure at each point. If your animal is sensitive, go to the corresponding alarm point of the organ on the abdomen or side and see if this is also sensitive. If so, a problem is probably occurring within the organ. If only the back point is sensitive, this could indicate an organ involvement or a local muscle or spine problem.

Cats and dogs have seven cervical (neck) vertebrae, thirteen thoracic vertebrae where ribs are attached, seven lumbar (lower back) vertebrae, three sacral (pelvic area) vertebrae, and twenty to twenty-three tail vertebrae.

A rib extends between two thoracic vertebrae. Two adjoining ribs make up a **rib space.** Cats and dogs have twelve rib spaces and thirteen ribs.

In between the depressions on either side of the spinal vertebrae, lying in the rib space, one can find six of the association points. These are the lung, pericardium, and heart, found between the shoulder blades, and the liver, gall bladder and spleen/pancreas in the last rib section. Just behind the last rib sits another association point, that of the stomach.

The association points in the lumbar area can be found in the thick muscle groups running along each side of the spine. Depressions between the lumbar vertebrae house three to five association points. They are the triple heater, kidney, large intestine, and in some cases, the small intestine and urinary bladder. I say some cases, because in most animals, the small intestine and urinary bladder association points are found in the two sets of depressions that can be felt over the sacrum. The reason for the discrepancy as to where to find the small intestine and urinary bladder association points stems from the fact that humans and animals have different vertebral numbers and association points were extrapolated from human data. Additionally, the nerves that serve the small intestine and bladder may have slightly different grouping origins, which account for the alternate places. I suggest that you feel along the lumbar spine *and* the sacrum. If there is sensitivity at a point in either section, it may indicate a problem with the small intestine or bladder.

The alarm points have no specific order and relate directly to their corresponding organ.

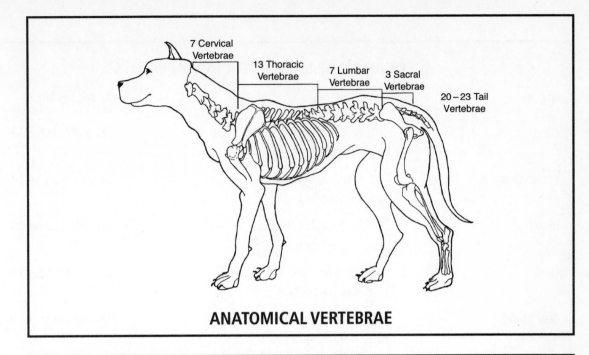

ANATOMICAL VERTEBRAE

7 Cervical Vertebrae

13 Thoracic Vertebrae

7 Lumbar Vertebrae

3 Sacral Vertebrae

20 – 23 Tail Vertebrae

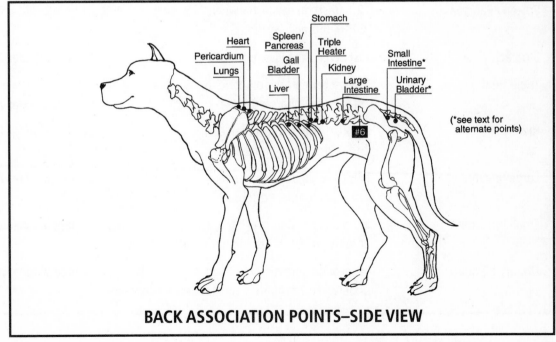

BACK ASSOCIATION POINTS–SIDE VIEW

Stomach

Heart

Spleen/ Pancreas

Triple Heater

Pericardium

Gall Bladder

Kidney

Small Intestine*

Lungs

Liver

Large Intestine

Urinary Bladder*

#6

(*see text for alternate points)

LOCATION OF BACK ASSOCIATION POINTS[7]

Organ	Location	Acupoint No.
Lung*	3rd rib space, between 3rd & 4th thoracic vertebrae	Urinary Bladder 13
Pericardium*	4th rib space, between 4th & 5th thoracic vertebrae	Urinary Bladder 14
Heart*	5th rib space, between 5th & 6th thoracic vertebrae	Urinary Bladder 15
Liver	10th rib space, between 10th & 11th thoracic vertebrae	Urinary Bladder 18
Gall Bladder	11th rib space, between 11th & 12th thoracic vertebrae	Urinary Bladder 19
Spleen / Pancreas	12th (last) rib space, between 12th & 13th thoracic vertebrae	Urinary Bladder 20
Stomach	Just behind the last rib	Urinary Bladder 21
Triple Heater	In muscle depression between 1st & 2nd lumbar vertebrae	Urinary Bladder 22
Kidney**	In muscle depression between 2nd & 3rd lumbar vertebrae	Urinary Bladder 23
Large Intestine	In muscle depression between 4th & 5th lumbar vertebrae	Urinary Bladder 25
Small Intestine	In first depression over sacrum or between 6th & 7th lumbar vertebrae	Urinary Bladder 27
Urinary Bladder	In second depression over sacrum or between 7th lumbar and 1st sacral vertebrae	Urinary Bladder 28

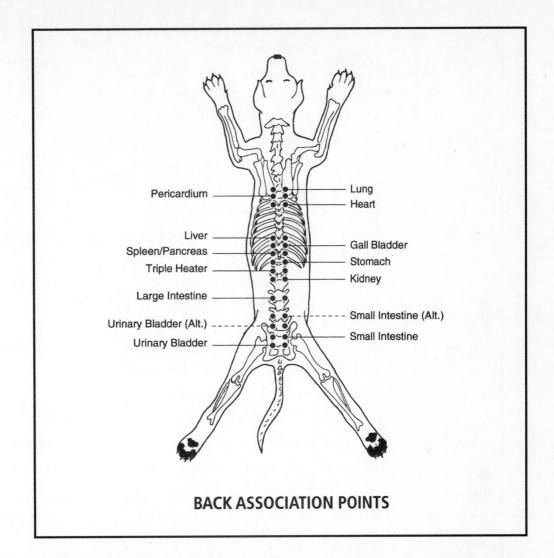

Pericardium — Lung

Heart

Liver

Spleen/Pancreas — Gall Bladder

Triple Heater — Stomach

Kidney

Large Intestine

Urinary Bladder (Alt.) - - - Small Intestine (Alt.)

Urinary Bladder — Small Intestine

BACK ASSOCIATION POINTS

* An easy way to locate lung, pericardium or heart points is to have your animal in a standing position. The area between the shoulder blades at the level of the spine encompasses these three points. The lung point can be found at the beginning of the shoulder blades, the pericardium in the middle, and the heart just behind the blade.

**An easy way to find the kidney association point is to locate the widest part of the arc that forms the last rib. Place your thumb here, and extend your index finger up to the spine. The kidney point is found here.

LOCATION OF ALARM POINTS

Organ	Location	Acupoint No.
Lung	In the deep brisket or pectoral muscle in the dog, and under the collar bone of the cat.	Lung 1
Pericardium	On abdominal midline, approximately at the level of the upper set of nipples.	Conception Vessel 17
Heart	On abdominal midline, on the extension of the last bone of the sternum, known as the xyphoid process.	Conception Vessel 14
Stomach	On the abdominal midline, halfway between the tip of the last sternum bone and the umbilicus.	Conception Vessel 12
Liver	Due to anatomical variations between human and animal, point is located near the bottom end of the 6th or 9th rib space.	Liver 14
Gall Bladder	Due to anatomical variations, the point is usually located near the bottom of the 10th rib space.	Gall Bladder 24
Spleen/Pancreas	At the end of the 11th (last enclosed) rib space, just in front of 12th rib.	Liver 13
Kidney	At the end of the last (floating) rib.	Gall Bladder 25
Large Intestine	1/2 inch on either side of umbilicus (naval)	Stomach 25
Triple Heater	If abdomen divided into fifths between naval and pelvis, this point is 2/5 down from naval	Conception Vessel 5
Small Intestine	If abdomen divided into fifths between naval and pelvis, this point is 3/5 down from naval.	Conception Vessel 4
Urinary Bladder	Abdominal midline, overlying pelvic bone	Conception Vessel 3

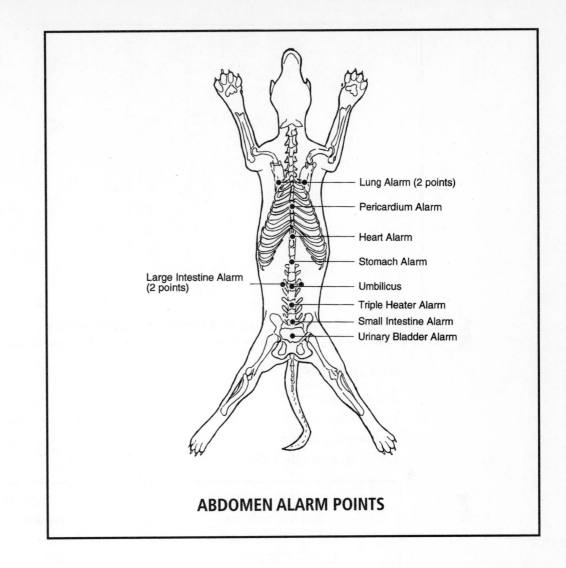

Lung Alarm (2 points)

Pericardium Alarm

Heart Alarm

Stomach Alarm

Large Intestine Alarm
(2 points)

Umbilicus

Triple Heater Alarm

Small Intestine Alarm

Urinary Bladder Alarm

ABDOMEN ALARM POINTS

Both the association points and the alarm points can be used for treatment as well as diagnosis. They can also be included in regular daily massage routines.

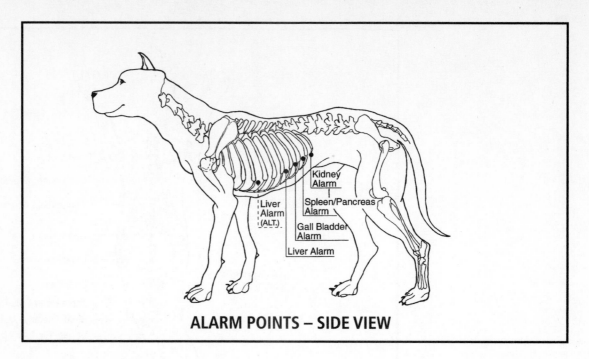

ALARM POINTS – SIDE VIEW

OLFACTION

The final aspect of the TCM exam employs your nose. Odors abound where animals are concerned, and attempting to classify these odors is helpful in pinpointing a problem area. You will remember that each element is associated with a specific odor:

Spleen/Pancreas, Stomach	Sickly sweet
Lung/Large Intestine	Rotten
Kidney/Urinary Bladder	Putrid
Liver/Gall Bladder	Rancid
Heart/Small Intestine	Scorched, burnt

Discharges can be extremely odoriferous and an unmistakable indicator of illness. They can arise from the skin itself, or from the ears, nose, vagina or penis. The breath may also have a distinctive or strong odor, as can the urine or stool. In fact, one of the first symptoms that an animal may exhibit is a peculiar odor. Because some of us have a more sensitive sense of smell than others, odors may not become a factor until they are quite strong. Usually the stronger the odor, the more serious the imbalance has become. So it would not be unusual to see the TCM veterinarian sniffing around your animal. The animals don't seem to mind this, but some of their humans think it's odd.

Once a TCM exam is performed, with its observation, auscultation, palpation and olfaction, the practitioner will step back and review the patient in her/his entirety before making up a treatment plan. Treatments may include massage, acupuncture, dietary or herbal therapy, all of which are intended to bring the individual back into a healthful balance.

Endnotes

1. Maciocia, Giovanni. *Tongue Diagnosis in Chinese Medicine.* (Seattle, WA: Eastland Press, 1987), 15.
2, 4. Connelly, Dianne M. *Traditional Acupuncture: The Law of the Five Elements.* (Columbia, MD: Center for Traditional Acupuncture, 1979), 32, 52, 72, 87, 104, 114.
3. Wiseman, Nigel, Andrew Ellis, Paul Zmiewski. *Fundamentals of Chinese Medicine.* (Brookline, MA: Paradigm Publications, 1985), 141–149.
5. Klide, Alan M., Shiu H. Kung. *Veterinary Acupuncture.* (Philadelphia, PA: University of Pennsylvania Press, 1977), 12–16.
6. Schwartz, C., DVM. North American Veterinary Conference, Orlando, FL, 1993.
7. Schoen, Allen M., DVM, MS., ed. *Veterinary Acupuncture, Ancient Art to Modern Science.* (Goleta, CA: American Veterinary Publishers, 1994). Canine Atlas by Y-C Hwang, 107–140.
Janssens, Luc A.A., DVM, PhD. *Acupuncture Points and Meridians in the Dog.* (Boulder, CO: International Veterinary Acupuncture Society, 1984). *Acupuncture, A Comprehensive Text.* J. O'Connor and D. Bensky, trans. ed., (Seattle, WA: Eastland Press, 1974).

Exact anatomical locations and nomenclature listed in these references.

CHAPTER SIX

Herbology

Throughout our history, herbs have been used for healing. Herbal medicines are derived from plant, animal and mineral sources and have been handed down as traditional folk remedies for countless generations. Virtually every culture on earth has contributed to this vast store of knowledge. Herbal medicines have also been studied and formalized, along with medical education in general, in both the East and West. Our current use of this ancient medical art is supported by empirical evidence and scientific phytotheory. In fact, it was only in recent times that synthesized drugs, like antibiotics, were developed to combat disease. It is interesting to note that many synthesized drugs are derived from plants — a prime example is the heart drug digitalis. Made from the foxglove plant, it has been used to treat heart conditions for more than a century.

It is also interesting to note that there is currently an explosion of interest in the study of the vast array of virtually unknown plants from the world's tropical rain forests. Aware of the potential beneficial uses and applications that these plants could have, pharmacologists and herbalists from all parts of the world are attempting to collect, identify, and preserve this wealth of flora before their fragile environment is destroyed.

Since ancient times, herbalists have studied the physical environments of plants, minerals and animals. They looked at where and in what season they flourished and grew, what extremes of climate and weather they were able to withstand, and which conditions were most harmful. They studied the resemblance of a substance in nature to that of a specific component of the human body. All these features guided the herbalist in recognizing natural patterns and how they resembled patterns in people. In Traditional Chinese Medicine, herbalists categorized these substances according to the philosophies of the Five Elements and Eight Principles. In the West, herbs were categorized according to Galen and the Greek and Roman system of the Four Elements of earth, air, fire and water. As Western herbology developed, the herbal matching system became known as the **doctrine of signatures**. Although this phrase was coined by European herbologists, the Chinese herbology system adheres to the same principle. Just as each individual signs her name differently, each natural substance has a signature of its own.

For example, plants with large leaves service large surface area organs such as the skin, the lungs or the liver. Burdock is one such plant. Plants with fuzzy, soft, flannel-like short hairs that resemble lung or intestinal cilia, or which contain slimy, mucous-like sap, may be used to soothe throats, coughs or diarrhea. Mullein and marshmallow are examples. Plants that have long growing seasons, whose buds first appear in spring, but that do not flower and fully mature until winter, such as the sour mountain date in China, are known as longevity herbs because they can withstand several seasons and harsh conditions.[1] The shape of an oyster shell resembles a kidney, and the way it functions by filtering water through its valves in its watery habitat is similar to the way the kidney filters and purifies fluids in the body. Crushed oyster shell is often used by the TCM practitioner to improve the vitality (qi) of the kidney.

Ancient Chinese legends tell of animals that guided humans to the use of plants. Henry Lu relates the legend of Asiatic plantain (cheqian). During the Han Dynasty in the first century, a famous Chinese general and his troops were forced to stay in an uninhabited area where the troops suffered from famine, thirst and blood in their urine. A groom noticed that his horses, who were grazing on a certain plant in the area, did not have blood in the urine. The groom alerted the general who had all his troops boil the plant and drink the decoction. The debilitating condition disappeared, and the horses were acknowledged as saviors.[2] In North America, a relative of the Asiatic plantain was used by Native Americans and European settlers for easing inflammation and stopping hemorrhage.

HISTORICAL BACKGROUND OF CHINESE
AND WESTERN HERBS

Historically, herbal therapy in China dates back to the third century B.C., the earliest known medical treatise being *The Yellow Emperor's Classic of Internal Medicine.* During the first and second centuries A.D., another book was compiled called *The Classic of the Agriculture Emperor's Materia Medica.* It listed 365 plant, animal and mineral substances that could be used to treat 170 diseases.[3]

Later in the third century A.D., a very famous book by Dr. Zhang Zong-Jing was written called *The Shang Han Lun.* The diagnosis and herbs in this book are still studied today in Oriental medical schools. The *Shang Han Lun* discusses the stages and severity of diseases, alerting doctors to a favorable or unfavorable prognosis. About one fifth of the herbs listed 1,600 years ago are still in use today.

Over many centuries, Chinese medicine developed different schools of thought as to the underlying causes of imbalances and disease. These philosophies came from further study and interpretation of the Eight Principles and Five Elements. Imbalance and disease were thought to be the result of interlocking patterns of all of nature's forces which are never static. As part of this philosophy, the herbal system understands that many causes make up an imbalance. And formulas are used to rebalance the entire system, treating the symptom and the root causes.

Native peoples on the American continents have used herbs for centuries, handing down their knowledge primarily in their oral traditions. Like the Chinese, both spiritual and physical aspects of the plants and animals were observed and studied in order to best utilize their healing properties. Native Americans in this country saved many European settlers' lives by introducing them to local herbs. One example is Indian sage, or boneset, which was used for epidemic fevers, flus, colds and grippes.[4]

Unlike Chinese and Native American herbologies, modern European herbology is based upon the quantitative aspects and functions of specific herbs. At one time European herbologists adhered to the doctrine of signatures, which you may recall, encompassed the qualities of the herbs in their environments. Today, European herbologists study the specific chemical particles contained within the plant. These are called the active constituents. This system is called pharmacognosy or phytotherapy, and is the forerunner of our synthesized Western drugs. Here specific complaints are addressed by specific plant substances in a more linear manner. Much of the Western research that is recognized by the pharmaceutical industry is based upon phytotherapy. In the Western tradition, herbs are used singly or in smaller formulas than their Chinese counterparts.

HERBS TODAY

Today herbs are on the cutting edge of treating many cancers, viruses and chronic debilitating diseases with which Western drugs have had limited success. Chinese, indigenous North and South American and European herbs are all being sought as alternatives, and in some instances, replacements for Western drugs. Because herbs are in the forefront of many modern therapies, scientists are looking at exactly how they work. Studies are underway that examine: the active constituents of these plant, mineral and animal substances; patients' responses to them; and possible methods of synthesizing them. I would like to point out here that many traditional herbalists, myself included, disagree with relying on finding the active constituent of an herb. Instead, we use parts of the entire plant to include their synergistic effects and to maintain a link to the natural environment.

In veterinary medicine, practitioners have been using Chinese herbs in this country for approximately twenty years, and Western herbs for much longer. Personally, I have been using herbs for over a dozen years, and find them both practical and effective on their own or in conjunction with Western pharmaceutical medications. In order to get the best results, I prefer using the Traditional Chinese diagnosis system whether I'm using Chinese or Western herbs.

ADVANTAGES FOR USING HERBS

With the exception of conditions that require surgery, herbs can be used to treat almost any condition. In Traditional Chinese Medicine, both the ailment *and* the type of individual are taken into account for diagnosis and treatment. For example, an antibiotic would be prescribed by a Western practitioner to kill the bacteria causing an infection, regardless of the type of individual she was treating. But to a TCM practitioner, antibiotics belong to a category of cooling or heat clearing herbs. Giving a cooling type herb to a cold type individual with a constitution prone to diarrhea, water vomiting, weak digestion or problems in cold weather, might cause diarrhea or vomiting as a side effect. Instead, she would use a combination of herbs that would clear the infection *and* protect the digestion of the cold type patient. Thus, advantage number one is that herbs can be tailored to the individual.

Herbs can also increase vitality and fluids in the body. These herbs are called **tonics** and can be used to gently nurture and strengthen an individual for long periods of time without unwanted side effects. By strengthening an organ system, you can often prevent future problems. So, advantage number two is **tonification** and **prevention** of further disease.

For example, a cat with kidney problems is at higher risk of getting urinary bladder infections because the entire urinary system is weakened by the dysfunctional kidney. Herbs that help tonify the kidney also keep the bladder in better shape by allowing the kidney to successfully filter toxins and fluids. This keeps urine passing more freely and the bladder working regularly, not letting its guard down to infectious agents.

By working with the immune system, herbs can increase lymph flow and activate T-cells to fight off infections.[5] Herbs can fight bacteria, as antibiotics do, and also viruses. Herbs such as *radix isatisdis sue baphicacanthi* are being used to help treat the AIDS virus in humans and the FeLV and FIV viruses in cats.

Some herbs have been shown to have specific action against the bacteria that cause tuberculosis. This disease is on the rise in the U.S. among humans, and many of the Western drugs are no longer effective. Studies in China have shown the herb *rhizoma coptidis* to be effective in treating TB.[6] Some cats and dogs who suffer from chronic lung infections may become resistant to many antibiotics. These cases can benefit greatly from herbs.

Herbs are being used to treat certain types of **cancer**. Studies being done in Japan, Taiwan and China, show promise in halting or delaying tumor growth, and herbs such as *ganoderma mushrooms* appear to help stop the metastasizing, or spread, of certain tumors.[7] Herbs are used as a first line of defense in the debilitated, older animal or in conjunction with chemo- or radiation therapy to help strengthen the individual and mitigate side effects. So, advantage number three is that herbs can be used as an adjunct to Western treatments.

Herbs are also employed to help treat **pain**. Animals who suffer from chronic, degenerative conditions such as arthritis and hip dysplasia, can usually benefit from taking herbs. As mentioned earlier, the Chinese believe that pain stems from a blockage of qi or circulation along the pathways of energy called meridians. When herbs are prescribed, they address the blockage problem, and also help to strengthen the bones and the tissues surrounding the painful area.

A TCM exam can often pinpoint a *pattern* of imbalance that would not be identified in a Western exam. For instance, an animal may exhibit loss of appetite in the mornings or evenings on a regular basis. A Western practitioner may not identify this as a problem, but a TCM diagnosis would view this as a problem occurring between the liver and the spleen/pancreas. Herbs would be used to harmonize the workings of these two organ systems and restore normal appetite.

Finally, herbs have the advantage of being better tolerated in some drug sensitive individuals. This is especially true with cortisone preparations which are good for decreasing inflammation, but can cause uncontrollable urination, vomiting or panting in some animals.

• Tailored to individual

• Improve vitality,
blood, fluid balance

• Act as a preventative

• Strengthen the
immune system

• Antiviral and
antibacterial
activity

• Anti cancer activity

• Pain relief

• Unidentified Western
disease patterns

• Drug sensitive
individuals

It's important to state here that although I believe herbs are wonderful, they are not a panacea. Nor is it my intention to minimize the good effects of Western medications. They are often necessary and in many situations, the only substances that are completely effective. Herbs simply offer a more gentle and acceptable alternative to some animals.

QUALITIES AND CATEGORIES OF HERBS IN TRADITIONAL CHINESE MEDICINE

Herbs have **flavors**, **meridian associates**, **thermal energies**, **directions**, **actions** and **categories**. These qualities are used to restore the balance of yin and yang within the individual, which is vital to health.

◆ Flavors and Meridians

Each herb when ingested imparts a flavor, and each flavor, has a specific function and is associated with a specific meridian. **Sweet** herbs strengthen and are usually associated with the **spleen/pancreas** and **stomach** meridians. **Sour** herbs dry, restore and soothe inflamed mucous membranes of the respiratory, digestive and urinary systems. These herbs are also known as **astringents** and most are related to the **liver** meridian. **Hot/spicy/pungent** and **acrid** herbs disperse circulation and energy. These herbs are usually associated with the **lung** meridian and respiratory system. **Bitter** herbs help clear infection, detoxify the system and are usually associated with the **liver** or **heart** meridians. **Salty** herbs help soften masses or nodules such as cysts or tumors, and are usually associated with the **kidney**. In the treatment section of this book, when a meridian and organ system is discussed, herbs will be recommended that are beneficial for restoring balance.

◆ Temperature and Directions

Each herb has a **thermal** and **directional energy**. When an herb is consumed, it imparts its own internal temperature quality. Herbs can be **hot, cold, warm,**

cool or **neutral.** Herbs can also direct more circulation to the areas of the body that need them. For example, an herb can have an **upward** direction and help the yang of the body by increasing circulation to the head and chest area. An herb can also have a **sinking** or **downward** direction, which helps the yin of the body to calm and cool itself. An herb can have a **dispersing** and **outward** direction which acts to increase circulation near the body's surface.

◆ Actions and Categories

There are 37 actions or functions currently listed for herbs.[8] These stem from eight traditional classifications that have been expanded and specialized.

Herbs are categorized according to patterns described by the Five Elements and Eight Principles. They include, yin/yang, cold/hot, deficiency/excess, and interior/exterior. Their qualities also encompass dryness, dampness, wind invasions along with the earth, metal, water, wood and fire elements. A TCM herbalist matches a diagnosis category with an herb category.

EIGHT TRADITIONAL HERB CLASSIFICATIONS AND THEIR FUNCTIONS.[9]

Sweating herbs are used in humans *and* animals when there is an acute condition, like the flu or a high fever. Although animals do not sweat the way humans do, there is an internal reaction that transfers heat to the body's surface as a result of ingesting sweating herbs. It appears as a vapor-like moisture at the skin's surface.

Vomiting herbs induce the patient to vomit up toxic matter. We rarely use this in veterinary medicine, as Western drugs are usually preferred.

Draining downward herbs act to induce bowel movements in cases of severe constipation. They are used for short-term treatments only, as extended use can damage the qi.

Harmonizing herbs help with the interior organs and their relationships. They are especially helpful in digestive disturbances between the liver and the spleen/pancreas, or the gall bladder and stomach. These herbs are also useful in patients who have contracted viral or bacterial infections and are unable to shake them. Any prolonged illness can weaken the internal organs, leaving the patient susceptible to serious disease. These herbs help strengthen the organs while at the same time, help to expel the pathogen.

Warming herbs address the individual with a cold type constitution. Certain pains in the body are classified as cold and can be severely aggravated by cold weather. Warming herbs can be extremely helpful in regulating the internal temperature of a cold type individual.

Clearing herbs clear heat from the body and are useful in treating infections. Fever, inflammation and skin problems, such as hot spots, scabs or other bleeding eruptions, also respond well. Any uncontrolled bleeding from the body, whether from a stomach ulcer, colitis, respiratory infection, etc., is a sign of heat.

Reducing herbs are used to soften and diminish tumors, lumps, cysts, or phlegm. In Chinese medicine, the liver is responsible for smoothly circulating the blood and the energy. If there is a stagnation in the circulation, tissue substances will tend to accumulate like flotsam around a log jammed in a narrow stream. As the water rushes by, dead leaves, branches, silt, pebbles and waste products become caught and block the stream creating a stagnant pool. In the body, any circulatory slowdown, say from a narrowed blood vessel, an inflamed portion of intestine or a thickened sinus area, can act like a jammed log slowly choking the pathway with debris. The normally cool fluid becomes heated and sticky and turns to stagnant phlegm. If left untreated, lumps or cysts may form. Reducing herbs help to liquefy this phlegm, clear the blockage and send it on its way.

Tonifying herbs comprise one of the largest categories used in veterinary herbology. These herbs strengthen the different components in the body and increase vitality, blood building, fluid building and warming.

An expansion of one of the eight classic herb categories used in veterinary herbology is the "astringing" herb. Astringents strenthen and tighten the

EAST-WEST CROSS MATCH FOR
HERB ACTIONS AND INDICATIONS

Eastern Action	Western Indications
Sweating, warm, acrid herb	Flu with stiff muscles, worse in cold
Sweating, cool, acrid herb	High fever, sore throat
Harmonizing liver & spleen, stomach & intestines	Loose stools, depressed a.m. appetite, finicky eater, gas, burping, food sensitive
the **exterior with interior**	Slow recuperation from infection with body weakness, chills & fever
Clearing	Infections, skin eruptions, hot spots, hemorrhages, fevers, abscesses
Reducing & Phlegm Transforming	Fatty tumors, cysts, malignant tumor shrinkage, abscesses, chronic coughs
Astringing Qi with warm, sweet herb Blood with neutral salty herb Water with cooling, acrid herb	 Low odor diarrhea with undigested food Hemorrhage Urinary incontinence
Tonifying Qi with warm sweet herb Yang with warm sweet herb Blood with warm, sweet, or bitter herb Yin with cool, sweet, or bitter herb	 Poor appetite, weight loss Weak hind legs, impotence Anemia, palpitations Dry chronic cough

cell membrane and thus limit leakage of material through the cell wall. This makes them useful in curbing diarrhea which leaks fluid and protein from the gut. They are also useful in cases of hemorrage from blood vessels and involuntary urine leakage from the bladder.

There are now thirty-seven different herb classifications used to address the complex illnesses of the modern veterinary and human world. These include specific categories for arthritis, hormonal and immune-induced disorders.

SINGLE HERB EXAMPLES

Although most Chinese herbs are used within formulas, here are some examples of single herbs that fit into the above classifications.

I'm sure you've all heard of **Ginseng**. Ginseng is an example of a qi tonic that is warming and sweet with an upward direction. Ginseng helps the spleen and stomach meridians and is used to enhance the immune system, to help stimulate appetite and weight gain, to help modulate blood pressure and to tonify the yang and male assertiveness tendencies of the body.

Another herb that you many be familiar with is **Tang Kuei**. Tang Kuei is a blood tonic that is warming, sweet and sour. It works with the liver meridian to nourish and move the blood. It is used to treat anemia, dry skin, dizziness and to tonify the yin and female calmness and internal nurturing tendencies of the body.

Pinellia is a warm, acrid herb with a downward direction that transforms cold phlegm and is considered a reducing herb. It works with the spleen/pancreas and stomach meridians. It is helpful with vomiting of water or mucous, watery diarrhea and coughs with sticky, clear-colored phlegm.

The **Ma-Huang** twig is an example of a sweating herb which is used as a first-line defense against colds and flus. It is warm and acrid, working with the lung and urinary/bladder meridians. It has an outward dispersing direction, and is used in cases of acute upper respiratory problems that have watery nose and eye discharges. It's also helpful for fatigue.

The preceding table is an example of how an herbalist would classify and choose herbs from the TCM diagnostic groupings already discussed to treat common modern problems.

PUTTING IT ALL TOGETHER

Now that you've had an introduction to the different aspects of the single herbs, let's put it together so you can see how herbs are used in a practical clinical setting.

Felix is a long-haired black and white cat who has had chronic diarrhea for over a year and is losing weight. He lives near the ocean in a damp basement apartment. Felix's person is bringing him to see me because the Western medications that had been prescribed were not working. During our initial exam, I notice that Felix is showing cold type symptoms. His person reports that Felix doesn't seem particularly thirsty, that he does like to bury himself under the covers or sit on top of the heater vent, and that he's sluggish. His diarrhea began during a cold spell the previous winter. I examine his tongue, which is pale and flabby. His pulse is weak, deep and slow. These symptoms tell me that Felix does not have enough yang or qi to keep his spleen/pancreas and stomach warm and dry. This has been made worse by the cold, damp environment in which he lives.

The spleen/pancreas has the job of transforming the food we eat into usable energy and qi. The stomach has the job of transporting this food to other parts of the body so that it can be used. In Felix's case, the spleen/pancreas is sensitive to cold and damp and has become weakened. In the Five Element System the stomach (earth element) feeds the colon (metal element). The colon, in turn, can become stressed and malfunction. This results in the diarrhea, causing malabsorption and weight loss.

To treat this condition, I recognize that using herbs to help only the colon would not solve the problem. All of the issues need to be addressed so I prescribe an herb combination that will: (1) warm the individual, (2) center its energy by upwardly re-directing the downward flow of diarrhea, and (3) tonify the qi thereby helping to strengthen the spleen/pancreas and stomach.

This will indirectly help the colon stop the diarrhea and balance out its underlying cause. Happily, Felix responds well to this treatment.

Because of the complex nature of herbs, a more detailed study needs its own book. Suffice it to say here that herbal formulas include four components.[10] A **chief** herb is chosen which addresses the main problem. A **ministerial** herb addresses a secondary problem which helps the chief herb perform effectively. **Assistant** and **envoy** herbs are added, which help direct herbs to their destinations and ameliorate any potential side effects, such as digestive disturbances.

HERBAL PREPARATIONS, PATENT HERBS AND DOSAGES

Herbs can be purchased fresh, in dried or freeze-dried powders, tinctures, teas, syrups, tablets, and in round pellets of different sizes.

Fresh or dried, whole herbs are cooked into strong teas known as **infusions** or **decoctions**. The milder herbs such as chamomile, catnip or plantain prepared this way are more suitable to animal use, as the stronger smelling and tasting herbs prepared like this are usually refused. In cases where stronger or larger doses are required, the best preparations are usually the powdered or freeze-dried powders. Freeze-dried herbs are made from brewed teas and then dried, like many instant coffees.

Tinctures are made from dried or fresh herbs steeped in alcohol or glycerine for a specific period of time so that their properties can be extracted into the liquid. Cats and some dogs are very sensitive to alcohols and the tinctures need to be diluted as indicated in the specific treatment section, or by actually boiling off the alcohol. To do this, place the opened herb bottle in the top of a double boiler for five minutes so that the steam rises and the alcohol evaporates. Tinctures are very efficient ways to use herbs with animals.

Patent herbs are ready-mixed preparations which are based on frequently used traditional formulas prescribed by herbal practitioners. The formulas use the qualities and classifications already discussed. Ordinarily, a prescription is made by combining exact amounts of the dried herbs together in a packet which is then boiled and drunk as tea. But some formulas have become so common, that it is easier for manufacturers to make them into already mixed pills, granules or liquids, thus eliminating the weighing and cooking steps. These patent medicines can then be purchased over the counter, similar to drugs sold without prescriptions in our pharmacies. The Chinese formulas listed in the treatment section of the book are patent medicines.

Some of the Chinese herbal formulas contain domestic animal substances. Ethically, I do not believe in using these products if at all possible. In some cases, where there are no substitute formulas, I find myself in a bind as to whether or not to use an animal substance, to heal another animal. If any formula listed in Part Three includes animal products, it is identified. It is up to you to decide whether to use it.

There are over 1,000 commonly used patent combinations.[11] According to a regulatory law passed in 1985, all pharmacies producing these herbs are inspected by government agencies in China. However, some manufacturers are noted for the excellent quality of their herbs. The F.D.A. regulates the importation of many patent herbs and medicines. They are available in local Chinese neighborhoods, health food stores, herb companies or through acupuncture and herbal practitioners.

As an ecologist, I am drawn to using herbs that grow in the part of the world where I practice. While I prefer the traditional Chinese concepts of differentiation and diagnosis, of course, I don't live in China. Therefore I use the principles of Chinese medicine with Western herbs. Several books have been published on this subject,[12] and more are being written, as herbalists endeavor to combine both systems.

Some herbs are best given on an empty stomach or between meals, although most of the herbs listed in this book can be given with food. It is sometimes best to mix the herbs with a small amount of food and feed it to your dog or cat with a fifteen-minute break before giving him the rest of his meal. This way the herbs don't get lost in the shuffle and diluted by a lot of food. However, when this is impossible, the herbs can be given with the entire meal.

The dosages and dilutions listed in this book are based upon my personal experience in practice. They are listed along with the herbs for the various conditions in the treatment section of the book.

Endnotes

1, 2, 3. Lu, Henry C. *Legendary Chinese Healing Herbs.* (New York: Sterling Publishing Co., Inc., 1991), 55, 74, 13.

4. Holmes, Peter. *The Energetics of Western Herbs, Vol. I.* (Boulder, CO: Artemis Press, 1989), 130.

5, 7. Dharmananda, Subhuti. *Chinese Herbal Therapies for Immune Disorders.* (Portland, OR: Institute for Traditional Medicine and Preventive Care, 1988), 11, 28, 53.

6. Bensky, Dan and Andrew Gamble. *Chinese Herbal Materia Medica.* (Seattle, WA: Eastland Press, 1986), 459.

8, 9, 10. Bensky, Dan and Randall Barolet. *Chinese Herbal Medicine Formulas & Strategies.* (Seattle, WA: Eastland Press, 1990), 9–11, 14, 37.

11. Naeser, Margaret A., PhD. *Outline Guide to Chinese Herbal Patent Medicines in Pill Form.* (Boston, MA: Boston Chinese Medicine, 1990), 22.

12. Holmes, Peter. *The Energetics of Western Herbs, Vol. I & II.* (Boulder, CO: Artemis Press, 1989).

Tierra, Michael. *Planetary Herbology.* (Santa Fe, NM: Lotus Press, 1988).

CHAPTER SEVEN

Food Therapy

To many of our furry friends, *the* most important thing in life is food. They don't think of calories, just the enjoyment of odors, flavors and chewing (or not chewing). Above all, eating is fun. As responsible human companions for our animals, we want to feed them what is the best for their health *and* enjoyment.

When most of us think of nutrition, we usually think of calories that we burn as energy, vitamins and minerals, proteins, carbohydrates and fats. We have all been taught that to be healthy we must "eat a balanced diet," and that a balanced meal has at least one type of food from each category.

In Traditional Chinese Medicine, foods are considered quite differently. They are looked upon as an extension of herbs, with all the herbal qualities we discussed in the previous chapter. There is a lot of crossover, as many mild herbs are foods, and many foods are considered herbs. So, rather than proteins or carbohydrates, we have foods that warm us or cool us off, foods that direct energy or fluids upward or downward, and foods that help certain organ systems to function optimally.

Traditional Chinese Medicine practitioners and scholars have evaluated foods over many centuries, observing their interaction within the body. By studying food substances in nature, scholars assessed the physical conditions in which plants and animals lived, where and when they flourished and under which conditions they struggled to survive. For example, the observation of rice being planted and grown in paddies in very damp, humid conditions, may have inspired the first Chinese herbalists to use this grain in aid of the digestive process of the spleen/pancreas and stomach, which are affected by dampness. They also observed and assessed individuals of different body constitutions as they ate certain foods. Over time, as the data was gathered and conclusions were drawn and gradually systematized, the practice of Food Therapy evolved. Today, TCM practitioners recommend certain foods for balancing and improving a variety of conditions and restoring and maintaining good health.

I'm sure you have experienced changes in your own body temperature after eating certain foods. For example, we drink iced tea in the summer to cool us off. It is not only the ice that cools us, but also the **quality** of black or green tea itself, which is a **cooling** and **bitter** food. After eating a very spicy meal with garlic or curry powder, we tend to sweat or feel hot in the upper part of the body. This is due to the **thermal quality** of garlic or curry powder as it interacts within our bodies. These spices have a **warming** and **pungent quality.** Additionally, some foods have the capacity to increase urination, such as the grain barley, which has a **cooling, sweet** and **salty quality.** Other foods strengthen certain organ systems in our bodies, such as beef, which aids the digestive process of the stomach and spleen/pancreas and builds strong bones, or millet which helps relieve inflammation in the joints.

Just as with herbs, each food is affiliated with the qualities of **direction, flavor, organ system** and **nature** or **temperature.**

THE DIRECTIONS OF FOOD

Each food directs the movement of qi, blood or fluid in a particular fashion in TCM. These directions are: **upward, downward, inward** or **outward.** For example, if your animal friend has a problem with fluid retention in the body as in heart failure, the TCM practitioner might recommend a food such as barley that has a **downward** direction in order to direct fluid away from the lungs and the abdomen and out through the bladder. On the other hand, if your animal friend has a problem with urinary incontinence, where the urine leaks down and out of the body, foods with an **upward** direction might be prescribed to balance the outward, downward tendency. In such a case, oats might be indicated. If an animal has a flu or a cold, a food such as garlic can be used with its **outward** direction, to help fluids move across the cell membrane and then direct them out of the body through breath moisture or urine. If your animal friend tends to be hyperaggressive, foods with a **downward** direction, such as lettuce with its calming, cooling quality, may be prescribed. Foods with an **inward** direction are most often recommended in the winter, to help with preserving energy. They are usually salty, like seaweed, or bitter, such as celery, rye or burdock root.

There are two other types of foods that are associated with directions. These are the **slippery** or **sliding** foods and **obstructive** foods. Honey is an example of a slippery food which acts as a lubricant and helps fluids or solids move through the body more easily. On the other hand, if we eat foods that obstruct the passage of food or fluid, such as leeks,[2] we can slow down the leakage of stool or urine.

FLAVORS OF FOOD

The **flavors** of foods are similar to the **flavors** of herbs, as discussed in the previous chapter. They are: **sweet, sour, pungent (spicy), salty** and **bitter.** Each flavor has a different function, and if one tends to eat more of one flavor than another, imbalances may develop that can create problems.

Sweet foods are often used to help digestion and qi. Sweet foods do not necessarily mean cookies or cakes. The "sweetness" is an inherent quality within the food. Rice and corn are examples of sweet foods.[3] You can discover the flavor quality of a food yourself by choosing, say, a vegetable like the yellow squash, holding a piece of it in your mouth, then slowly chewing and savoring its flavor. See if you can taste the sweet quality of the squash. Then try this experiment with other foods.

Salty foods, such as seaweeds, are often used to "soften" tumors or cysts. This is the first step a TCM practitioner will use to try to dissolve a mass without surgery.

Sour foods are often used to "astringe" or dry the mucous membrane surfaces. Astringents are substances that help keep the cells from leaking mucous or moisture along intestinal, urinary, reproductive or respiratory surfaces.

Drinking a beverage with lemon helps dry mucous in a sore throat. It also helps to stop diarrhea and soothes the intestinal tract. Raspberry leaves are fed to pregnant animals to help strengthen the cells in the uterus because they are astringent, sour and sweet in nature and help to avoid miscarriages.[4]

Pungent foods such as garlic and onion are used to promote sweating, stimulate circulation, and help digestion. They also help to break up mucous if too many mucous type foods, such as red meat and dairy products, are eaten.

Bitter foods aid digestion. They are good for regulating the bowels, whether constipation or diarrhea is the problem. Some of you might be familiar with "Swedish bitters" which are taken before a meal to help digestion. Some bitter foods also have cooling or anti-inflammatory effects on the body, helping to clear internal heat. Skin conditions that feel hot to the touch, itchy, scabby, dry or bleeding are manifestations of internal heat. Eating foods such as lettuce or celery, as well as topical applications of cooled green tea can benefit these skin conditions.

MERIDIANS AND FOOD

Certain foods have affinities for certain organ systems or meridians of the Five Element System. In TCM, the consumption of a specific food can affect changes in a related organ. While eating the proper amount of these foods will help to restore a weakened organ, eating too much can cause *another* imbalance and effect all the other organs of the body. Because each food has a specific flavor and affinity for an organ and its meridian, it is vital to choose foods with the right qualities *and* consume them in the appropriate quantities.

Spleen/Pancreas/Stomach meridians have affinities for foods such as barley, rice, chicken, egg, ginger, and beef.[5]

Lung/Large Intestine meridians have affinities for bean curd (for moistening), cabbage, castor beans, mushrooms, corn, figs, garlic, honey (also for moistening), yams, taro, and licorice.[6]

Kidney/Urinary Bladder meridians have affinities for carp, chestnut, egg yolk, cinnamon bark, clams, duck, fennel, grape, kidney, chicken liver, mutton, pork, salt, string beans, wheat and yam.[6]

Liver/Gall Bladder meridians have affinity for celery, leek, beef liver, pork liver, plum, vinegar, or wheat.[6]

TEMPERATURE OR THERMAL NATURE OF FOOD

In addition to directions and flavors, each food has a **temperature** or **thermal nature**. The temperatures are: **cooling, warming, hot** and **neutral**. The thermal nature of a food is described by the way you feel after you have eaten it. For example, adding small amounts of celery, millet or pork liver, which are all cooling foods, help to decrease internal inflammation and cool the body. This applies to physical cooling *and* emotional cooling. So, if your animal friend seems to overheat easily, cooling foods may be of assistance in making him more comfortable. If your animal friend is aggressive with a hot temper, cooling foods may help to calm him down and even out his temper.

Warming foods are used to aid circulation and digestion. This does not mean that the food is warm to the touch, as if you had heated it on the stove. Rather, it describes a feeling of internal warmth after consumption. Warming foods such as lamb, chicken or oats, may be used to help digestion and food assimilation. They may also be helpful in treating arthritic conditions that become worse in cold weather, as they invigorate the circulation. Animals who sleep in front of the heater all the time, or those with cold feet or ears, may benefit from eating warming foods. Dried ginger can be added to their meals for this purpose.

Neutral foods are the best balancers. Because they don't create a specific thermal quality, they can be added to the diet to modify milder conditions. Potato, rice and corn are examples of foods with neutral temperatures. Pork and rabbit are neutral meat proteins and eggs are another source of neutral protein.

YIN AND YANG FOOD QUALITIES

Now that we have looked at the individual qualities of foods, let's step back and look at the broader view. Since Traditional Chinese Medicine is based upon the all-inclusive concepts of yin and yang, this, of course, includes all the foods we eat. Designating foods into strict categories according to their yin or yang nature is a complex issue because, as with all aspects of TCM, everything is relative. But, it is important to understand the basic concept. If an animal has a predominance of yin which is causing health problems, avoiding yin type foods would be one of the ways to treat the imbalance. Conversely, if the animal were showing signs of too much yang, one would prescribe a diet low in yang type foods.

Yin is everything that has physical substance. Yin is also anything that is relaxing, calming, cooling, moistening, introspective, dark, gentle, graceful, receptive and yielding.

Yang is everything that is active and functioning. It is the movement without the substance. For example, when the brain is functioning, it's thoughts cannot be weighed on a scale. The thought of food is not food itself, so thinking might be classified as yang. Yang creates tension, stimulation, warmth, dryness, strength, activity and aggression. This is all relative, how-ever, because if we were to just sit quietly and be introspective in our yang thoughts, this would be considered a yin action.

Without becoming too philosophical, each food has *both* yin and yang qualities. When we choose certain foods to balance an individual animal, we are looking at as many aspects of that food as possible. For example, Paul Pitchford, author of *Healing with Whole Foods, Oriental Traditions and Modern Nutrition,* considers meat a yin and jing essence food because it is dense, heavy, causes weight-gain and an increase in physical mass.[7] Jeffrey Yeun and Henry Lu, noted Chinese nutritionists and authors, categorize different meats according to their classifications of energies and flavors. Dr. Lu writes, "Hot and warm energies are yang; cool and cold energies are yin. Pungent and sweet flavors are yang; sour, and bitter, and salty flavors are yin."[8] According to this interpretation, some meats are yang and some are more yin.

In my veterinary practice, I tend to use meat in both its yin and yang classifications. For deficient, thin or weak individuals, I may use nearly all meats to help restore muscle and mass to the body. In sluggish, yin individuals, I may use certain meats to increase the circulation and yang of the body. In hyper individuals, I tend to decrease any meat that has an upward direction, such as chicken, while I might use chicken in cases of sluggishness or prolapsed hernias *because* of this upward direction.

THE METHODS OF MIXING AND MATCHING

As one of the possible treatment plans for home use, diet modification may be the best and easiest way to begin to experiment with TCM. Dietary guidelines are listed for individual conditions in the treatment sections later in the book. Here we will go over some basics of Chinese Food Therapy.

In order to know which foods are appropriate for a certain type of animal, we have to think back to the Eight Principles of yin/yang, cold/hot, interior/exterior, deficiency/excess and the constitutional types for the Five Elements.

If your animal friend is more yin than yang, he may be sluggish, very laid back and calm, thirstless, slightly overweight with a tendency to have a distended abdomen, gentle, graceful and very sensitive emotionally. To balance these overly yin tendencies, you would want to add yang foods to his diet to help activate the metabolism and give your friend more energy and zing. But if, on the other hand, your animal friend tends to be too aggressive, tense, loud and hyperactive, this would indicate more yang tendencies than yin. Here you might want to cool your animal's tension and help descend his energy by adding yin type foods to the diet.

If your animal friend is too cold and needs a personal heater, gets up frequently at night to urinate, or has become incontinent, warming foods will help counter these overly cold traits. On the other hand, if she seems hot, behaves aggressively, has inflamed, smelly ears, red, itchy skin or hives, then cooling foods are called for.

If your animal friend gets the flu or an upper respiratory condition, which is considered an exterior problem, foods that help disperse energy to the body's surface are used. Unlike humans, our dog and cat friends do not sweat through their skin pores. Although, in my practice I have experienced a moist, vapor-like quality that resembles a light sweat in animals with weakened qi. I am not certain how this occurs physiologically. Like humans, animals have areas of small blood vessels called capillary beds near the body's surface. Foods that have an outward directional quality will "push" the circulation and qi outward toward the region of these capillary beds. So, in addition to toxins being expelled through the breath (by panting) and through the urine, toxins are also expelled through this vapor-like exchange or "claminess," if you will, at the skin's surface.

If your animal friend has a chronic illness which effects an internal organ, this is considered an interior problem. Depending upon the nature of the illness, different foods can be useful. For example, some interior problems have a central core of heat, in which case cooling foods would be helpful. Some interior problems have a cold central core, in which case energizing and warming foods would be prescribed.

An important distinction to make is whether your animal friend is an **excess** or **deficient** individual. This is in no way a criticism of his personality. It's just a categorization. The excess individual is assertive and always in your face, with a very strong bark or meow. He is often overweight or stocky, with strong, hard and over-abundant muscles with fat spread between them. You know the kind of animal I'm talking about — cats who look like bulldozers where there is no loose neck skin to grab. They are totally solid. This solid framing enhances their robustness. When excess individuals are thin, they are quick, lithe, and dominant. In either case, excess individuals are confident and vocal and always wanting attention. When they become ill, it's usually with high fevers which they are able to kick very quickly.

The deficient individual tends to be more shy, timid and introverted, with a weak meow or bark, poor digestion and frequently ill. When this animal is overweight, it is with soft, pudgy fat, weaker muscles and a sway back. When a deficient animal is thin, the bone structure is slight and the muscles are small.

An excess individual will usually benefit from raw and yin type foods. When animal protein is used, fish may be better than red meat. Foods should be cooked, even if only slightly, for a deficient individual in order to help with assimilation and absorption and increase vital energy or qi.

In association with the Eight Principles, there are foods that create conditions of **dryness** and **dampness**. These are foods that create moisture in the body, or dry the dampness in the body. Remember that dry conditions can mean dry, itchy skin, an increased thirst, constipation, or a dry cough. Foods that create moisture within the body help remedy these imbalances. A damp condition can manifest itself as a distended, heavy abdomen, cool swellings in the limbs, mushy stools, or a wet chronic cough. Foods that counter these tendencies by drying the excessive moisture or dampness are used to help alleviate the condition.

Because not all good foods are necessarily good for all animals, it is important to understand, not only the condition you are treating, but also the type of individual your animal friend is.

These are examples only, and should not be over-used, because eating too much of a certain food can produce another imbalance! Just as there are foods that aid certain conditions, there are also foods that aggravate or may even cause certain conditions. Be certain you know which foods to avoid or limit if your animal friend has a tendency toward particular problems. Again, for individual conditions, food suggestions will be made in the third part of this book. These are just preliminary guidelines.

INDIVIDUAL CONDITION	FOODS TO BALANCE
Yin	Yang
Yang	Yin
Cold	Warm
Hot	Cool
Exterior	Pungent, Outward
Interior	Depends on Type of Condition
Deficient	Mostly Cooked
Excess	Raw, Cooked, Bitter
Dry	Moistening, Yin
Damp	Drying

EXAMPLES OF FOOD TYPES [9]

Yin	Salt, Clam
Yang	Salmon, Lamb, Quinoa
Cold	Kelp, Banana
Hot	Trout, Dried Ginger
To Clear Exterior	Onion, Garlic
To Clear Excess	Celery, Burdock, Greens, Lima Beans, Grains
To Strengthen Deficiency	Oats, Rice, Buckwheat, Beef, Lamb, Eggs, Sardines
To Dry Dampness	Mackerel, Amaranth, Rye, Celery, Turnip
To Moisten Dryness	Pork, Sardine, Mussel, Barley, Potato, String Bean

IF YOUR ANIMAL FRIEND HAS . . .	LIMIT THESE FOODS
Cold Conditions	Raw Foods, Clams, Kelp, Wheat
Hot Conditions	High Fat Foods, Ginger, Venison, Trout, Chicken, Shrimp, Salmon, Chicken Liver
Dry Conditions	Garlic, Rye, Celery, Lettuce, Asparagus
Damp Conditions	Tofu, Dairy, Citrus, Wheat

BALANCING WITH THE SEASONS

If, by now, you think you have grasped how this food therapy works, let me throw in a little twist at this point. The last consideration that is important to remember is that in Traditional Chinese Medicine, we try to balance the individual with her external environment and each season creates a different environment. In summer, we are usually very active, as well as warm. In winter, we tend to slow down, spending more time indoors, in response to the shorter days and lack of daylight. In the spring, we awaken from our winter doldrums and begin to stretch our minds and bodies. In the fall, we slow down again, storing our reserves in preparation for winter. Remember that each food has an affinity for **direction, lifestyle** and **thermal quality** which mimics each season. Therefore, it is important to add a small amount of a food that has the corresponding quality for the given season to our diet. It's the age-old principle that "like cures like." Dr. Henry C. Lu quotes the master herbalist Shi-Chen Li, who describes this in *An Outline of Materia Medica* from 1578: "In spring, one should eat more pungent, sweet and neutral foods which have an upward direction to stay in harmony with the upward movement of the season. . . . "[10] While it is important to balance the internal body condition or type with foods that counter the tendency, we must remember to take into account the surroundings in which we live. If we look closely at the yin/yang symbol, we see that inside each of the halves there is a dot representing the other one. It is this small portion of each aspect that keeps us in harmony. Likewise, eating small amounts of food that remind us of the current season is helpful in maintaining balance.

SEASON	FOOD TO MIMIC THE SEASON[11] (Eat small amounts to stay in harmony)
Summer (Hot foods)	Black Pepper, Cayenne Pepper
Fall (Sour & Sweet foods)	Barley, Clam, Sweet Potato, Duck, String Bean
Winter (Salty & Bitter foods)	Kelp, Pork, Celery, Burdock Root
Spring (Pungent & Sweet)	Corn, Carp, Garlic, Kohlrabi, Leek

The best reference books I have found in English for an extended discussion of Chinese food therapies are listed in the Endnotes.

PUTTING IT ALL TOGETHER

Now that we have basic guidelines, how can we use them? If you have the time to cook, healthy cats and dogs can eat a mixture of grains, vegetables and animal proteins. Organically grown foods, that are free from pesticides, hormones, antibiotics and excessive stress are best.

I am a firm believer that we are what we eat, and if we buy animal products that have been raised in inhumane conditions, the suffering of the animal is retained in the meat that is consumed. There is also the ethical question of eating animals in general. The fact that we kill animals to use their flesh to nurture our own, should not be taken lightly.[12] I also believe that most of us living in the United States probably eat more meat than is necessary for maintaining health. Our animal companions may also require less meat than we think. A fuller description of meat protein will be discussed later in this section.

I believe that all foods, whether from plant or animal sources, carry with them their experiences from life, and that is what makes them so powerful an influence on both humans and animals. Looking at as many characteristics of the foods we consume as possible gives us the information we need to use them properly and responsibly. Examining the physical conditions under which the foods grow, their colors, the thermal energy we sense after eating them, are all factors in determining their effects on the body and spirit. I also believe that cancer, which is on the rise in animals as well as people, has a basis in the overly processed, stress-filled, quick-fix foods that are consumed by many of us and our animal friends.

And now a word about water. Most animals will drink water anytime, anywhere, no matter how dirty, muddy or stagnant it may appear to you and I. Many public water supplies, however, contain low levels of heavy metals, like lead, which leech in to the water system from old pipes. Even "natural" water supplies, like picturesque mountain streams, carry harmful micro-organisms such as *giardia*. While we can't control every water source we, or our animals drink from all the time, we can keep from ingesting some of these contaminants by drinking filtered water whenever possible.

MEAT AND YOUR DOG OR CAT FRIEND

Dogs can be vegetarians, especially if their constitutions are excess. However, full-range vitamin and mineral supplements are needed to include nutrients such as L-Carnitine. If you want your canine companion to be vegetarian, but the animal is thin or excessively timid and frightened, meat proteins may be needed to bolster the diet. I think it is best if puppies are given meat protein sources for at least the first six to eight months while their bones and eyes are developing.

Cats *cannot* be vegetarians in my opinion, as they require meat sources with specific amino acids in order for their eyes to develop properly. As a vet student, I was taught that cats needed an enormous daily caloric intake to maintain health. Commercial cat foods were developed using high-fat meat products to meet those needs, the rationale being that cats in the wild eat meat. However, they do not do this on a daily basis. The average house cat may not require the high-calorie intake that is needed by wild felines who hunt for a living. As a result of this over-feeding, we have "fat cats," and "diet" cat food was developed. Holistic veterinarians are now questioning whether such high meat or calorie requirements are really necessary.

Another important difference between our canine and feline friends is that dogs can convert B-carotene into vitamin A, whereas cats need pre-formed vitamin A to complete their diets.

Before suggesting guidelines for home-cooked diets, I would like to present a brief discussion of some of the common foods we use for our animal friends.

MEATS

Meat is commonly used to nourish the muscles, blood and jing essence of the body. It provides flesh and substance and is traditionally used to tonify weak individuals. If you have an overweight animal friend, limiting the amount of meat as well as the overall amount of food, may be advisable. Meat can also create different moods and thermal sensations in the body. Many meats create warming in the body, so they are helpful in keeping those animals warmer who tend to feel the cold, but it should be used sparingly in those who over-heat. I have seen cases when meats have caused aggressive tendencies in my patients, which disappear when the meat is eliminated or reduced.

The literature I have read about food therapy applies to the interaction of different foods with humans. Since everything is relative, I have been studying the size and disposition difference between humans and our smaller animal friends. While every individual is different, it seems to me that smaller animals have a slightly different relationship with other animals than do humans. For example, a prime diet for cats might be canned rat and rice, or sparrow and corn, thus incorporating what they might eat in nature. Dogs probably wouldn't go after cows, but they might hunt rabbits, rodents and smaller game. Because of this, I have found that the traditional aspects of meats listed for humans are sometimes transferable to animals and sometimes not. The following is a list of foods with some of their aspects as I have noted in my experience as a practicing veterinarian.

Chicken. Chickens are quick-moving animals, bobbing, pecking, and constantly chattering in high-pitched tones. They are prolific breeders, laying eggs and hatching chicks. In light of this, chicken is considered a warming food, nourishing for the blood and jing essence, and nurturing to the spleen/pancreas, stomach and kidney.[13]

Turkey. Free-range turkeys are also quick-moving, and companionable with other turkeys. They are heavier birds than chickens, and relatively more yin. The dark meat of the turkey contains tryptophan, which apparently has a calming effect on animals and humans. Turkey is both warming and wet and the dark meat creates more moisture than the light meat. Turkey can cause damp heat and gout in humans, which is calcified arthritis in the joints. In animals, I have found it useful for treating intestinal problems that have underlying yin deficiencies or dryness. These might include some irritable bowel syndromes where there is blood in the stool or frequent vomiting of dry hair balls. It is especially helpful when there is constipation with blood.

Beef. The cow is calm and laid back, slow-moving and large, structurally dense and sweet-tempered. These are all yin qualities. Beef has dense tissues which are good for building blood, bones and yang muscle strength. It is considered neutral and sweet, especially good for nourishing the spleen/pancreas and stomach.[14] Although it is neutral for humans, beef may have a more downward, yin effect on small animals. It is good for the thin, spare animal who lacks confidence.

Liver. Liver is a dense, internal organ, excellent for building jing essence. Because of its density it can also create stagnation and mucous in the digestive tract leading to constipation, abdominal swelling and weight gain. Use it in small amounts for your animals. Beef liver is cooler than chicken liver.

Lamb. Lamb is young, which means it can impart jing essence, feed the muscles, blood, bones, and organs as well as yang sexual energy. Unlike cattle, lambs and sheep seem more timid and fearful. Since fear is the emotion associated with the kidneys, eating lamb or mutton may adversely heighten insecurity and affect the kidney. Observe your animal friend for heightened insecurity. Because of its fat content which can create internal heat to break it down, it seems more warming than chicken. Since lamb is *so* tonifying, it should be used cautiously with animals who overheat or overeat.

Rabbit.[15] Because rabbits procreate so prodigiously, they are considered to be nourishing to the jing essence and to the kidney. They are quick, and will nourish the yang and warming aspect of the kidney. Because they live underground, they also have strong yin tendencies. However, because of their inherent emotional nature of fearfulness — you've all heard the expression "running scared like a rabbit" — they may adversely affect the kidney. Because of their mixed yin and yang makeup, I consider them to be neutral. Rabbit seems to be in the right size category for our small animal companions, but rest assured, I am not trying to make enemies of our rabbit friends!

Venison.[16] Considered yang, spare and quick, like most wild game, venison does not tend to be overfed, and therefore would not necessarily impart excessive muscle flesh as would cattle. This would make venison good for the sluggish animal who gets cold easily.

Tuna and Mackerel. These are very strong fish that live in the deep, cold oceans of the world. Because of this, I consider them to have yin and yang aspects. They affect both the kidneys and the spleen/pancreas. They should be used sparingly in the animal who suffers from urinary tract problems with blood. However, they may be good additions to those sluggish individuals who tend to have heavy, hanging abdomens, moist lung problems, or arthritis that is worse in damp weather.

Pork. In human food therapy, pork is considered one of the most cooling of the animal meats. It is used to restore fluids to the body in such diseases as diabetes.[17] I have found pork loin or butt a good meat protein for inflammatory bowel problems where there is dryness and blood. You need to boil the pork and remove all the fat from the water. Contrary to fears that cats cannot tolerate pork, I have used this defatted meat in cats who show the wasting type disease symptoms.

GRAINS

Grains provide primarily qi, blood and yin to the diet. They are usually more cooling than meat sources. Grains should be the primary component of dog diets, and a major component in cat diets. Grains nourish the moisture in the body. The qi energy they provide is more sedate than meat sources, and many individuals thrive primarily on grains in a more balanced fashion than with meats.

Rice. Rice helps to nurture the center of body, including the spleen/pancreas and stomach. It is neutral and sweet in nature.[18] Because of its hulled coating, brown rice helps to clear the liver and gall bladder of toxins and has many B vitamins, but may be more difficult for some animals to digest.

Corn. Corn is sweet, neutral and nurtures the spleen/pancreas and the heart. It is also helpful at drawing water from certain areas of the body, so it can aid the kidneys.[19] When corn is fed to horses it is considered a hot grain, and those who eat too much can become hyper and full of excessive energy. In light of its effect on the heart, which supports joy and exuberance in Traditional Chinese Medicine, this is easy to understand. Since corn affects both the heart and the kidneys, if a horse tends to be kidney yin deficient and appears nervous and unusually thirsty, eating corn may exaggerate the imbalance and be "too hot" for him.

Barley.[20] This is a cooling grain that helps the intestines, the stomach and spleen/pancreas. It helps to nourish dryness. It is both sweet and salty in flavor, and thus, also affects the kidneys which have an affinity for salt. Barley is helpful in treating an animal that is suffering from burning, painful urination.

Wheat. This is cooling, sweet and salty with an affinity for the liver. It also has a calming effect on the mind, and Paul Pitchford notes that it nourishes both the kidneys and the heart. Wheat counters hyper-excitability in some animals. (We can relate to this if we think of how we feel after eating a big plate of pasta — most of us long for a nap!) If the animal tends to be sluggish after a primarily wheat-based meal, it may have too sedating an affect. Many food-sensitive individuals, both human and animal, have allergies to wheat, but this may be to processed forms only. Whole wheat that is organically grown is more nutritious, carrying vitamins and minerals in the hull.

Vegetables. Vegetables provide mostly moistening and qi for the individual. Because many vegetables and fruits grow above ground and are not structurally dense, they are considered yang. However, because they contain a lot of water, they are also very yin. Additionally, their thermal temperatures for the most part are cool, with the root vegetables being warmer and more meat-like. Vegetables are calming. Dogs usually benefit from vegetables in their diets, while cats only tolerate very small amounts.

THERMAL FOOD NATURES AT A GLANCE

	PROTEINS		GRAINS	VEGETABLES		
Cooling	Clam		Millet	Lettuce	Tomato	**Cooling**
	Duck		Barley	Celery	Napa Cabbage	
	Egg		Wheat	Broccoli		
	Pork			Spinach		
Neutral	Beef		Yam			**Neutral**
	Beef Liver		Rice		Beet	
	Rabbit		Corn		Turnip	
	Chicken Gizzard		Rye		Carrot	
	Sardine		Potato			
Warming	Tuna		Sweet Potato			**Warming**
	Turkey	Chicken			Cabbage	
	Salmon	Chicken Liver	Oats		Squash	
	Lamb	Shrimp			Kale	
	Venison	Trout				

THERMAL FOOD NATURES

I have found that the thermal qualities of food give good primary guidelines toward balancing an individual animal's nature and condition. Since all foods are combinations of yin and yang, I have listed what I consider to be the *overall* thermal qualities. This information is based upon texts by Henry C. Lu, Paul Pitchford, Bob Flaws[21] plus my own observation and experience.

DIETS FOR DOGS

The following section includes a compilation and explanation of some homemade diets for the puppy, adult and senior dogs. Providing your animal friend with the best diet *for him* is fundamental to good health. I understand that these days it can be difficult to find the time to cook for ourselves, let alone the animal members of our families. If, however, you do have the time, and the desire, here are some options à la TCM.

Grains must be very thoroughly cooked for animals as they don't really chew their food. Their teeth are designed primarily for tearing meat, rather than chewing and their intestinal tracts are much shorter than ours. I recommend adding 2½ cups of water for each cup of grain and cooking for 1¼ hours over low heat, until all the water is absorbed. If your animal has excess grain in its stool, he may not be digesting the grain properly. Try soaking grains overnight, cooking longer with more water, or using flakes or a cracked grain product rather than whole grains. If this doesn't work and excessive grain is still seen in the stool, consider other grains such as corn, quinoa or barley. It is natural to see some grain in the stool as every particle may not be completely digested.

Let's discuss raw versus cooked meat. Many experts in the veterinary field recommend feeding raw meats, except, of course, for pork which may contain parasites. My feeling is that most healthy animals *can* tolerate raw meat, because the meat's own enzymes are not lost and the food can be digested more easily. If you do choose to feed raw meat to your cat or dog, be sure to cut it into small pieces. On the other hand, some apparently healthy animals have difficulty digesting raw meat as evidenced by vomiting, loose stools, gas or obvious discomfort. In Traditional Chinese Medicine, these individuals have deficient spleen/pancreas tendencies. If your animal friend belongs to this group, it is best to cook the meat slightly, approximately five minutes. This actually begins the digestive process. Remember, your dog friend hardly chews. He seems to inhale the food with quick gulps. When cooking meat, either parboil, broil, bake or pan fry it with a cover to help keep nutrients intact. An alternative is to make a stew with the meat and vegetables cooked together. If you notice that your dog's assimilation seems poor, which would be indicated by weight loss, excessive burping or flatulence, natural enzymes from papaya extracts can be added to the meal. These are available through your holistic veterinarian or natural foods stores.

The basic difference between the puppy/young adult and adult diet is the distribution of protein, grain and vegetables. The younger animal requires a higher protein level than the grown animal.

In the adult years, meat/legume proteins may be varied and should include: kidney beans, which increase yin fluid, are cooling and sweet; lentils, which are neutral and aid the heart; and aduki beans, which are neutral, sweet and sour, and help the kidney and adrenal glands.[22] Tofu is cooling, moistening and helpful to the colon and lungs. Tofu may be difficult for some dogs to digest. Additionally, if your dog friend suffers from loose, pasty stools or mucous in the lungs, tofu is contraindicated. Many large breed, barrel-chested dogs are prone to bloating. Because tofu or bean products may increase this tendency, I do not recommend that either of these be used as the sole protein source. Lentils and other beans, if pre-soaked, washed and cooked well (1½ hours) can be used as a partial protein, with chicken or fish.

SAMPLE DIETS

These diet choices are based on the yin/yang, cooling/warming, deficiency/excess, and meridian influences that combine to form an individual animal's temperament or make-up. At the end of this chapter, a more complete listing of foods found in prepared commercial diets with their inherent qualities is given.

◆ Puppies / Young Adults

Puppy and young adulthood are obvious growth phases. Because of this, and also because different puppies have different metabolic rates and exercise re-

CANINE DIETS TO BALANCE TEMPERAMENT		
	Hyper (++Yang)	**Normal**	**Sluggish (++Yin)**
Cooked	1/3 Brown Rice	2/3 Brown Rice	Rolled Oats
Grain	2/3 Millet or Bulgar	1/3 Barley or Corn Meal	
Meat (Choose one at a time)	Raw Beef (medium cut)	Beef	Chicken
	Pork (defatted, cooked)	Rabbit	Venison
	Eggs (2) (not daily)	Chicken	Turkey
	Carp/Cod/Whitefish	Turkey	Rabbit
	Duck	Beef Heart/Liver	Lamb
	Chicken Gizzards	Chicken Gizzards	Chicken Liver
	*Meats can be raw	*Meats raw/cooked	*Meats cooked
Vegetables	Celery, Lettuce	Broccoli, Squash	Kale, Squash
	Seaweeds, Spinach	Seaweeds, String Beans	Carrots, Beans

quirements, exact amounts cannot be given. Remember that with fresh, whole foods your animal friend is receiving a biologically high-quality diet, which should maximize health and assimilation. While commercial products may be more convenient, they also have more filler and bulk and, cup for cup, may not equal your home-cooked food. The preceding sample recipe yields 5 cups of cooked food. Because puppies grow so quickly, I usually recommend beginning with ⅔ cup of food three times daily for puppies weighing up to 15 pounds. Increase the amount as your puppy grows. If your puppy seems hungry all the time, or if he appears thin and there is inadequate weight-gain, you will need to increase the amounts accordingly. You will, of course, be taking your young friend to your vet for regular puppy check-ups while he is still growing. She will help you to make these decisions. Puppy diets can be fed up to 10 months of age. Thereafter, adult diets can be adjusted appropriately for decreased meat proteins and increased grain sources.

◆ Adult Dogs

Obviously, the amount of exercise and work done by your animal friend will influence how much he will eat. If there is unwanted weight gain or weight loss with a home-cooked diet, it may be necessary to adjust the amounts fed accordingly or to increase or decrease your dog's exercise time. If changing the exercise pattern or adjusting food amounts does not rectify the problem, I suggest changing the grain and/or the meat protein source. For example, foods that are more cooling often bring more fluid into the body which can cause weight gain in some individuals, or increased urination with weight loss in others.

If your animal friend is losing weight and tends to urinate too copiously, adjusting the meat or grain protein to a more warming source would be beneficial. If your animal friend cannot maintain a good body weight, please check with your veterinarian, as this may indicate a more complicated problem.

Supplements. In order to make certain that all your canine companion's needs are being met, I recommend commercial vitamin and mineral supplements for puppies and young adults that can be purchased in pet food sections at natural foods stores. I also recommend adding extra vitamin C in the form of sodium ascorbate to the diet, as I believe the stress factors of modern living warrant it. Puppies should get 250 mg of vitamin C daily, as should small dogs; 500 mg daily for medium-sized dogs, and 750 mg daily for large dogs. Too much vitamin C will cause loose stools, so adjust down until the stools are firm again. Additionally, an oil supplement is required, such as cold-pressed olive oil or unrefined peanut oil, ranging from 1 teaspoon for small dogs, to 1½ tablespoons for large dogs. Cod liver oil can be used in addition to olive oil, as it provides a good source of vitamin A and antioxidants which help in arthritis conditions. Use 1 teaspoon for medium-sized dogs.

I like to recommend kelp powder or other seaweeds as a seasoning to one meal daily. One quarter teaspoon is a good inducement to eating, as the seaweeds are tasty and smell good. There is also evidence that many seaweeds help prevent cancer. *For specific conditions, see Part Three of this book for vitamin or mineral supplementation.*

SKIPPY'S STORY

Skippy is a medium-sized mixed-breed dog, about fifteen months old, who was brought to me because he kept eating the furniture — not just pulling apart couch material, but actually eating wood, fabric and stuffing. He even ate part of the doggy door. Skippy's regular veterinarian had prescribed an Elizabethan collar for him to wear around his neck to help stop this behavior. The veterinarian had also suggested to Skippy's human that behavioral modification and disciplinary action was needed.

When I examined Skippy, I was immediately struck by his continual motion. He was unable to focus on anything. In the exam room, he simply could not stay still, but was preoccupied with exploring his surroundings, listening to sounds, pacing about and sniffing everything. In fact, he did not, or could not, hear his human's voice asking him to be still. I was told that he hardly ever paid attention to commands. Fortunately, he was a good natured, happy dog. Skippy was always overjoyed to see everyone — too overjoyed, in fact. His person also reported that Skippy consumed copious amounts of water, liked to sleep on cement, linoleum or near an open window, and in fact, seemed very uncomfortable whenever the temperature went above 70 degrees F. His appetite was sporadic. He seemed more interested in playing than eating, and when he did eat, it was either late at night or in small picky amounts. His human often heard gurgling and rumbling from Skippy's stomach, and on the rare occasions when Skippy did sit down, he panted continually and his tongue was very red. His skin felt very warm to the touch. When I felt his pulse on the inside of the hind legs, it was rapid and pounding, tight like a stretched rubber band. I asked Skippy's human what she fed him and if she had tried altering it. She told me it was a lamb and rice dry food, and that when she switched to another commercial dry food, Skippy had gas and diarrhea.

According to Traditional Chinese Medicine, Skippy was exhibiting all the signs of internal heat and excessive fire which can come from the heart (fire constitution) or the liver (wood constitution). The fire constitution exhibits extreme joy and hyperactivity, because there is not enough cooling fluid in the body to keep one calm. This means that there is *relatively* too little yin to overcome the fire signs. The wood constitution shows anger and frustration. Clearly Skippy was showing more heart fire signs. Additionally, when one is not calm, but flailing out in all directions, there is no center. The center in TCM is the focus of the earth elements, the spleen/pancreas and stomach. And in the Five Element System, the fire element nourishes the earth element. With so much energy stuck in the fire element, the spleen/pancreas and stomach were not adequately nourished and so could not digest properly. The intestinal tract was inflamed, and very agitated. Dry foods are warming in nature because of the processing procedure of being baked and heated. The hypoallergenic diet of lamb and rice that he was being fed added to the fire condition, with the lamb being very warming and the rice being neutral.

Skippy was also showing signs of internal heat by his preference for sleeping in cool places, his inability to tolerate warm temperatures, his constant thirst, panting, pounding rapid pulse, red tongue *and* his continual motion. When his stomach was too hot, he tried to put the fire out by eating the furniture, including the stuffing that might sop up the burning hyperacidity.

I prescribed a diet of cooked millet, brown rice, pork, celery, spinach, turnips and string beans. The millet is cooling, moistening, calming and downward acting. This aids the spleen/pancreas, stomach and kidney fluids. It also calms the heart. The brown rice, is neutral, aiding the liver, spleen/pancreas and stomach. The pork is cooling and helpful to the kidneys. If the kidneys are stronger, they control the heart fire better in the Five Element System. Celery and spinach are also cooling and string beans are neutral and help the kidney. Turnips are root vegetables and help to strengthen the center of the body. We added a vitamin supplement, including vitamin C and trace minerals. After two weeks, Skippy began to calm down. There have been no more episodes of furniture-eating, and he is even listening to his human!

SENIOR DIET

1½ Cups Cooked Grain

Choose one or mix equal parts of two of the following:

  white rice (neutral > warming, upward direction); mixed with ⅓ pre-soaked, well-cooked brown rice

  rolled oats (warming with upward direction)

  barley flakes (cooling, moistening, downward direction)

  hulled millet (cooling, moistening, downward direction)

  wheat cream (cooling, calming with the heart)

Meat Protein – ½ Cup

  baked chicken breast, without skin or baked fish (not trout or shellfish) or

  2 eggs (lightly scrambled) (can use 1 to 2 times per week) or

  1 to 2 ounces cooked beef liver (free-range cow if possible) (can use 3 times per month)

Vegetables ¼ Cup

  cooked squash, potato, string bean, carrot or broccoli

THE OLDER DOG

Just like humans, older animals will change their dietary needs as they age. As life progresses, the vital energy and fluids that we were born with are used up. Daily exercise and performance requirements will dictate our dietary needs. Most importantly for the older animal, remember that the spleen/pancreas, stomach, liver and gall bladder may be at least partially impaired. This does not mean actual pathology, but simply the weakness of advancing age. To help facilitate absorption and ease of digestion, it is essential to thoroughly cook foods and grains so that they are easily digestible.

As a dog ages, it may be difficult for him to handle, for example, brown rice, whole barley or whole oats with the hulls intact. Although these grains are more nutritious than their processed, polished, flaked or rolled counterparts, the older animal may not be able to assimilate these nutrients. Additionally, warming foods that are lower in fat, such as chicken (without the skin), if the animal chills easily, or cooling foods such as ground pork (defatted) if the animal overheats easily, can be offered. Baked fish such as carp or cod, are also excellent for this purpose. If dairy products are desired, it might be better to use goat's milk products as these do not create as much mucous as cow's milk.[23] Additionally, because a goat's lifestyle is usually more free-roaming than a modern dairy cow's, goats may suffer less stress and pass on fewer stress-related by-products in their milk. Unlike cattle, goats are rarely fed antibiotics prophylactically.

In older animals with arthritis, it has been shown that diets high in red meat may increase joint pain by stimulating the inflammatory response of a substance called prostaglandins. A high intake of red meat also increases the saturated fats in the body which impede circulation. Therefore, the older animal should have only a limited amount of red meat, as beef, lamb, or beef liver. In Traditional Chinese Medicine, these foods enhance the bone marrow, red blood cells and strengthen the spleen/stomach or earth element. Alkaline-producing grains such as millet, may also be helpful to the joints.

Older dogs can be fed smaller meals twice daily to reduce the stress on the digestive tract. However, if they have been on a once-daily feeding schedule for most of their lives and seem comfortable with it, you might not need to make a change.

Dietary recommendations for specific conditions are listed in Part Three.

THE SENIOR DOG DIET

The preceding diet is adequate for a medium-sized, 40 to 50 lb. dog. However, if your dog loses or gains weight on this amount of food, adjust the amounts accordingly. If you find a particular food combination that suits your dog friend, stay with it, as variation may cause problems. If the dog has a strong digestive system and can tolerate whole grains, they are still preferable, but as dogs age their digestion may not remain as strong as it once was. Pre-soaking whole grains helps. Also, because whole grains allow for more bulk and improved bowel movements, if flaked or cracked products are used, you may need to add 2 to 3 tablespoons of oat or wheat bran to the diet.

If your dog friend develops gas, try decreasing the vegetables. If constipation occurs, increase the vegetables and add bran or pumpkin. If abdominal distention or diarrhea develops, decrease or eliminate vegetables, and use rice and chicken *only* as a base diet. It is very important to cook the grain thoroughly (for a long time), using 2½ to 3 cups of water to 1 cup of grain and cooking over slow heat. Flaked grains need less cooking time.

Supplements for 40 to 50 pound dog:
>Vitamin E, 200 IU
>Vitamin C, 500 to 1,000 mg
>Kelp powder, ¼ to ½ teaspoon
>Nutritional yeast, 1 tablespoon
>Lecithin granules, 2 teaspoons
>Bone meal, 1 teaspoon
>Cod liver oil, 1 teaspoon
>Olive oil, 1 to 2 tablespoons
>Or a Senior Dog Vitamin/Mineral Mix from a natural
>foods store or holistic veterinarian.

TOPO'S STORY

Topo was a lovely German Shepherd. Her human had prepared homemade meals for her all her life. Because of this, and all the love she received (and her good genes), she grew robust and remained healthy and strong well into old age. When I began seeing Topo, she was ten years old, and the only major problem she seemed to have was a weakness in her hind quarters.

I treated her with acupuncture and herbs, and she did well. But eventually, she developed diarrhea, and was obviously having difficulty digesting her food properly. Her abdomen began to sag and her pulse in the hind legs seemed somewhat mushy. Her tongue was slightly pale and wide, showing some teeth imprints along the sides and had very little coating on it.

For most of her life Topo's diet had been raw ground meat, brown rice and vegetables. The vegetables were originally fed to her raw, but as she got older, her human cooked them for easier digestion.

The diarrhea, saggy abdomen, mushy pulse and wide tongue all reflected problems with the spleen/pancreas and stomach. You will remember that the spleen/pancreas and stomach are responsible for transforming and transporting the food we eat into usable qi and energy. Topo was definitely having a problem transforming the food, as indicated by her saggy abdomen and diarrhea. I believe that the problem lay in the fact that she could no longer digest the raw meat and whole grain. We changed her diet to white rice and cooked chicken, and minimized the vegetables. The cooked chicken and white rice were warming and drying for the spleen and stomach and much more easily digested. Topo's human, in the interest of wanting the best whole foods for her' dog, was actually overworking the dog's capability to digest the food. The best compromise was to mix some proportion of thoroughly cooked brown rice with the white rice, to provide bulk and nutrition. As Topo grew older, her qi transforming capacity had diminished and she needed simpler, *cooked* foods.

DIETS FOR CATS

It is much more difficult to satisfy a cat with home-cooked food than a dog. Dog's seem to love "people" food, while cats find it mostly unappealing. If, however, you have that rare, adaptable type of cat, home-cooked foods are definitely superior to commercial diets.

◆ The Basic Active Cat Diet

Cats require a higher calorie and higher protein intake per pound than dogs. At least that's what we were taught in vet school. Over the years, however, as I have seen more and more over-weight cats, I am beginning to wonder if this is true. Many veterinarians now recommend feeding a less "dense" diet to their clients' cats. The ratio of meat to grain is one-half to two-thirds meat, to one-half to one-third grain. Most cats will eat vegetables in very small

FELINE DIETS TO BALANCE TEMPERAMENTS

	Hyper (++Yang)	Normal	Sluggish (++Yin)
Cooked	cracked wheat	cornmeal	rolled oats
Grain	+/or barley flakes	+/or sweet potato	+/or potato
Meat	beef stew meat	ground lamb	chicken
(Choose One)	chicken gizzards	beef liver/heart	turkey
	cod	beef stew meat	ground lamb
	egg (not daily)	tuna or mackerel (once weekly)	venison
	duck	chicken ground/whole	sardine
	+ / − rabbit	rabbit, turkey	+ / − rabbit

amounts, if at all. I like to sneak a few raw carrots and sprouts to my cats on the off-chance they will eat them. Some cats even seem to like some fruits, such as apples or cantaloupe and these are fine to give in small amounts.

Most cats will eat five to six ounces of food daily, either in one meal, or divided into two meals. This will vary, of course, depending upon lifestyle, exercise and hunting capabilities, if permitted. If your cat becomes too fat, or begins to lose weight, adjust the amount you are feeding accordingly. Most cats will eat their fill in half an hour. In her book *The New Natural Cat*, Anitra Frazier recommends removing the food after half an hour, in order to help your cat's digestive system stay toned.[24] She also provides tips on how to change your cat over to a diet of raw foods. As far as raw versus cooked, I believe that feeding raw meats is fine for the healthy individual. However, cooking is necessary for individuals with a sluggish or internal cold tendency.

Most cats do not like either brown or white rice. I'm not sure if it's the texture or particle size, but from what my clients tell me, rice is not delicious to our feline friends. Occasionally, some cats will eat rice cakes crumbled up with their meat, especially if there's some soy sauce on it!

Three to four ounces of meat per day is plenty for most cats. The older or less active the cat, the less meat she may need.

Supplements: Powdered cat vitamin supplements are available through your veterinarian or natural foods store. Alternatively, there are children's vitamins that are suitable for cats. They should include: 1,000 mg vitamin A, folic acid, vitamins B1, B2, B6, biotin and B12 in low dosages of approximately 1 mg; pantothenic acid of approximately 6 mg; vitamin K of approximately 10mcg; plus minerals including 2 mg phosphorus, 3 mg calcium, 500 mcg magnesium and other low dose trace minerals, usually from algae sources.

Vitamin C in the form of sodium ascorbate or ascorbic acid is helpful at 250 mg daily. Vitamin E at 50 IU daily or 100 IU every other day can also be given.

Meat digestion produces acids in the body which must be neutralized by calcium. The high percentage of meat in a cat's diet, therefore, utilizes a high amount of calcium. So, it is important to remember to include a calcium source in the suppliment. The calcium-phosphorus ratio should be approximately 1.1 to 1. A good source of calcium and trace minerals like magnesium and silicon are the seaweeds, such as kelp or kombu. Cats usually like their salty flavor. Sprinkle ¼ teaspoon daily on your cat's food. If your cat won't eat seaweed, alfalfa is an excellent alternative. Add ¼ teaspoon of alfalfa or alfalfa sprouts to your cat's meal. Some of my clients tell me that when their cat friends eat the sprouts, they do not need to go outside and eat grass to vomit. Alfalfa in Western herbology has long been used as a stomach soother.

Cat's also like the taste of nutritional yeast flakes which are high in B vitamins. Most commerical vitamin powders have nutritional yeast as a base. If a commercial powder is not being used, mix ½ teaspoon of yeast flakes to your cat's food daily.

An oil supplement, such as olive oil or butter, can be added to the diet in the amount of ¼ teaspoon per day for palatability, increased fat and essential fatty acid composition. If the cat suffers from arthritis, it is better to avoid dairy products such as butter, because the mucous produced may further injure the joints.

MITZI'S STORY

Mitzi was a bad-tempered Domestic Shorthair who regularly attacked her human without provocation. Mitzi had intermittent diarrhea with blood and mucous present, and spent hours excessively grooming her belly or tearing clumps of hair out of her back. Her regular veterinarian suspected a problem with inflammation in the intestine and colon, and had recommended a food high in fiber. The result was only to infuriate Mitzi further, making her constantly thirsty and her abdomen distended. She attacked her owner even more often than before.

When I first saw Mitzi, she looked like a rounded pear with little legs. Her abdomen was taut and her pulse was rapid. Her tongue was dark pink in color with a slightly yellowish coating. This last item I noted as Mitzi sat on the exam table hissing and spitting at me.

Mitzi's angry attacks and biting response alerted me to a potential liver problem. Remember that in TCM the liver keeps everything running smoothly, and if there is liver imbalance, the individual will become angry, aggressive and hot. Signs of heat are a dark pink tongue with a yellow coating, rapid pulse, excessive thirst, blood and mucous in the stool and *fury*. The random attacks on her owner were indications of Mitzi's mood swings, another symptom of a compromised liver. The hair-biting made me think there was an element of stagnation involved, where the energy or blood flow had gotten stuck. Again, this would be a function of the liver not regulating the circulation properly. When the liver becomes so unbalanced, it compromises the spleen and digestive problems, including diarrhea and inflammation, can occur. The diarrhea with blood is considered heat with dampness.

Unless I wore steel gloves, Mitzi was not a candidate to receive acupuncture treatments, nor was her human able to administer medication in Mitzi's intractable state. So, first we tried a diet change. I prescribed cracked wheat (for calming, cooling and thirst quenching), barley flakes (for calming, cooling and strengthening the stomach and spleen), and beef stewing meat alternating with chicken gizzards. Both of these meats are neutral, with the beef having a more sinking quality. We added some mixed, powdered seaweeds to cool her liver and alleviate it's stagnancy.

Mitzi began to calm down after ten days on this diet. Her attacks on her human became fewer, she gradually began to stop biting her fur and the excessive grooming decreased. After three weeks, she was calm enough for her human to give her herb capsules to clear the heat from the liver and balance both the spleen and the liver. It took several months before Mitzi was completely out of discomfort, but without the diet change, we would never have gotten to first base.

◆ The Senior Cat Diet

Many cats can grow old on a 30 to 40% fresh meat/fish diet, along with 60% grains and supplements. Although this seems high relative to commercial diets, if whole grains and whole foods are used rather than processed filler, this percentage does not seem to overly tax the kidneys. This is probably due to the high biologic value of the protein sources. Obviously, if your cat has kidney or liver problems, she will need a special diet, and you should consult with your veterinarian. You may also follow the guidelines for kidney or liver diets listed later in the book.

As cats grow older it is extremely important to make sure they get a small amount of fresh organ meat such as liver, heart, or kidney, three times monthly, to maintain blood, vital essences, bones and teeth. As your cat ages, it is also important to check in with your veterinarian twice yearly.

COMMERICAL PET FOODS
FOR BOTH CATS AND DOGS

Although many of us would like to cook for our animal friends, it is sometimes not practical because of busy schedules and lifestyles. Because we love our animal friends and want to do the best we can for them, an alternative to home-cooking might be to supplement commercial diets with fresh foods.

Many pet foods sold in supermarkets are made from fillers, poor quality meat and grain protein sources, food additives and colorings and potentially carcinogenic preservatives. But, with the advent of "natural" and "health" foods for people, there is now a wide selection of "natural" foods available for pets, which use vitamin E as a preservative, whole grains, and good, clean, quality protein sources. A word of caution however: watch out for any pet food containing the preservative ethoxyquin as this chemical is a known carcinogen.

While there are many good foods currently on the market, they may not be right for your particular animal friend. As you now know, Traditional Chinese Medicine categorizes foods according to their inherent qualities. The purpose of the categories is to match them with the qualities of the individual (animal or human) so as to bring about a balance. For example, let's say that your animal friend always seems cold, urinates frequently, even needing to go out during the night. In TCM, this indicates too much cold inside the body. You would therefore want to find a food containing warming ingredients to balance the body's cold tendencies. So, you go to the pet food store and find a good quality, hypoallergenic food that is made from wheat, avocado and chicken, and you decide to try it because, even though wheat and avocado are cooling and moistening, thereby increasing the potential cold inside the body, chicken is warming and may counterbalance the coolness of the other two ingredients. But you will have to experiment and observe the results. If your animal friend needs to get up more often in the night, or if she becomes incontinent, you'll know the food is too cooling for her. If she has a hard time digesting her meals, is sluggish with a distended abdomen and she tends to be either too fat or too thin, a lamb and rice diet may be a good choice. The warming lamb and neutral rice will warm the digestion, aiding the spleen and stomach, and increasing metabolism.

Dry foods are made by condensing ingredients, baking the moisture out of them and then usually spraying them with animal fat to improve their taste. Adding water to dry food does not compensate for its drying and heating qualities. They may not be best for the animal who is always thirsty and who has dry, flaky skin and a brittle coat. Also, think about living on a diet of

FOOD	DIRECTION	FLAVOR	THERMAL NATURE	MERIDIAN INFLUENCED
Chicken	Upward	Sweet	Warm	Spleen / Stomach
Turkey	Upward	Sweet/Sour	Warm / Moist	Spleen / Stomach Gall Bladder
Beef	Downward	Sweet	Neutral	Spleen / Stomach
Lamb	Upwards	Sweet	Warm	Spleen / Kidney / Heart
Rabbit	Upward	Sweet	Neutral	Spleen / Stomach / Kidney
Beef Liver	Upward	Sweet	Neutral	Liver
Chicken Liver	Upward	Sweet	Warm	Kidney / Spleen
Kidney	Upward	Sweet	Warm	Kidney / Spleen
Tuna	Up/Downward	Sweet, Salty	Neutral	Spleen
Sardine	Up/Downward	Sweet, Salty	Neutral	Spleen / Stomach
Egg, Chicken	Upward	Sweet	Neutral	Stomach
Rice	Upward	Sweet	Neutral	Spleen / Stomach / Liver
Corn	Upward	Sweet	Neutral	Stomach Large Intestine
Wheat	Downward	Sweet, Salty	Cooling	Spleen / Heart / Kidney Liver
Barley	Downward	Sweet, Salty	Cooling	Spleen / Stomach
Oats	Up/Down	Sweet, Bitter	Warming	Spleen / Stomach
Rye	Upward	Bitter	Neutral	Liver / Gall Bladder / Heart
Potato	Upward	Sweet	Neutral	Spleen / Stomach
Soybean	Downward	Sweet	Cooling	Spleen / Large Intestine

chips. Your digestion would have a pretty hard time breaking down all that fat all the time. Bagged food also lacks vitality. Remember that food imparts its life's experience when prepared and eaten. A diet of dry food is so over processed that its life experience is forgotten.

In cases where dry foods are fed, and the animal suffers from a hot or dry condition, I would suggest supplementing the food with well-cooked grain and vegetables. See the chart for the grains or vegetables that best fit your animal friend's particular situation.

As a weekly treat, feed your healthy dog or cat a meal of fresh meat or fish. Cut-up stewing meat is best, either raw or very slightly cooked. Fish can be fed the same way.

Canned foods of good quality are available, and can be used without the addition of dry foods. I usually recommend supplementing these foods with fresh grains or vegetables. Bones can be supplied weekly to keep the teeth clean. For dogs, I recommend raw knuckle bones from organic, pesticide-free animals. Since bones contain marrow, the richness may cause diarrhea or vomiting in some dogs with weak spleen qi or excessive internal heat. The size of the bone should fit the size of the dog — make sure it's not too small for the larger dog to swallow whole, and not too big for the smaller dog to harm his teeth or jaw. Above all, do not feed chicken bones that splinter to a dog of any size. Cats, on the other hand, enjoy and are not harmed by chicken neck bones.

Digestive enzymes can be added to food in cases where digestion is problematic. Papaya enzyme is an excellent supplement and is readily available.

TRADITIONAL CHINESE MEDICINE QUALITIES OF THE MOST COMMON PET FOOD INGREDIENTS

The preceding is a chart of the most common ingredients and their qualities found in commercial pet foods according to Chinese Medicine. The information is gathered from *The Chinese System of Food Cures, Healing With Whole Foods, and Prince Wen Hui's Cook* (see Endnotes), and my clinical experience.

Endnotes

1, 2, 6, 8, 10, 11, 13, 21. Lu, Henry C. *Chinese System of Food Cures, Prevention & Remedies.* (New York: Sterling Publishing Co., Inc., 1986), 21, 181, 179–183, 35, 45, 175–178, 179.

3, 4, 12, 17, 18, 19, 20, 21, 22, 23. Pitchford, Paul. *Healing with Whole Foods.* (Berkeley, CA: North Atlantic Press, 1993), 432, 425, 583, 117, 432, 421, 467, 111.

5, 14, 21. Flaws, Bob and Honora Wolfe. *Prince Wen Hui's Cook.* (Brookline, MA: Paradigm Publications, 1985), 146, 176, 152, 153, 158, 147.

7. Pitchford, Paul, Lecture, American College of Acupuncture, San Francisco, CA, April 15, 1995.

9. Flaws, Bob and Honora Wolfe. *Prince Wen Hui's Cook.* (Brookline, MA: Paradigm Publications, 1985), Directory listing, P. Pitchford, *Healing with Whole Foods* for Oats, 429.

15. Personal communication, P. Pitchford.

16. Yeun, Jeffry, Lecture, San Francisco, CA, 1994.

24. Frazier, Anitra. *The New Natural Cat.* (New York: E.P. Dutton Book, 1990), 57.

CHAPTER EIGHT # Introduction to Acupressure and Massage Techniques

Massage is the touch of the physical and energetic body with a healing purpose. Therapeutic massage is recognized as one of the primary forms of "hands-on healing" the world over, with most cultures having developed specific techniques for purposes both therapeutic and pleasurable. Most of all, massage is fun and can enhance your relationship with animals.

Any of us who live with an animal knows the joy of touching and petting and hugging our furry friends. They may not understand every word we say, but they always understand our body language.

Besides communication and affection, massage can be used to comfort tired muscles and relieve pain. By increasing the circulation to an area, massage can be used to strengthen areas of the body by stimulating muscles and restoring flexibility. When circulation is enhanced, the blood flows unhindered through the muscles which helps alleviate pain. Increased circulation can also enliven thoughts and energize the mind.

Acupressure is a specialized finger-tip technique which employs the diagnostic and meridian system of Traditional Chinese Medicine. Acu*pressure* can be used as a treatment for almost any condition that can be treated with acu*puncture*.

As part of my treatment programs, I invariably instruct clients to perform either acupressure or massage techniques on their animals as part of the home healing process. I often suggest that clients massage even young and healthy animals on a regular basis because, not only can acupressure and other forms of massage be used to treat various conditions and keep them from worsening, but such treatments can often prevent imbalances from occurring in the first place.

MASSAGE AS THERAPY

First we will discuss massage therapy in general, and then discuss acupressure.

How exactly does massage work? By increasing the circulation of blood and lymph to the skin and underlying muscles, massage allows the tissues to relax, stretch and maintain a healthy tone. While bones provide structure, muscles hold the bones in place. They are the workhorses of the body. Without muscles, their blood supply, tendons and ligaments, the bones would have no cushioning, and virtually no energy to do any work. Along with the tendons and ligaments, the muscles are the slings, ropes, pulleys, and rotators of the body.

When muscle tissue is injured or damaged, inflammation and pain invade the area. Chemical substances like histamines and lactic acid are released into the muscle cells causing abnormal contraction, tension and spasms. Normally free movement is restricted. Because muscles are usually attached by tendons to joints, injured muscles can cause a pulling or tightening of the joint. The result is an animal "holding" his limb, neck or back in a compensating posture, distributing his weight unevenly, creating new stresses on the bones and joints. Eventually the animal may begin to limp, unable to bear weight on a leg. Perhaps you have seen an animal stand "all humped up" in the middle or lower back area. They may walk "low" in the hind end, or stiff-legged, favoring a particular limb. These things are the result of muscle injury. Massage works with the muscles to help them relax and restore them to their original elasticity and position, freeing the animal from pain.

Another benefit of increasing the blood supply to the muscles by massage is that it can bring added nutrients to support and tonify a weak and fatigued area, such as the weakened hind quarters of your older animal friend.

Part of the treatment plan that I work out with my clients includes sending home a massage chart. No matter what kind of problem your animal friend may have, massage can be used between vet visits to facilitate healing. Love and physical contact seem to enhance almost all healing processes. Massage time is a more focused time with the animal, when the human pays close attention to their animal friend's well-being, rather than just a quick pat or stroke here and there. Some of my clients have their children do the massage with the animal. The focused massage time gives the child a sense of responsibility along with a feeling that he is helping his animal friend feel better. The trust that develops through touch between a human and animal is invaluable to both.

Some of you may be familiar with Linda Tellington-Jones, who has developed a method of massage, using random circular movements along the body to specifically help with behavior problems. Her method, known as the *T-Touch* (trademark) is an amazing process that she originally developed to train horses. Ms. Tellington-Jones expanded her work to include all animals. Many behavioral problems in animals have their root in fear. For example, if a horse has suffered an injury while going through a gate, he may always be nervous when asked to walk through any gate. If his fear is great enough, he may refuse to go through a gate whenever this is asked of him. Instead of punishing the horse for his refusal, the T-Touch method can be used to reprogram his fear and turn it into trust. When a horse trusts his human, he will do what is asked of him despite his fear. Ms. Tellington-Jones has produced several books and videos demonstrating the T-Touch method. I recommend her massage techniques to my clients, and highly recommend her learning materials.

Massage is a time-honored method of reducing stress and tension that usually brings a feeling of calmness to both the participants. This is particularly true for people and their animal friends. It has been shown through projects developed and publicized by Dr. Leo Bustad, while Dean at Washington State University Veterinary School in the 1980's, that stroking and touching an animal can help lower a person's blood pressure, increase self-esteem and establish a feeling of well-being. Programs now exist all over the country where animals are brought to visit senior citizens in retirement facilities, and children in centers with learning and behavioral disabilities. The humans look forward to these visits, and the animals, for their part, love the attention and seem to enjoy their visits immensely.

Massage is most helpful in restoring proper movement to injured limbs and joints. When injured muscle tissue is held in a fixed, unnatural, shielded position, it develops a new "muscle memory" or "holding pattern." Muscle memory is a term athletes use while training their muscles for a given sport. For a bike rider, it's the muscle memory and balance that occurs once you get on the bike after a long absence and you discover that you still remember how to ride. For surfers, muscle memory is in the spine for quick take-offs from a prone position on the board to a standing position to ride down the wave. Muscle memory is the unconscious way you hold your body in a given physical or emotional situation.

Animals can develop holding patterns as a result of any trauma which injures a bone or the alignment of the spine, such as being hit by a car, or even surgery. Holding patterns can also result from emotional traumas, when your animal friend tries to protect herself out of fear. Because of hereditary skeletal structure, holding patterns can develop due to poor conformation. The resulting joint dysplasia can decrease flexibility because the muscles and bones are no longer correctly synchronized. Although one cannot change entirely what nature gives, it is sometimes helpful to massage muscles along the body, especially the legs, during your animal's growth phases to keep her flexible. Try to notice any peculiar changes in her gaits that may occur during growth. The muscles that protect the underlying structure will change shape to try to accommodate change. Muscle tissue that is "held" appears smaller, of a tighter or denser weave, harder and more narrow. In many cases, the muscle memory can be reprogrammed by using massage to achieve greater flexibility and proper alignment.

Finally, massage can be used to create balance. In structural terms, balance is most vulnerable at places where the vertebrae change shape or direction, such as where the neck vertebrae end, just in front of the shoulders, and the thoracic vertebrae begin. The thoracic vertebrae are attached to the ribs, and where the thoracic vertebrae end, the lumbar vertebrae (without the ribs) of the lower back take over, finally meeting the sacrum and the tail vertebrae.

Meridians

Lungs

Large Intestine

Stomach

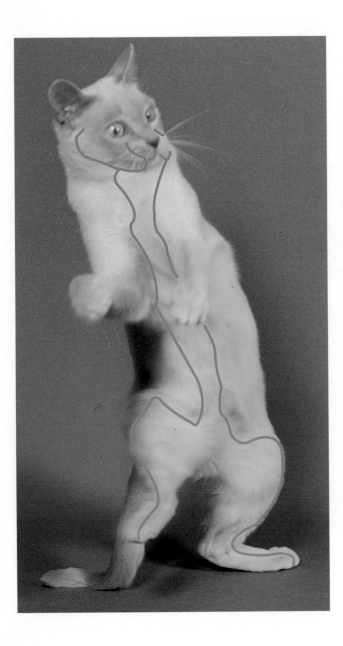

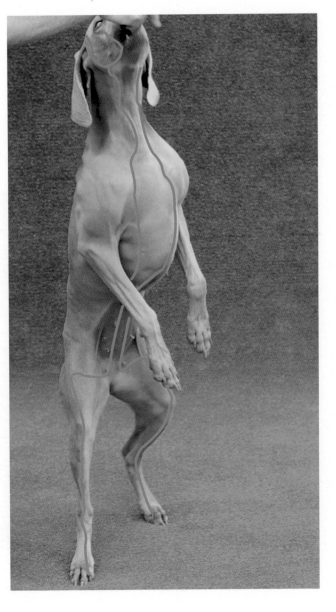

PLATE   C

Spleen / Pancreas

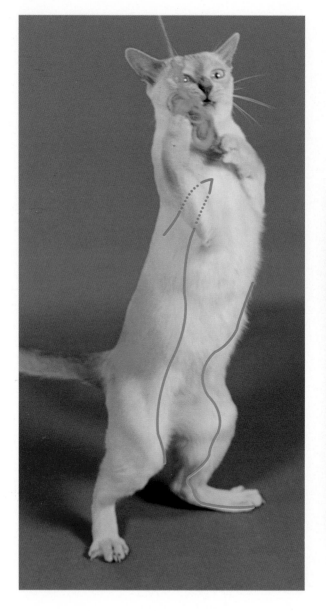

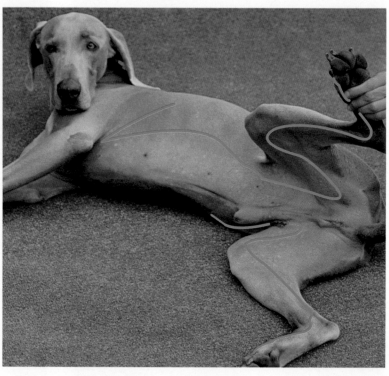

PLATE   D

Heart

Small Intestine

Urinary Bladder

Kidney

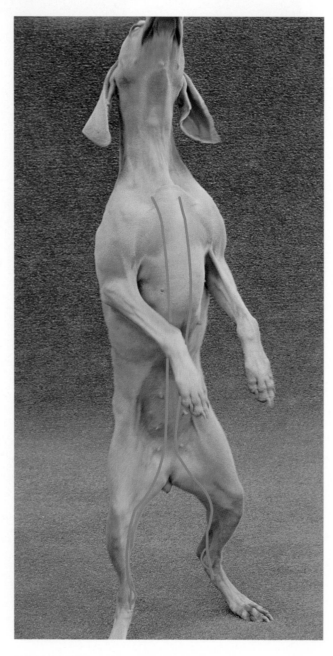

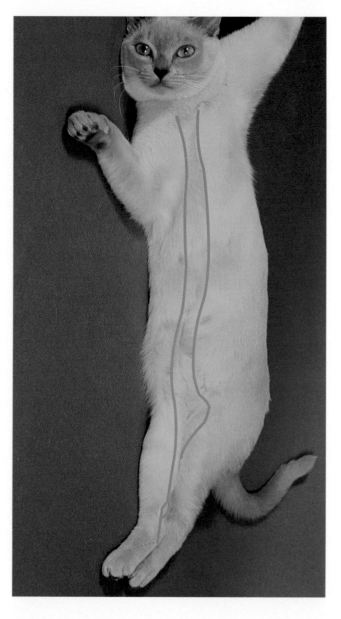

PLATE H

Pericardium

PLATE I

Triple Heater

Gall Bladder

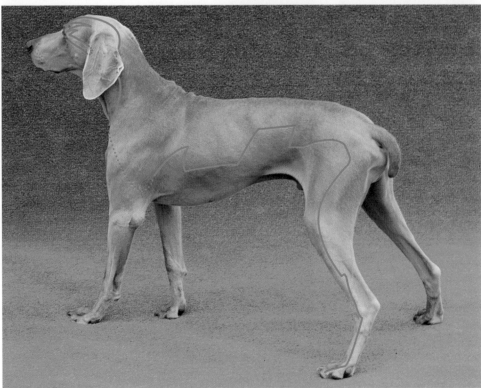

Liver

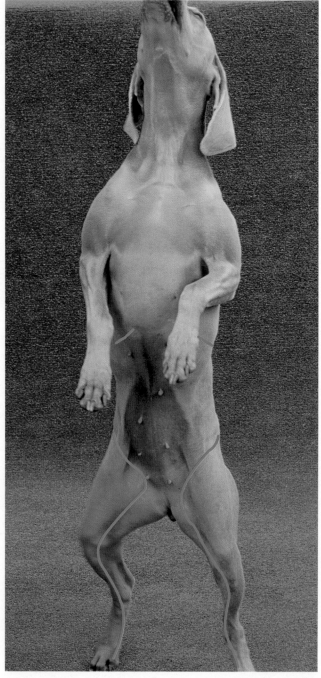

PLATE L

Conception Vessel

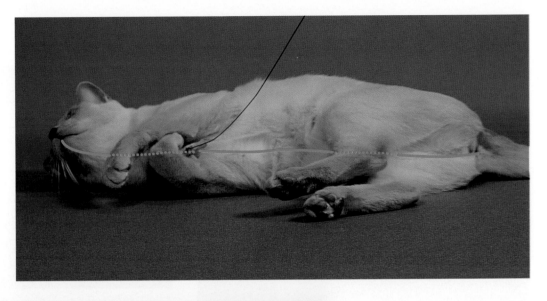

Governing Vessel

Acupressure Points

Eyes

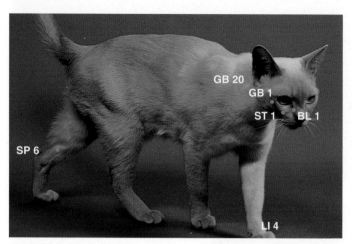

Red, Itchy, Dry Eyes, p.152
GB 20, LI 4 p.152; BL 1, GB 1, ST 1, SP 6 p.153

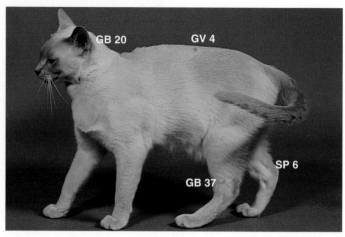

Light & Wind Sensitivity, p.162
GB 20 p.152; GB 37, GV 4 p.162; SP 6 p.153

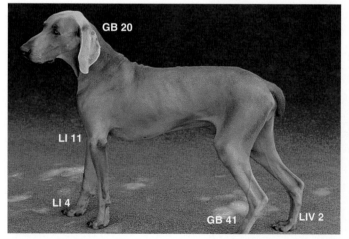

Conjunctivitis, p.156
GB 20, LI 4 p.152; LIV 2, LI 11 p.156; GB 41 p.157

Colds / Sinus Problems

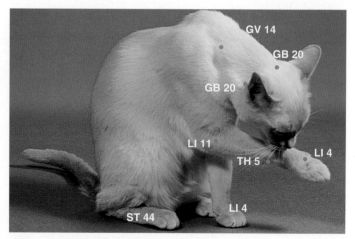

"Wind Cold, Wind Heat", p.166–76
GB 20, LI 4 p.152; GV 14 p.166; TH 5 p.157;
LI 11 p.156; ST 44 p.176

Ears

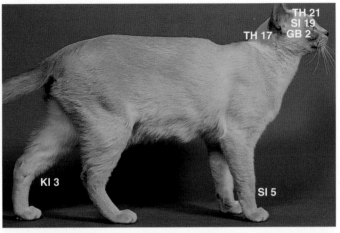

Hearing, p.187
TH 21, SI 19, GB 2, TH 17, KI 3, SI 5 p.187

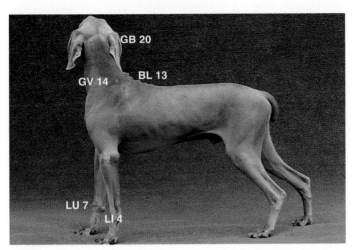

Kennel Cough, p.173
GB 20, LI 4 p.152; BL 13, LU 7 p.173; GV 14 p.166

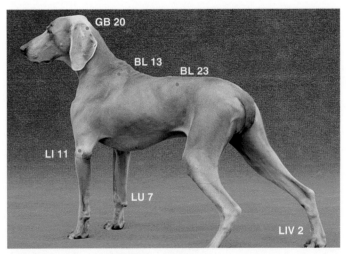

Dry Ears, Wax Buildup, p.188–92
GB 20 p.152; LI 11, LIV 2 p.156; BL 23 p.189;
BL 13, LU 7 p.173

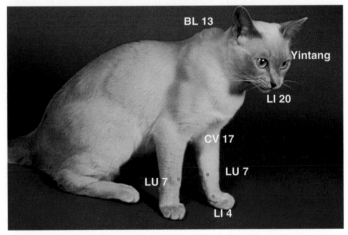

Chronic Sinus Support, p.179
CV 17, LI 20 p.179; BL 13, LU 7 p.173, LI 4 p.152;
Yintang p.180

Ears *(continued)*

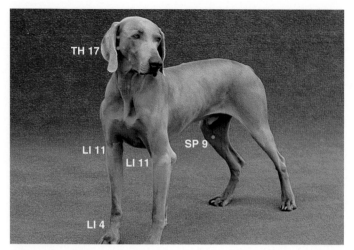

Moist Ear Infections, p.194
SP 9 p.194; LI 4 p.152; LI 11 p.156; TH 17 p.187

Teeth & Gums

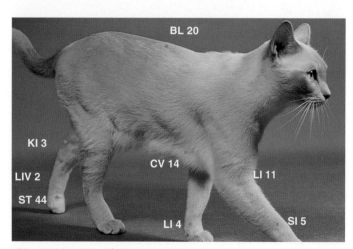

Gingivitis, Mouth Sores, p.203–6
ST 44 p.176; LIV 2, LI 11 p.156; LI 4 p.152;
KI 3, SI 5 p.187; BL 20 p.204; CV 14 p.204

Lungs

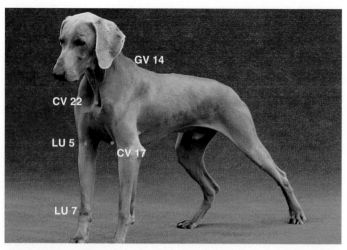

Bronchitis, p.211
CV 22, LU 5 p.211; LU 7 p.173; GV 14 p.166 CV 17 p.179

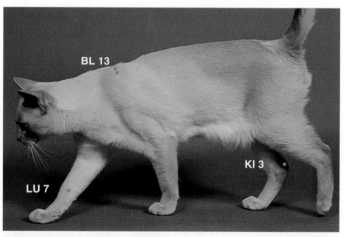

Dry Wheezy Cough, p.213
BL 13, LU 7 p.173; KI 3 p.187

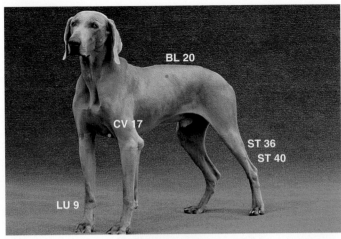

Moist Cough & Breathing, p.219
CV 17 p.179; LU 9, ST 36 p.219; ST 40 p.220;
BL 20 p.204

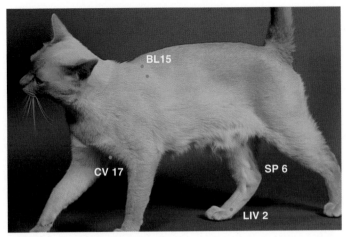

Cardiomyopathy, p.238
BL 15 p.229, CV 17 p.179; LIV 2 p.156; SP 6 p.153

Heart

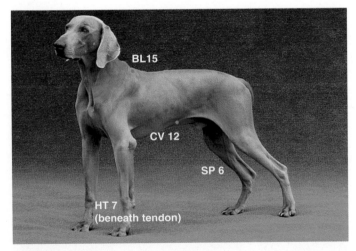

Early Heart Signs, p.229
SP 6 p.153; HT 7, CV 12, BL 15 p.229

Liver & Gall Bladder

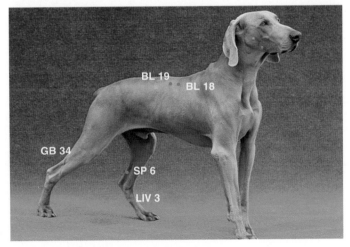

Liver Blood Deficiency, p.248
LIV 3 p.241; SP 6 p.153; GB 34, BL 18, 19 p.249

Liver & Gall Bladder (continued)

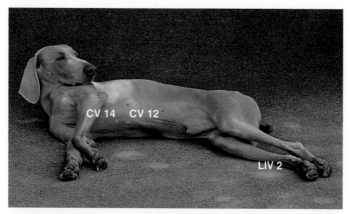

Vomiting Food & Bile, p.257
CV 14 p.204; CV 12 p.229; LIV 2 p.156

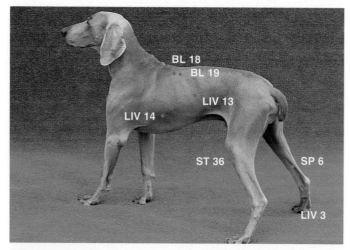

Hepatitis, p.258–60
LIV 13 p.235; LIV 14 p.259; BL 18, 19 p.249; LIV 3 p.241;
SP 6 p.153; ST 36 (do not use if fever) p.219

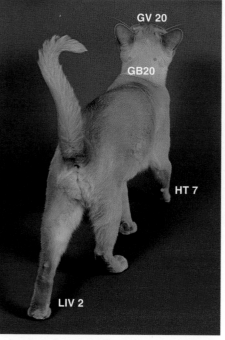

Seizures, p.250, 258, 263
GV 20 p.241; GB 20 p.152; LIV 2 p.156; HT 7 p.229

Spleen / Pancreas & Stomach

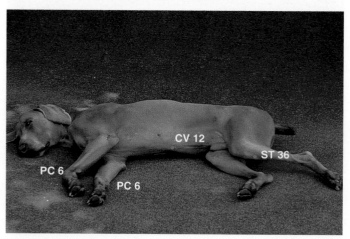

Weak Spleen Qi, p.274
ST 36 p.219; PC 6 p.241; CV 12 p.229

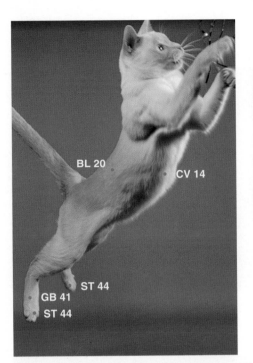

Stomach Fire & Strange Appetites, p.278
CV 14, BL 20 p.204; ST 44 p.176; GB 41 p.157

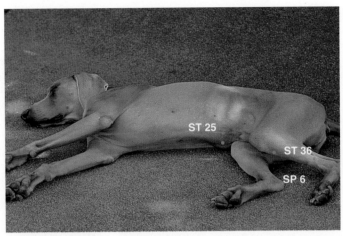

Soft Pasty Stools, p.282
ST 25 p.282; SP 6 p.153; ST 36 p.219

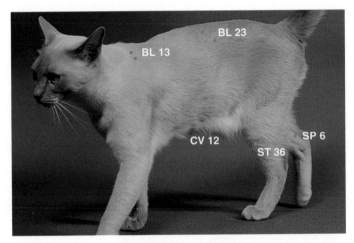

Diabetes, p.273, 283
BL 13 p.173; CV 12 p.229; BL 23 p.189;
ST 36 p.219; SP6 p.153

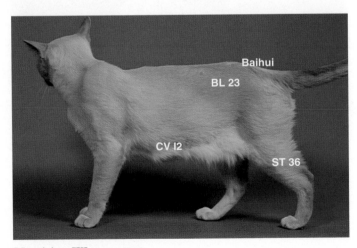

Vomiting Water, p.280
CV 12 p.229; ST 36 p.219; BL 23 p.189; Baihui p.280

Spleen / Pancreas & Stomach (continued)

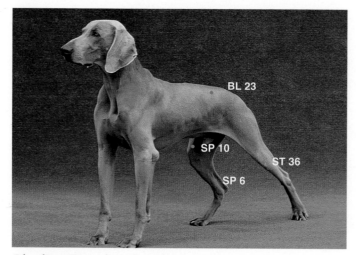

Bleeding Disorders A, p.286
SP 6 p.153; SP 10 p.286; ST 36 p.219; BL 23 p.189

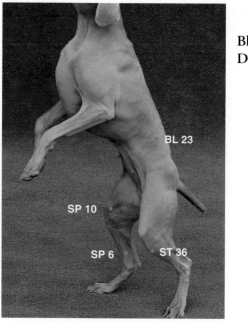

Bleeding
Disorders B

Kidneys & Urinary Bladder

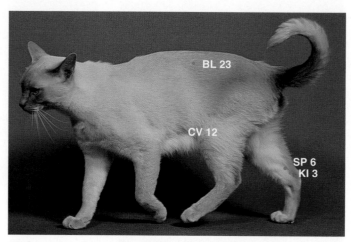

Kidney Yin Support, p.295
KI 3 p.187; SP 6 p.153; CV 12 p.229; BL 23 p.189

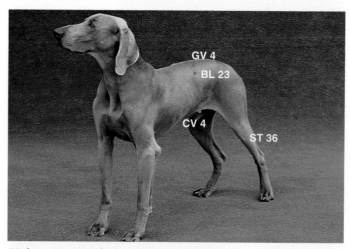

Kidney Yang/Libido Support, p.301
GV 4 p.162; BL 23 p.189; CV 4 p.250; ST 36 p.219

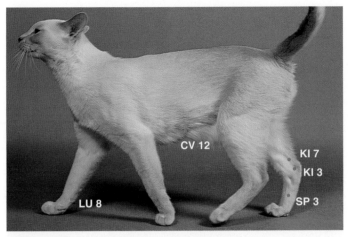

Kidney Failure, p.305
SP 3 p.305; KI 3 p.187; LU 8, KI 7 p.306; CV 12 p.229

Urinary Bladder

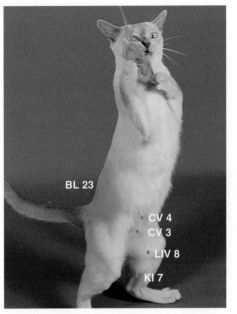

Cystitis Straining & Blood, p.311–14
CV 4 p.250; CV 3 p.312; KI 7 p.306; BL 23 p.189

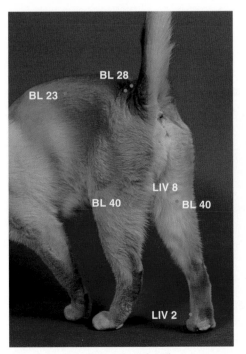

Cystitis, Straining & Blood, p.311–14
BL 40 p.250; LIV 2 p.156; BL 23 p.189; BL 28 p.312;
LIV 8 p.313

Large Intestine

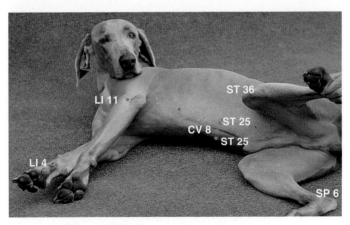

Acute or Watery Diarrhea, p.323–326
LI 4 p.152; LI 11 p.156; SP 6 p.153; CV 8 p.326;
ST 36 p.219, ST 25 p.282

Large Intestine (continued)

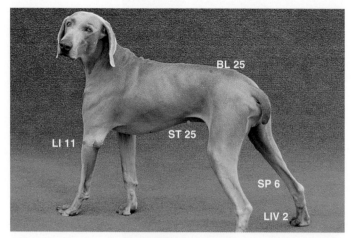

Diarrhea & Straining, p.327
LIV 2 p.156; SP 6 p.153; BL 25 p.327; ST 25 p.282;
LI 11 p.156

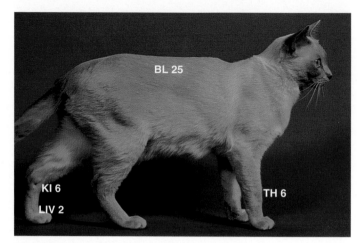

Constipation from Liver Excess, p.333
TH 6, KI 6 p.333; LIV 2 p.156; BL 25 p.327

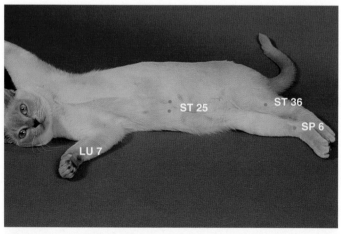

Constipation from Deficiency, p.331
ST 25 p.282; SP 6 p.153; ST 36 p.219; LU 7 p.173

Bones & Muscles

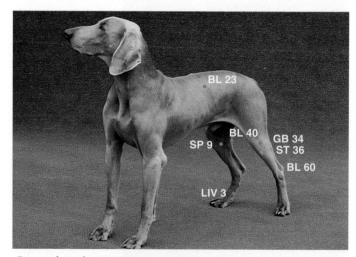

General Arthritis Points, p.340
BL 60 p.340; GB 34 p.249; BL 40 p.250; LIV 3 p.241;
BL 23 p.189; SP 9 p.194; ST 36 p.219

PLATE V

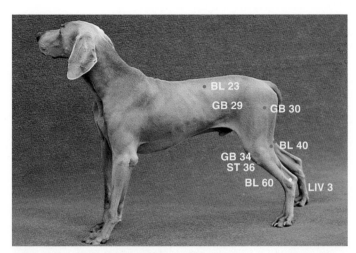

Hip Joint Arthritis, p.342

GB 29, 30 p.342; LIV 3 p.241; BL 60 p.340; BL 23 p.189; or
GB 34 p.249; BL 40 p.250; ST 36 p.219

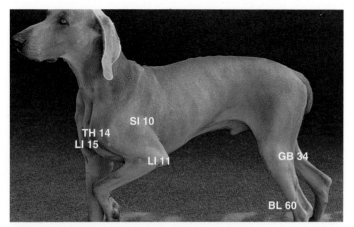

Shoulder Joint Arthritis, p.343

LI 15, TH 14, SI 10 p.343; LI 11 p.156; BL 60 p.340;
GB 34 p.249

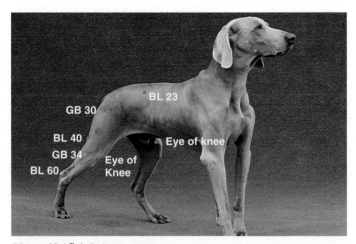

Knee (Stifle) Joint, p.342

Eyes of Knee, p.342; BL 23 p.189; GB 30 p.342;
GB 34 p.249; BL 60 p.340; BL 40 p.250

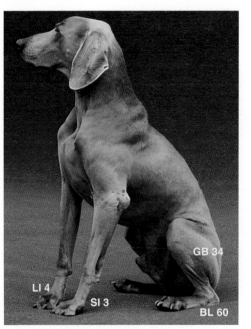

Elbow & Wrist Joints, p.344–45

Encircle Elbow, Wrist; LI 4 p.152; BL 60 p.340;
GB 34 p.249; SI 3 p.345

Skin

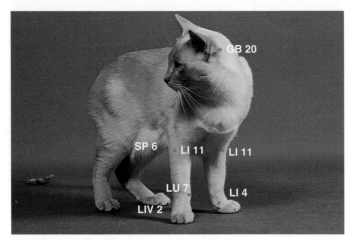

Hot, Itchy, Dry & Scabs, p.358–62
GB 20, LI 4 p.152; SP 6 p.153; LU 7 p.173;
LIV 2, LI 11 p.156

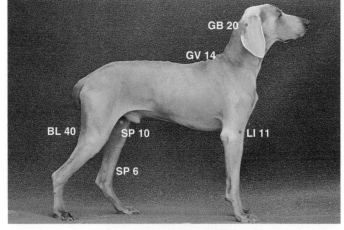

Doggy Odor, Itching, Oozing Scabs & Hot Spots, p.365
GV 14 p.166; LI 11 p.156; BL 40 p.250; SP 6 p.153;
SP 10 p.366; GB 20 p.152

PLATE X

Immune System & Glands

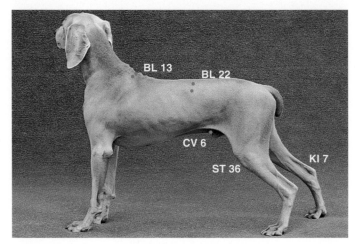

Hypothyroid, p.377–79
KI 7 p.306; CV 6 p.378; BL 22 p.379; ST 36 p.219;
BL 13 p.173

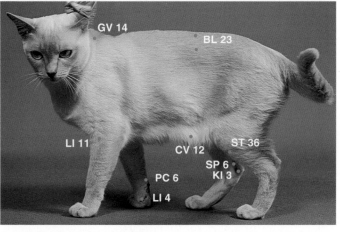

Immune Support, p.386
LI 4 p.152; LI 11 p.156; ST 36 p.219; PC 6 p.241;
CV 12 p.229; GV 14 p.166; KI 3 p.187; BL 23 p.189

It is at these transitional regions that structural changes cause directional changes in the angles of the body. These are stress points which require reinforcement to maintain their integrity. The muscles attached to these areas are subject to greater tension and stress. Massage can help these transitional areas to maintain integrity through alignment, dimension, tone and mobility.

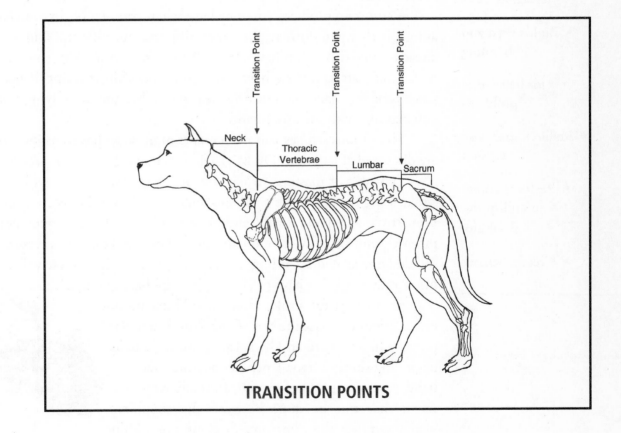

TRANSITION POINTS

WHAT MASSAGE DOES

- Increases blood and lymph circulation

- Brings strength to weakened muscles

- Disperses pain in tensed muscles

- Builds trust and bonding

- Aids behavioral problems

- Reduces stress and tension

- Restores proper mobility and flexibility

- Creates balance

Muscles run in layers, or what anatomists call fascial planes. They also run in certain directions. Think of a carpet with high pile. Run your hand in one direction and you will see the pile lie down. Go in the opposite direction and the pile stands up. Well, the muscles are similar, only on a somewhat more subtle level. On our animal friends, the fur is usually a good guideline. When you stroke the fur in one direction, along the grain so to speak, the hair lies down and the animal is comfortable. If you run your hand the other way to make the hair stand up, against the grain, there is more resistance and many animals don't like how this feels.

A common problem you may have when you first begin to massage your animal is that you don't realize how thick and movable the skin is. You may already know this if you have a Shar Pei whose "extra" skin is noticeable, but in fact, all cats and dogs have thick, movable skin, making it necessary to place your free hand on a nearby area to stabilize the underlying tissue while you massage with the other hand.

The various strokes and movements of massage have specific names, and are discussed at length in Dr. Michael Fox's book *The Healing Touch*.

The type of massage stroke you may be most familiar with is the long stroke using the flat of the hand and finger tips. This is known as "effleurage."[1] Long strokes are good for the abdomen and larger muscle groups along the neck and back. Most animals enjoy these strokes. The pressure should be regulated according to what the animal tells you. He will move away if it is too hard or closer if it is not hard enough.

Another useful stroke is like a rubbing motion, called "friction."[2] Use the tips of your fingers and apply pressure in a forward and backward motion, usually beginning slowly, about 1 per second, and gradually increasing to 2 per second. I usually recommend that this be done between the shoulder blades and over the rump area or along the midline

Stabilizing Technique

of the chest between the front legs extending down toward the abdomen. This sternal massage, along with the rub between the shoulder blades is useful for treating breathing problems and to quell coughing especially for cats who have asthma or allergic bronchitis.

Another technique I find helpful, especially with tight and stiff back muscles is the "rock 'n roll." Stand behind your animal and place the flat of your hands on the upper sides of the rib cage if the animal is tense in the shoulders, or around the sides of the belly if the animal is tense in the low back area. Ideally, your animal should be in a relaxed position, lying on her sternum and belly. Gently rock the animal from side to side. Then, very gently roll her body in an upward direction, first from left to right. Then rock again from side to side. This alternating, very gentle rocking and rotating is helpful in relieving muscle tension.

You can also gently extend the animal's spine by standing behind her and grasping the area in front of the thighs under the belly, while she is standing. Gently lift the hind legs off the floor while pulling up from the abdomen.

Lift Technique

The last massage technique I want to describe is from the Tellington T-Touch program. As I have already mentioned, the T-Touch uses as one of its main techniques a circular motion that is drawn with the finger tip at random places on the animal's body. As discussed in the Tellington books and videos, and as described in Diane Stein's book *Natural Healing for Dogs and Cats,* the circle is drawn beginning at an imaginary 6 o'clock position and goes around almost one and a quarter times until it reaches just past 8 o'clock. These circles have the effect of awakening brain waves that alert, calm and relax the individual. The result is that the Tellington-Jones techniques have been used successfully not only for physical conditions, but for all types of behavior problems as well, including aggression, such as snapping in dogs and biting and scratching in cats.

On either side of the spine are long muscle groups that run parallel to the spine from the neck to the tail. I instruct my clients to use a version of the T-Touch circles that I use myself when working with the spinal muscles.

Using your index fingers, begin at the spine and draw outward circles using T-Touch technique of one to one-quarter times per circle, gradually moving downward toward the next area. Use this technique in the area that your animal has the problem, starting just in front of where the pain, weakness or stiffness begins, to just behind the problem area. Remember that pressure is very minimal. Do this routinely for three to five minutes daily, and you may be surprised at the results.

JOEY'S STORY

Joey is a long-haired cat who grooms himself so excessively that he has removed most of the hair from this belly. It seems that he grooms most intensely about half an hour after breakfast and dinner and then again at bedtime, about 11:00 p.m. Because Joey prefers to be on the bed, his grooming keeps his human companion awake.

When I examined Joey he had a tense look on his face. He burped, which is highly unusual for a cat and his breath was slightly off, smelling of the fish he ate the night before. Joey had a distended hanging belly, which swayed when he walked. When I looked at his tongue, it was dark pink with a slightly yellow coating. His stomach was gurgling and his spine was sore to the touch at the transitional region just behind the rib cage, where the thoracic vertebrae meet the lumbar vertebrae.

According to the Chinese circadian clock, the times of Joey's intense grooming coincided with the times when food began to empty from his stomach and as his gall bladder was called upon to furnish bile to break down fats. The gall bladder meridian is most active around 11 p.m. when Joey and his human were getting ready for sleeping. The dark tongue with the yellow coating indicated heat or inflammation in the stomach, and his hanging belly indicated weak qi of the spleen/pancreas and stomach. Remember that the spleen and stomach are responsible for breaking food down into usable products of qi and blood and transporting them to needed places in the body. All in all, Joey's excessive grooming pointed to digestive problems. He needed a diet change and treatment for inflammation in the digestive tract.

I prescribed herbs and showed Joey's human certain massage points and strokes to replace Joey's problematic self-massage. I taught her to use long strokes on the abdomen with the flat of her hand and fingertips, running from the bottom of the rib cage to the groin area, repeating this six times. According to the philosophy of T'ai Chi, six is a number for sedation, and I wanted to sedate, or calm the digestive tract. I recommended that the massage be done just prior to eating, to be repeated about fifteen minutes after eating. The pressure was to be light to moderate. Because Joey was extremely sensitive on either side of his spine, just behind the ribs, (which coincides with the diagnostic point for the stomach, see diagnostic charts, pages 59–64), I thought he would be too uncomfortable to treat with acupuncture at first. Instead, I had Joey's person use the "rock'n roll" technique described earlier in the mid-back area, just before bedtime. After several weeks of herbs, diet change and massage, Joey's grooming began to diminish. Even after the completion of the herb treatments, Joey's human continued his daily massage, believing it good for Joey's digestion.

TRIGGER POINTS

Many times an animal will come into the office ripping its fur out of various places on the body, or licking other places raw. Generic treatment usually includes an injection of an anti-inflammatory drug such as cortisone or a prescription for a course of pills. This usually takes the symptoms away, but when the drug wears off, the ripping or licking often resumes. These traumatized areas may be the results of trigger points.

A trigger point is a localized area in a muscle that you can actually feel. A chiropractic colleague says it feels like "a marble in mud." It is a tight knot that forms as the result of repeated stress to a specific muscle. When a muscle is injured it becomes weak, short and tight. These changes put stress on the area surrounding the original injury site. This new area is known as a site of "referred pain." However, because the referred pain area is *not* the origin of the pain, treatment in the referred zone does *not* relieve the problem. Only treatment at the trigger point site will relieve the pain.

The difficulty is that trigger points set up areas of referred pain that do not have the usual anatomical nerve pathways that doctors are used to seeing. Dr. Janet Travell,[3] known as the godmother of Trigger Point Therapy, identified this problem after many years of research in the human medical field. In the veterinary field, Dr. Luc Janssens, has been able to describe nine trigger points on dogs.[4] There are probably many more, but they have not yet been identified. The most common are located in the (1) shoulder muscle, (2) the long muscle on the outside of the arm, below the shoulder (the long head of the triceps), (3) in the croup area in front of the pelvis, (4) in the big rump muscle, (5) on the front of the hip in the quadriceps muscle, (6) below the knee near the top part of the tibia and fibula in the Peroneus Longus muscle, and (7) inside the groin on the inside of the thigh.

MEDUSA'S STORY

A highly strung tortoise-shell cat named Medusa had been biting and ripping the fur from her back, just in front of the pelvis. She had concentrated her efforts on the right side only and had created a bald patch about two inches long by the time I saw her. She was quite normal otherwise, but when she had one of her spells, she became frantic. The skin in the area was normal in color, not red, and I could find no scabs or fleas. There was no sign of digestive disturbance, no sign of limping. However, when I examined her, she was sensitive all along the lower back on the right side. I ran my hand over the back of her rump and felt a small knot in the muscle, about the size of a pea. When I pressed on it, Medusa began to frantically lick her low back area. I treated the knot in the muscle, believing it to be a trigger point, by injecting it with a small amount of diluted vitamin B-12. The spells stopped for six months and the knot disappeared. The problem recurred later in the year, and I treated her again the same way. Somehow she must have been overusing a portion of her hind leg which caused the trigger point to recur. So, if your animal is experiencing pain that is not being helped by conventional treatment, try to see if a trigger point is involved.

ACUPRESSURE

Acupressure is a fingertip technique that uses the meridian system and acupuncture point locations. Acupuncture uses a needle to pierce the skin. Acupressure uses fingertip pressure on the skin's surface. Both systems effect change by stimulating or fatiguing the acupoints that are part of the meridians.

Remember that meridians are energy pathways that travel just beneath the skin's surface. They connect the body's surface with the interior organ systems and regulate energy and blood flow throughout the entire body. Professional acupressure therapists study at great length and use this system as their sole form of treatment. Although acupuncture is usually considered a deeper type of treatment, acupressure has the advantage that, with a guide to the points, it can be done by individuals at home.

HOW TO FIND AN ACUPRESSURE POINT

Most acupressure points lie in the depressions between the muscle bundles and bones. My first teacher, Dr. Alice DeGroot, used to say, "Acupoints are in the valleys, not on top of the mountains." So, rule one is to find the dip between the muscles, or tendons, or ligaments. Acupressure points are almost never on a bony prominence, such as the point of the elbow or knee. They are usually just to one side, in front of, or behind that prominence.

Try to find an acupressure point on your own body by flexing your arm, and noticing the crease that appears on the inside of your elbow. There are four acupoints connected with this elbow crease. On the inside of the arm, at the inside tip of the elbow crease, find the first point which lies between the end of the crease and the bony prominence of your elbow. This point is on the heart meridian and is used for calming, and to relieve chest pain and

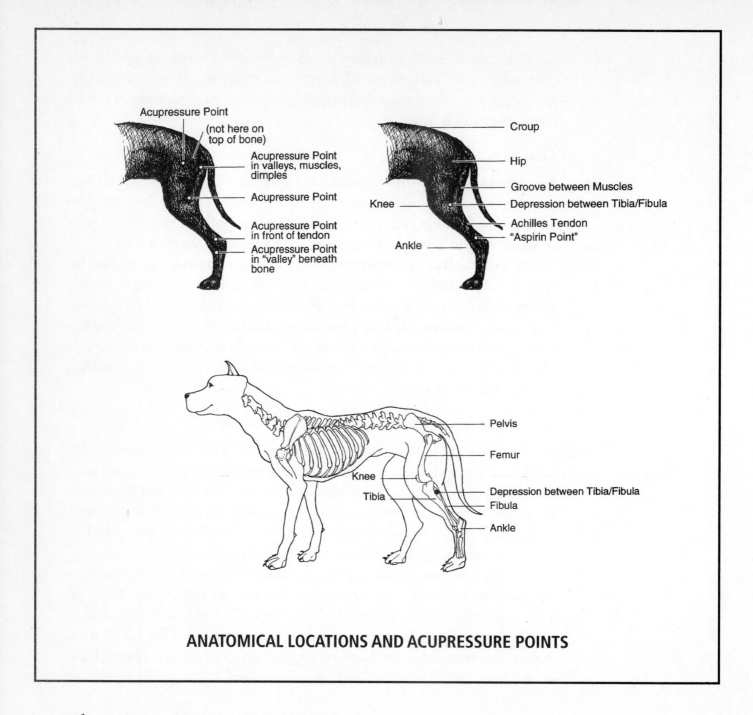

Acupressure Point
(not here on top of bone)

Acupressure Point in valleys, muscles, dimples

Acupressure Point

Acupressure Point in front of tendon

Acupressure Point in "valley" beneath bone

Croup

Hip

Groove between Muscles

Depression between Tibia/Fibula

Knee

Achilles Tendon "Aspirin Point"

Ankle

Pelvis

Femur

Knee

Depression between Tibia/Fibula

Tibia

Fibula

Ankle

ANATOMICAL LOCATIONS AND ACUPRESSURE POINTS

palpitations.[5] In the center of the crease you will feel a large tendon which is part of the biceps muscle. The second point is just to the inside of this tendon, on the crease. This point lies on the pericardium meridian and is used to diagnose and treat bronchitis and acute vomiting and diarrhea.[6] The third point is just on the other side of the biceps tendon. This point lies along the lung meridian, and is used to treat pneumonia and fluid in the chest. The last point is on the outside end of the elbow crease, in front of the radial bone. This point is found on the large intestine meridian and is used to lessen heat and inflammation, particularly with arthritic conditions and skin diseases.

Now try to find acupressure points on your animal. Let's start at the rump by running the palm over the outside of the thigh. You can find the thigh by starting on the back over the pelvic, or sacral area, in front of the tail. In horses and dogs this area is called the croup. It is the highest part of the lower back. Use your fingers to feel all the depressions in this area. First, run your entire hand (if your dog is large) or your fingers (for cats and smaller dogs) down the hind leg, beginning at the top of the sacral spine, or croup area. Feel the bony prominences. The bony prominence just below the tail on the outside of the leg belongs to one of the pelvic bones. Pick up the rear leg by the paw. If you follow the leg upward from the paw to the thigh, you will find the hip joint near the top of the leg because you will see it move when the hind leg is lifted.

When you come to the hip joint, it will feel like a ball fitting into a socket. The muscles here are thick, so you may need to use more pressure if you don't feel it immediately. On either side of the bone are two depressions. These are acupressure points — not on the bone itself, but in front of, and behind the movable hip joint (where the head of the thigh bone, the femur, fits into the socket of the pelvis). Continue to run your fingers down the outside of the hind leg, just below the stifle or knee. When cats and short dogs are standing, the knee is approximately at the level of where the belly meets the hind legs. This may be confusing at first, as you will want to think of the knee as being lower down the leg. Just below the knee, where the two bones of the lower leg begin, the tibia (which is the larger, lower leg bone), and the fibula (which is the small, thin, outside bone running alongside the tibia), there is a depression. This depression can be found just below the head of the fibula on the outside of the leg in the depression between the two bones.

Continue to run your fingers down the leg. Just above the ankle, there is a hollow depression that feels like an empty space containing just skin which is actually in front of the Achilles tendon. This hollow contains an acupressure point that is known as the "aspirin" point for treating painful joints.

Next, try running your fingertips along the backside of the hind leg. Here you will find two big muscle groups. Run your finger in the groove between them. Just above and behind the knee, there is a deep groove and here lies another acupressure point. This one is good for clearing inflammation or heat from the lower part of the body, and can be used for treating hot skin conditions, or inflamed joints.

HOW ACUPRESSURE WORKS

Acupressure is based on a system that was developed in Chinese medical schools over a thousand years ago.[7] Its treatment principles rely on the same diagnostic methods used in acupuncture that we have been discussing. Because it works with the meridians, acupressure can redirect energy flows, strengthen or tonify the muscles, bones and internal organs, or disperse pain. Acupressure creates balance in the body. Using specific acupoints, acupressure can be used to treat almost any medical condition except those requiring surgery. In Part Three of the book, the acupressure points are listed for various conditions as the main part of the treatment program.

◆ Directing and Regulating Energy Flow

Stimulating acupressure points strengthens the tissues surrounding the energy pathways or the underlying organ system. This strengthening is considered a "tonifying process."

In Traditional Chinese Medicine it is believed that pain occurs when the circulation of blood or qi is blocked. Acupressure can be used at specific locations to disperse this stagnant or stuck energy which relieves pain. Such dispersing techniques can be considered a "sedating process." In conditions such as blocked sinuses, acupressure can disperse the energy flow to encourage drainage.

◆ Creating Balance

Acupressure also creates balance in the body. As we have seen, the underlying balance of the body revolves around equality of the yin and yang forces, the yin being the nurturing, soothing, calming and moistening influences, the yang being the aggressive, assertive, quick, forceful ones. The underside of animals and the front of humans are considered yin. The top sides of animals and the backs of humans are considered yang. Acupressure can play a major role in balancing these two primary forces. If an individual is too yin, balancing can come from stimulating points along the back or yang meridians. In the same way, if an individual is too yang, the yin aspects need to be enhanced. It is also said that to massage an acupressure point in a clockwise direction, you can encourage the yang, while massaging an acupressure point in a counterclockwise direction, will nurture the yin.[8]

Traditional Chinese Medicine also believes in the concept of the **three burners.** Each burner is a compartment of the body. The **upper burner** is composed of the head and chest; the **middle burner** is composed of the liver, gall bladder, spleen/pancreas and stomach, and the middle region of the body; and the **lower burner** is comprised of the kidneys, adrenals, intestines, bladder and sex organs. The burners of the body help keep energy, blood and fluid flowing continuously and smoothly. They are the regional managers of the body. Each organ has its job within a region and each region functions as part of the entire body. Massage works at the transition points between the burners to keep each region in balance with the others. At the risk of sounding like a broken record, health comes from balance and when balance exists, the body, mind and emotions are happy and peaceful. This is true for animals as well as humans.

ACUPRESSURE TECHNIQUE

Now that you have an idea of where acupressure points can be found, what they feel like, and how they are used, let's discuss technique. Of course, professional acupressure therapists spend a great deal of time learning acupressure techniques. The following is a brief description of the basic principles.

When doing acupressure on your furry friend, fingertip pressure is used, with the finger extended, not bent. Some people like to use the thumb, some the index finger.

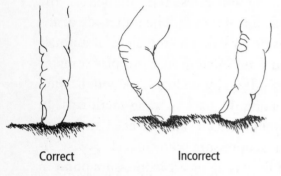

Correct   Incorrect

HOLDING A POINT

According to Dr. Kuan Hin, the success of the massage depends on even pressure, rather than intensity.[9] When you apply pressure, begin slowly and lightly, gently deepening with steady movement. When the muscle and/or animal begins to resist or become tense, stop the pressure, relax just a bit, and hold the point for five seconds.[10] This steady pressure at a given depth that you and the animal agree upon is called **holding a point.** If you are uncertain as to how deeply or how hard to press, listen to the animal. They will make you aware of their discomfort by squirming or moving away, by giving you a warning look, or, when they become uncomfortable enough, by snapping. As you practice these massage techniques, you will become more aware of the subtle signs that the animal gives you. Remember that touch is a whole experience. Your aim in holding a point is to match the energy of the individual you are working with. Pay attention to your animal friend and trust yourself to find the right degree of pressure.

CALMING THE AGITATED ANIMAL

When dealing with an animal who is very agitated, I find that holding three points around the head is helpful. Very light pressure is used at first, with a steady increase as the animal responds. The points are just below the back of the head, in the indentations at the nape of the neck, midway between the

spine and the base of the ear, as
well as the point just in front of
the bump on the top mid-
line of the head. This
bump, known as the
external occipital pro-
tuberance, is very promi-
nent in some breeds, such as Golden
Retrievers and Siamese cats, and
not so prominent in others. There

THREE-POINT HOLD

is a small notch just in front of this protuberance which can be found by running your fingernail forward from the highest point on the midline of the top
of the head toward the forehead. Using very light pressure, this three-point
hold is an excellent calming mechanism. The points are Gall Bladder 20, for-
mally known as "Wind Pond," to relieve tension coming up from the liver,
and Governing Vessel 20, known as the "Meeting Point of One-hundred
Points," used to rebalance the energy.

If your animal is agitated, use long strokes along the neck first, then try to
massage the ear flaps. Finally, finish with the three-point hold for ten to fifteen
seconds.

A CASE OF LAMENESS

One of my clients came to me with her older Collie, Milly, who had a lameness in her shoulder. It was a problem that occurred intermittently, when she
and Milly were out on the trail, or running on the beach. When Milly was at
rest there was no sign of a problem, and radiographs showed nothing. When I
examined Milly, I could feel muscle tightness on the inside of the arm-pit and
along the back of the arm above the elbow, although no trigger points were
palpable. The tight, large muscle groups were going into spasm during intense
exercise and then relaxing somewhat at rest, granting Milly a reprieve from
the pain. It appeared that a reflex muscle memory pattern was triggered during

exercise. Milly might have injured herself originally from over-exertion at some point, causing a chronic sprain or excess stretching of a tendon.

I instructed my client as to which acupressure points to press around the shoulder, elbow, and wrist. These points are along the meridians of the front leg that span the involved muscles. The purpose of the acupressure was to disperse the blocked energy that was causing the spasms. I asked my client to hold the set of points for a total of three minutes before she took Milly out to run. If, during exercise, Milly pulled up lame, my client was to massage the points again.

The following week I received flowers from my client because Milly was doing much better, with little sign of lameness. More importantly, my client wanted to thank me for showing her how help her dog *herself*.

STEP-BY-STEP DAILY MASSAGE

First, greet your animal friend in whatever fashion you both are used to. My cat insists on raising her hind quarters to me so that I can scratch her just in front of her tail. Some dogs are head shy and would rather be greeted by a pat under the chest, while others insist upon a vigorous head or ear rub.

The daily massage has a number of purposes. First, it gives you private and special time with your animal that is mutually relaxing. Second, it stimulates your animal friend's circulation and enlivens the muscles which helps keep them toned, fit and flexible. Third, it stimulates the meridians. As Dr. Kuan Hin so beautifully states, "It stimulates a meridian simply to pass your hand over it; however simple and inadequate. . . . it may appear to an outsider, you will find its action manifold and most beneficial."[11] During massage time, you might notice a change in the texture of the skin or fur, or an area of discomfort. As you become more familiar and comfortable with this type of work with your animal friend, you will become more sensitive to subtle changes in her behavior, mood, and general condition. Such close observation can alert you to small problems before they become serious.

Notice how your animal friend moves as he approaches you. Does it seem fluid? Is there stiffness? Is he shuffling? I always notice how an animal carries his head, because a tilt to one side may mean neck or leg problems. Notice the expression on his face. Is it happy or sad, is his brow furrowed with worry? I always laugh when people ask me if animals have feelings. *Of course* they do. We just need to notice them.

Next, make sure the animal is in a comfortable position. Many dogs and cats like to lie on their sides. Others like to sit up on their haunches, resting their paws in front or tucked underneath them.

Begin the massage in the neck or head area, using long petting strokes, along the top of the head and down the spine. The longest meridian of the body, the urinary bladder meridian, runs parallel to the spine. The massage begins in the neck area where the bladder meridian branches into two pathways on either side of the spine. It runs along the neck, between the shoulder blades, all the way to the base of the tail and down the hind legs. Find the pressure your animal likes with the long strokes. If it is too hard, he will move away. If it is not hard enough, he will move closer toward your touch.

Using your thumbs and fingers, stroke from the center of the chin upward in both directions along the jaws to the base of the ears. Try to make the animal grin. The chin and corners of the mouth stimulate the stomach meridian. As you travel to the base of the ear, you will touch the large intestine and small intestine meridians. Use either straight strokes or small circular motions.

Rub the ears from the base to the tip of the flap. This is very relaxing to most animals. In Traditional Chinese Medicine, the ear flaps and outer ear areas are a hologram for the entire body. (An entire system of acupuncture was developed in France by Dr. Nogier, based on the ear.) The triple heater meridian, which acts as the traffic controller that manages the three main body areas, encircles the ear flap. Massaging the ear and the flap will relax and invigorate all the organs of the body.

Next, work down the sides of the neck in a circular fashion, using the Tellington-Jones technique of one and one-quarter circles from the spine outwards. If the skin is excessively moveable, you may need to stabilize the area with one hand and massage with the other. You will be stimulating the bladder meridian which keeps the circulation moving along the spine, decreasing tension. Rub back and forth between the shoulder blades and continue to massage along the spine using the same circular motions. When you come to the rump area, use the flat of your hand with larger motions and rub first in one direction to make a circular sweep, and then the other.

If your animal friend is sensitive in a particular area, please check the charts of diagnostic association points on pages 59–64, so that you can be aware of a potential problem. Remember, sensitivity along the spine can mean a local pain reflex or indicate a problem with an internal organ system. In any event, please notice if there is any sensitivity at these particular points, and if it recurs.

Return to the front legs. Place your animal friend on his side, for the next part. At this point he should be relaxed and compliant. Lay the hand you are not using lightly on his neck to stabilize the tissue. (See stabilizing illustration on page 122.) Begin at the top of the shoulder, using downward strokes along the outside of the front leg. You will be massaging along the large intestine, small intestine and triple heater meridians. If you feel a tender spot or a swollen or tight area, pay closer attention. Either hold the area or massage it using small circular motions. If these areas of sensitivity or swelling persist, you need to check with your veterinarian.

After stroking the outside of the leg down to the paws, move toward the front of your animal and gently lift the arm forward and, using both hands (or the entire hand if it is a cat or small dog), gently encircle the limb and run your hands in a downward direction toward the paws. You are now massaging the inside surface of the foreleg which encompasses the heart, lung and pericardium meridians. If your animal friend will allow it, massage the pads of the feet, and very gently pinch between the pads in the webs of the feet. This brings the circulation to the tips of the digits before it returns to the heart. These toetips are the places where the yin and yang meet and transform one into the other.

When I perform the belly massage I use the palm of my hand or my

Urinary Bladder Meridian Massage

fingertips in a gentle, circular motion starting under the chest, then moving below the rib cage, down to the groin area. An alternative is to use straight strokes with the palm of your hand. Many animals like this and won't want you to stop. Use light to moderate pressure and notice if your animal friend is sensitive in any particular abdominal area. If there is any sensitivity, be sure to keep an eye on it and if it worsens, consult your vet.

The abdomen houses five meridians: the liver, spleen, stomach, kidney and conception vessel. It is very important to aid digestion and elimination by massaging the abdomen. If you feel lumps, especially in the center of the abdomen, deep below the skin, or in the groin area, these are probably lymph nodes. If they are hard, painful, or large, bring it to the attention of your veterinarian.

Finally, work on the hind legs, beginning on the outside of each thigh. You will be massaging the gall bladder meridian which runs along the outside of the thighs. Because the muscles are usually thicker here, more pressure may be needed to effect a response. Test it out and see how your animal friend responds. If necessary, remember to stabilize the hind leg with your free hand just in front of the rump area.

Either long strokes or large circles can be used on both the outer and inner thigh areas. The three meridians that run along the stomach down to the groin and continue to travel along the inside of the upper thigh are the kidney, liver, spleen and stomach.

The knee is the most complex joint in the body, housing many ligaments, and a great deal of cartilage. Cup your hand over the knee and hold the area. Then gently massage behind the knee with your thumb and fingers. Continue down the leg, encircling the lower limb with your palm. The stomach meridian crosses from the inside of the leg to the outside of the leg around this area of the knee. The outside of the lower leg has the gall bladder and stomach meridians. The urinary bladder meridian runs along the back of the leg, and finally on the outside of the ankle. Find the spot in front of the Achilles tendon, just above the ankle, and use your thumb and forefinger to massage this space — it will feel like two pieces of skin rubbing together. This is a special meeting place for meridians. On the inside of the ankle, meridians of the kidney, spleen and liver cross. On the outside of the leg, the urinary bladder meridian has its point for joint pain for the entire body.

As you continue down the foot, the foot bones will seem longer than you think they should be. Remember that the foot bones in animals have a more vertical angle than ours, which are parallel to the ground. Gently take each paw and push upward from the bottom of the pads to flex the limb. Finish with some pressure between the toes and a final pad massage.

Take a deep breath. Let it out. The entire session should take ten to twenty minutes, depending upon both of you. Hopefully this has been a very enjoyable and relaxing time for both you and your animal friend.

Endnotes

1, 2, 10. Fox, Michael W. B., Vet Med, MRCVS, PhD. *The Healing Touch.* (New York: Newmarket Press, 1981), 64, 68, 66.

3. Travell, Janet. *The Trigger Point Manual.* (Baltimore, MD: Williams & Wilkens, 1983).

4. Janssens, Luc A.A., DVM, PhD. *Trigger Point Therapy. Problems in Veterinary Medicine Veterinary: Acupuncture.* A. Schoen, ed. (Philadelphia, PA: J.B. Lippincott Co. Vol. 4, No. 1, March 1992), 121.

5, 6. O'Connor, John and Dan Bensky, trans. ed. *Acupuncture, A Comprehensive Text.* (Seattle, WA: Eastland Press, 1981), 251, 246.

7, 8, 9, 11. Dr. Kuan Hin. *Chinese Massage and Acupressure.* (New York: Bergh Publishing, Inc., 1991), 74, 103, 45, 65.

Part 3

THE TREATMENT

An Introduction to Treatment

*T*he purpose of this section is to introduce you to a new way of viewing the health imbalances of your animal friend. In Parts One and Two of the book, I have outlined some of the basics of Traditional Chinese Medicine, including its theory, diagnosis and modes of treatment. The diagnosis uses the meridian system of the Five Elements and the location and substance system of the Eight Principles. Treatment incorporates the use of acupressure and massage, herbs and food therapy. Now, we will see how to *apply* all this knowledge to specific health imbalances in our animals.

The first thing you will need to do is observe and assess your animal friend according to the Five Element Theory and the Eight Principles. To make this a little easier for you, please refer to the appropriate Assessment Worksheet on pages 144–45. The worksheets are designed to help you create a "map," of your dog or cat friend's current condition. This will help you to determine the most effective ways to improve his or her health, both specifically and generally.

Remember that in TCM each individual is viewed in a multidimensional way. An animal's constitutional nature will make her suseptible to different imbalances. This individuality affects the type of treatment that will best bring the body into balance. This is what makes the system unique.

This book, however, is *not* meant to be a substitute for professional veterinary care. While some treatments are listed for situations where Western medicine has little or nothing to offer, many of the treatments can be used very successfully in conjunction with Western medicine. Most importantly, Traditional Chinese Medicine is practical and sensible, and I ask you to be practical and sensible about when to seek professional advice from your veterinarian.

The following listings give simple home procedures to follow for *non-emergency* conditions. I have started at the head of the animal and worked down to the toes of the hind leg, covering the most common imbalances or ailments that I have encountered in my practice. In TCM terms, this anatomical layout corresponds to the specific compartments or **burners** of the body. The **upper burner** refers to the head, chest and foreleg areas. The **middle burner** refers to the liver, gall bladder, spleen/pancreas and stomach, that is, everything between the diaphragm and the lower compartment of the body. The **lower burner** refers to the kidneys, urinary bladder, intestines, sex organs and lower limbs.

In each listing, I have combined a Western problem, or imbalance, and its TCM diagnosis. This is followed by its TCM treatment which may include acupressure, massage points, herbal and food therapy. I have also included nutritional supplements that I have found to be helpful in specific situations. While not usually part of TCM treatment, I do feel that supplementation is too important to omit.

First complete your worksheet, so that you have a good idea of your animal friend's general condition and specific imbalance(s). Then look up the Western term for the problem, such as "sneezing," or "liver disorder." You will find a description of the problem in both Western and TCM terms, and in some cases, an example of how I treated one of my animal patients.

A detailed description of appropriate acupressure /massage treatment follows, including the specific locations of the points, meridians and the techniques to be used. The acupressure points are listed with their meridian name, meridian abbreviation and number, followed by a translation of the point name, ie., "Large Intestine (LI)4. Known as 'Adjoining Valleys'…"

Acupuncture and acupressure professionals use these terms to locate specific points. The numbers help to locate approximately where the point sits on the meridian. Refer to the section on the meridians in Chapter One beginning on page 26, to refresh your memory.

Traditionally, Chinese physicians named each point according to either its anatomical location or its function so as to help the student and/or practitioner identify where and how to use the point. [*Please see the Endnotes for the sources for these translations.*]

As you will see, many of the same acupressure points can be used for multiple situations. It is not uncommon to see the same point listed for an eye problem, an ear problem and diarrhea. Remember that points are chosen according to their physical locations along the meridians, their internal meridian or organ connection, or their interaction within the Chinese systems of the Five Elements and Eight Principles. Therefore, one point can be used to treat a multitude of conditions.

A QUICK REFERENCE FOR ACUPRESSURE / MASSAGE

- Focus yourself for 1 or 2 minutes before you begin.
- Think of the treatment goal: rebalance an organ, relieve pain, etc.
- Find the point in the "valley" between muscles and bone.
- Treat acupressure points of 12 major meridians on *both* sides of the body.
- Apply steady, light to moderate pressure.
- Breathe to facilitate energy movement.

When I ask you to "hold" the point, remember to use even pressure at a depth that's comfortable for the animal. Hold the point for 15 to 60 seconds, unless otherwise indicated.

After the acupressure and massage instructions, you will find detailed descriptions of herbal treatments: the herbs themselves (both Western and Chinese), their preparations, dosages and how to administer them to your animal friend. This is followed by appropriate vitamin and mineral supplements and dietary recommendations.

This is a great deal of information, so please don't hesitate to go back to the relevent chapters in Parts One and Two to refresh your memory when necessary.

DIAGNOSIS CHART FOR YOUR DOG FRIEND

Current Symptom(s): _____

_____

Five Element Constitution Types

(fire, earth, metal, water, wood): _____

Circadian Clock (when symptoms occur)

hour: _____

season: _____

Environmental Influences

(conditions when symptoms worsen/improve): _____

_____

Condition Location

exterior (acute): _____

interior (chronic): _____

Condition Type, yin:_____ yang:_____

cold:_____ hot:_____

Patient's Constitution Type

excess (strong):_____ deficient (weak):_____

hot:_____ cold:_____

Listening to Sounds

breathing (loud, shallow, weak, dry, rapid): _____

coughing (deep, dry, moist): _____

voice (loud/strong, soft/weak: _____

Tongue

color (pink, red, pale, spotted): _____

coating (white, yellow, absent): _____

shape/size (swollen, shrunken, teeth imprints): _____

_____

Hair Coat

(dry, oily, brittle, falling out): _____

Odors (scorched, rancid, rotten, sweet)

breath: _____

ears/nose: _____

skin: _____

genitals: _____

Discharges (clear, colored, thick, watery)

eyes: _____

ears: _____

nose: _____

genitals: _____

Pulse   small dogs   large dogs

rate: rapid   >110   >80

slow   <60   <40

shape (threadlike, large, knotted, normal, surface, deep):

_____

force (strong, bounding, weak): _____

Gait (strong, favoring): _____

Elimination Habits

urination (frequency, color, odor, pain): _____

_____

defecation (frequency, texture, color, odor, straining):

_____

Mood/Behaviorial Changes

(anger, restlessness, fearfulness, etc.): _____

_____

Qi Assessment

appetite: _____

energy (a.m./p.m.): _____

vomiting: _____

Yin Assessment

thirst: _____

heat tolerance:_____

Yang Assessment

cold tolerance:_____

Nutrition

current diet: _____

_____

supplement: _____

Current Medications: _____

DIAGNOSIS CHART FOR YOUR CAT FRIEND

Current Symptom(s): _____

_____

_____

Five Element Constitution Types

(fire, earth, metal, water, wood): _____

Circadian Clock (when symptoms occur)

hour: _____

season: _____

Environmental Influences

(conditions when symptoms worsen/improve): _____

_____

Condition Location

exterior (acute): _____

interior (chronic): _____

Condition Type, yin:_____ yang:_____

Patient's Constitution Type

excess (strong):_____ deficient (weak):_____

hot:_____ cold:_____

Listening to Sounds

breathing (loud, shallow, weak, dry, rapid): _____

coughing (deep, dry, moist): _____

voice (loud/strong, soft/weak: _____

Tongue

color (pink, red, pale, spotted): _____

coating (white, yellow, absent): _____

shape/size (swollen, shrunken, teeth imprints): _____

_____

Hair Coat

(dry, oily, brittle, falling out): _____

Odors (scorched, rotten, rancid, sweet)

breath: _____

ears/nose: _____

skin: _____

genitals: _____

Discharges (clear, colored, thick, watery)

eyes: _____

ears: _____

nose: _____

genitals: _____

Pulse

rate: rapid >180 _____> slow <80 _____

shape (threadlike, large, knotted, normal, surface, deep):

_____

force (strong, bounding, weak): _____

Gait (strong, favoring): _____

Elimination Habits

urination (frequency, color, odor, pain): _____

_____

defecation (frequency, texture, color, odor, straining):

_____

Mood/Behaviorial Changes

(anger, restlessness, fearfulness, etc.): _____

_____

Qi Assessment

appetite: _____

energy (a.m./p.m.): _____

vomiting: _____

Yin Assessment

thirst: _____

heat tolerance: _____

Yang Assessment

cold tolerance: _____

Nutrition

current diet: _____

_____

supplement: _____

Current Medications: _____

_____

CHAPTER NINE   *The Eyes*

In Traditional Chinese Medicine the eyes and vision are associated with the **wood** element of the liver and gall bladder.

Three of the yang meridians used in acupuncture begin around the eye. These are the gall bladder, urinary bladder and stomach meridians. Though it may sound strange, sometimes the functions of digestion and fluid elimination can affect the eyes.

IMBALANCES OF THE EYE

Since the eye is so closely associated with the liver, it stands to reason that they both share the same sensitivities. Problems will develop if there is not enough moisture to nourish the eye, or if there is too much internal heat rising up from the liver. Both conditions can cause dry, red, itchy and inflamed eyes. In addition, the eyes are very sensitive to the wind and will respond by tearing or drying out.

The Western treatment for most eye problems is antibiotics or cortisone. However, in TCM, it is important to distinguish whether your animal is exhibiting eye problems from a deficiency of fluids or an excess of heat, as the treatment for each is different.

DEFICIENCY OF LIVER BLOOD AND YIN:
RED, ITCHY AND DRY EYES

When there is a deficiency of the blood and yin fluid in the liver, an overall body dryness can develop, manifesting as dry skin, increased thirst and itchy, dry, red-rimmed eyes. Your animal friend anxiously rubs them against the rug or with his paw. His eyes become worse as the day wears on, and they may be sensitive to sunlight and heat. With chronic inflammation, discharges and infections can occur.

Many animals with such a deficiency may be skittish, fearful or restless. Use a gentle touch and a patient attitude to overcome the sensitivity while medicating their eyes.

Other characteristics of a deficiency of blood or fluids is a dry tongue, with little or no coating, and a thin, weak pulse felt on the inside of the hind leg. I have seen many huge Rottweilers with red, itchy eyes as a result of a liver blood deficiency whose femoral pulse is no bigger than a strand of spaghetti. (Because of their size, Rottweilers often have pulses that resemble ball point pens!)

In TCM, the liver not only stores the blood but "smoothly circulates" it as well. When there isn't enough blood to bathe the organs, circulation begins to stagnate. This, in turn, can lead to accumulated pockets of heat or cold and more dryness resulting in red, itchy dry eyes.

CONJUNCTIVITIS, HOT TEARING EYES, DRY EYE

In TCM, these conditions are caused by excess liver heat or fire rising. As we will discuss in the section on the liver, when the liver malfunctions, it tends to overheat or stagnate.

It's not by chance that the liver is part of the wood element. Wood fuels fires and fire burns. If the liver has enough blood circulating and functions in a body with an excess constitution, the liver can overheat. When excess heat rises from the liver it creates inflammation, especially in the upper part of the body—one of the prime targets being the eyes. Red, burning, itchy, moist, swollen eyes and eyelids can result.

You may remember that the emotion associated with the wood element is anger. Think of the phrase, "She's so angry, she's seeing red." We're all aware of nervous anger causing our faces to go red. Continual stress and anger can, in fact, cause eye redness and inflammation in dogs who are continually barking for attention or guarding their territory. Cats who would rather be the only cat in the household but who have to compete with other feline house-mates, may become susceptible to eye problems.

Eye conditions caused by excess liver heat often have a thick discharge that is grey, yellow or green in color and may have a noticeable odor. Streaming tears that burn the hair off around the eyes, may also occur from excess heat. The discharge will be most apparent in the morning, upon rising, as the liver is responsible for circulating the blood while we sleep. Itching and rubbing may be worse between 11:00 p.m. and 3:00 a.m., which are the times the liver and gall bladder meridians are most active.

When the liver is out of balance, it tends to influence and even overpower the spleen/pancreas. This plays havoc with the digestion and with the way moisture moves through the body. Eyes whose surrounding tissues are wet, hot, inflammed and sticky, are the result of a liver and spleen/pancreas imbalance with heat and dampness.

Many of these problems are worse after eating. An individual will become extremely thirsty and will drink excessively. Animals with excess heat and fire rising are *not* amenable to being touched around the eyes. No matter how gentle you are, it hurts too much.

CONJUNCTIVITIS: HEAT AND STAGNATION

When there is excessive heat and dampness, the result is congestion of the tissues which is a form of stagnation. The tissues are very painful, inflamed and puffy. Chronic conjunctivitis is a form of excess heat with stagnation.

Conjunctivitis looks as painful as it is; the inside of the lower lid looks like raw hamburger. The discharge can range from hot, burning tears to green or yellow pus. Conjunctivitis can be acute with a sudden onset when an external pathogen invades a susceptible individual. The suddeness is like a "gust of wind." The Chinese call acute conjunctivitis a wind heat or damp wind heat condition, depending upon the amount of moisture stuck in the tissues.

I once had a dog patient, named Sammy, who used to jump the fence and run away whenever he had the chance. His person got tired of this, so he hooked Sammy up to a long clothesline pulley in his backyard. He felt it would give the dog maximum exercise to run back and forth while not allowing him to escape.

Sammy ran alright, but in a frenzy and barking continually. Before long, Sammy developed an eye problem. His eyes became dry, itchy and very red and eventually there was a greenish, smelly discharge. His eyes itched so much, that Sammy rubbed them on the grass causing more inflammation. It was a huge struggle for Sammy's human to administer the medications prescribed by his usual vet. The medications helped for a while, but as soon as they were stopped, the problem reappeared.

When I saw Sammy, his eyes were dry and his head felt hot to the touch. It was my belief that the dog's living situation had created enough internal anger and stress to cause stagnation and damage to the liver. This allowed the liver fire to rise, causing the eye problem. I discussed changing the backyard situation with Sammy's human companion. When Sammy was released from the clothesline lead and allowed to interact in his backyard and home more normally, his frenzied barking decreased. We treated him with acupressure and herbs in his food that helped calm the liver and clear the heat in the upper body. Slowly, Sammy's eyes began to improve, and after three months they were almost normal. During the entire treatment period, we used no eye medications, just acupressure and internal herbs.

WIND, TEARING AND DRY EYE

The liver and the eye are associated with the environmental factor of the wind. Many dogs love riding in the car with their heads hanging out the window. This causes runny, streaming eyes in many dogs. If the wind is warm, or if the dog has a predisposition for overheating, the streaming tears may have a burning sensation. You will know this if your animal becomes sensitive to the sunlight (called photophobia), causing tearing even without the wind. There may also be an area where the hair falls out around the eye because of the hot, burning nature of the tears. Cats may also experience this if they are regularly outdoors on windy days.

In Western medicine, when the eyes or nose are affected by the outside environment, they are known as inhalant allergies. In Traditional Chinese Medicine, it is known as a wind invasion.

It is an individual's underlying predispositions that will affect her wind sensitivity in general. There may be imbalances in the Five Element Control System where the lungs are deficient, and can't keep the liver in balance. There may also be imbalances in the Five Element Creation Cycle where the kidneys are deficient, and can't nourish the liver and eyes properly. Both of these conditions can cause continual tearing.

An individual that must continually produce tears may use up internal fluid stores of the liver and not be able to manufacture the tears needed to keep the eye surface moist. A severe dryness of the eye surface may result. Such an individual who has a problem with the liver can develop dry eye. Dry eye in this case is a combination of wind, plus dryness, plus heat.

FOOD ALLERGIES AND THE EYES

Another factor affecting the eyes is diet. We know from Western medicine that our liver is affected by what we eat. Our eyes, also, are affected by what we eat. Many food allergies, especially in cats, can show up as eye discharge or inflammation. If your cat has a chronic eye discharge, try an experiment. First, notice the type of protein in the food you are feeding. If it is poultry, change it to beef, lamb or fish. Also, some animals are sensitive to yeast, so check the ingredients list on your commercial food container. Many discharges will respond to changes in the diet.

In addition to food allergies, certain foods create an upward and heating action in the body. One such food is garlic. Try eating a clove of garlic. Some of you will notice that your head begins to feel warm or that you begin to sweat. Others may notice their eyes begin to get dry. It depends upon your internal makeup, and state of your liver and other digestive organs. Garlic helps to deter fleas in many dogs and cats and is also a digestive aid. But if your animal is prone to red, itchy eyes, you may need to reduce or eliminate garlic from the diet. Some seafoods such as shrimp, and wild game such as venison, create excess heat that rises in the body. Dry foods high in fat can also create heat and stagnation. So, if your animal friend tends to get red, itchy eyes, notice the type of proteins or supplements you are feeding and change them accordingly.

TREATMENT OF EYE IMBALANCES

Refer to the preceding text to distinguish whether the cause is a deficiency of fluids or an excess of heat from the liver. Remember that most animals with deficiency conditions are uncomfortable, but they will usually allow treatment around the eye. Most animals with excessive conditions are in pain, and will resist treatment around the eye.

◆ **Acupressure Points for Red, Itchy, Dry Eyes from Liver Blood and Yin Deficiency**

Treatment is aimed at nourishing the liver blood and yin fluid stores, as well as eliminating wind symptoms.

Gall Bladder (GB)20. Known as "Wind Pond," this point not only dispels wind but also dispels heat and redness from the eyes.

Location: Below the back of the head, in the depression found in the nape of the neck, approximately halfway between the spine and the bottom of the ear. The points are easily found when the head is moved up and down. These "dimples" are found on both sides of the body. Hold the point for approximately 20 seconds.

Large Intestine (LI)4. Known as "Adjoining Valleys," this is the master point for the head. It helps circulate the blood and qi around the eyes.

Location: The point is located in the web between the dewclaw and first long toe of the paw on the front leg. It can be treated by massaging the entire webbing using your index finger and thumb. Massage between the dewclaw and paw in a back and forth motion.

- **Points Surrounding the Eye:**

Urinary Bladder (BL)1. Known as "Eyes Bright."
Location: On the skin at the inner corner of the eye.

Gall Bladder (GB)1. Known as "Pupil Seam."
Location: On the skin at the outer corner of the eye.

Stomach (ST)1. Known as "Contain Tears."
Location: Below the middle of the eye, in line with the pupil, in the skin over the tip of the boney eye orbit.

These points are used for local nourishment and tonifying of the meridians and their organs. Use light steady finger pressure for 10 seconds on each point. An alternative would be to use the small circular strokes around the eye, temple and face.

Spleen (SP)6. Known as "Three Yin Junction," this point moistens and tonifies blood and fluid.
Location: On the inside of the hind leg, just behind the tibia bone and below the beginning of the group tendon (Achilles) that extends from the muscle bellies, or widest part of the muscle.

- **Herbal Treatment**

Lycium, Chrysanthemum and Rehmannia.[1] This formula treats deficiency of liver and kidney yin and blood. It is a variation of the basic kidney yin and blood tonifying formula, Rehmannia Six. It is used for dryness of the eye, poor vision and dizziness (for example, your cat may be uncertain about jumping down from a chair or table, or your dog may be reluctant to walk downstairs).

It contains the blood, qi and yin tonics of rehmannia, dioscorea and lycium; the moisture-moving herbs of cornus, alisma and hoelen; the heat-clearing herb of moutan; plus the wind and heat-clearing herb of chrysanthemum. It is available in small, round pills. Use for 3 weeks on and 1 week off:

> **Dosage:** cats/small dogs: 1 to 2 pills, twice daily
> medium dogs: 4 pills, twice daily
> large dogs: 6 pills, twice daily

Euphrasia (Eyebright).[2] This Western herb, provides nutrition to the eye itself and can be used internally and as an eyewash tea for topical use. It improves vision and has astringent, pungent, bitter and cooling qualities. It can be used both in deficient conditions when the eye is dry and has begun to form mucousy discharges, or in hot type infectious conditions with conjunctivitis and copious green or yellow-colored discharges.

> **Dosage :** Prepare by steeping 1 tea bag or ½ teaspoon powdered dry herb in 1 cup boiled water. Strain any particles through a coffee filter. Cool.
> **Topical:** Use as a wash by squeezing contents of gauze pad soaked in the tea over the eye, or from a dropper into eye three times daily. Store the tea in an airtight container in the refrigerator. Prepare fresh every 2 days. If redness of the eyes develops, discontinue use.
> **Internal:** Make tea as above, and add to wet foods or cooked grains at 1 teaspoon for cats and small dogs; 1 tablespoon for larger dogs.

◆ Nutritional Supplements

Vitamin A, as cod liver oil or alone:

> cats/small dogs: 2,000 mg (½ teaspoon) daily
> medium dogs: 5,000 mg (1 teaspoon) daily
> large dogs: 10,000 mg (2 teaspoons) daily

Vitamin E, as evening primrose oil, for its essential fatty acid and antioxidant effect which decreases inflammation:

cats/small dogs: 50 to 100 IU daily
medium dogs: 200 IU daily
large dogs: 400 IU daily

Vitamin C, as sodium ascorbate or ascorbic acid. Overdosing can cause diarrhea. Decrease dosage if the animal develops loose stool.
cats/small dogs: 125 mg, twice daily
medium dogs: 250 mg, twice daily
large dogs: 500 mg, twice daily

Bioflavonoids are helpful in the assimilation of vitamin C.

Vitamin B Complex, including niacin and pantothenic acid. Try to avoid products high in yeast, as these can cause eye allergies. Use one quarter to one half the human dosage in the mid-range human potency.

Trace Minerals as seaweeds or blue-green algae with quercitin for allergic type itching and dryness. Use 1/16 to 1/2 teaspoon, depending upon product and size of the animal to be treated. If diarrhea develops, cut dosage in half or eliminate if necessary.

◆ Dietary Recommendations

In deficiency eye conditions, it is best to use neutral and bitter type foods, along with foods that strengthen the liver. Neutral foods include potato, eggs, rabbit, cod, beef and beef liver, chicken gizzards and ground pork (defatted). Neutral grains are thoroughly cooked brown rice and corn. Bitter foods, such as celery, spinach and lettuce, clear inflammation. Foods that help the liver are poultry, wheat and rice. Now here we come into some conflict, as some cats and dogs are allergic to poultry and wheat. However, in many cases, once the liver blood is strengthened with acupressure and/or herbs, these allergies seem to disappear and poultry and wheat can gradually be reintroduced into the diet.

EXCESS HEAT AND CONJUNCTIVITIS

Treatment is aimed at cooling the liver, calming the excess fire and smoothing the circulation to decrease the tendencies of congestion and stagnation.

In cases of excess heat and dampness, where the tissues are moist, congested and inflamed, fluid-moving points may be added.

In cases of wind heat, as in conjunctivitis, points are used to clear heat and cool the liver, but in addition, points to dispel or relieve wind are added.

◆ **Acupressure Points for Treating
   Excess Heat and Conjunctivitis**

Gall Bladder (GB) 20. Known as "Wind Pond," this point dispels wind and heat and can be used in *all* cases of excess heat and/or wind invasion.

Location: See page 152. The technique is holding the point with steady pressure, or small circular strokes. Since there is an excess of heat, remember to breathe as you may feel a rush of energy.

Large Intestine (LI) 11. Known as "Crooked Pool," this point clears heat from the upper body and regulates the immune system. It is used in all excess heat and wind invasions.

Location: On the outside of the front leg, at the end of the elbow crease when the elbow is flexed. Use a circular motion at the point with steady pressure.

Large Intestine (LI) 4. Known as "Adjoining Valleys," this is the master point used for the head and face. It can be used as a balancing point, being useful for immune stimulation, excess heat, wind and dampness conditions.

Location and technique: See page 152.

Liver (LIV) 2. Known as the "Walk Between," this point relieves liver heat, cools and calms the liver, the eyes and the head. As it cools the liver, it also sedates the upward rising of qi and blood to the head.

Location: In humans, this point lies between the big and second toes. Unless your animal friend has his hind leg dewclaw still intact, there is no "big toe." Instead, most dogs and cats have four toes on each hind foot: toes II through V. Although there is some controversy over exactly where Liver 2 is located, in my experience, it lies along the inside top aspect of the hind paw, at the level just above where the toes meet the foot bones. Massage in a *downward* direction. This is opposite to the normal flow of qi in the liver meridian and therefore sedates the point. You can also "sweep" the energy downward along the inside portion of the foot bone down to the claw in order to make sure you have treated the exact point.

Gall Bladder (GB) 41. Known as "Near Tears on the Foot," this point aids in decongesting and moving circulation through the gall bladder and liver as well as clearing heat and dampness. It is used in conjunction with Liver 2, to rebalance these two organs. Because of its ability to drain the dampness, it is useful in excess damp heat conditions.

Location: In the hollow just in front of the joining of foot bones (metatarsals) IV and V. Hold the point.

SUDDEN CONJUNCTIVITIS:
AN ACUTE WIND CONDITION

Use **Gall Bladder (GB) 20,** page 152 and **Large Intestine (LI) 11,** page 156.

Triple Heater (TH) 5. Known as the "Outer Gate," this point relieves exterior and hot conditions.

Location:[3] If you divide the front leg between the elbow and wrist into six portions, this point is located in the last sixth closest to the wrist. It is on the outside (lateral) of the forearm, in the depression just behind the major tendon of the extensor muscle, known as the common digital extensor. Rub the point in an up and down direction with the fingertip.

◆ Herbal Treatment

Lung Tan Xie Gan Wan.[4] This formula is good for excess heat from the liver, and also the damp heat that can occur in conjunctivitis. It includes herbs that drain excess liver fire, including gentiana, gardenia and scutellaria; plantago to break up congestion and dampness; rehmannia and tang kuei to strengthen liver blood and bupleurum to regulate the liver.

> **Dosage:** cats/small dogs: 1 pill, twice daily
> medium dogs: 3 to 4 pills, twice daily
> large dogs: 5 pills, twice daily

If diarrhea develops, cut the dosage in half. Because of its cooling nature, a very prolonged course may damage the qi of the animal. Usual duration of treatment is one to two weeks.

Golden Seal (Hydrastis canadensis).[5] This Western herb has bitter and astringent actions and is excellent for clearing bacterial infections and drying congestion caused by damp heat and to clear the heat from the liver. Because golden seal lowers blood sugar, it is not advised with diabetics on a fixed insulin dosage. Golden seal also stimulates uterine contractions and is therefore, not to be used during pregnancy. The herb can be used both internally and as an eyewash for up to two weeks.

Dilute tincture 10 to 15 drops in 1 ounce distilled water. If the alcohol content is too high for the animal, he will salivate. Give three times daily.

> **Dosage:** internal: cats/small dogs: 10 drops of diluted tincture
> medium dogs: 20 drops diluted tincture
> large dogs: use powdered herb and place in capsules
> (due to bitter taste) 1 to 2 #0 capsules

To make the eyewash, steep ¼ teaspoon powdered herb in 1 cup boiled water. Cool and strain through a coffee filter to remove any particles. Use 1 dropperful per eye. As with other eye medications, if redness worsens, discontinue use.

Euphrasia (Eyebright). Use as directed on page 154, as eye wash or internally.

Marigold + Dandelion + Chamomile. This combination in equal parts can be used as an eyewash to bathe red, swollen, itchy and dry eyes. Combine ¼ teaspoon of each herb and use to 1 cup boiled water. Steep and cool. Strain through a coffee filter and drop into eye 2 to 4 times daily.

NUTRITIONAL SUPPLEMENTS

Vitamin C, as sodium ascorbate or ascorbic acid. Use as high a dose as possible before instigating diarrhea. For this condition, use up to 5,000 mg per day for large dogs, divided into two doses of 2,500 each.

Trace Minerals, from seaweed sources:
> cats/small dogs: ⅛ teaspoon daily
> medium dogs: ¼ teaspoon daily
> large dogs: ½ teaspoon daily

Zinc: cats/small/medium dogs: 5 mg daily
> large dogs: 10 mg daily

Multiple Vitamin B from non-yeast source: 10 mg daily.

DIETARY RECOMMENDATIONS

In any heat situations, avoid overly warming or upward directional foods. Limit or exclude dry food during an outbreak of conjunctivitis, as this may create more heat and dryness. If dry food is being used, a lower fat and preferably "baked, unsprayed" food should be used. Supplement a dry food diet with very thoroughly cooked brown rice, potato, whole wheat pasta, barley or millet, up to 25% of amount being fed. If a home-cooked diet is being used, the grain can be up to 60% for dogs and 33% to 40% for cats. The grains must be well cooked, for 1¼ hours at 1 cup grain to 3 cups water. Animal protein sources of up to 25% for dogs and 67% (two thirds) for cats should be neutral to cooling foods such as pork, pork kidney, small amounts of beef, white fish. Aduki beans can be added. For dogs, celery, mushrooms, spinach, alfalfa sprouts, carrots, broccoli and Napa cabbage can be added up to one fifth of their diet. Cats usually eat very small amounts of vegetables, if any. *Avoid* chicken, shrimp, venison and lamb, as these foods are warming and may increase heat.

DRY EYE IN DOGS

Dry eye is a chronic condition. It usually starts from excess heat rising upward, evaporating the eye fluids, or an underlying deficiency of blood and fluid. By the time the eyes become dry, it is necessary to clear the heat before restoring fluid.

◆ Acupressure Points for Treating Dry Eye

Heat-clearing acupressure, herbs and diet are the first line of treatment. This means you should follow the regimen listed above for excess heat conditions. After an initial course of treatment of up to one month, you can switch to a deficiency blood and fluid regimen.

Once heat has been cleared, and the animal is less sensitive around the eyes, it is especially important to use the local acupressure points surrounding the eye. These are **Stomach (ST) 1**, **Urinary Bladder (BL) 1**, and **Gall Bladder (GB) 1**,—all found on page 153. The technique to use is light, steady pressure on these points.

In his book, *Chinese Massage and Acupressure*,[6] Dr. Kuan Hin describes a daily exercise that encourages healthy eyes. Massage in a circular direction on the skin from the inside corner of the eye, under the eye and then to the outside corner, around the top of the eye back to the inside corner. Then change direction and go from the inside corner around the top of the eye to the outside corner, under the eye, and back to the inside corner. Do each direction several times with light steady pressure. Also massage in front of the ears, from the top to the bottom. These points encourage facial circulation.

◆ Herbal Treatment

The surface cornea of dogs with dry eye becomes thickened and pigmented due to lack of normal lubrication. Eye washes made from **bilberry fruit, eyebright** and **marigold** are helpful in restoring functional tissue to the eye surface. Use ⅛ teaspoon bilberry, ¼ to ½ teaspoon of eyebright and marigold to 1 cup boiled water, steeped, strained and cooled.

Shou Wu Pian.[7] This is a single patent herb which moistens and cools the liver and kidney fluids. It helps to supply the eye with an increased blood supply. Use 1 to 3 tablets, twice daily.

◆ Nutritional Supplements

Essential fatty acids, which produce prostaglandins from linoleic acid, are helpful in restoring tear duct lubrication. **Evening primrose oil** is an excellent source.[8] I recommend 250 mg daily. **Vitamin C** and **trace minerals** are also beneficial.

LIGHT AND WIND SENSITIVITY

Many cats and breeds of toy dogs seem prone to developing this problem. When the eyes tear in windy weather, it is a wind condition. Treatment is aimed at dispelling the wind.

Eye sensitivity in general extends to the sunlight and, in some cases, indoor light. Because tears are watery, this can be a cold and yin condition. You need to look at the other characteristics of your animal friend to determine her predisposition. (see Chapter Three, the Eight Principles, page 25). If the eyes are tearing due to a cold condition, treatment is aimed at eliminating the wind and warming the yang and circulation. If the tears are burning, as you will see if the eye looks inflamed and the hair is burned off around the eye, then it is a wind *heat* condition. Here the treatment is aimed at eliminating the wind and cooling the eye.

◆ Acupressure Points for Treating Light and Wind Sensitivity

Gall Bladder (GB) 20. Known as "Wind Pond," this point dispels wind to the surface.

Location: See page 152. Hold the point for 20 seconds.

Gall Bladder (GB) 37. Known as "Bright Light," this point clears the vision and regulates the liver.

Location: On the outside of the lower hind leg, below the knee, just behind the small bone (fibula). The point lies between two muscle bellies: the cranial tibialis and the peroneus longus. If you divide the leg between the knee (stifle) and the ankle (tarsus) into three parts, this point is approximately one third of the way up from the ankle. The technique is to massage in an up and down motion. Find the muscle bellies, or the widest part of the muscle, and massage between them, from approximately the middle of the leg to the end of the muscle groove.

Governing Vessel (GV) 4. This point, known as "Life's Fire Gate," is one of the main warming points of the body. It helps to regulate the inner fire. If the tearing is a cold type phenomenon, acupressure here will help to relieve the cold.

Location: On the midline of the back between the second and third lumbar vertebrae. The technique is to use mild finger pressure in a back and forth motion.

Spleen (SP) 6. Known as the "Three Yin Junction," this point nourishes the yin and blood of the liver, kidney and spleen.

Location: See page 153. Use small, circular strokes or hold the point.

Endnotes

1. Naeser, Margaret A., PhD. *Outline Guide to Chinese Herbal Patent Medicines in Pill Form.* (Boston, MA: Boston Chinese Medicine, 1990), 307.

2, 5. Holmes, Peter. *The Energetics of Western Herbs, Vol. I & II.* (Boulder, CO: Artemis Press, 1989), 410, Vol. I, 553, Vol. II.

3. Hwang, Yann-Ching, DVM, PhD. *Problems in Veterinary Medicine: Veterinary Acupuncture,* A. Schoen, ed. Volume 4, No. 1 March 1992, (Philadelphia, PA: J.B. Lippincott Co., 1992), 22.

4, 7. Fratkin, Jake. *Chinese Herbal Patent Formulas.* (Boulder, CO: Shya Publications, 1986), 82, 182.

6. Dr. Kuan Hin. *Chinese Massage and Acupressure.* (New York: Bergh Publishing Inc., 1991), 58.

8. Pitchford, Paul. *Healing with Whole Foods.* (Berkeley, CA: North Atlantic Press, 1993), 131.

CHAPTER TEN

The Nose and Upper Respiratory Conditions

Have you ever wondered why certain individuals become ill while others escape unscathed? The reason is that some individuals have strong wei qi. As discussed in Part One, the wei qi acts as the first barrier to disease entering the body. If an animal is weakened by overexertion, poor nutrition or exposure to windy environments, viral or bacterial pathogens can gain entry. The outcome of the struggle between the wei qi and the invading pathogens determines whether the animal becomes ill or remains healthy.

Once an animal is sick, his response to the illness depends on whether he is of the excess or deficient type of constitution and whether the pathogen is of the hot or cold type.

The excess individual tends to throw off the illness quickly, while the deficient individual may suffer for a prolonged period.

There are two types of pathogens that travel in the wind and assault the wei qi: these are the cold type pathogen and the hot type pathogen. The Chinese refer to these acute attacks of illness as "wind cold" or "wind heat." The Chinese believe that an individual's vulnerability to wind attacks is at the back of the head, at the base of the neck. *(For a review of this information, see Chapter Two, page 32.)*

WIND COLD ATTACKS

The cold pathogen causes an internal coldness with chills. The animal wants to be in the sun, near a heater, under the covers or on your lap. Accompanying the chills is lethargy and a clear, watery eye and/or nasal discharge. The patient is often too tired to eat and doesn't want to drink water. Your animal may experience a dull headache or earache, which can be relieved with massage. (Yes, your animal friend does get headaches, which you can see in his furrowed brow, his reaction to loud noises, or hiding his head under or pressing it against things.)

WIND HEAT ATTACKS

The hot pathogen causes fever and your animal becomes hot to the touch, irritable and restless. She may not want to be touched or very near you as your body warmth will be too much for her to take. She will have a tremendous thirst, especially for cold water, and you may notice that she wants to drink from the toilet where the water is very cold. As the internal heat rises, the internal body fluids evaporate, creating a redness around the eyes, ears or muzzle. If there is pain, it will be piercing and sudden, rather than dull and achy.

◆ Treatment

The first line of treatment is to try to eliminate the assault through the places where it originally entered the body: namely, the back of the head and base of the neck. Acupressure uses "wind releasing points" to accomplish this.

If this is a wind heat condition, points are added to eliminate or cool the heat. In both wind heat and wind cold attacks, basic immune points are included to strengthen the wei qi.

Deficient, weaker animals are treated with lighter acupressure work and milder herbs. Excess, over-reactive individuals are treated with stronger acupressure and more potent herbs. Both deficient and excess animals are subject to wind cold and wind heat type flus. When treating either type, immune points are added to strengthen the wei qi.

◆ Acupressure Technique for Deficient and Excess Individuals

For deficient individuals, light pressure for approximately 1 to 2 minutes is sufficient. For excess individuals, light to moderate pressure should be used. In cases when the individual is very restless, stronger pressure for short periods of time may be necessary. The goal is to try to "match" the pressure with the state of the individual. The animal will let you know if the pressure is too much by moving away, or too little by moving into your fingers.

When the body is assaulted through a wind invasion at the back of the neck, it can be viewed as an "excess of energy" at that particular place on the meridian. This excess creates stagnation and leads to pain and inflammation. The purpose of the acupressure is to get rid of this excess of energy by awakening the point and then overstimulating it. Once the nerve fibers have fired, the point becomes fatigued, and the acupressure begins to "sedate" the point. As the point is sedated, its opening to the surface relaxes, becomes slightly enlarged, and releases the energy from the depths of the body up to the surface. Western practitioners call this "sweating out" a cold.

◆ Acupressure Points for Treatment of Wind Cold Conditions

Gall Bladder (GB) 20. Known as the "Wind Pond," this point is used to dispel wind to the surface, thereby releasing energy to the outside environment.

Location: See page 152. The technique is to hold the point with steady pressure.

Governing Vessel (GV) 14. Known as "Big Vertebra," this point, like GB 20, is used to dispel the wind invasion and to relieve a stiff neck.

Location: On the midline of the back, in the depression between the last cervical (neck) vertebra and the first thoracic vertebra, directly over the spinal column. The point is found by moving the neck downwards and forward. The point is the place where the spine is stationary and the neck moves. It is, in fact, the "big vertebra," being the first thoracic vertebra, or T-1. Use the tip of the finger or nail and move the finger back and forth on the point. Pressure should be as much as the animal can tolerate without discomfort.

Large Intestine (LI) 4. Known as "Adjoining Valleys," this is the master point influencing the head. This means that it can be used for every condition involving the head, face, eyes, ears, nose, mouth and throat. Because the large intestine meridian ends at the nose, points along this meridian affect upper respiratory conditions. It is a major point used for headaches and to relieve sinus congestion and it is also utilized for sore and painful throats and difficulty swallowing.

Location: See page 152. Rub the web up to its highest point for 10 to 60 seconds, using your thumb and index finger. Place the animal in a sitting position or lying down, as the paw should not bear weight when locating the point. In dogs who have had their dewclaws removed, the point is actually in the scar tissue formed on the second toe.

◆ Herbal Treatment

Gan Mao Ling.[1] This formula, translated as "Common Cold Effective Remedy," is effective in both cold or hot type infections. It includes herbs that are bitterly pungent such as chrysanthemum, vitex and menthol, to increase surface circulation and to relieve wind, along with lonicera, isatis and illex roots which relieve heat, and evodia fruit to relieve cold chill signs, nausea and headache. Use for 3 to 5 days.

> **Dosage:** cats/small dogs: 1 tablet, 3 times daily
> medium dogs: 2 tablets, 3 times daily
> large dogs: 3 to 4 tablets, 3 times daily

This herbal formula is also useful if the animal has been exposed to the flu virus but has not yet shown any symptoms.

Echinacea purpurea and Angustifolia (Purple Cone Flower, Missouri Snakeroot). Used for centuries by Native Americans, echinacea has antiviral and antibacterial properties. It not only decreases the duration of an illness, but can be used as a preventative as well.[2] It has also been shown to be dose effective, so that if you think it is not working at the dosages listed below, you can increase the dosage by one third of that listed. Duration of treatment is for 10 to 14 days. It has bitter, pungent and cooling characteristics and works mostly on the lungs, stomach and liver.[3]

Powdered forms can be placed in capsules or sprinkled directly over food. If herbal tinctures are used, dilute as indicated below, and boil the alcohol off the mixture if used with cats or small dogs. This is done by setting the diluted mixture in an open bottle over steam heat for 2 minutes.

Dosage: cats/small dogs: Mix 15 drops in 1 ounce distilled water. If the animal salivates, the alcohol content is too high. Use 10 drops of diluted mixture, 3 to 4 times daily.

medium dogs: tincture: 30 drops in 1 ounce distilled water. Use 15 drops of diluted mixture 3 to 4 times daily.

large dogs: Use the powdered herb at ½ teaspoon, 3 to 4 times daily.

Vaporizing is a good way to medicate the cat or dog who doesn't want to be handled or is having difficulty breathing. For watery, clear discharges, warming and wind relieving herbs such as oregano, sage, yerba buena, peppermint and basil can be added to the vaporized steam. Add one or more in small amounts to the vaporizer and place it with the animal in an enclosed space such as a bathroom, for 5 to 30 minutes. Once they realize that the steam helps them to breathe, most animals feel quite comfortable in this kind of situation.

◆ Nutritional Supplements

Vitamins and minerals for wind cold conditions are the same as for wind heat conditions, and are listed on pages 171–72. Deficient individuals with wind cold conditions, may need lower dosages of vitamins and minerals because these individuals get diarrhea more easily.

◆ Dietary Recommendations

For most illnesses involving mucous production, dairy products and high amounts of red meat should be avoided as much as possible. These foods tend to increase sticky phlegm and mucous production in many animals.

There are two schools of thought as far as what to feed when an animal is ill. Some believe in fasting the animal to "starve the cold," while others advocate "feeding the animal" to nourish the individual. In my opinion, if your animal is of a deficient constitution, feed him. If your animal is of the excess constitution, then fasting to starve the cold may be appropriate.

If you are fasting your animal friend, broth can be given as the sole food, along with vitamins. Broths made with chicken and miso are warming and nutritious. If you are feeding your animal friend, serve small meals with small amounts of skinless chicken cooked in its own broth along with a larger amount of well-cooked brown rice. Warming spices such as garlic, ginger, basil and cinnamon twig or bark can be included. Feel free to add sardine or other fish oil. This will tempt your friend's tastebuds, as well as provide essential fatty acids.

◆ Acupressure Points for Treatment of Wind Heat Conditions

Governing Vessel (GV) 14, page 166 and **Large Intestine (LI) 4**, page 152. As listed above for wind cold.

Triple Heater (TH) 5. Known as the "Outer Gate," this point is used to dispel wind in hot type conditions. It decreases fevers, acts as an anti-inflammatory to ease sore throats and alleviate headaches. This point is also used to foster the wei qi.

Location: See page 157. Use a circular motion on the point from 10 to 60 seconds. It may be difficult for you to precisely locate this point, but don't worry, your fingertip is larger than the point and if you are in the general area you will be able to facilitate a response.

Large Intestine (LI) 11. Known as "Crooked Pool," this point is a major anti-inflammatory point for the entire upper body, especially the head, neck and front leg regions. LI 11 is used to lower fever, and reduce swelling and pain. It is usually the choice in hot type conditions, but may also be used to balance the entire immune system.

Location: See page 156. Use a circular motion in both directions or to just hold the point for approximately 30 seconds.

◆ Herbal Treatment

Boneset (Eupatorium perfoliatum, Indian Sage).[4] This Native American herb was introduced to the European settlers in the 1600s. It is very bitter, cold and drying. It has been used extensively for lung and bronchial infections and is excellent for the acute onset of fevers with cough.

> **Dosage:** Use as a tincture, diluting 15 drops in 1 ounce distilled water. It is a very bitter herb. Use the diluted mixture 3 times daily.
>
> > cats/small dogs: 10 drops
> > medium dogs: 20 drops
> > large dogs: 30 drops

Eyebright.[5] This herb relieves fever and breaks up congestion of the sinuses. It is also beneficial to the eyes, clearing redness, swelling and discharges. Make a tea infusion by steeping ½ teaspoon to 1 cup boiled water. Cool, and mix with food or give by mouth.

> **Dosage:** cats/small dogs: 1 to 2 teaspoons
> > medium dogs: 1 tablespoon
> > large dogs: 2 to 3 tablespoons

Osha (Ligusticum porteri, Colorado Cough Root).[6] This is another herb used by Native Americans, which grows in the western mountain ranges at high elevations. It is especially useful for sore and painful throats, coughing or wheezing. This herb is also indicated if your animal appears to have a headache around the sinuses, but allows her head to be massaged gently.

> **Dosage:** It is usually available in tincture form, and is diluted at 20 drops to 1 ounce distilled water. Dosage is as for boneset, above.

Echinacea purpurea and Angustifolia. Use as listed on pages 167–68.

If your animal is having difficulty breathing or doesn't want to be handled, vaporizing with cooling aromatic herbs like eucalyptus, catnip and elderflower can help clear congestion. For instructions, see page 168.

NUTRITIONAL SUPPLEMENTS

The following vitamin supplements may be given during the illness and for approximately 3 to 5 days after symptoms have ceased.

Vitamin C. Use sodium ascorbate, ascorbic acid or rose hips. Vitamin C should be used in as high a dose as possible. Overdose will appear as indigestion or diarrhea. Although it is true that dogs and cats manufacture vitamin C, under stressful situations, including illness, the body appears to need more vitamin C than it can produce.

> cats/small dogs: 125 to 500 mg, twice daily
> medium dogs: 250 to 1,500 mg, twice daily
> large dog: 500 to 1,500 mg, twice daily

Quercitin.[7] This is found in blue-green algae or can be purchased under its own name. Quercitin is a bioflavinoid that helps with vitamin C absorption, and is useful in mouth ulcers, bruising of tissue and lowering cholesterol. Only small amounts are necessary, usually about 200 mg, and can be given at the same time as vitamin C.

Vitamin A. Although dogs can convert beta carotene to vitamin A, cats do not have this ability. Therefore, they need preformed vitamin A. The best source I have found is cod liver oil.

> cats/small dogs: ½ teaspoon daily
> medium dogs: ⅔ teaspoon daily
> large dogs: 1 teaspooon daily

Vitamin E. This vitamin is wonderful as an anti-inflammatory. Care needs to be taken, however, because it can raise blood pressure if the dose is too high.

> cats/small dogs: 50 to 100 IU daily

medium dogs: 100 to 200 IU daily
large dogs: 400 IU daily

Vitamin B Complex. Try to avoid yeast based products, as nasal infections and antibiotic use can sensitize the animal to an overgrowth of yeast. Use one quarter to one half the recommended dosage for humans. If too much vitamin B complex is given, the animal may have diarrhea or appear "over alert" and hot to the touch.

Trace Minerals. Seaweed powder or other trace mineral supplements are helpful during times of stress in regulating the body's metabolism and overwhelming the invading pathogen. Zinc, at 5 to 10 mg daily, is especially helpful in painful, red sore throats.

DIETARY RECOMMENDATIONS

For most illnesses involving mucous production, dairy products and red meats should be kept to a minimum, as described for wind cold conditions. For wind heat illnesses, fasting with broths seems most reasonable, since many of these conditions include sore throats and swollen glands. Broths made from a mild white fish and white miso, honeysuckle, celery, carrots and mung bean sprouts are excellent. Supplements such as pediatric fluid replacements from the grocery store are useful in making sure the animal stays hydrated. With fevers, it is essential to check with your veterinarian for guidance.

KENNEL COUGH

Kennel cough is a form of wind cold *or* wind heat invasion that targets the nose, sinuses and wind pipe. In addition to the wind signs described earlier, there is also an annoying cough, which can linger if your animal friend is in a vulnerable and deficient state.

The cough can be dry, gagging and ticklish on the outset, and then progress to a more hoarse, moist and deep croup-type sound.

The treatment principle centers around expelling the wind cold or heat and either quieting the cough if it is dry, or helping the animal expectorate if there is phlegm and excessive moisture.

◆ Acupressure Points for Treatment of Kennel Cough

Points indicated for wind invasion can be used, primarily:

Gall Bladder (GB) 20. Known as "Wind Pond," to dispel the pathogen.
Location and technique: See page 152.

Governing Vessel (GV) 14. Known as "Big Vertebra," to dispel the pathogen.
Location and technique: See page 166.

Large Intestine (LI) 4. Known as "Adjoining Valleys," which is the master point for the head and throat area.
Location and technique: See page 152.

To these points, you can add:

Urinary Bladder (BL) 13. Known as "Lung's Hollow," this is the association diagnostic point for the lungs. It is important to protect and strengthen the lungs in order to prevent the upper respiratory virus from going deeper.
Location: This point is found on both sides of the spine, in the depression at the tip of the third thoracic vertebra, approximately at the level of the front end of the shoulder blades. When the animal stands, there are usually three rib spaces covering the area between the shoulder blades. The Lung Association Point, BL 13, is located in the first of these three spaces. Use a back and forth motion on the points inside the shoulder blades.

Lung (LU) 7. Known as "Broken Sequence," this point is used for dry coughs. It is the meeting place of the lung and conception vessel channels and therefore, helps to moisten the lung meridian as well as stop coughs.
Location: Just above the wrist on the side closest to the body (medial), in the depression above the small protuberance, called the styloid process, at the end of the long bone called the radius. Massage in an up and down and circular motion.

◆ Herbal Treatment for Dry Cough

Fritillaria and Loquat Syrup.[8] This syrup includes fritillaria, schizandra, glehnia, prunus and honey to moisten the lung and help stop the cough. It also includes herbs to eliminate sticky phlegm such as eriobotrya and platycodon. Citrus and tussilago are added to help circulate the qi and stop the cough. Menthol is used to eliminate wind. This is a very mild herb combination that may be given 3 to 4 times daily.

> **Dosage:** small dogs: 1 teaspoon
> medium dogs: ½ tablespoon
> large dogs: 1 tablespoon

Boneset or **Osha.** Dosages listed under wind heat conditions, page 170.

Wild Cherry Bark.[9] This cooling, astringing bitter herb helps to moisten the lungs and wind pipe, stop coughing and decrease inflammation in the throat. Tinctures, teas and syrups are available. For syrups, follow the dosage indicated for children, using slightly more for large dogs. Tinctures can be mixed at 30 drops per 1 ounce distilled water.

> **Dosage:** small dogs: ½ teaspoon, 4 times daily
> medium dogs: 1 teaspoon, 4 times daily
> large dogs: up to 1 tablespoon 4, times daily

TREATMENT FOR MOIST PHLEGM COUGHS

Usually these coughs with phelgm are of the clear and therefore, cold variety. Hot type phelgm would be colored and thicker. Unfortunately, most dogs swallow the phlegm before they cough it out. So you must open your dog's mouth to see if any excess watery or sticky saliva is present in the mouth (which would indicate cold phlegm), or if the mouth is very dry which might indicate colored, thicker phlegm.

Yerba Santa (Eriodictyon californicum).[10] The leaves are used to make strong teas or tinctures which function as an expectorant and mild decongestant.

Dosage: Make a diluted solution, using 15 to 25 drops of tincture in 1 ounce of distilled water. Of this dilution use:

> small dogs: ½ teaspoon, 3 to 4 times daily
> medium dogs: 1 teaspoon, 3 to 4 times daily
> large dogs: ½ tablespoon, 3 to 4 times daily

If you suspect the cough has progressed from the thin, watery type to the thick, colored type, or if the dog is running a fever, use the herb **white horehound** to expel the mucous and heat. For tincture dosage, use as yerba santa.

◆ Nutritional Supplements

Use those listed for wind conditions on pages 171–72.

CAT UPPER RESPIRATORY INFECTIONS WITH MOUTH SORES

An upper respiratory infection in your cat that includes ulcerations on the gums and tongue can be a very serious situation. Mouth sores make it painful and difficult for the cat to eat and drink. In Traditional Chinese Medicine, this can be considered a virile wind heat situation that attacks the susceptible cat, creating a fierce response. Once ulcers form, it means that the organism was able to gain entry to a deeper layer, destroying the protective mucous membrane on the mouth's surface. The first sign that something is wrong will probably be when your cat begins drooling. The saliva may be thick and putrid and sickly sweet smelling. There may even be blood in the saliva and your cat may have her tongue extended due to swelling in the back of the mouth. This is a more serious problem than just sneezing or coughing.

Gum inflammation in TCM involves the stomach, and indicates heat coming up from that organ. If there is ulceration, this is severe stomach heat or fire. Stomach fire can cause a burning sensation in the stomach lining which may be another reason that the cat won't eat. In this situation, more aggressive treatment than home care may be necessary. I would recommend you consult your veterinarian for treatment.

◆ Acupressure Points for Upper Respiratory Infections with Mouth Sores in Cats

Gall Bladder (GB) 20. See page 152.

Large Intestine (LI) 4. See page 152.

Large Intestine (LI) 11. See page 156.

Stomach (ST) 44. Known as "Inner Court," this point cools and drains heat from the stomach, and relieves the inflammation and pain in the mouth.

Location: In the web of the hind foot between the second and third toes. Remember that the back leg has only four toes, named II–V. Rub back and forth between the toes as much as your cat will allow. Massage along the angle of the jaw from below the ear around toward the chin. Use long, light strokes. These points are affiliated with the stomach meridian.

◆ Herbal Treatment

Echinacea. Dosage and dilution on pages 167–168. This can be used along with antibiotics your veterinarian has prescribed.

Golden Seal.[11] This is a Native American herb used to clear heat and dry dampness, which includes all the saliva produced by the ulcerations. Golden seal is a superb antibiotic type herb. It is bitter, cold and astringent. The tincture is easiest to use. Golden seal can lower blood sugar and because of its uterine stimulating effect, is contraindicated during pregnancy. Golden seal is used for shorter periods of time, usually up to two weeks at this dosage.

> **Dosage:** Of the tincture, use 15 drops in 1 ounce distilled water. Use 10 to 20 drops of this diluted mixture, depending on the size of the cat and severity of the condition, 3 to 4 times daily.

Mouth Flush. Unfortunately, we cannot ask the cats to gargle or rinse their mouths. We can however, try to flush the mouth, very gently from the sides of the lips. Boil a small panful of water for 10 minutes, allowing it to bubble and roll. To ½ cup boiled water, add ⅛ teaspoon iodized salt. Cool the mixture and use this as a mouthwash. Altnernatively, if the cat is able to drink water on her own, boil the water for 10 minutes. Cool, and steep with some chamomile flowers to make a mild tea to use instead of water.

◆ Nutritional Supplements

All the vitamins listed for wind conditions on pages 171–72, are indicated. Most important are quercitin with vitamin C which helps reduce symptoms of oral herpes in humans[12] and zinc which decreases gum inflammation.

◆ Dietary Recommendations

Offer soft food of any type that the cat will eat. Try to include sardines as they contain omega-3 oils, to strengthen the immune system.

◆ After the Acute Situation: Fatigue, Dryness and Sinusitis

Traditional Chinese Medicine has the advantage over Western medicine in its ability to strengthen the individual in the aftermath of illness. So often in my practice I hear clients say that Brandy, Taffy or Joey has "never been the same since...."

As part of the respiratory system, the nose is affiliated with the lungs. The nose and the lungs are very susceptible to dryness. The nose filters the air, helping the lungs extract moisture and then sending it downward into the body. If the filtering system has been weakened by a severe or lingering upper respiratory infection, the internal lung and body fluids are affected. This can result in dry, caked, ulcerated muzzles and nostrils, constipation and dry skin.

If the lung fluid deficiency becomes more pronounced, the individual will become more thirsty, and the breathing may become dry, loud or asthmatic. Serious lung conditions, such as bronchitis or allergic bronchitis may develop. The skin, which acts like the third lung of the body, can also become dry. Since the lung is coupled with the large intestine in the Five Element System, the first place the lung will leech the fluid that it needs will be from its partner, the large intestine. This can cause constipation and dry stools.

I see many cats who have had a severe upper respiratory condition and now have either intermittent bouts of sneezing or a chronic runny nose with an egg-white discharge. The cats snuffle and seem slightly congested. You can hear them breathe from across the room. This is **chronic sinusitis**.

More subtle signs of a weakened respiratory system might develop, such as the cat who tires easily, doesn't run around much or tends to get sick repeatedly with either fevers or mild colds. These cats may also develop a black-colored crust at the tips of their nostrils. The black crust appears because the fluid that bathes the mucous membranes inside the nose dries up.

In dogs, too, chronic upper respiratory conditions seem to manifest as a crusted muzzle or nostrils that seem to be "mud-caked." Small ulcerations at the tip of the nose may also form as a result of their body fluids drying up.

Because Traditional Chinese Medicine views these symptoms as a depletion of the moistening fluids in the lungs, treatment is aimed at lubricating and rebalancing these organs.

Heidi is a Basset Hound who came to see me several months after she had recovered from an upper respiratory infection. Since her recovery, not only were her nostrils dry and caked, but her coat became dry, brittle and flaky. She was extremely thirsty, especially following her afternoon walk, and during exercise, needed to stop and pant. Heidi also seemed to be dreaming alot, running and paddling in her sleep. She was restless and slept fitfully, often awakening at 4:00 a.m. to drink water.

Heidi was showing signs of a lung yin or fluid deficiency. The thirst, dry coat and nostrils all indicated lung dryness or deficiency of yin. Additionally, she was so depleted of fluids that the yin was insufficient to keep her calm, making her jumpy when awake or fitful when asleep. (Remember, the lung's energy is strongest from 3:00 a.m. to 5:00 a.m., exactly the time when Heidi became thirsty enough to awaken for a drink.)

SYMPTOMS OF
CHRONIC UPPER
RESPIRATORY
INFECTIONS

• Sneezing, snuffling,
loud breathing

• Mud-caked or sooty black
nostrils

• Dry, flaky fur and skin

• Constipation

• Increased thirst

• Easily fatigued

I treated Heidi with acupressure and herbs to rebalance her lungs, and she slowly returned to her normal state of energy and sweet temperment. Eventually her sleep became less active and she stopped getting up in the middle of the night to drink. Her coat became soft and beautiful again!

◆ Acupressure Points for Treatment of Chronic Upper Respiratory Infections

Urinary Bladder (BL) 13. Known as "Lung's Hollow," to balance the lung meridian.
Location and technique: See page 173.

Conception Vessel (CV) 17. Known as " The Women's Long Life Point," this point is used to benefit the diaphragm, regulate the breathing and yin fluid when the patient is wheezing, panting or experiencing chest pain. It is also considered the "influential" point related to breathing and lung tissue.
Location: Found on the midline of the abdomen between the top set of nipples. It is usually at the level of the widest area of the breast bone in the 4th rib space. Hold the point or use a small up and down motion for 1 minute.

Lung (LU) 7. Known as "Broken Sequence," this point is the energetic connection between the lungs and large intestine to aid water movement between the upper and lower body. It is also a meeting place between the lung and the conception vessel meridian so that moistening is one of the major effects on the lungs. Use this point for constipation and dryness of skin.
Location and technique: See page 173.

Large Intestine (LI) 4. Known as "Adjoining Valleys," this is the master point for the head and face, sinuses and nose.
Location and technique: See page 152.

Large Intestine (LI) 20. Known as "Welcome Fragrance," this point on either side of the nostrils is a major point for the nose. Traditionally it is treated along with LI 4 for chronic sinusitis.

Location: In the depression at both ends of the sides of the nostril where it meets the face. Hold the point for 10 to 30 seconds.

SINUS ACUPRESSURE POINTS

In addition to the points listed above, use light fingertip pressure around the eyes and at the bridge of the nose (**yintang**) to relieve sinus congestion.

◆ Herbal Treatment

Bi Yan Pian.[13] This formula works well on very stuffy noses with egg-white or greenish discharge from the nostrils. It includes magnolia flower, cocklebur fruit and schizonepeta to clear wind, dampness obstruction and to promote easy breathing, along with platycodon to clear phlegm and phellodendron and forsythia to clear heat. Licorice is used to aid digestion that might be hindered from the heat clearing effects of the herbs.

> **Dosage:** cats/small dogs: 1 tablet
> medium/large dogs: 4 tablets
> Use 2 to 3 times daily after food, for up to 6 weeks.

Eyebright. This herb is effective for problems of the eyes and for swollen, congested mucous membranes of the nose and sinus headaches.

> **Dosage:** See page 170.

Calendula officinalis (Marigold).[14] This herb has four of the five flavors: sweet, bitter, salty, and pungent, and is neutral with a potential to dry and cool. Calendula is wonderful in ointment form to soothe nostril tips and dried out muzzle areas. Internally, calendula tincture is good for the dry, inflamed, stuffed up sinusitis without discharge. For internal use, dilute 15 drops of tincture in 1 ounce distilled water. Use for up to one month. Decrease dosage if diarrhea occurs.

> **Dosage:** cats/small dogs: 10 drops, diluted mixture, twice daily
> medium dogs: 20 drops, diluted mixture, twice daily
> large dogs: 30 drops, diluted mixture, twice daily

Echinacea. A more diluted version is used for long periods of time[15] to decrease an individual's susceptibility to recurrent illness. Dilute 15 drops in 1 ounce distilled water. Use once a day for 30 days.

    Dosage: cats/small dogs: 10 drops
                  medium dogs: 25 drops
                  large dogs: 30 drops

- **Vitamin Supplements to Support the Lungs and Restore Balance and Immunity**

Vitamin C. Sodium ascorbate or rose hips combination, with diarrhea as the limiting factor.

          cats/small dogs: 250 mg, twice daily
          medium dogs: 500 mg, twice daily
          large dogs: 1,000 to 1,500, twice daily

Quercitin + Bromelin. Bioflavinoid and enzyme combination for allergic type respiratory conditions and to strengthen the lungs in general. It may be helpful for sinusitis. Give 250 mg, twice daily with vitamin C. Quercitin can also be found in blue-green algae.

Evening Primrose Oil: 100 to 250 mg daily, depending on the size of the animal.

Cod Liver Oil: ½ to 1½ teaspoons daily, depending on the size of the animal.

Vitamin B Complex: from a non-yeast source, ¼ to ½ human dosage.

Seaweeds. Kelp or nori for trace mineral supplementation and regulation of metabolism: ⅛ teaspoon cats to ½ teaspoon dogs.

◆ Diet to Support and Moisten the Lungs

As rice is the grain associated with the lung,[16] a combination of white and brown rice, or brown rice alone, can be added to the diet. See sample diets in Chapter Seven, page 82. If added to a commercial diet, grain can provide up to 25% of the total diet. It must be cooked with extra water for $1\frac{1}{4}$ hours (1 cup of rice to 3 cups water). Millet can also increase fluids if there is a dry lung problem with thirst and dry breathing. Additionally, a small amount of honey can be added for very dry breathing, usually $\frac{1}{2}$ teaspoon.

Garlic should be minimized because it creates an upward surge of heat in the body, and may dry the eyes and nose.

Meat and fish protein should be in the moisture-giving or neutral range, which includes beef, beef liver, lamb and sardines. Unless an individual is of the cold type, poultry, venison and shrimp should be avoided as these foods are quite warming. Vegetables such as avocado, spinach, broccoli, most greens, string beans, celery and yams are cooling or moistening, as are carrots which are high in vitamin A and aid the lungs.

Since this is a dry condition, dry food should be used in moderation, and supplemented with cooked grains and vegetables when possible. The drying process itself creates heat in the body when it is digested. If your animal is already hot and dry, these foods may make the situation worse.

Endnotes

1. Fratkin, Jake. *Chinese Herbal Patent Formulas.* (Boulder, CO: Shya Publications, 1986), 53.

2. Hobbs, Christopher. Echinacea: A Literature Review, *Herbal Gram,* No. 30, Winter, 1994, 38–41.

3, 4, 5, 9, 11, 14. Holmes, Peter. *The Energetics of Western Herbs, Volume I & II.* (Boulder, CO: Artemis Press, 1989), 681, 130, 410, 459, 553, 565.

6, 10. Moore, Michael. *Medicinal Plants of the Mountain West.* (Santa Fe, NM: Museum of New Mexico Press, 1979), 119, 168.

7, 12. Balch, James and Phyllis. *Prescription for Nutritional Healing.* (Garden City Park, NY: Avery Publishing Group, Inc., 1990), 10.

8, 13. Naeser, Margaret A., PhD. *Outline Guide to Chinese Herbal Patent Medicines in Pill Form.* (Boston, MA: Boston Chinese Medicine, 1990), 73, 54.

15. Wagner and Jurcic, as reported by Christopher Hobbs, *Herbal Gram,* No. 30, Winter, 1994, 38–41.

16. Connelly, Dianne M., PhD, MAc. *Traditional Acupuncture: The Law of the Five Elements.* (Columbia, MD: The Center for Traditional Acupuncture, Inc., 1979), 89.

CHAPTER ELEVEN

The Ears

A very large number of our domestic, four-legged friends seem to have ear problems. The conical shape acts like radar stations, honing in on sounds that are beyond the range of human hearing. Their ears are much more movable and versatile than ours and they're also incredibly expressive. Entire behavior patterns can be gleaned from ear positioning. Cats show flattened, airplane ears, for example, just before they are ready to pounce into aggressive action. Dogs' ears perk up in joyous greeting when their people come home. For whatever the reasons, animals' ears work hard and seem to be susceptible to all sorts of ills.

Western medicine actually considers certain ear problems to be normal for some breeds. Many animals shake their heads, for instance, for no apparent reason. Because dogs tend to have longer ear canals than humans, along with longer ear flaps, the propensity for air and moisture to be trapped inside is greater. Ear problems may start out acutely, but they often linger. It is not uncommon for dogs especially to suffer from chronic ear problems all of their lives. Aside from ear mites, cats seem to have fewer ear problems than dogs, but recently I have seen more ear problems cropping up in our feline friends.

The most common types of ear problems seen in veterinary practice are: hearing imbalances, red, dry inflamed ears with and without waxy discharge, and soupy, smelly, moist ears.

THE EARS AND THE MERIDIANS

The meridians surrounding the ear are the three yang meridians of the gall bladder, small intestine and triple heater. In addition to the meridians, traditionally, "The ear is the meeting place of all the channels of the body."[1] There is an entire branch of acupuncture based on how the embryo of the body is mapped out on the outer ear, or auricle. Charts show the head pointed down toward the base of the ear, with the eye at the ear lobe. The feet are in the upper large flat area toward the top of the ear. The spine is aligned along the curve of the "anti-helix." The internal organs are in the central portion of the ear surrounding the ear canal opening. There are over 200 acupuncture points located on the ear.

Although the ear connects all the channels of the body, the specific element it is related to is the kidney. The kidney is the underlying yin essence of the body, and it is through its water and blood movement that the ear apperati are bathed properly so that we can hear. When the kidney is deficient in its ability to produce the fluid necessary to adequately moisten the inner workings of the ears, hearing problems can result.

Many factors can weaken the kidney including heredity, life in a very dry environment and an overabundance of fear. If an animal is constantly under stress from fearful situations, the kidney suffers. This is especially seen in catastrophic situations like fires, earthquakes and tornedos.

When the kidney is deficient in the Five Element System of Creation, it cannot nourish the liver properly, and the liver blood stores will be affected. This can create an increased dryness of the body, resulting in dry skin, eyes, ears and fur. When the kidney is deficient in the Five Element Control Cycle, it cannot control the fire organs of the heart, small intestine, pericardium and triple heater. Any excess fire in the body rises upwards and causes inflammation and dryness, especially in the upper parts of the body, including the ears.

HEARING IMBALANCES

Most of the problems discussed in human texts deal with ringing in the ears, called "tinnitus," which can eventually lead to loss of hearing or balance. These problems are considered to be deficiency kidney type patterns. They are deficient because proper fluid balance is not present to feed the ear components. This can cause inflammation and the development of ear-ringing. Although this phenomenon occurs in animals, we usually don't recognize it until it is quite advanced. Dogs and cats show their discomfort by reacting irritably to loud, sudden noises. They will startle easily and run for cover, hiding wherever they can.

It is interesting that Western medicine recognizes that many animals with kidney failure begin to lose their hearing. One very special dog named Corky was my patient for many years. When her kidneys finally began to weaken, her human realized that Corky was also losing her hearing because Corky wouldn't respond to the phone or doorbell. I treated acupuncture points for hearing along with kidney points. Corky's person soon reported that Corky could hear the phone and doorbell again. Half-jokingly she asked if she could get on the table next!

In the Five Element System, the water element of the kidney has to keep the fire elements under control. If the kidney fluid is weak, such as appears with ear-ringing, the fire can rise up, increasing the discomfort and distorting the hearing. Some of my senior patients seem to acquire selective hearing. You know, those dogs who can hear a banana being peeled in the kitchen from outside, but cannot hear their human calling them to come in.

The two fire elements of the small intestine and triple heater are connected to hearing. It is said that they separate the "pure from the impure sounds,"[2] similar to how the small intestine separates foods for use or disposal. A canine patient came to me with the peculiar complaint of not knowing where specific sounds came from. His human said that she would call to him from across the road, but the dog became bewildered, running in all directions looking for her. He would only come to her when he could see her. His human thought the problem was a distortion of hearing. The dog was also thirsty and restless, which pointed to disharmony between the water and fire elements. I treated acupuncture points along the kidney, small intestine and triple heater meridians, and the dog quickly recovered his sense of direction.

TREATMENT OF HEARING IMBALANCES

The treatment is aimed at supporting the yin of the body especially of the kidney, along with the vital essences of the other blood-making organs of the body. Additionally, local fire meridian points can be used to increase local circulation and rebalance the fire and water elements.

◆ Acupressure Points

Triple Heater (TH)21. Known as "Ear's Door."
Small Intestine (SI)19. Known as "Palace of Hearing."
Gall Bladder (GB)2. Known as "Confluence of Hearing."
Location: All of these points are located just in front of the ear and can be gently massaged in an up and down manner several times daily.

Triple Heater (TH)17. Known as "Shielding Wind."
Location: Just below the ear. Massage in a circular motion.

Kidney (KI)3. Known as "Great Creek," this point strengthens the kidney.
Location: It is found on the inside of each hind leg, just above the ankle (tarsus), at the midpoint between the Achilles tendon and the protuberance of the ankle bone (medial malleolus). Hold the point for 15 to 30 seconds.

Small Intestine (SI)5. Known as the "Valley of Yang," this point cools the fire of the small intestine.
Location: Lift the front paw of your animal, the nails pointing upward. This overextends the wrist forming a crease at the wrist. SI 5 is located at the outside end of this crease, just on the outside of the protuberance called the styloid process of the ulna. Hold the point for 15 seconds.

◆ Herbal Treatment

Liu Wei Di Huang Wan.[3] This is a classic kidney tonic formula, containing the blood and yin tonics of rehmannia and cornus; the spleen/qi tonic of dioscorea; the heat-clearing herb of moutan; the "empty fire-clearing" herb alisma; and the dampness clearing herb hoelen.

Dosage: cats/small dogs: 1 to 2 pills, twice daily
medium dogs: 3 to 4 pills, twice daily
large dogs: 6 pills, twice daily

Tso Tzu Otic.[4] This formula is a modification of Liu Wei Di Huang Wan, with magnitite and bupleurum added to clear upward heat coming from the liver in addition to strengthening the kidney. **Dosage** is the same as for Liu Wei Di Huang Wan, above.

RED, DRY, INFLAMED EARS

Redness and dryness around the ear, inside the canal or on the ear flap can be caused by a lack of fluid. When the fluid stores get low enough, there is not enough moisture to cool the normal internal fires of the body. This creates a relative increase in heat, known as "false fire." This heat does not come from an "aggressive, overpowering flame," but rather, from the weakness of not being able to generate enough fluid to keep the heat at bay. It is therefore known as a deficient condition. The blood and fluid-making organs of the body are the kidneys, liver and spleen/pancreas. When the fluids are deficient enough, the ears become dry, red, inflamed and thickened. Your animal friend will be slightly sensitive to your touching his ears. But if you use a light, gentle touch, he will usually accept it.

If a deficiency of blood is the underlying cause, the animal will exhibit such signs as a dry tongue with little or no fur on it, dry, flaky skin, moderate thirst and sometimes skittishness.

◆ Acupressure Points for Treating Dry, Red, Inflamed Ears

The treatment is aimed at tonifying the yin and the blood and clearing the false heat so that proper moistening can be restored to the ear tissue.

Gall Bladder (GB) 20. Known as "Wind Pond," this point relieves wind, discomfort and heat from the ears.

Location: See page 152. Hold the point for 15 seconds.

Large Intestine (LI) 11. Known as "Crooked Pool," this point relieves heat from the upper body.

> *Location:* See page 156. Use small, circular motions for 10 to 15 seconds.

Lung (LU) 7. Known as "Broken Sequence," this point moistens the upper body.

> *Location and technique:* See page 173.

Urinary Bladder (BL) 23. Known as "Kidney's Hollow," this is the association point of the kidney and will balance the blood and underlying fluid of the body.

> *Location:* In the depressions in the muscle on both sides of the spine, between the 2nd and 3rd lumbar vertebrae. The technique is to use circular motion outward from the spine or a gentle, rocking, back and forth motion.

◆ Herbal Treatment

Shou Wu Pian. This single herb nourishes the blood of the kidney and liver. It has a slightly cooling nature.

> **Dosage:** cats/small dogs: 1 tablet, twice daily
> medium dogs: 2 tablets, twice daily
> large dogs: 3 tablets, twice daily

Chih Pai Di Huang Wan.[5] This is a combination of Liu Wei Di Huang Wan, listed for hearing imbalances, which nourishes the kidney and liver blood and essence, with the added herbs of anemarrhena and phellodenron, which clear false fire. Dosage is the same as for Liu Wei Di Huang Wan, pages 187–88.

◆ Topicals

Vitamin E cream, aloe vera gel, almond or **olive oil. Chamomile** or **black tea** compresses are soothing and healing.

◆ Nutritional Supplements

Vitamin E: cats/small dogs: 50 IU daily
medium dogs: 100 to 200 IU daily
large dogs: 400 IU daily

Cod Liver Oil: ½ tsp to 1½ teaspoon daily

Kelp Powder: cats/small dogs: ¹⁄₁₆ teaspoon daily
medium/large dogs: up to ½ teaspoon

Vitamin C: cats/small dogs: 125 mg, twice daily
medium dogs: 250 to 500 mg, twice daily
large dogs: 500 to 1,000 mg, twice daily

◆ Dietary Recommendations

Foods that have neutral to cooling qualities are useful because these foods create moisture. For dogs, you can choose more vegetables and less meat. Red meat is good for generating blood, but can create internal heat if eaten in excess. For cats, neutral meat proteins are good choices such as rabbit, ground pork (boiled with the fat skimmed off), chicken gizzards, mackeral and eggs. For non-meat choices, try sweet potato, brown rice, millet, barley and whole wheat pasta. Vegetables include green beans, broccoli, Napa cabbage, carrots, peas and beans which can be raw or steamed and beans, of course, must be cooked thoroughly. Avoid venison and high-fat foods, as they can heat up the liver. Remember that dry food creates heat in the body when it is digested and usually has a higher fat content. Supplement dry food with ⅓ to 1 cup of thoroughly cooked brown rice, depending upon the size of the animal.

CHRONIC EAR WAX BUILDUP

Discharges are usually categorized in terms of the Eight Principle characteristics of yin or yang (see Chapter Three, page 26), interior or exterior, cold or hot, excess or deficient, and dry or damp.

If there is a discharge, it usually indicates an excess of some substance. Ear discharges are usually dry or damp, as well as excess. If an offensive odor is present it is considered a hot condition. The odors can be assessed with the five elements:

Sour rancid = Liver (Wood) imbalance
Sickly sweet = Spleen/pancreas (Earth) imbalance
Scorched = Heart/small intestine (Fire) imbalance
Putrid = Kidney (Water) imbalance
Rotten Decay = Lung (Metal) imbalance

Dry, crusty, sticky ear wax indicates that there is enough fluid present to form ear lubrication, but that heat is rising up and consuming that fluid. When heat or inflammation rises upward, the liver is usually the culprit. The deficient, red, hot, dry ear patient mentioned above is so devoid of fluid vital essence that no discharge can be produced. On the other hand, the dry, crusty, sticky earwax patient tends to have a more excess constitution. This patient is producing a discharge showing a heated liver which is marginally out of balance. This causes the heat to rise or block the circulation. The normal lubricating and cleaning capacity of the ear is out of balance. Any odor is usually mild at this point, with a hint of sour rancidness, reflecting a liver imbalance. These patients are more sensitive to touch than the dry-eared individual, but once touch is initiated, the animal will usually like the rubbing to disperse the stagnant wax buildup.

◆ Acupressure Points for Treating Earwax Buildup

Treatment is aimed at clearing the heat, while helping the liver to rebalance by breaking up stagnation.

Large Intestine (LI)11. Known as "Crooked Pool," this point clears heat from the upper part of the body.
Location and technique: See page 156.

Liver (LIV) 2. Known as the "Walk Between," this is the "fire point" on the liver meridian, and is used to drain heat from the liver. The point is especially useful if there is a sour, rancid odor present.
Location: See page 156. The technique is to "brush" in a downward direction along the inside of the back paw.

Urinary Bladder (BL) 13. Known as "Lung's Hollow," this is the association point of the lung, and is useful for moistening the upper part of the body.

Location and technique: See page 173.

◆ Herbal Treatment

Self Heal, Eyebright in equal parts, **and Licorice** in ½ part, in powdered form. Self heal and eyebright are cooling herbs. Eyebright unclogs congestion in the head area. Self heal clears the heat, calms the liver, and dries up discharges.[6] Self heal is a type of prunella which is used to clear heat from the liver and break up liver stagnation. Licorice is neutral and moistening. This herb combination is given orally, to rebalance, cool and moisten the liver.

Dosage: cats/small dogs: ¼ teaspoon
medium dogs: ⅓ to ½ teaspoon
large dogs: ¾ teaspoon

Use this combination for three weeks, once or twice daily, depending on the severity of the problem.

◆ Topicals

Aloe vera gel ½ cup + 1 capful **distilled white vinegar** + 1 capful **hydrogen peroxide** + 1 tablespoon **yucca root tea** + 1 drop **cedar** or **lavender oil.** Apply several dropperfuls into the ear, massage and remove excess with a cottonball.

Alternatively, aloe vera gel or hydrogen peroxide can be used to clean the ear. In order for the condition to clear, the liver and kidneys need to be working optimally. Therefore, it is the acupressure and internal herbs that will probably help the condition, rather than the topical preparations.

◆ Nutritional Supplements

Multiple B Vitamins, at one quarter to one half human dosage.
Vitamin C, as sodium ascorbate: 150 to 1,000 mg twice daily, depending on diarrhea.
Trace Minerals, including zinc: 5 mg daily.

◆ Dietary Recommendations

Cooling and neutral foods such as barley, millet and whole wheat are useful to balance the liver, along with green vegetables, cabbage and celery. Avoid excess poultry and shellfish, as these foods heat the liver.

CHRONIC MOIST EAR PROBLEMS

One day, a Cocker Spaniel named Tony came into my office waiting room. From the back of the clinic I could smell his ears. The odor was so strong that I wondered how Tony himself could tolerate it. It was sour, rancid and putrid. Just from that smell, it was clear that Tony had problems with all the five elements of his body.

Tony's human told me that the problem had been recurring for five years. His genetic heritage and drooping ears probably predisposed him to ear problems. His human reported that Tony's mother and brother also had ear problems. As if this was not enough, Tony also had recurrent loose stools or diarrhea that had a strong odor and he tended to urinate in the house at night. He also drooled excessively, his tongue dripping saliva.

When I examined Tony's ears, they had a soupy, pus-like yellowish discharge that had burned the hair off the side of his face. It obviously hurt him to have his ears examined. In Traditional Chinese Medicine, such moistness is a dampness problem. The odor, burning discharge and sensitivity make it a heat problem as well. Thus, the moist and chronic ear discharges are damp heat imbalances. If the moisture predominates, there is more dampness. If the odor, redness or sensitivity predominate, there is more heat.

The organ most sensitive to dampness is the spleen/pancreas. The original heat problem between the kidney and liver, as discussed in the section on ear wax, page 190, also involved the spleen/pancreas in Tony's case. In the Five Element System, the spleen/pancreas keeps the kidney under control and the liver keeps the spleen/pancreas under control.

When there is dampness, water may accumulate in odd places, such as in the abdomen, as in Tony's case. This soggy feeling can lead to increased urination and soft stools. The odor in the stool indicates that the liver, as well as the spleen/pancreas, is involved. Tony's tongue, which appeared wide, moist and had tooth imprints on the sides, and his drooling also reflected a dampness problem in the spleen/pancreas.

When treating chronic moist discharges, it is essential to understand the underlying imbalances, because unless these are corrected, the discharge returns as soon as the ear medication stops. Western medicine will try to identify the organism growing in the ear and use an antibiotic that addresses that organism. Eastern medicine knows that the organism in the ear is the result of a deeper imbalance occurring within the individual and tries to rebalance that underlying problem. Because of the deep-seated nature of the imbalance, chronic moist ear discharges are difficult to treat.

◆ Acupressure Points for Treating Chronic, Moist Ear Problems

Treatment is aimed at drying the dampness and clearing the heat. After this initial phase, the underlying imbalances may be addressed. Usually this includes balancing the liver and spleen. (See Chapters Fifteen and Sixteen.) Unless otherwise noted, all points can be held for 10 to 30 seconds.

Spleen (SP) 9. Known as "Yin Tomb Spring," this point helps dry dampness all over the body.

Location: On the inside of the hind leg, just below the knee (stifle), in the groove between the long (tibia) bone and the muscle closest to it (gastrocnemius).

Large Intestine (LI) 4. Known as "Adjoining Valleys," this is the master point for the head.

Location: See page 152.

Large Intestine (LI) 11. Known as "Crooked Pool," this point clears heat in the upper body.

Location: See page 156.

Triple Heater (TH) 17. Known as "Sheilding Wind," this point relieves wind and unblocks the meridians allowing for free circulation of fluids.

Location: See page 187.

◆ Herbal Treatment

The following tinctures of these Western herbs can be used internally.

Ribwort plantain 15 drops + 5 drops **witch hazel** + 3 drops **lavender** in 1 ounce of distilled water.

> **Dosage:** 1 to 3 dropperfuls, twice daily, depending upon the size of the animal. Treatment lasts for two weeks. Do not use with pregnant animals.

Lung Tan Xie Gan.[7] This Chinese herb contains the heat and damp-clearing herbs of gentiana, gardenia, scutellaria, alisma, moutan and plantain, plus the blood herbs of tang kuei and rehmannia, along with licorice to harmonize the formula.

> **Dosage:** cats/small dogs: 1 pill, twice daily
>
> medium dogs: 2 pills, twice daily
>
> large dogs: 3 pills, twice daily

If loose stool occurs, decrease dosage by half. Treatment lasts for up to two weeks.

◆ Topicals

Mix the following tinctures together in 1 ounce of distilled water:

Calendula 10 drops + 1 drop **agrimony** + 1 drop **lavender.** Apply 1 dropperfull in each ear, massage, and remove excess debris. The alcohol in the tinctures can irritate some animals, and if this occurs use tea made with ½ teaspoon **calendula** + ¼ teaspoon **lavender flower** + 1 drop **agrimony** tincture.

As with any other ear medication, if redness or irritation develops, discontinue use.

◆ Nutritional Supplements

Vitamin E, as anti-inflammatory: 50 IU for cats/small dogs
medium/large dogs: up to 400 IU

Vitamin C, as sodium ascorbate, with diarrhea being the limiting factor:
cats/small dogs: 125 mg, twice daily
medium dogs: 250 mg, twice daily
large dogs: 1,000 mg, twice daily

Intra-cellular antioxidants, available at your natural food store as catalase or sulfoxydismutase, may be helpful in clearing toxins from the body. **Dosage** is from one quarter the human dose for cats and small dogs, to one half to two thirds of the human dose for large dogs.

Trace minerals, in the form of kelp powder or other seaweed, at ¼ teaspoon for cats and small dogs, and ½ to ⅔ teaspoon for large dogs.

◆ Dietary Recommendations

If heat predominates, the individual will be stubborn and irritable, and extremely resistent to treatment. If this is the case, cooling or neutral foods, as listed on page 190, for heat conditions of the ears are suggested. Avoid poultry, shellfish, venison and lamb, as these are warming foods that encourage liver heat.

If dampness is the dominant problem, foods that aid the spleen/pancreas and are more warming or neutral should be used. Usually the excessive damp individual is mild mannered, quiet, slightly stubborn, often stocky and leaning toward overweight with soft flesh. The best foods to try here are mackeral, lamb, rabbit, oats, well-cooked brown rice, white rice, potatoes, corn, carrots, squash.

ACUTE EAR INFECTIONS

If your dog or cat shows sudden signs of ear pain when you touch her around the ear or lift the flap, if there is inflammation of the ear flap, ear odor or discharge, continual head shaking or drooping of the ear, have your veterinarian check it out. There may be an infection or a foreign body present causing an ear infection. If there is no foreign body and you wish to try herbs and acupressure, consider the following options.

Acute ear infections, as all acute conditions in Traditional Chinese Medicine, are considered **wind** conditions. Just as in conjunctivitis and upper respiratory infections, the wind enters suddenly, overpowering the individual's immune system. The wind in acute ear infections is usually accompanied by heat.

◆ Treatment

The treatment is aimed at alleviating the wind and cooling the heat. The animal's ear may be very painful, and treatment of local points surrounding the ear may not be tolerated well by your normally tractable animal friend. Unless otherwise indicated, points can be held from 15 to 30 seconds.

◆ Acupressure Points for Treating Acute Ear Infections

Governing Vessel (GV) 14. Known as "Big Vertebra," is used to dispel wind invasions.

Location: See page 166. Use small, back and forth motions.

Large Intestine (LI)11. Known as "Crooked Pool," this point is used to dispel heat and wind in the upper body.

Location: See page 156.

Gall Bladder (GB) 20. Known as "Wind Pond," this point alleviates wind and heat. This point is optional and may be too painful for the animal.

Location: See page 152.

◆ Nutritional Supplements

Vitamin C: cats/small dogs: 125 mg, twice daily
medium dogs: 250 mg, twice daily
large dogs: 1,500 mg, twice daily, with diarrhea being the limi-
ing factor.

Bioflavonoids and/or **Blue-Green Algae**, with diarrhea being the limiting
factor: cats/small dogs: 1/16 teaspoon, daily
medium/large dogs: 1/2 teaspoon, daily

Zinc: 5 to 10 mg daily.

HEAD SHAKING

Some animals shake their head and ears excessively and it drives their humans
crazy! When the veterinarian checks the ears, there seems to be nothing wrong.
There is no discharge, odor, pain or inflammation of any kind.

I believe that the head shaking is caused by a blockage or stagnation
along the meridians serving the ear area, especially the gall bladder meridian.

I had a very dear patient, Tia, a Doberman Cross, who was diagnosed
with liver cancer. We were able to keep her going much longer than the Western practitioners thought possible. One of the strange behaviors she exhibited
was to shake her head continually when she was having a flareup with the
liver. When we were able to subdue the liver and gall bladder, the head shaking diminished. Sometimes exercise also seemed to help this condition. Exercise unblocks stagnation along the meridians.

Another cause for head shaking is a difference in the internal pressure in
the eustacian tube. This connection is between the ear and the back of the
throat. It's what gets clogged during rapid changes in altitude when descend-
ing in an airplane and we have to yawn or open our mouths wide in order to
"pop our ears." This also occurs in dogs and cats, especially if there is some
sort of sinus problem. They shake their heads to equalize the pressure.

Some animals will shake the head when there is a food allergy involved. The head shaking may begin as soon as ten minutes after the meal, or up to one hour later. Experimenting with different foods may be of assistance.

Look at the meridians surrounding the ear, especially the gall bladder, triple heater and small intestine.

◆ Acupressure Points for the Treatment of Head Shaking

Acupressure at any points listed for wind releasing, heat clearing or blood nourishing may be helpful.

Endnotes

1. Nei Jing, chapter Kou Wen Pien, reported in *Outline of Chinese Acupuncture*. (Peking, China: Foreign Language Press, 1975), 269.
2. Connelly, Dianne M., PhD, MAc. *Traditional Acupuncture: The Law of the Five Elements*. (Columbia, MD: The Center for Traditional Acupuncture Inc., 1979), 50.
3, 7. Naeser, Margaret, PhD. *Outline Guide to Chinese Herbal Patent Medicines in Pill Form*. (Boston, MA: Boston Chinese Medicine, 1990), 291, 169.
4, 5. Fratkin, Jake. *Chinese Herbal Patent Formulas*. (Boulder, CO: Shya Publications, 1986), 209, 204.
6. Holmes, Peter. *The Energetics of Western Herbs, Vol. II*. (Boulder, CO: Artemis Press, 1989), 503.

CHAPTER TWELVE

The Teeth and Gums

How is your animal friend's breath today? Sweet enough to kiss? Dogs especially like to lick and kiss you so you should know the answer to this. Cats will let you know when they are grooming or yawning—if their breath is bad, you can smell it.

Although mouth washes to clear the breath are not yet on the market for animals, almost everything else is. Dental hygiene has become an important part of veterinary medicine. Due to the increased life expectancy of most domestic animals, teeth tend to show increased wear, needing cleaning, cavity fillings, root canals or extractions. Gums need attention for inflammatory gum disease known as gingivitis. Since the mouth has a high bacteria count, if an animal's teeth or gums are compromised, this may place added stress on the rest of the body, including the heart.

Many dogs exhibit worn down teeth at an early age because of excessive chewing on themselves from irritations of the skin. Many young cats exhibit severe gum disease because of compromised immune systems and suseptibility to viruses. Still others have tartar buildup due to digestive problems.

In Traditional Chinese Medicine, the teeth are part of the skeletal system, and are governed by the kidneys and the water element. When the kidneys are weak, the teeth decay more easily, or become transluscent and fall out. Also, when the kidneys are weak, the inherited part of the immune system, known as the kidney jing, is weak. Weak kidney jing or essence can affect the other systems of the body.

In looking at the Five Element Control Cycle, it is the earth element of the spleen/pancreas and stomach that keeps the kidney balanced. If the kidney is weak, the earth element can become overpowering. Since the kidney's job is to keep all the organs cool and moistened, if it is weak, excessive heat in the stomach can arise, creating havoc with the digestion. Stomach (or gastric) inflammation causes changes in hydrochloric acid production, saliva viscosity and vomiting. Since the digestive system opens up to the mouth, an imbalance in the earth element can therefore weaken the tissues of the mouth, including the gums, cheeks and tongue surface. It is said that the digestive juices of the stomach create a healthy tongue coating which appears thin and white. If the stomach and spleen/pancreas are not functioning optimally, problems with the soft tissues in the mouth occur. Gums that are spongy, bleed easily or are ulcerated are a result of too much stomach fire which can create bad breath and tartar buildup.

An animal with excess stomach fire will become voraciously hungry and thirsty in an attempt to "put out the fire." In fact, she may want to eat paper, rocks, kitty litter, lick cement, all kinds of strange things.

Just as the spleen/pancreas keeps the kidney under control in the Five Element System, the kidney, in turn, keeps the heart in balance. If the kidney is weak, the heart can be affected. This is interesting, because we know from a Western point of view that bad teeth and gums can cause heart valve and kidney problems by depositing an excessive load of bacteria into the circulation. Therefore, from both a Traditional Chinese *and* Western medical standpoint, poor teeth and gums involve the kidney and the heart.

TRUE HEAT, FALSE HEAT

It is important to discuss the difference between **true heat** and **false heat**, as the treatment for mouth problems caused by these conditions will be different in each case.

True heat is the inflammation that occurs when an *excess* type of individual gets out of balance. An excess type of individual is strong-willed, assertive, and confident. When this individual becomes ill, she will be irritable, with a high fever, swollen glands, and excessive thirst. Here, heat needs to be cleared and the fire causing elements need to be subdued. The strong, heat-clearing herbs needed in this case can weaken the qi and cause diarrhea so are better tolerated by strong, excess type individuals.

A deficient individual is mild-mannered and quiet, and gets out of balance because his cooling capabilities fail to keep the normal internal heat under control. Here there is a relative heat that arises. The deficient individual's reaction to infections is milder, with chills, little fever and a great need to be consoled. If there is thirst, it is for small amounts frequently. The deficient heat needs to be cleared, but in a gentler manner, and at the same time, the underlying organs need strengthening.

Mo is a sweet, five-year old domestic short-haired kitty who was brought to see me because he was eating paper tissues and as much grass as he could find. His mouth was very odorous and his gums looked like the inside of a ripe strawberry. His lymph glands under the throat were so enlarged, that opening his mouth was painful. He was always thirsty, but only drank a few sips at a time. His tongue was dark red with very little tongue fur. (The central area of the tongue almost appeared bald of fur!) After questioning his human, I found out that as a kitten, Mo had a severe upper respiratory condition that seemed to take a lot out of him. Although he had no mouth ulcers at the time, his immune system was compromised, making him susceptible to colds. His human told me that Mo often vomited his food, but then ate it again. She said that Mo demanded food almost all day long. Since he didn't appear to be overly fat, she wondered where all the food was going. She also said that Mo had become irritable, and was eating more tissues in between meals.

Mo's condition was a rather severe example of stomach fire from underlying false heat. Eating the tissues was an attempt to sop up the burning acids in his stomach. The severe upper respiratory infection he couldn't kick as a kitten indicates that Mo probably had weak kidney jing from birth. Mo's qi in general was not optimal. Since it is the spleen/pancreas and stomach that make the qi from the food, an imbalance here further weakens the immune system and can create false (deficient) fire in the stomach.

The center of the tongue corresponds to the earth element, and seeing this bare indicates the status of the qi, with heat eating up the tongue fur. The lack of tongue coating reflects a deficiency type condition, as does Mo's persona in general. Because of the chronic nature of the problem, it was difficult to turn it around. The moral of the story is: Don't wait until your animal friend is in such dire straits! If you notice any changes in the breath, gum color, tartar buildup or early tooth-wear, check with your veterinarian.

◆ Treatment

Treatment is aimed at clearing the heat, but also at trying to restore and balance the kidney with the spleen/pancreas and stomach. The following points are used for cooling and balancing the stomach and spleen/pancreas while strengthening the kidney's moisture. They can be used in both deficient and excess individuals.

◆ Acupressure Points

If your animal will allow it, gently masssage around the mouth, especially at the corners of the lips, chin and jaw. The circular massage of the Tellington-Jones technique (Chapter Eight, page 119) is most effective.

Stomach (ST) 44. Known as "Inner Court," this point drains heat from the stomach and decreases pain.

Location: See page 176. Usually this point is very sensitive and the technique is to quickly and gently press at the top of the web.

Large Intestine (LI) 4. Known as "Adjoining Valleys," this is the master point for the head.

Location: See page 152. Hold the point for 15 seconds.

Kidney (KI) 3. Known as "Great Creek," this point increases the kidney moisture.

Location: See page 187. Hold the point for 15 seconds.

For strong, excess individuals, do not use Kidney 3, but replace this point with:

Liver (LIV) 2. Known as "The Walk Between," this point clears heat from the liver.

Location: See page 156. Use a small, downward, brushing action for 10 to 15 seconds.

Small Intestine (SI) 5. Known as "The Valley of Yang," this point clears heat from the heart's partner, the small intestine. This helps to reduce the inflammation.

Location: See page 187. Massage in a counterclockwise direction to sedate the point.

◆ Alternative Points for Weak Individuals

Urinary Bladder (BL) 20. Known as "Spleen Hollow," this is the association point for the spleen/pancreas. It will help balance the organ and strengthen the qi.

Location: On both sides of the spine, in the depression between the last two ribs and the back. Hold the point.

Conception Vessel (CV) 14. Known as "Great Palace," this is the alarm point of the heart. It is useful in clearing heat from the stomach that we recognize as heart burn.

Location: On the abdominal midline, at the tip of the last bone of the sternum (under the chest), known as the xyphoid process. Gentle massage in a downward direction is helpful in clearing heat.

◆ Herbal Treatment

Chamomile.[1] This mild Western herb has a bitter and sweet taste that can be used to calm the stomach and heart fire and reduce inflammation. Use it internally as tea, and add to food, or use it externally on the gums with a cotton swab.

Dosage: cats/small dogs: 1 to 2 teaspoons, twice daily
medium dogs: 1 to 2 tablespoons, twice daily
large dogs: 3 tablespoons, twice daily

Plantain. A mild herb that is used as an astringent to relieve pain, decrease inflammation and act as an antiseptic. This can be used internally at 5 drops of tincture diluted in 1 ounce distilled water, at 1 to 3 droppers twice daily, or topically. Make a "packet" of the dried or fresh herb by wrapping ½ teaspoon of herb in a gauze pad as a small package. Dip the packet in warm water and let it soak to liberate the effects of the herb for 10 minutes. Use the packet to compress the gums daily.

Strawberry + Raspberry Leaves + Eyebright.[2] These are mild herbs, suitable for weakened individuals. Because of their astringent action, they help to strengthen the mucous membranes and reduce inflammation and bleeding. They can be used internally as a tea or topically, by making a packet (see instructions for plantain, above).

SEVERE STOMACH FIRE AND MOUTH SORES: AN ACUTE SITUATION

This condition is a true heat situation, both in a weakened, deficient individual who is overpowered by fire, or a strong, excess individual who has other signs of internal heat. When it occurs suddenly, like conjunctivitis or the flu, the Chinese call it a "wind invasion."

◆ **Acupressure Points for Treating Stomach Fire with Mouth Sores**

Treatment is aimed at clearing the heat and dispelling the wind.

Governing Vessel (GV) 14. Known as "Big Vertebra," this point dispels wind and heat.

Location: See page 166. Hold the point for 15 to 30 seconds.

Stomach (ST) 44. Known as "Inner Court," this point drains heat from the stomach and decreases inflammation.

Location: See page 176. Hold the point.

Large Intestine (LI) 11. Known as "Crooked Pool," this point relieves heat from the upper body and cools the mouth.

Location: See page 156. Hold the point.

◆ Herbal Treatment

Niu Huang Shang Zing Wan.[3] This combination has the heat-clearing herbs of cow gallstone, coptidis, borneol, platycodon and lotus; the wind-clearing herb of chrysanthemum; the blood-moving herb of tang kuei; and the harmonizing herb of licorice. It is contraindicated with pregnant animals. Use for 3 days only. If diarrhea develops, discontinue use.

> **Dosage:** cats/small dogs: 1 tablet, once daily
> medium dogs: 2 tablets, once daily
> large dogs: 4 tablets, once daily

Golden Seal. This herb clears heat and excessive moisture, as well as bacteria. Dilute 15 drops to 1 ounce of distilled water, and use 1 to 3 dropperfuls three times daily, depending upon the size of the animal. Do not use with pregnant animals.

◆ Topicals

Yarrow tea as a wash if you can get it into the mouth, or **watermelon frost ointment** which is available in Chinese pharmacies.

◆ Nutritional Supplements

For mouth inflammation and restoring healthy gums:

Vitamin B, from a non-yeast source. Avoid yeast, as there is an imbalance of bacteria and the animal may be more susceptible to yeast infections. Use half the human dosage.

Acidophilus or mixed culture. Use powdered supplements at one to three quarters human dosage.

Vitamin C, as rose hips with bioflavonoids. The bioflavonoids, especially with quercitin work synergistically with the vitamin C to help increase absorption and resolve mouth sores.

> cats/small dogs: 125 mg, twice daily
> medium dogs: 250 mg, twice daily
> large dogs: 1,000 mg, twice daily

Vitamin E: cats/small dogs: 50 IU, daily
> medium/large dogs: 400 IU, daily

Vitamin A: 2,000 to 5,000 mg for gum inflammation, depending on the size of the animal. Use three times weekly. If your animal has a history of liver problems, decrease dosage by half.

Zinc, 5 to 15 mg daily. This is especially helpful for red, inflamed, sore gums.

Bone Meal or **Alfalfa Tablets**, for calcium to strengthen bone around teeth.
> cats/small dogs: ¼ teaspoon daily
> medium/large dogs: ½ teaspoon daily

Kelp or **Dulce Powder**: cats/small dogs: ⅛ teaspoon, daily
> medium/large dogs: ⅔ teaspoon, daily

Co-Enzyme Q 10, an antioxidant developed in Japan used for healing the mucous membranes and detoxification.
> cats/small dogs: 5 to 10 mg daily
> medium/large dogs: 30 mg daily

Pancreatic Enzymes, to help digestion in the stomach. Use one third to one half the human dosage.

DIETARY RECOMMENDATIONS

This is the most important facet of the treatment. I recommend foods that strengthen the kidney and cool the stomach such as barley, millet, corn, well-cooked brown rice, asparagus, lentils, kidney beans, string beans, celery, ground pork (boiled, with fat skimmed off), sardine, eggs and carp. Raw beef cut into small chunks can be given. **Avoid** dry foods, as the processing of these foods incorporate heat and fat and will generate more heat in the body. If you cannot avoid dry food, use a clean "health food" commericial diet that's lower in fat with highly digestible protein. Supplement this food with well-cooked grain.

Endnotes

1. Holmes, Peter. *The Energetics of Western Herbs, Vol. II.* (Boulder, CO: Artemis Press, 1989), 463.
2. Moore, Michael. *Medicinal Plants of the Mountain West.* (Santa Fe, NM: Museum of New Mexico Press, 1979), 150.
3. Naeser, Margaret A., PhD. *Outline Guide to Chinese Herbal Patent Medicines in Pill Form.* (Boston, MA: Boston Chinese Medicine, 1990), 154.

The Lungs: The Metal Element

With every breath we take, we inhale the life force of the universe. This furnishes the lungs with "cosmic qi."[1] In addition to taking in oxygen, the lungs remove water from the air and direct it downward for utilization in the rest of the body.

The lungs are coupled with their yang partner, the large intestine to form the metal element. Both organs excrete waste: carbon dioxide and feces. The season associated with metal is autumn, and it is not uncommon to have asthma, bronchitis or allergy attacks at this time of year. The hours associated with the lungs in the Circadian Clock are 3 a.m. to 5 a.m., a time when lung problems may worsen.

In the Five Element Creation Cycle, the earth element of digestion (the spleen/pancreas and stomach) feeds the lungs, while the lungs feed the water element of the kidney. Thus, weak digestion or water supply to and from the kidneys may affect an individual's ability to breathe.

In the Five Element Control Cycle, the lung controls the liver and is controlled by the heart. Therefore, a weakened lung can alter the workings of either of these organs.

The emotion associated with the lungs is grief. Too much grief or sadness can create imbalance in the lungs. All too often, I have seen animals come down with bronchitis after the death of a human or animal loved one.

The lungs are sensitive to dry weather. Individuals living in dry climates may suffer from allergies, bronchitis or asthma. When the lungs are insulted, they produce mucous, lose their elastic nature and fail to inhale or exhale properly.

BREATHING

Breathing requires energy and tools. The energy is supplied by the lung qi, the digestive qi of the spleen/pancreas and the yang energy of the kidney. The tools are the lung tissues with their cells, air pockets and cartilage tubes, supplied by the lung yin with the aid of the underlying kidney yin.

When we inhale, we activate the lung qi. As the lung expands to receive the breath and air moisture, the yang of the kidney is said to "rise up and grasp" the breath at the end of inhalation. The partnership between the lung qi and the kidney yang helps move air moisture through our bodies.[2] The digestive qi from the spleen/pancreas and stomach also helps to fuel the breathing muscles of the chest and diaphragm.

If the lung qi, kidney yang or digestive qi are weak the individual may have weak, shallow breathing, especially when inhaling. If the lung or kidney yin is weak, exhalation is impaired.

COUGHING

Coughing can be caused by an external insult from the environment that first affects the nose and head (see wind and upper respiratory infections), or from an internal imbalance in the breathing process. From either cause, excess mucous forms in the air passages, causing irritation and coughing.

Individuals with good stores of lung and digestive qi, and lung and kidney yin and yang, will have an easy time shaking off a cough from an external insult. But those individuals with a weak breathing process can have a tougher time of it.

BRONCHITIS

When bronchitis attacks, it is usually from a wind heat condition. Instead of staying in the upper airway passages of the nose and the windpipe, the susceptible individual experiences a deeper invasion. The lungs' usual response to such an insult is for the mucous to become thick and yellow or green in color. This mucous replaces the normal lung fluids. It is unusual to see much mucous when our dogs and cats cough, because they tend to swallow it. Usually we just hear them gagging on it or notice their rough breathing. Because breathing difficulties can be life threatening, professional veterinary care should be sought immediately. In addition, the following suggestions may be of use.

◆ Acupressure Points for Treating Bronchitis

In acute bronchitis, we try to clear the heat from the lungs, stop the cough and alleviate the wind invasion. If mucous is sticking in the wind pipe, herbs can be used to help bring it up as well as soothe the irritated mucous membranes.

Lung (LU) 5. Known as "Cubit Marsh," this point clears heat from the lungs and helps to stop the cough.

Location: On the inside of the elbow, just to the outside of the major tendon of the biceps muscle. Flex the elbow. You will feel a strong tendon. The point is in the elbow crease to the outside of this strong tendon. Hold the point for 15 seconds.

Lung (LU) 7. Known as "Broken Sequence," this point aids the cooling fluid, or yin, of the lungs. Together with Lu 5, it is used to dispel phlegm from a wind invasion cough.[3]

Location: See page 173. Use a circular motion.

Governing Vessel (GV) 14. Known as "Big Vertebra," this point dispels a wind invasion.

Location and technique: see page 166.

Conception Vessel (CV) 22. Known as "Heaven's Prominence," this point is used to regulate movement of the lung qi[4] and stop the coughing in both bronchitis and bronchial asthma.

Location: On the sternal midline of the neck, just above the beginning of the rib cage. There is a notch in the center, where the neck enters the chest area. Apply light pressure on the point or a stroke in a downward direction.

◆ Herbal Treatment

Pleurisy Root.[5] Also known as yellow milkweed, this Western herb is used as an expectorant to relieve coughing, congestion and inflammation. For short-term use, up to 2 weeks. As tincture, dilute 15 drops to 1 ounce distilled water. Of the diluted mixture, use 2 to 3 times daily, depending on the severity of the symptoms.

> **Dosage:** cats/small dogs: 1 dropperful
> medium dogs: 2 dropperfuls
> large dogs: 3 dropperfuls

Fritillaria Extract Tablets.[6] This formula helps resolve coughing. It contains fritillaria and platycodon to clear lung heat; polygala to calm the heart and spirit; schizandra to dry the mucous and help the lungs; citrus peel to stop the cough and regulate the qi; and licorice root to stop the cough and harmonize the other herbs.

> **Dosage:** cats/small dogs: 1 tablet, 3 times daily
> medium dogs: 2 tablets, 3 times daily
> large dogs: 4 tablets, 3 times daily

Echinacea or **Golden Seal.** For descriptions and dosages, see pages 167, 176.

◆ Nutritional Supplements

See the recommendations for **wind heat attacks** in Chapter Ten, pages 171–72.

DRY, HACKING COUGH; DRY, WHEEZY BREATHING

Percy is a Toy Poodle who had a bout with bronchitis about a month before he was brought to see me. Ever since he was a puppy, Percy has had a hard time breathing normally. He could never really take a deep breath in. His breathing was short, shallow and rapid. Then, when his humans moved to

Palm Springs he had a hard time breathing in *and* out. The dry desert air made him extremely thirsty, his skin feel dry and his chest muscles lose their elasticity. It just seemed harder to expand and contract his ribs.

When his favorite family member left home to go to school, Percy became very sad. Out of the blue, he caught a cold that went to his chest. He was on antibiotics for two weeks which got rid of the infection, but the dry cough persisted and the whistly, almost asthmatic breathing sounds became worse whenever he exerted himself. His bark sounded hoarse and crackly. Percy avoided the sun because overheating seemed to make him itchy, which was a new development. He was tired, always thirsty, his mouth was dry and his tongue was cracked.

Percy was susceptible to the bronchitis attack because of his inherited weak lung qi. This was further weakened by the move to the hot, dry desert climate. Grieving for his departed human friend depleted his lungs even more. Percy needed nourishment for his lungs immediately to prevent asthma from developing later on.

Percy's treatment was aimed at nourishing the fluids of the lungs, and the yin in general which is supported by the kidney.

◆ Acupressure Points for Treating Dry Cough with Wheezing

General Note: For any of the lung problems which result in coughing or problematic breathing, general massage on the midline of the chest, starting either under the throat over the windpipe, or between the front legs and extending downward toward the belly can be used. Make a sweeping, stroking type pattern in a downward direction, with pressure that is invited by the animal. If the animal doesn't want to be touched under the chest, the other general area to massage is between the shoulder blades, along the back, in a back and forth motion. Usually the animal who is coughing or having a breathing problem will appreciate having one of these two areas massaged. The massage will decrease the frequency or severity of the cough.

Lung (LU) 7. Known as "Broken Sequence," this point opens up the lungs for greater expansion, and also connects with the yin surface of the body along the conception vessel meridian. This point increases the yin of the lungs. It is used for coughing and asthma.

Location and technique: See page 173.

Urinary Bladder (BL) 13. Known as "Lung's Hollow," this is the association point of the lungs and is used to balance the lung organ.

Location: See page 173. Use a gentle back and forth motion between the shoulder blades.

Kidney (KI) 3. Known as "Great Creek," this point will strengthen the kidney yin.

Location and technique: See page 187.

◆ Herbal Treatment

Mei Wei Di Huang Wan ("Eight Immortals Long Life Pills").[7] This is the classic kidney formula Rehmannia Six, used to moisten the blood and yin of the kidneys and liver, with herbs added to both moisten and astringe the lungs. It is used for chronic, dry coughing associated with lung yin and kidney deficiency. It contains rehmannia to nourish the kidney yin and blood; cornus to nourish the liver and kidney yin; dioscorea for spleen qi; plantago and moutan to cool the kidneys; hoelen to promote urination; ophiopogon to moisten the lung yin; and schizandra to strengthen and astringe the lung and kidney. Astringents keep the fluid where it belongs within the tissues so that mucous won't develop.

> **Dosage:** cats/small dogs: 1 to 2 pills, twice daily
> medium dogs: 4 pills, twice daily
> large dogs: 6 pills, twice daily

If the formula is too moistening, diarrhea or more difficult breathing may develop, because the lungs may be too weak to move the increased fluid. If this happens, cut dosage in half or eliminate it.

Yang Yin Qing Fei Tang Jiang (Nourish the Yin, Clear the Lung Sweet Syrup).[8] This formula strengthens the lungs, soothes sore throats and helps stop dry, chronic coughs, all after an insult has weakened the lung tissue. It has been used in treating tuberculosis and lung cancer. It contains rehmannia, peony, and ophiopogan to nourish the yin; moutan and scrophularia to clear internal inflammation; fritillaria to stop coughing; menthol to soothe the throat; and licorice as a harmonizer.

> **Dosage:** cats/small dogs: ½ teaspoon, twice daily
>
> medium dogs: 1 teaspoon, twice daily
>
> large dogs: 2 teaspoons, twice daily

Grindelia (Gumweed).[9] This Western herb is good for dry hacking coughs, especially if the animal is also very itchy from a depletion of lung yin, bronchitis and asthma.

> **Dosage** as tincture: dilute 15 drops in 1 ounce water. Of the diluted tincture, use 1 to 2 times daily, depending on the severity of the symptoms.
>
> cats/small dogs: 1 dropperful
>
> medium dogs: 2 dropperfuls
>
> large dogs: 3 dropperfuls

Coltsfoot.[10] This is the Western equivalent to the Chinese herb tussilago, which is used for coughing in general. In both traditions it is a "stop the cough" herb. It is astringent, bitter, sweet, cool, dry and moist, all at the same time. As tincture, dilute 15 to 25 drops, depending upon the severity of the coughing, to 1 ounce distilled water. Strong teas can also be used up to 3 times daily.

> **Dosage:** cats/small dogs: 1 dropperful
>
> medium dogs: 2 dropperfuls
>
> large dogs: 3 dropperfuls

◆ Nutritional Supplements

See suggested supplements on pages 221–22.

◆ Dietary Recommendations

Provide moistening and tissue-building foods. Meat proteins include pork, beef, beef liver, lamb, sardines, tuna, cod, clams and eggs. Grains include corn (polenta), brown rice, barley and millet. Rice is the grain associated with the lungs, so brown or white rice may be the only grain needed. Vegetables can be raw or cooked and should include asparagus, string beans, broccoli and spinach. Dry foods, because of their dry processing, should be minimized or eliminated during recovery period. Foods that are high in fat or very spicy such as garlic, should be minimized as they dry the body out more.

SHALLOW BREATHING, ASTHMA AND MOIST COUGHS

Some animals, like Percy, are born with shallow breathing. Some acquire it at a young age after a mild upper respiratory problem. Others may acquire it later in life after a bout with a serious lung infection. Shallow breathing along with shortness of breath upon exercise is a lung qi deficiency.

Qi deficiencies are almost always worse after exercise or stress. But in addition, if an animal is predisposed to having weak qi, he will show other signs, such as digestive difficulties and sluggishness, a weak bark or meow. Depending upon the severity of the condition, the animal may have a weak chronic cough.

Weak qi also affects the warming or yang of the body involved with the kidney. If the animal's kidney thermostat is not working properly (requiring him to have his own pet heater), the yang of the kidney may be low. This often accompanies a lung qi deficiency and results in excessive moisture getting trapped in the lungs. The dog or cat then develops moist breathing or coughing.

Asthma can come from a deficiency of yin fluids causing dry asthmatic breathing, or a deficiency of qi and yang warming causing moist asthmatic breathing. The individual's predisposition dictates which condition develops. If the yin is weak the animal is restless, thirsty, easily overheated and has a reddish tongue. If the yang and qi are weak, the animal is fatigued, cold, sluggish, thirstless and has a pale, flabby tongue.

Ryan is a large German Shepherd Cross who was brought to me because his breathing was shallow and he couldn't keep up with the other dogs or humans on walks in the hills. Ryan is very sweet, but timid around strangers. He tends to put on weight and is easily chilled. He hardly ever drinks water. He loves his walks, but needs time to recover from them. His early history is unknown as he was a foundling, so we don't know if he suffered from an upper respiratory condition as a pup. But his person reported that Ryan was susceptible to catching colds. He used to jump and run around with his dog playmates, but he no longer has the energy and seems either sad or disinterested. His bark has become weak and low and he coughs after exercise—the cough having a slight, gurgling sound.

When I examined Ryan, he had some weakness in his lower back and his hind legs trembled almost imperceptibly. His favorite position was lying down, and I could barely see his chest move when he breathed. His tongue was pale and slightly moist and his pulse was weak. His breathing sounded harsh and moist.

Ryan had signs of weak lung qi and spleen qi, as indicated by the weak, shallow breathing, the propensity for catching colds, the weak voice and the sadness. He also showed signs of weak spleen qi, such as fatigue, sluggish digestion, and his pale, slightly moist tongue. Weak kidney yang was indicated by the weakened hind end, wanting to lie down, the low bark and pale tongue.

We treated Ryan with acupuncture to strengthen his lung, spleen and kidney qi and yang. We changed his diet to include warming foods, which seemed to help his digestion and boost his energy level. Slowly, Ryan began to improve. He caught fewer colds and became noticeably stronger. He loves his walks, and can keep up with his friends. We were never able to completely get rid of his shallow breathing, but there has been definite improvement.

Lung imbalances can come from an underlying digestive or spleen qi problem. Cats who develop chronic allergic bronchitis or asthma are often large, sluggish and overweight. They have allergies to pollens, causing teary eyes and sneezing, and allergies to foods. They have pasty stools, and moist, rattling breathing. They may also have occasional bouts with bladder problems with frequent urination. The situation is similar to the weak lung and spleen qi and kidney yang problem discussed in Ryan's story, but here, the problem begins in the digestive system. Because of this, and because it is usually a long-standing problem, the liver becomes involved adding stagnation to the picture.

When these cats cough, they will gag and eventually dispel a small amount of frothy, white mucous or phlegm. But most of it remains trapped in the chest, causing very labored breathing.

Brutus was a cat with such a condition. He was a very regal large, black, short-haired cat with a white chest and alot of charm! He came to me because he had been diagnosed some years earlier with chronic allergic bronchitis. He was given Western drugs, including something to dilate his bronchioles and anti-inflammatory cortisone. Despite this, he was having a very hard time breathing. He had moved up to the San Francisco Bay area which is cool and damp, from Los Angeles where it is warmer and drier. When Brutus breathed, you could see his abdomen pumping and his rib cage moving only very slightly. His breathing sounded like a cross between a locomotive and a whistling bird. Because of his bulk and breathing problem, he was not very active. Brutus tended to have loose stools, and a pale, sometimes blue-purplish, moist tongue. It was difficult to find his pulse on the hind leg because it was buried so deep and pulsated without much force. During one exceedingly rough breathing spell, when the humidity was high, the coating on his tongue became very thick, white and greasy. This was a clue that there was an increase in the phlegm stuck inside the body. Increasing the Western medication proved ineffective. Acupuncture and herbs which dissolved the phlegm and warmed the interior of the body helped Brutus out of an emergency situation.

After each acupuncture session he seemed to feel better, and slowly the thick, white, greasy coating on his tongue disappeared and the blueness was replaced by pale pink.

◆ Acupressure Points for Treatment of Shallow Breathing, Weak and Moist Coughs

General Note: The general massage points listed for lung yin deficiencies can be used for any of the breathing or coughing problems in this section.

Conception Vessel (CV) 17. Known as "Women's Long Life," this point strengthens the diaphram and expands the chest. It is especially good for bronchial asthma and any coughing problems with or without moisture.

Location: See page 179. Hold the point with light pressure or use circular motions for 15 seconds.

Lung (LU) 9. Known, as the "Great Abyss," this is the tonification and source point of the lung. It is used for strengthening the lungs, clearing phlegm and helping to stop the cough, whether from asthma or bronchitis.

Location: Lift the front paw and flex the wrist. The point can be found on the innermost side of the wrist crease on the underside of the paw. Hold the point for 15 seconds.

Urinary Bladder (BL) 20. Known as "Spleen Hollow," this is the association point for the spleen/pancreas and helps the spleen qi with digestion. This point is useful in cases of lung and spleen deficiencies, including moist asthma and impeded phlegm type breathing.

Location: See page 204. Hold steady pressure on the point or use circular motion.

Stomach (ST) 36. Known as "Three Mile Run," this point is used for boosting the general qi of the body.

Location: On the outside of the hind leg, just below the knee, outside of the vertical portion of the main leg bone, the tibia. The point is in the middle of the muscle belly. Use steady pressure or a circular motion.

Stomach (ST) 40. Known as "Abundance and Prosperity," this point is an important phlegm transforming point. It is used for coughing with abundant mucous. It is especially important for individuals who get cold easily and whose breathing is moist and rattling.

Location: Located on the outer side of the hind leg between the bottom of the knee (stifle) and the ankle (tarsus). Divide this space in half. The point is located at this level just to the outside of the small leg bone called the fibula. There will be a depression between the two muscle bellies. Hold the point or use circular motion for 15 to 30 seconds.

◆ Herbal Treatment

Er Chen Wan.[11] This is the formula that regulates phlegm and moisture accumulation from weak spleen qi. The animal will have sticky saliva on the tongue or bubbly saliva on the gums or back of the throat. This formula contains pinellia which transforms cold, sticky or watery phlegm and sends it downward out of the lungs and stomach; hoelen, which moves dampness in a downward direction out through the bladder; licorice which helps spleen qi; and citrus peel which regulates spleen qi. Do not use if there is great thirst, which is a heat sign, as these herbs are neutral to warming.

Dosage: cats/small dogs: 2 pills, twice daily
medium dogs: 4 pills, twice daily
large dogs: 6 to 8 pills, twice daily

Inmortal (Milkweed, Asclepias).[12] This is a Western herb, traditionally used by the Spanish and Native Americans of New Mexico. It is a bronchodilator and helps expel mucous from the lungs via drainage of the lymph system. It can be used for asthma and bronchitis, and is especially indicated in kidney and spleen yang deficiencies and lung qi deficiencies. Make a strong tea by boiling ½ teaspoon of the powdered root in 1 quart water for 20 minutes. Do not give to pregnant animals as it increases uterine contractions.

Dosage: cats/small dogs: ½ teaspoon, twice daily
medium dogs: 1 teaspoon, twice daily
large dogs: 2 teaspoons, twice daily

◆ Dietary Recommendations

Foods that are warming and neutral are useful for shallow, weak breathing and moist coughs. Foods that create extra fluid, such as dairy products and raw vegetables, should be avoided. Choose from animal protein sources such as chicken, salmon, tuna, lamb venison and beef. Too much red meat or turkey will cause excess mucous production in some animals. Grains to choose from are white or brown rice, buckwheat, rye, corn and oats. The best vegetables are kale, carrots, cabbage and squash. These should be slightly cooked.

◆ Nutritional Supplements

These supplements are beneficial to the lungs in general and can be used in almost all cases of lung imbalances.

Vitamin C, as sodium ascorbate: 125 mg to 1,000 mg, twice daily, with diarrhea being the limiting factor.

Vitamin B Multiple: from ¼ human dose for cats and small dogs, up to ½ human dose for large dogs.

Cod Liver Oil, as a source of Vitamin A and fatty acid supplement. Use ½ teaspoon for cats/small dogs, 1 teaspoon for medium dogs, up to 2 teaspoons for large dogs.

Vitamin E or **Evening Primrose Oil**. Vitamin E can raise blood pressure, so if hypertension is a problem, stay in the lower levels.

cats/small dogs: 50 IU, daily
medium dogs: 200 to 400 IU, daily
large dogs: 800 IU, daily

Kelp Powder or **Seaweeds:** from ⅟₁₆ teaspoon for cats and small dogs, up to ½ teaspoon for large dogs, daily.

Quercitin and Bromelin:[13] 125 mg to 500 mg, twice daily, to help absorption of vitamin C.

Coenzyme Q-10. This substance helps with oxygenation of the blood. Researched at length in Japan, it helps to lower blood pressure, and acts as an anti-histamine and anti-cancer supplement.

THE SENIOR PATIENT

As our animal friends get older, they use up their hereditary qi and stores of yin and blood. Their respiratory tracts become less resilient and elastic. The muscles, which are serviced by the spleen qi, may also weaken, hampering the action of the diaphragm.

Many older animals, especially dogs, will begin to pant while at rest and seem to have something actually impeding their breath. They will tire easily, and although they may not cough, they huff and puff whenever they do any exercise. Western medicine calls this "chronic obstructive lung disease." In Western medicine this includes chronic bronchitis, allergic asthma, emphysema and any process that causes thickening of the cartilage in air passages. All these conditions decrease elasticity and oxygen exchange in the lungs. Once chronic obstructive lung disease takes hold, there is no real treatment offered by Western medicine.

Although we can't turn back the clock with total rejuvenation, Traditional Chinese Medicine is helpful in alleviating some of the symptoms and strengthening the qi that is left. Chronic obstructive lung disease falls into the patterns listed for lung imbalances. Because of its long-standing duration, and the roles played by the kidney and spleen, the liver may also be involved, adding stagnation in the chest and worsening all symptoms.

Because of its complex nature, and because of each individual's singular constitution, you will need to differentiate between the different syndromes listed earlier, and treat them accordingly. To help you differentiate which pattern fits your dog, here are some basic signs to look for.

Weak lung and kidney yin =
Dry, hacking cough or dry wheezing; thirst; restlessness; reddish tongue.

Weak lung qi and kidney yang =
Shallow breathing; moist wheezing; weak hind legs; lack of thirst.

Weak lung qi, spleen and kidney yang =
Excessive phlegm with coughing up little mucous; cold; all symptoms worse with movment.

Follow the appropriate acupressure, herbal and dietary recommendations for each condition. The following acupressure points and massage may be done as a tonic for the older animal with a propensity for lung problems.

◆ Acupressure and Massage to Help the Lungs of Seniors

- Rub between the shoulder blades back and forth for 2 minutes, using light pressure. This covers the association points for the heart, pericardium and lungs.
- Rub along the chest midline from the beginning of the first rib space to the second set of nipples. This covers the alarm points for the heart and pericardium.
- Acupressure at **Urinary Bladder (BL) 23** between the second and third lumbar vertebrae. This covers the association point for the kidney.
- Rub the outside of the lower hind leg from the knee to the ankle. Use random circular motion (the Tellington-Jones technique, see page 120) and light pressure. This helps the qi and disperses the phlegm.
- Using your fingers, brush downward and upward along the inside of the hind paws. This decreases liver stagnatinion.

Endnotes

1. Dr. Kuan Hin. *Chinese Massage and Acupressure.* (New York: Bergh Publishing, Inc., 1991), 76.

2. Kaptchuk, Ted. J., OMD. *The Web That Has No Weaver.* (New York: Congdon & Weed, 1983), 240.

3, 4. O'Conner, John and Dan Bensky, trans. ed. *Acupuncture, A Comprehensive Text.* (Seattle, WA: Eastland Press, 1981), 244, 174.

5, 10. Holmes, Peter. *The Energetics of Western Herbs, Vol. I.* (Boulder, CO: Artemis Press, 1994), 198, 206.

6, 11. Fratkin, Jake. *Chinese Herbal Patent Formulas.* (Boulder, CO: Shya Publications, 1986), 65, 64.

7, 8. Naeser, Margaret A., PhD. *Outline Guide to Chinese Herbal Patent Medicines in Pill Form.* (Boston, MA: Boston Chinese Medicine, 1990), 94, 90.

9, 12. Moore, Michael. *Medicinal Plants of the Moutain West.* (Sante Fe, NM: Museum of New Mexico Press, 1979), 80, 89.

13. Balch, James F., MD, and Phyllis Balch, CNC. *Prescription for Nutritional Healing.* (Garden City Park, NY: Avery Publishing Group, Inc., 1990), 10.

CHAPTER FOURTEEN

The Heart and the Pericardium: The Fire Element

The heart is the "prince of circulation," leading the blood through the vessels of the body. Of all the organs, it is considered the basis of the yang, whose warmth and activity maintain the fire in the body. Obviously, without your heart, you cannot live. In fact, it is said that the axis of the individual revolves around the balance between the yin of the kidneys and the yang of the heart.

In addition to its circulating responsibilities, the heart in Traditional Chinese Medicine is said to be the guardian of the spirit or shen. In animals, the state of the shen is seen in their behavior patterns. Normal emotional and mental responses are guided by the heart, and also by its protector, the pericardium.

In the Five Element System, the heart is one of the four fire organs. Its yang partner is the small intestine, while its cousins are the pericardium and triple heater. The heart and small intestine meridians are most active from 11:00 a.m. to 3:00 p.m., while the pericardium and triple heater are most active between 7:00 p.m. and 11:00 p.m.

The pericardium guards the heart, absorbing the first blows of insult. This is especially true in cases of mental or emotional trauma. Physically, the pericardium is the membrane sac that covers the heart. It can also be thought of as the boundary between the heart and the lungs.

Heart problems are usually indicated by difficult breathing and the curtailment of vital functions. When the heart malfunctions, fluids build up in the chest causing shortness of breath, coughing or pain. Such life-threatening symptoms will alert you to bring your animal friend in for veterinary care. However, these signs occur toward the final stages of heart disease. Emotional or behavioral changes or digestive disturbances may be early signs of heart problems.

The Chinese place great importance on the emotional and spiritual makeup of an individual. The emotion joy is associated with the heart. The puppy who is always romping and playful is considered "all heart." This is wonderfully normal. However, there are dogs who get carried away, becoming over-excited, barking with joy until they go into a frenzy. Some get so excited, they nervously pee at the arrival of their human. Still others are so emotionally taxed by abandonment or loss of a human or animal friend, they literally pine away and die of a "broken heart." Many of our animal friends are emotional sponges and take on the emotional state their households. Noticing and rebalancing these early disharmonies may prevent the onset of heart disease. Although Traditional Chinese Medicine cannot change heredity, it can mediate the way organs interact and therefore, minimize heart problems.

THE BEATS AND MURMURS MEET
YIN, YANG AND THE FIVE ELEMENTS

In TCM, heart imbalances can be divided into three main groupings: those with **too little blood or fluid**, those with **too little warmth or power**, and those with **too much heat** which causes the circulation to become stuck. Early signs of heart imbalances are usually of the first two categories, and to the Western practitioner, often may seem unrelated to the heart.

Let's review the heart in its Five Element interactions so that we may understand how these disharmonies manifest themselves.

First, remember that the heart's job is to circulate the blood which bathes the organs so that they stay calm and moist. So, the heart directly interacts with all the organs.

In the Creation Cycle, the heart feeds the spleen/pancreas and stomach element. If the heart is weak, the spleen/pancreas has to work harder to transform the food we eat into blood and energy. If the heart is weak, this can cause problems with **digestion of a nervous origin**, and/or **fatigue** or **excessive panting** after exercise or eating.

Without an adequate volume of blood circulating forcefully through the heart to nourish the spleen/pancreas, your animal friend may become nervous, restless or emotionally sensitive, especially about food. This can manifest as a picky appetite, diarrhea, vomiting or constipation that is emotional in origin, and brought about by nervous agitation.

The more agitated the animal becomes, the more fluids are used up through overheating and panting. This affects the kidney which keeps the heart's fire under control. With too little fluid, the animal will become very thirsty. When the control system between the kidney water and the heart fire of the body is disturbed, the animal will show other signs of nervousness, known as **disturbed shen of the heart**. This includes nervous peeing, more than normally active dreaming and paddling during sleep, excessive barking and a racing heart or palpitations during periods of excitement.

When the energy or qi component of the spleen/pancreas is depleted because the heart cannot supply enough circulating power, the individual will tire easily and not be able to keep up with her playmates. After exercise she pants and her heart races.

These imbalances are caused by the heart having too little blood or fluid and too little power and warmth to keep the circulation moving.

Individuals with too little blood or fluid are more sensitive during the summer and in hotter climates. They may also exhibit changes in the tongue. A healthy, pink tongue with good muscle, moisture and vitality show a heart in good working order. When there are cracks, especially deep and running down the center, it is said to be related to a weakness in the energy of the heart. Puppies who appear perfectly healthy can have very noticeable central cracks in the tongue. I always keep an eye on this as the animal grows older, because this is a sign of hereditary heart weakness. Regular exercise and good diet are important to avert further heart problems with these puppies. These

- **Nervous digestion from emotional disturbances**

- **Agitation, pacing, howling, excess barking**

- **Nervous urination**

- **Excessive panting, thirst and fatigue after exercise**

- **Unhealthy tongue with cracks**

symptoms are usually not recognized in Western medicine as potential preludes to heart disease, with the exception of excessive panting. However, in Traditional Chinese Medicine, they are early hints of heart imbalances.

Julie is an adolescent German Shepherd who was brought to see me because of frequent diarrhea and difficulty gaining and maintaining weight. She was a nervous dog who barked at everyone she knew, and was afraid of people and things she didn't know. Julie was supposed to be a watch dog and guard the house when her people were away. But instead, she cowered in a corner and even allowed a burglar to break in. Her person reported that after this incident, Julie was so upset she couldn't eat for a week. She absolutely refused any food in the mornings, although she would drink water. The diarrhea continued along with increased thirst after exercise. She had become extremely sensitive to noise and touch and seemed to be panting more.

When I examined Julie, I noticed that her tongue was dry and had a very obvious crack down its center. In the exam room, Julie paced and whined. I was told that at home she paced in the evenings at about 8:00 p.m. She was sensitive on the back diagnostic points for the heart, spleen/pancreas and the kidney and her heart rate was slightly elevated.

I felt that Julie was showing an early heart imbalance that was affecting the spleen/pancreas which accounted for the diarrhea and nervous appetite. This was worse during breakfast when the spleen/pancreas is most active. She also had an imbalance of the kidneys which created the excess thirst and panting. Her pacing occured during the hours when the pericardium, the heart's protector, was most active. The deep tongue cracks were in keeping with the diagnosis of a weakness of the heart.

I treated Julie by changing her diet to foods that helped the spleen/pancreas and heart such as millet, potato, mushrooms and string beans. Foods that nourish the blood, such as small amounts of beef and beef heart were prescribed, along with small amounts of chicken and rabbit. The association points along the spine for the heart, spleen/pancreas, stomach and kidney were massaged twice daily. We also added a vitamin supplement, including vitamin E, trace minerals and enzymes. Julie began to improve immediately.

◆ Acupressure Treatment of Early Heart Imbalances

Treatment is aimed at restoring balance between the heart and the spleen/pancreas and kidney.

Spleen (SP) 6. Known as "Three Yin Junction," this point nourishes the yin and blood of the body. It is the meeting place for the spleen, kidney and liver channels, thereby helping all three organ systems.

Location: See page 153. Hold the point for 15 seconds.

Heart (HT) 7. Known as "Spirit's Door," this point calms the shen and decreases palpitations. It balances the heart while stabilizing emotions.

Location: On the back (under) side of the wrist above the crease, just under the major tendon called the superficial digital flexor. The point is found just under the triangular depression formed between the tendon and the wrist bone. Flex the wrist while lifting the paw and gently massage the point in a circular fashion.

Conception Vessel (CV) 12. Known as "Middle Cavity," this is the alarm point of the stomach. It aids digestion and helps the stomach work smoothly with the spleen/pancreas. It is useful for vomiting and nervous indigestion.

Location: On the midline of the abdomen, halfway between the end of the cartilage extension of the sternum (xyphoid process) and the umbilicus. Hold the point or use a small downward motion.

Urinary Bladder (BL) 15. Known as "Heart's Hollow," this is the back association point for the heart. It communicates directly with the heart and helps to balance its energy.

Location: In the muscle depressions on both sides of the spine, at the level just at the end or behind the shoulder blades, in the fifth rib space. Use a slow back and forth motion.

♦ **Herbal Treatment**

For easy overheating, extra sensitivity, nervous urination, pacing, howling or excessive barking, especially at night: Tian Wang Pu Hsin Wan.[1] This formula is a combination of kidney yin and blood tonics; herbs to cool heat brought about by deficient kidney fluid and heart imbalances; herbs to calm the spirit; and herbs to promote the circulation. It contains rehmannia, tang kuei, schizandra, ophiopogon and asparagus to help yin and blood; scrophularia and platycodon to clear heat; zizyphus, biota, polygala and hoelen to calm the spirit; and salvia to promote blood circulation. Use once or twice daily, depending on the severity of the problem. Start with 1 dose and increase if no response. If diarrhea occurs, cut dosage in half.

    Dosage: cats/small dogs: 2 pills
                medium dogs: 3 to 4 pills
                large dogs: 5 pills

For nervous vomiting, loose stool that worsens with emotional upset, picky appetite, especially in the mornings: Kwei Bi Wan.[2] This formula addresses imbalances between the heart and the spleen/pancreas and stomach. It contains codonopsis, atractylodes and astragalus to help the spleen qi; saussurea to move stuck qi; tang kuei and longan fruit to help the blood of the spleen and heart; and hoelen, zizyphus and polygala to calm the spirit. **Dosage** is the same as for Tian Ma Pu Hsin Wan, above.

For distinguishable tongue cracks, easy overheating and panting, mild restlessness and agitation with new situations: Hawthorne Berries.[3] This cooling, nourishing and calming Western herb is a good all-around heart tonic herb. It helps the heart and kidney balance. As a tincture, use 10 drops in 1 ounce distilled water.

Dosage: cats/small dogs: 1 dropperful, twice daily
medium dogs: 2 dropperfuls, twice daily
large dogs: 3 dropperfuls, twice daily

◆ Nutritional Supplements

Vitamin C + Bioflavonoids. Vitamin C acts as a natural bronchodilator and antioxidant to keep the arteries clear of toxins and prevent thickening. Diarrhea is the limiting factor.

cats/small dogs: 125 mg, twice daily
medium dogs: 500 to 750 mg, twice daily
large dogs: 1,000 mg, twice daily

Vitamin B Complex[4] including thiamine and niacin, at ¼ human dosage for cats and small dogs, and ½ human dosage for medium to large dogs.

Vitamin E. For antioxidant use. High doses can increase blood pressure.

cats/small dogs: 50 IU, daily
medium dogs: 100 IU, daily
large dogs: 200 to 400 IU, daily

Essential Fatty Acids:

cats/small dogs: ⅛ teaspoon, daily
medium dogs: ¼ teaspoon, daily
large dogs: ½ teaspoon, daily

Taurine. An amino acid needed for heart contractility. Use 500 mg, 1 to 2 times daily, depending on the severity of the condition.

Lecithin Granules:

cats/small dogs: ½ teaspoon, daily
medium dogs: 1 teaspoon, daily
large dogs: 1 tablespoon, daily

Seaweeds. Low in sodium and high in trace minerals.

        cats/small dogs: 1/16 teaspoon, daily

        medium dogs: 1/4 teaspoon, daily

        large dogs: 1/2 teaspoon, daily

Bone Meal, for helping heart contraction and calming the nerves.

        cats/small dogs: 1/8 teaspoon, daily

        medium/large dogs: 1/2 teaspoon, daily

Coenzyme Q 10. An enzyme developed in Japan to help modulate blood pressure and increase oxygenation. It is used as a preventative in lower doses.

        cats/small dogs: 5 to 10 mg, daily

        medium dogs: 15 mg, daily

        large dogs: 25 mg, daily

Pancreatic Enzymes, to aid digestion.

◆ Dietary Recommendations

For agitation, poor appetite, vomiting and diarrhea: Neutral and nourishing foods for the blood and qi of the spleen are helpful. Such foods are beef, beef heart, lamb or rabbit. Because red meats can cause narrowing of the arteries, they should be alternated with fish and chicken. Grains include millet and brown rice. Green vegetables in season, potatoes and 1/2 teaspoon of grated beets can be added to the diet. If dry food is used, choose a "natural" type food with whole grains and one in which red meat is not the only protein source. Supplement the commercial diet with cooked grains and vegetables.

For agitation, thirst, panting, constipation and excessive dreaming: Cooling and moistening, as well as neutral foods that help the heart and kidney are emphasized. Dogs can be on commerical, vegetarian diets with small amounts of fish, rabbit, beef or turkey as a supplement. Grains such as millet and barley can be used, as well as celery, asparagus and mushrooms, lentils and kidney beans. Alternatively, stews with meat bones can be made with rice and vegetables,[5] non-fat dairy products such as cottage cheese or yogurt, are also moistening.

For cats, use fish and sardines in small amounts to provide omega-3 oils which help keep the arteries[6] clear of plaque. Rabbit and turkey are moistening meats. Dry foods should be minimized as the problem is a deficiency of fluid and dry foods are, of course, drying.

LIFESTYLE

It is very important to give the animal a calm atmosphere in which to live and particularly to eat. Feeding twice daily will reduce the burden on the spleen/pancreas. It is also important to provide regular exercise on a daily basis to keep the circulation from becoming stagnant.

LATER STAGES OF HEART IMBALANCES AND DISEASE

All individuals are different and are born with different propensities. Some tend to be dry or hot, others weak and cold. The later stages of heart disease in Traditional Chinese Medicine reflect these hereditary differences. They fall into progessive forms of **too little power or warmth to keep the circulation moving** and **heat that obstructs the heart openings.** In Western Medicine, this condition falls under congestive heart failure and forms of cardiomyopathy.

Later stages of heart conditions involve the qi or warming energy aspects of the spleen/pancreas, the lungs and the kidneys, which allow too much water to accumulate in the body. The signs are: coughing during exercise and at rest, especially at night; a clear, watery, nasal discharge; panting; short, shallow breaths; and extreme fatigue.

In more serious, advanced conditions fluid builds up in the chest and abdomen, giving the animal a "hanging belly" or distressed, labored, breathing. Your animal friend will stand with his front legs spread as wide as possible to give the chest room to expand. His feet or ear-tips will seem cool to the touch because the circulation isn't getting to the ends of the extremities. Also, the animal's tongue will appear slightly blue or purple, indicating inadequate

- Severe fatigue

- Coughing at rest or
during exercise

- Excessive panting or
distressed breathing

- Blue or purplish
tongue

- Heart murmurs

- Weight loss,
diarrhea

- A hanging belly

- Irritability when
touched around
the rib cage

oxygenation due to poor circulation. If you see any of these signs, take your animal to the veterinarian for immediate attention.

If, however, an individual is born with excessive and forceful tendencies, another type of heart problem can develop. This one comes for an **overactive liver** which leads to blood that moves in an uneven, jerky fashion.

In the Five Element System, the wood element of the liver feeds the heart, like wood fuels a fire. The liver is responsible for storing and circulating the blood smoothly. When the liver malfunctions, the circulation can become either heated, causing the heart rate to rise, or stagnant, causing the heart to contract more forcefully. Your animal friend appears to be on a short fuse, becoming angry easily and not wanting to be touched around the rib cage. He is also restless and very thirsty.

If the condition progresses, blood clots can form causing paralysis or strokes. The animal will have a very difficult time breathing. He will try to cough up mucous, but nothing comes up because it is very sticky and tenacious. This is an emergency situation, and the animal needs immediate veterinary care.

This condition in Western medicine occurs as end stage heart failure or forms of cardiomyopathy. In Traditional Chinese Medicine, it is known as heated phlegm that obstructs the openings of the heart.

◆ Treatment

Because of the extremely serious nature of the problem, the animal should be under veterinary care. The following acupressure points, nutritional supplements and dietary recommendations may be helpful in conjunction with medical treatment. There are herbs that can be used for heart conditions, but they are beyond the scope of this book. They can be found in professional guides.

◆ Acupressure

Heart patients are usually fragile. Acupressure is done by lightly holding the points or using very gentle, circular or back and forth motions. Choose only one or two points to work on per session. If the animal is too sensitive to touch, work energetically above the skin surface, about ½ inch.

Lung (LU) 5. Known as "Cubit Marsh," this point helps drain fluid from the lungs, enabling the animal to breathe more freely.

Location and technique: See page 211.

Stomach (ST) 40. Known as "Abundance and Prosperity," this point transforms and moves phlegm and excess moisture accumulation in the body. It is especially good for the individual who cannot cough up sticky mucous.

Location and technique: See page 220.

Liver (LIV) 13. Known as "Gate of Symbol,"[7] this is the alarm point of the spleen/pancreas. It influences all the yin organs of the body, helping to move fluid that is trapped in the abdomen, which gives the animal a "hanging belly" look. It is also helpful in clearing tightness in the chest because it removes pressure on the diaphragm and rib cage.

Location: This point is found at the end of the next to last, that is, the twelfth rib, in the last enclosed rib space. The enclosed rib spaces attach to the spine and to the sternum on the abdomen.

Stomach (ST) 36. Known as "Three Mile Run," this point tonifies the energy of the body, helping with circulation and strength of the lower legs. It also aids in the digestion and absorption of food.

Location: See page 219.

Urinary Bladder (BL) 13, 14, 15. Known as "Lung Hollow," "Pericardium Hollow," and "Heart Hollow," they are the association points for the lungs, pericardium and heart. These points help balance the organs of the chest and relax the diaphragm.

Location: On either side of the spine, between the shoulder blades, covering the 3rd – 5th rib spaces. Use a back and forth motion.

◆ Nutritional Supplements

All those listed previously for prevention and earlier signs of heart imbalance are useful, especially:

Vitamin C + Quercitin and Bromelin, to enhance oxygenation and reduce any asthmatic breathing.

> cats/small dogs: $\frac{1}{16}$ teaspoon, daily
> medium/large dogs: $\frac{1}{4}$ teaspoon, daily

Taurine: 500 to 800 mg, daily.

Lecithin Granules: 1 to 3 tablespoons daily.

Co-Enzyme Q-10, in higher dosage for oxygenation and blood pressure modulation:

> cats/small dogs: 10 mg, twice daily
> medium dogs: 20 mg, twice daily
> large dogs: 30 mg, twice daily

Proteolytic Enzymes to aid in digestion and relieve the load on the spleen/pancreas.

Trace Minerals, as the seaweeds.

◆ Dietary Recommendations

Just as with human heart problems, it is important to minimize the amount of salt and animal fat in the diets of our animal friends. There are special veterinary diets available which accomplish this. From the Chinese Food Therapy point of view an animal that has too much fluid accumulation in the chest or abdomen should avoid foods that bring extra moisture into the body. These include tofu, millet, and wheat. Grains to choose from are rye, oats, buckwheat, corn and brown rice. Although brown rice has salt in its hull, overall it helps the body to eliminate excess fluid. Meat protein sources include white meat chicken, mackeral with its high omega-3 oils and broiled carp or cod. Garlic is helpful to the heart and to eliminate fluids. Lentils are good filler to decrease meat protein and can be added to animal sources up to one fourth for cats and one third for dogs. Helpful vegetables include carrots, spinach, celery, kohlrabi, beets, broccoli and squash. Banana is a good source of potassium for those animals on diuretics.

For animals who show signs of heat, anger and irritability, have a history of high blood pressure or a tendency to throw blood clots, choose foods that are calming or neutral without being overly damp. These foods include fish, corn, rice, wheat occasionally, baked potato with the skin, beets, lettuce, celery, broccoli, avocado and chard.

CARDIOMYOPATHY IN CATS

The most common type of cardiomyopathy in cats is the thick muscle type. In this condition the heart muscle walls widen and the interior chambers of the heart that house the blood during pumping, shrink.

I believe this stems from a combination problem of too little blood or fluid for the heart to circulate, together with too much heat in the liver. Most cats with this form of cardiomyopathy are large, robust and assertive "liver" types. Because the liver's job is to smoothly circulate and store the blood, liver problems lead to erratic, forceful and uneven circulation. The other problem is an increase in heat as the hard-working liver overfuels the fire of the heart.

This physical workout causes the heart muscle to become enlarged. But the amount of room in the chest is finite, and part of it belongs to the lungs. At the same time, the rising internal heat uses up the fluid part of the blood, making the blood thicker and forming clots. As the heart's muscle enlarges, its inner chambers shrink. Some of the thickened blood becomes stuck in the heart or arteries.

You may see your cat's nose turn from pink to white occasionally, indicating a problem with the circulation. Or you may notice some behavioral changes. Many cats exhibit mood swings that match their irratic circulation. "Touch me, I love you," to, "Don't touch me. I'll bite you." Other cats seem generally apathetic. Unfortunately, these may be the only signs you will see before a sudden collapse with difficulty breathing, or paralysis if a blood clot forms in a main artery.

◆ Treatment

Because cats who develop this problem often hide symptoms until an "attack," it is difficult to know when to initiate preventative measures. Some of the early signs of heart imbalance listed here may be helpful. Cats with cardiomyopathy have a serious, life-threatening condition and should be under veterinary care. In addition, acupressure and nutritional supplementation may be helpful.

◆ Acupressure for Treatment of Cardiomyopathy in Cats

Urinary Bladder (BL) 15. Known as "Heart's Hollow," this is the association point for the heart, used to balance this organ.
> *Location and technique:* See page 229–30.

Conception Vessel (CV) 17. Known as "Women's Long Life Point," this point is used to aid the diaphragm, calm the patient and decrease palpitations.
> *Location and technique:* See page 179.

Liver (LIV) 2. Known as the "Walk Between," this point is used to smooth the liver circulation and cool the heat caused by an excessive liver.
> *Location and technique:* See page 156.

Spleen (SP) 6. Known as "Three Yin Junction," this point is used to nourish the blood and fluids of the body.
> *Location and technique:* See page 153.

◆ Nutritional Supplements

Taurine: 250 to 500 mg daily, depending on the size of the cat.

Co-Enzyme Q 10: use dosage as listed on page 236.

Chlorophyll and/or **Microalgae,** for B complex and for nervous tension: $\frac{1}{16}$ to $\frac{1}{8}$ teaspoon

Quercitin + Bromelin, as indicated on page 222, to enhance breathing.

Vitamin C: 250 to 500 mg, twice daily, if not experiencing diarrhea.

Vitamin E: Very small doses, 25 IU every other day, to help reduce cholesterol.

Lecithin Granules to help with fat metabolism: $\frac{1}{2}$ teaspoon daily.

Trace Minerals, as seaweeds.

◆ Dietary Recommendations

Unless there is anemia, minimize red meats, which increase cholesterol and hypertension. Small amounts of chicken heart once a week may help support the heart muscle. Use white meat chicken, carp, small amounts of mackeral and rabbit. If the animal is very restless and thirsty, small amounts of defatted ground pork can be used if mixed with cooked lentils or aduki beans. (See Chapter Seven for recipes.) Avoid dairy products which may induce mucous and clog vessels.

Grains to calm nervousness include whole wheat, brown rice and corn. If there is fluid accumulation use small amounts of amaranth and rye.[8]

THE PERICARDIUM AND STRANGE NEUROLOGICAL SIGNS

Lemon was a cat who looked like she had had one too many beers. She could barely focus her eyes, and kept falling over every time she tried to walk. She was frightened easily and didn't like loud noises. She would howl occasionally or make guttoral vocal sounds for no apparent reason. Sometimes she would walk around in circles, unaware of her surroundings. At other times she was lucid.

She had been to her regular veterinarian for lab tests, the results of which were normal. She did not have an inner or middle ear problem, although she was treated with antibiotics and cortisone. The drugs had no effect on her symptoms except to make her more hungry.

When I examined Lemon, she became agitated and began to tremble. She was so upset, she almost seemed to be having a seizure. This behavior along with her balance problems and intermittent awareness, led me to think that there was a problem with the pericardium.

In TCM, abnormal behavior falls under the auspices of the heart shen, but is usually treated by the guardian of the heart — the pericardium. Disturbed shen can manifest as circling, head tilts, stroke-like accidents, certain types of seizures, fear-biting or aggressive behavior, dizziness or lack of lucidity. Such mental/behavioral disturbances are considered a problem created when the normal fluids of the body are turned to "mucous" or "turbid, unclear fluids," that cloud the situation.[9]

When Lemon displayed her behavior pattern, I saw a problem that could be addressed by treating the pericardium and its disturbances. Acupuncture, using points on the pericardium, heart, gall bladder and liver meridians, helped to bring her back into balance. Additionally, I had her person give her daily massage on Governing Vessel 20, on top of the head, and Liver 3, on the inside of the hind legs, to aid blood circulation and clear channels. Lemon responded to treatment and returned to her normal behavior. This is an example of how Western medicine was unable to identify a pattern of imbalance and thus, was unable to successfully help the patient. However, Traditional Chinese Medicine was able to recognize a problem, effectively treat it and eventually return the patient to her normal good health.

◆ Acupressure for Treatment of the Pericardium Imbalances

Since there are too many types of problems that could fall under the category of pericardium imbalances, I will only list a few points that may be helpful. Please be aware that odd behavior can also be a symptom of a serious metabolic imbalance. Be sure to consult your veterinarian before making an at-home diagnosis.

Pericardium (PC) 6. Known as "Inner Gate," this point calms the spirit and regulates the flow of qi through the body. It can be useful in balance problems such as circling and falling over.

Location: On the back (under) side of the front leg, just above the accessory carpal pad which is the sole pad sitting just above the wrist. The point is between the two tendons that run very close together. Flex the wrist, and hold the point between the tendons.

Governing Vessel (GV) 20. Known as "Meeting of 100 Points," this point calms the shen and can be used for seizures, circling or confusion.

Location: On the top of the head, on the midline, in the notch just in front of the small bumpy protuberance between the ears. Use a small back and forth motion in the notch.

Liver (LIV) 3. Known as "Great Pouring," this point circulates the liver blood which bathes and calms all the organ systems, and restores blood deficiencies.

Location: On the inside aspect of the hind paw, midway between the toes and the ankle. Use an upward sweeping motion to encourage circulation along the liver meridian.

◆ Herbal Treatment

Calming herbs can be used to restore the nervous system.

Chamomile or **Catnip.** Either herb can be used as a tincture, at 10 drops to 1 ounce distilled water, using 1 to 3 dropperfuls, twice daily, depending upon the size of the animal, or as tea, ½ to 1 tablespoon per feeding.

◆ Nutritional Supplements

Use supplements similar to the heart imbalances, including **vitamin C, bioflavonoids, B complex, trace minerals,** and **oyster shell** at ⅛ teaspoon for cats; ½ teaspoon for large dogs, daily.

◆ Dietary Recommendations

Avoid foods that create an upward sensation in the body, such as garlic. Foods that produce mucous, such as dairy and red meats, should be minimized. Instead, use rabbit and fish as animal protein sources. Add foods that have a sinking effect, such as seaweeds. Pickled cucumbers are helpful for dogs as is dill. Celery and lettuce help calm the shen. Whole grains such as brown rice, whole wheat, millet and barley keep the system calm.

Endnotes

1, 2. Naeser, Margaret A., PhD. *Outline Guide to Chinese Herbal Patent Medicines in Pill Form.* (Boston, MA: Boston Chinese Medicine, 1990), 331, 272.

3. Holmes, Peter. *The Energetics of Western Herbs, Vol. I.* (Boulder, CO: Artemis Press, 1989), 257.

4. Balch, James F., MD, and Phyllis A. Balch, CNC. *Prescription for Nutritional Healing.* (Garden City Park, NY: Avery Publishing Group, Inc., 1990), 128.

5. Basko, Ihor, DVM. International Veterinary Acupuncture Accreditation Course. Philadelphia, PA, 1989.

6, 8. Pitchford, Paul. *Healing with Whole Foods.* (Berkeley, CA: North Atlantic Press, 1993), 126, 419.

7. Hwang, Yann-Ching, DVM, PhD. *Problems in Veterinary Medicine, Veterinary Acupuncture*, A. Schoen., ed. (Philadelphia, PA: J.B. Lippincott Co., Volume 4, No. 1, March 1992), 31.

9. Kaptchuk, Ted, OMD. *The Web That Has No Weaver.* (New York: Congdon & Weed, 1983), 214.

CHAPTER FIFTEEN

The Liver and Gall Bladder:
The Wood Element

In Traditional Chinese Medicine the liver is a resident of the middle compartment, or middle burner, of the body, along with its partner the gall bladder. It is large, dense and yin, and one of the few organs which can regenerate itself when damaged.[1] This is a useful trait in our modern life where the liver sustains so many insults, such as sudden or chronic inflammation, environmental toxicity and autoimmune diseases.

Due to its central location, the liver connects the breathing and circulating operations of the chest with the digestive functions of the abdomen. It acts as a pumping station in cooperation with the heart to filter and recycle the blood. The liver acts with the spleen/pancreas and stomach to properly digest food so that qi and blood can be made from what we eat.

The liver and the gall bladder make and then release bile into the intestinal tract. Bile and bile acids are necessary for digesting fats and absorbing fat soluble vitamins. The liver is also intimately related to protein synthesis and metabolism, breaking down and rearranging amino acids into useable or storable forms. It is during this process that the liver also clears toxic ammonia build up in the body. It stores excessive carbohydrates and participates in the conversion of these materials into glucose and energy.

In Traditional Chinese Medicine, the liver and the gall bladder form the wood element. In addition to its digestive functions, the liver is said to smooth the circulation of the blood and the qi, allowing the body to run smoothly without the stops and starts of a traffic jam. It is also said to store the blood, especially when the body is at rest. If you look closely at a piece of liver before it is cooked you will see that it is bloody and has an intricate pattern of vessels all through it. The liver is the picture of both storage and function.

Blood problems of all kinds, including high or low blood cell counts, abnormal blood cells, clearing old cells from the circulation, bleeding into the intestinal tract, bloody skin eruptions and eliminating toxins from the blood all fall under the guidance of the liver. In Western terms, this includes infections of the blood, anemia, blood cancers, inflammatory bowel diseases, skin and food allergies and autoimmune problems.

Blood is needed to bathe all the organs so that they stay moist, lubricated and functional. Since the liver stores the blood, it is responsible for moistening the sense and sex organs, the central nervous system, the skin and intestines, the joints and tendons. When the central nervous system is not properly bathed, seizures can occur. When our tendons and ligaments are dry, stiffness results. When the uterus or ovaries are undernourished, changes in reproductive cycles occur. Traditional Chinese Medicine is able to recognize and rebalance such patterns of illness before they develop into emergencies.

The liver is known as the "general of the blood," who keeps the troops in good spirits; moving when necessary and resting when possible.

The liver and gall bladder are said to be associated with the sinews and tendons of the body. A sinew is a tendon, but it is also defined as a "source of strength, power and vigor."[2] The general of the blood can be looked upon as the leader of the strength, power and vigor of the individual.

When the liver is out of balance it responds by becoming hot, dry or stagnant. Stagnation in the digestion is often the forerunner of most digestive upsets and pain. Because the liver is sensitive to the wind and the springtime, any condition brought on by either is a clue to liver imbalance. Additionally, the liver and gall bladder are most active from 11 p.m. to 3 a.m. in the circadian clock. So problems occurring then may point to a liver imbalance.

THE EMPTY STOREHOUSE:
HOW THE LIVER SHOWS ITS DEFICIENCY

Because the liver stores the blood and bathes the organs and sinews, if the liver blood is low, problems of dryness, such as anemia, constipation, infertility, irregular heat cycles, inadequate or inappropriate erections, stiffness, vision, dizziness, brittle fur or nails, fatigue or depression can occur.

The liver can become deficient in blood due to heredity or by environmental, dietary or emotional influences. In the Five Element Creation Cycle there are several situations that can weaken the liver such as: a weak kidney which nourishes the liver; a weak heart, which takes energy from the liver; or even a weak liver itself — all can cause a depletion of liver blood. A windy environment or continual toxic challenge in the air or water can overwork and weaken the liver. A diet high in fat requires excessive bile production which also taxes the liver, or a high volume diet can overburden the whole digestive system. Finally, anger, aggression or frustration can drain the liver. Rudy may want to be the only cat in the household and is stressed by the new kitten you just brought home, or Taffy may be bored and restless and need to run off leash more. Such emotionally stressful situations can create a drain on the liver.

◆ Stiffness and Inflexibility

When the liver is short on blood, it will first try to borrow it from its partner, the gall bladder. The gall bladder meridian runs along the head, neck, zigzags around the ribs and flanks, hips, knees and ankles to the fourth toe. This lengthy meridian serves many large and small joint surfaces and the tendons and ligaments along its course. If the gall bladder is short of blood to bathe the tendons and ligaments, the animal might have a stiff neck or hind limbs. You will notice that she is constantly changing her position in an effort to make herself more comfortable. The stiffness will appear to be worse after resting and improve with motion, as the blood begins to circulate. Your animal friend may experience numbness in the extremities which can cause her limbs to buckle under her, or you may see her dragging a leg. If the feet or ear tips don't get enough circulation they may feel cool to the touch. For the same reason, your cat might scratch a lot when she first gets up.

Stiffness and inflexibility of the body can also extend to behavior. These animals are downright stubborn. They want everything *their* way.

◆ Breeding Irregularities

Liver blood deficiencies can also cause breeding irregularities. The heat cycle comes approximately twice a year in dogs. Cats are spontaneous ovulators, which means that an egg does not drop until breeding is actually taking place. The feline cycle can be continuous depending on the season. Have you ever noticed that during the spring especially, cats are exceptionally amorous and many kittens are born? Remember that spring is the season of the liver. The kidney and spleen/pancreas initiate the first phases of the reproductive cycle, while the last phase is controlled by the liver. This is the time when the female animal is ready for breeding and is most receptive to the male.

When the liver is short on blood, it draws from the kidney. This can make the heat cycle weak, irregular or absent entirely. I have an intact female Toy Poodle patient, Priscilla, who has severe digestive problems. She cannot tolerate any fatty foods. As her digestive problems have worsened, Priscilla's heat cycles have become irregular. During the last year, she has not had any heat periods at all. She does become sexually excited but never fully cycles with blood. Priscilla's underlying problem is **deficiency of liver blood** which has affected her digestion *and* her reproductive system. Treatment has primarily focused on tonifying the blood stores of the liver.

If the liver's blood stores are weak, the liver can't move the qi or energy evenly. This makes the individual moody or irritable during the acceptance phase of the cycle. The female will never actually appear "ready." If approached, she may even be aggressive toward the male.

In the male, hormonal libido is under the auspices of the yang aspects of the kidney and the triple heater. However, sperm counts and stamina are affected by low liver blood stores. Low sperm counts, scrotal or penis irregularities or swelling, retained testacles and hernias all involve weak liver blood, stagnation and imbalances of the kidney and spleen.

On the other hand, if the liver is overly active, stagnation and heat can cause heavy bleeding with pain and downright meaness during breeding in the female, and inappropriate erections with aggression in the male.

SPAYING AND NEUTERING

As part of animal population control, we neuter the males and spay the females. I believe this is an important part of animal health, because it tends to keep aggression between males under control, to relieve an undue strain on otherwise continually reproducing females, and, of course, to prevent the killing of unwanted animals.

Whenever surgery is done on an animal, stagnation of the circulation or a disruption in the liver blood stores can occur. As we have seen, such liver imbalances can cause behavioral changes. After being spayed or neutered, many animals undergo what seem like personality changes. Some seem to be fatigued and have no interest in exercise, they just want to eat. This syndrome is caused by a deficiency of liver blood which is too weak to keep the qi moving. Treatment is aimed at nourishing the blood and qi with herbs, foods or massaging the appropriate acupressure points.

Other animals may become disobedient and willfull. They don't listen when called or they chew up shoes, papers or other household items. Most humans react with anger to such behavior, which in turn, frustrates the animal even more. In such cases, the liver (and the animal) becomes more stressed. These individuals show how a disruption of liver blood stores and stagnation of liver qi, can affect behavior. The best treatment is to give the animal a lot of exercise as well as restore some liver blood in the form of blood-rich foods. Exercise helps to smooth out the qi flow and the blood rich foods help to nourish the underlying deficiency.

LIVER BLOOD DEFICIENCY AND SEIZURES

Seizures can arise from liver malfunctions caused by too much heat or too much dryness. If the liver blood stores are severely weakened, they affect the fluids and yin of the rest of the body. Without enough fluid to cool the body, a relative internal heat or false fire can arise. The false fire tends to rise upward in a quick rush, and tremors are seen. If the false heat goes unchecked, the tremors can intensify to cause seizures. The upward "gush" is similar to a gust of wind and is considered an **internal wind** in Traditional Chinese Medicine. This type of seizure will usually be preceded by fatigue and shaking in an animal whose constitution is of a deficient type.

THE TONGUE AND LIVER DEFICIENCIES

Deficiencies of blood leave the tongue looking pale. If there is stagnation involved, the tongue will have a purplish tinge. The position of the liver and gall bladder on the tongue hologram is on the sides, so it is here that changes in the liver can be seen by signs of swelling, redness, roughness or dryness. If the fluids of the body are extremely depleted, the tongue will be a deep red with a purplish tinge.

◆ Treatment

All liver blood deficiency problems can be helped by nourishing the blood of the liver, kidney and spleen. These imbalances include anemia, low white blood cell count, impaired vision, joint or back stiffness that improves with movment, constipation, dry skin, irregular or weak reproductive cycles and deficiency type seizures.

◆ Acupressure Treatment for Liver Blood Deficiencies and Seizures

Liver (LIV) 3. Known as the "Great Pouring," this point is the source point on the liver meridian. It helps strengthen the blood and qi and can be used for *all* liver blood deficiency problems.

Location and technique: See page 241. Brush in an upward direction, along the direction of flow of the meridian to stimulate it, for 10 to 15 seconds.

Spleen (SP) 6. Known as "Three Yin Junction," this point is the meeting place of the liver, kidney and spleen meridians on the hind leg. It tonifies the blood and yin (fluid) of the body and can be used for *all* liver blood deficient imbalances.

Location and technique: See page 153. Hold the point for 30 seconds.

Urinary Bladder (BL) 18. Known as "Liver's Hollow," this is the association point for the liver. It is used to balance and strengthen the liver and can be used in *all* liver blood deficient imbalances.

Location: In the depressions on either side of the spine between the ninth and tenth ribs, in the ninth rib space. Find the point by counting backwards from the last rib space which is number twelve. Hold the point for 30 seconds.

◆ Joint Stiffness, Numbness and Weakness

Use any liver blood points plus:

Urinary Bladder (BL) 19. Known as "Gall Bladder's Hollow," this is the association point of the gall bladder and is used to balance it, help with joint stiffness and constipation.

Location: This point is located in the depression on both sides of the spine between the 10th and 11th ribs, in the 10th rib space. Hold the point for 30 seconds.

Gall Bladder (GB) 34. Known as "Yang Tomb Spring," this point benefits the liver and gall bladder, and strengthens the tendons and ligaments of the entire body. It helps in numbness and weakness of the lower legs and with constipation.

Location: On the outside of the lower leg, below the knee, in the depression just below the prominence of the head of the fibula (small bone of lower leg). Use circular motions or hold the point 15 seconds.

Gall Bladder (GB) 30. Known as "Encircling Leap," this point is good for low-back or hip pain, stiffness or numbness of the hind leg. It is also used for scrotal or genital pain or heat and skin rashes.[3]

Location: In the depression behind the hip, where the head of the femur (leg bone) fits into the pelvis. Use small, circular motions here, or use the palm of your hand over the entire hip in circular motions in both directions.

◆ Constipation and Skin Conditions

See Chapter Eighteen, pages 329–35, and Chapter Twenty, page 356.

◆ Reproductive Problems

Urinary Bladder (BL) 40. Known as "Commission the Middle," this point is used to clear heat and regulate water in the lower part of the body. It is useful in irregular cycling, groin pain, low back, hip and knee pain and stiffness and constipation.[4]

Location: On the back of the rear leg, behind the stifle (knee), in a depression in the middle of the crease of the knee. Hold the point or to use a short up and down motion for 15 to 30 seconds.

Conception Vessel (CV) 4. Known as "Hinge at the Source," this point is useful in irregular cycling, infertility, vaginal discharges, and premature ejaculation. It stabilizes the kidneys and qi of the lower body.

Location: On the midline of the lower abdomen. Draw a line connecting the umbilicus and the pelvis. CV 4 is approximately two thirds of the way down from the umbilicus. Use small circular motions or hold the point for 15 seconds. To insure treatment, massage the lower half of the abdominal midline to the pelvis.

◆ Seizures from Deficient Liver Yin

Governing Vessel (GV) 20. Known as the "Meeting of 100 Points," this point calms and balances the yang. It is useful in tremors and seizures.

Location: See page 241. Use a back and forth motion, or hold the point for 10 to 15 seconds.

Gall Bladder (GB) 20. Known as "Wind Pond," this point relieves wind in the body and is useful in treating seizures and tremors.
Location: See page 152. Hold the point for 15 to 30 seconds.

*Spleen (SP) 6, page 153, + **Urinary Bladder (BL) 18,** page 249, can also be treated.

◆ Herbal Treatment

Shou Wu Pian.[5] A general blood tonic for the liver and kidney, it is useful for eye redness and pain, dizziness, joint stiffness, dry skin and dull, brittle fur, short or weak heat cycles and low libido.

> Dosage: cats/small dogs: 1 tablet, twice daily
> medium dogs: 2 tablets, twice daily
> large dogs: 4 tablets, twice daily

Rehmannia Six or **Liu Wei Di Huang Wan.** This is a basic kidney blood and yin tonic, and is also useful for liver blood deficiency. It helps to relieve thirst, build blood stores, strengthen weak heat cycles and help impotence problems. It contains the blood and yin tonics of rehmannia and cornus; the qi tonic of dioscorea and hoelen; the false heat-clearing and draining herbs of moutan and alisma. If diarrhea occurs, cut dosage in half.

> Dosage: cats/small dogs: 1 to 2 pills, twice daily
> medium dogs: 4 pills, twice daily
> large dogs: 6 pills, twice daily

Alfalfa.[6] This salty, neutral and moist herb is helpful in restoring fluid and blood to the organs, especially the liver and slpeen/pancreas. It is helpful in anemia, dizziness, and depression.

> Dosage: cats/small dogs: ½ teaspoon powdered herb, daily
> medium dogs: ⅔ teaspoon powdered herb, daily
> large dogs: 1 teaspoon powdered herb, daily

◆ Dietary Recommendations

In cases of deficient liver blood, moistening, tonifying and blood building foods are needed. These foods are different from diets where the liver has been overtaxed and clearing is needed. If liver clearing diets are used here, the individual may become weaker. Also, as the liver is directly involved in digestion, feeding smaller amounts more frequently may be helpful for your animal.

Proteins such as small amounts of beef, lamb or chicken liver may be beneficial.

Muscle meat in general is beneficial for increasing tissue mass, and lean beef, rabbit, and white meat chicken are good muscle meat sources for the liver yin and blood. Enzymes help the liver to digest fats and other foods and eggs supply blood and yin. Grains such as wheat, millet and brown rice can be used and vegetables such as carrots, celery, broccoli, spinach and chard can be added to the diet. Dry foods should be minimized as this is already a dryness problem.

BILE FILLS THE MOUTH OR LACK OF SMOOTH LIVER FLOW CREATES QI STAGNATION AND HEAT

If the liver fails to do its job of smoothly circulating the blood, stagnation occurs. This affects the flow of qi as well as blood. The target organ most influenced is the spleen/pancreas.

In the Five Element Control Cycle, the liver controls the spleen/pancreas. When the liver becomes hot or stagnant, it creates digestive upsets, overpowers the spleen/pancreas, and causes vomiting, diarrhea and pain. Just as in the deficient blood conditions, prolonged stress, frustration, and emotional instability can unbalance the liver. Stress of all kinds is extremely hard on the liver, because one of the ways many of us, both human and animal, deal with it is by overeating or eating too quickly. Many situations can be stressful for our animal friends. Perhaps there is someone new in the neighborhood who likes to tease your cat, or a new member of the household who is getting the attention your cat is used to receiving. Maybe your house is being remodeled and your cat is spending her days hiding in a closet. Like humans, many animals will eat more when they are under stress. Because the liver breaks down fatty foods, increased consumption of dry food, which in many cases is greasy, will overtax the liver. In fact, almost any digestive upset manifested by vomiting or diarrhea that becomes worse when the animal is angry or irritable, is related to the liver. However, depending upon the predisposing constitution of the animal, different individuals will respond in different ways. An excess, alpha type, with an outgoing, in-your-face attitude, will become angry and exhibit a fiery digestive problem, with bile, blood mucous, straining and vocal pain. A deficient type, with timid inward tendencies, will be irritable, depressed or aloof and exhibit a more stagnant problem, with less blood, mucous or inflammation, but more straining and moisture.

If an individual overeats, particularly fatty foods or too many moisture producing foods, the spleen/pancreas can become overburdened and vulnerable to further attack from the liver. Such an animal may vomit bile, especially when the stomach is empty of food. Bile, along with other acids, causes acid-type indigestion, which will also make the animal uncomfortable. If the acid burns long enough or if the heat generated becomes excessive, ulceration of the digestive tract can occur. Your animal may smack her lips a lot or seem to want to eat something, but isn't sure what she wants. She may eat dirt if her stomach is burning from the excess acids. The rib cage area and stomach hurt and she will resist being touched in those places. In Western terms, this would be considered upper inflammatory bowel disorder.

If there is diarrhea, it will include frequent, labored straining. This occurs because stagnation causes blockage and pain along its route. From the inflammation there may be mucous, blood and a very foul odor. The animal will refuse to be picked up or touched. This is known in Western terms as lower irritable or inflammatory bowel disorder.

Sylvia is a Samoyed. She was diagnosed with irritable bowel syndrome by her regular vet but she responded only partially to the steriod and antibiotic therapy that was perscribed. When the medication was stopped, the symptoms returned. While on the medications, she had been losing weight steadily and this convinced her humans to bring her to see me.

Sylvia had been abused as a puppy by her original family and was given up for adoption. When she arrived in her new home, she was thin, nervous and highly strung. She seemed very hungry all the time, but vomited everything she ate hours after eating. Sometimes she even vomited bile alone between meals. Sylvia alternated between having constipation and diarrhea, and in either case the bowel movement seemed painful for her. Sometimes there was blood present and in both cases the stool was extremely foul smelling.

Sylvia had another problem, which her humans thought stemmed from her early childhood abuse. She was unpredictable around children. When they tried to pet her, sometimes she was fine but sometimes she would turn around and snap at them. She was the same way with other dogs she met while out walking. Because of this, her humans always kept her on the leash. This frustrated all three of them because Sylvia loved to run and her humans wanted her to have the exercise.

Sylvia was also constantly thirsty. She had an itchy right eye which looked very dry on the surface. She was sensitive to the sun, and sometimes the affected eye had a thick, greenish discharge.

When I examined Sylvia, she was very cautious with me. When I tried to touch her around the rib cage she cried out and her stomach was very noisy. When she burped in my face it smelled quite foul. The association points of the liver, gall bladder, spleen and stomach were extremely sensitive and her tongue was red in color with a yellowish moss on it.

My diagnosis was **liver fire and stagnation.** It was probably attributable to the anger of her puppyhood abuse, or to the fatty, dried foods she was fed. Because the situation had gone on for such a long time, the fire was beginning to consume her fleshy substance, underlying blood stores and tongue coating, making her thin, dry-eyed and ready to fly off the handle at the least provocation.

I treated Sylvia by first clearing the liver fire and then breaking up the stagnation. Later she was given herbs to strengthen her blood and qi.

◆ The Tongue and Excess Liver Fire

If you look at the tongue, it will appear red or reddish purple. The coating is thick and mossy and dirty white or yellow in color. Because this is an excess situation, there is excess tongue coating.

◆ Liver Qi Stagnation: Cysts, Food and Allergies

Sometimes stagnation can occur on its own, without the additional factor of excess heat. The symptoms are not recognized in Western medicine as a pattern, but I am mentioning it here because it fits some of the problems we see today in our animals. Stagnation can bind the body's energy, blocking circulation, digestion, or forming cyst-like lumps. Stagnation causes pain, discomfort and agitation. It is as though one were being bound by a rope. The Chinese call this "binding of the qi."[7]

This kind of stagnation can block the circulation in the digestive tract. Humans get what is known as a "plum pit" feeling in the throat. It's as though there is a ball stuck in the back of your throat, making it difficult to swallow. Animals may look as if they are swallowing repeatedly. They want to be stroked under the neck or they may vomit up water or mucous or have a nervous stomach with a poor appetite.

When there is a binding of the qi, swelling in the groin area may occur. Often an animal will lick or groom this area in order to try to move the qi such as the cat who licks all the hair off her abdomen for no apparent reason. The skin appears clear and free of redness or scabs. She just keeps licking and grooming. She is irritable and doesn't want to be touched except on her head. I believe this is qi stagnation occurring *before* irritable bowel syndrome sets in.

Liver qi stagnation causes inflammation in the digestive tract when the circulation becomes stuck, allowing heat to develop in some parts of the intestine and cold pockets in others. Think of stop and go traffic on the freeway during rush hour. Food is lurching along the intestine, sitting in some places while moving very rapidly through others. When this occurs, the digestive tract becomes sensitive to many foods and allergies can develop.

HEPATIC LIPIDOSIS

Stagnation can lead to a condition which in cats is called hepatic lipidosis. It is a congestion of the liver which causes the cat to stop eating. This is another case of the liver overpowering the spleen and is often a forerunner of hepatitis. It commonly happens to big, overweight or stocky cats with excess type personalities who tend to overeat or eat large amounts at one time. These traits overwork first the liver and then the spleen/pancreas, causing the cat to stop eating. This excess condition creates the stagnation that results in hepatic lipidosis.

◆ **After the Acute Incident of
   Lipidosis or Hepatitis**

Once the liver is damaged during an acute episode of lipidosis or hepatitis, it must be restored, or a chronic type of syndrome can occur called chronic hepatits or cirrhosis of the liver. Emotional stress or rich, high fat, high volume eating can trigger a return of the condition.

The chronic condition is one of stagnation and deficiency. The liver has been so excessively insulted that its stores are eventually used up. If poor eating habits or emotional anger and frustration continue, the liver cannot recover. Eventually, it hardens and shrinks in size.

SEIZURES FROM EXCESSIVE LIVER HEAT

As with the liver blood deficiency and stagnation, the rising heat can also come in gusts, like the wind. But with in an individual with a predisposition to a firey liver, the nature of the seizure is more violent and frequent. Your animal friend will be agitated and angry but not necessarily fearful. The seizures may happen at any time of the day or night and usually occur in clusters. Your animal will probably want to eat after the seizure.

◆ Treatment

In liver flow problems, treatment is aimed at clearing the heat if there is excess fire rising upward and unblocking the stagnation. Usually harmonizing the energy between the liver, gall bladder and spleen/pancreas and stomach is done. In all cases the goal is to restore the normal flow of qi and blood.

◆ Acupressure Treatment for Vomiting of Bile or Food

Conception Vessel (CV) 14. Known as "The Great Palace," this is the alarm point of the heart. I call it the heartburn point. It helps to calm the spirit and decrease vomiting of food or bile. It is also useful in chronic hepatitis.[8]

Location: See page 204. Hold the point with light pressure for 10 to 15 seconds.

Conception Vessel (CV) 12. Known as "Middle Cavity," this is the alarm point of the stomach. It is good for any kind of vomiting, including bile, mucous, water and food. It relieves stagnation and heat from the stomach and is also indicated for ulcers in the stomach.

Location: See page 229. Hold the point for 10 to 15 seconds.

Liver (LIV) 2. Known as the "Walk Between," this point clears heat and unblocks stagnation in the liver.

Location and technique: See page 156.

◆ Herbal Treatment

Golden Seal + Dandelion + Chamomile. This combination of Western herbs will cool the stomach, clear the liver and move and smooth the stagnant qi. Use once or twice daily, depending upon severity of the situation. In 1 ounce distilled or spring water, use tinctures as follows:

Golden Seal – 10 drops
Dandelion – 5 drops
Chamomile – 5 drops
Dosage: cats/small dogs: ½ to 1 dropperful
medium dogs: 1 to 2 dropperfuls
large dogs: 2 to 3 dropperfuls

Shu Gan Wan (Comfort Liver Pills).[9] This formula smooths the liver qi, unblocks stagnation and decreases vomiting due to hyperacidity such as when the animal is regurgitating food, mucous or bile from an empty stomach. The formula includes qi regulators and activators of melia toosendan, curcuma, aquilaria, saussurea, alpine katsumada seed, citrus and amomi. Qi and blood tonifiers hoelen and peony are added along with corydalis for pain relief in the liver and stomach area. Because of its qi activating herbs, this formula is contraindicated during pregnancy.

Dosage: cats/small dog: 1 pill, twice daily
medium dogs: 2 to 3 pills, twice daily
large dogs: 4 to 5 pills, twice daily

Herbs to harmonize the liver and spleen are discussed in Chapter Sixteen, page 276.

Treatment for diarrhea with blood, mucous and straining is listed in Chapter Eighteen, pages 326–29.

HEPATITIS

If the heat and stagnation of the liver become severe, it overpowers the spleen/pancreas and creates a congestion of moisture which blocks the bile ducts and cannot move. This moisture turns yellow from bile and acids and travels through the body. Your animal will have noticeable jaundice on the inside of the ears, the mouth and the visible skin. If an organism is involved, it is called infectious hepatitis. As this is a life threatening situation, the animal should be under medical supervision.

As your animal will be under the care of a veterinarian, the following list of acupressure points may be used along with Western treatment.

Liver (LIV) 14. Known as "Expectation's Door," this is the alarm point of the liver. It is used to balance the organ and helps spread the liver qi and transform dampness in the liver and spleen.

Location: Located along the rib cage, in the 6th rib space, toward the area where the rib connects with its soft cartilage extension. You can feel this because there is a slight bump at the joining point between the rib and the softer cartilage. The easiest way to locate this point is to count backwards from the last enclosed rib space which is the 11th rib space (between the 11th and 12th ribs). You may hold the point, or lightly stroke in a downward direction along the entire rib space to make certain you have covered the point. Use light pressure, as the animal may be very sensitive.

Liver (LIV) 13. Known as "Gate of Symbol," this is the alarm point of the spleen. It is used to balance the organ, and to remove the congested damp heat from it. It is also used for jaundice, enlargement of the liver and the spleen and pain.

Location: See page 235. Hold the point, or stroke downwards along the entire rib space. Light pressure is needed as the animal may be sensitive.

◆ Herbal Treatment

During an acute situation, the animal may not tolerate anything orally. See the following section on chronic hepatitis and cirrhosis, for herbal recommendations.

CHRONIC HEPATITIS AND CIRRHOSIS

In both of these cases there is a tendency for the liver qi to be stagnant. In chronic hepatitis there are flareups with heat that is still "true" or excessive heat. In cirrhosis, the liver is so damaged that it shrinks, and the yin substance of the organ is lacking. In both cases, supporting the liver qi with its spreading capacity, and renewing and restoring the blood and yin is helpful.

In chronic hepatitis, flareups with fever and jaundice should be treated as acute situations that require clearing. After the acute flareup, strengthening the liver is the most essential aspect of treatment. The symptoms include pain when touched around the rib cage, some agitation, anxiety or depression, intermittent diarrhea and constipation. If the fluid is very deficient there will be excessive thirst. There may be low grade vomiting, or vomiting of bile. The animal will be sluggish and somewhat fatigued, due to qi stagnation and deficiency. This may make the animal more prone to catching colds or viruses.

◆ Acupressure Treatment for Chronic Hepatitis and Cirrhosis

Urinary Bladder (BL) 18. Known as "Liver's Hollow," this is the association point of the liver and is used to balance and strengthen this organ.
Location: See page 249. Massage back and forth in small strokes.

Urinary Bladder (BL) 19. Known as "Gall Bladder's Hollow," this is the association point of the gall bladder. It is used to balance and strengthen the organ, allowing free bile formation and flow.
Location: See page 249. Rub back and forth in small motions.

Liver (LIV) 3. Known as "Great Pouring," this point strengthens the liver and spreads the qi. If heat is present, it clears the heat by opening the channels to allow the free flow of qi.
Location and technique: See page 241.

Stomach (ST) 36. Known as "Three Mile Run," this point helps the qi of the entire body. Don't use it if there is a fever present.
Location: See page 219. Use mild circular motions for 10 seconds.

◆ Herbal Treatment

Milk Thistle.[10] This Western herb clears dampness and promotes bile flow. It is especially useful in the stages of jaundice where there is a light yellow color. The herb helps protect the cell walls of the liver to avoid toxic substances from entering and is also useful in chronic situations. It can be found in natural food stores as the nutritional supplement silymarin. Both the fruit and seeds of the plant are used.

As a tincture, dilute 20 drops in 1 ounce of distilled water. Boil off the excess alcohol by heating the dilution without its cover for 3 minutes over boiling water.

Dosage: cats/small dogs: 1 dropperful, twice daily
medium dogs: 2 dropperfuls, twice daily
large dogs: 3 dropperfuls, twice daily

Celandine.[11] This herb known in homeopathy and botanically as chelidonium, is used for short periods of up to two weeks to help promote bile flow, open obstructions and to clear dampness. Use celandine with milk thistle.

As a tincture, dilute 15 drops to 1 ounce distilled water.

Dosage: cats/small dogs: 1 dropperful, once daily
medium dogs: 2 dropperfuls, once daily
large dogs: 2 dropperfuls, twice daily

Oregon Grape Root.[12] Useful to clear the liver of toxins, heat and dampness.
As tincture, dilute 15 drops to 1 ounce of distilled water

Dosage: cats/small dogs: 1 dropperful, once or twice daily
medium dogs: 2 dropperfuls, twice daily
large dogs: 3 dropperfuls, twice daily

Dandelion + Burdock Roots + Agrimony, to clear dampness and facilitate liver blood and bile flow. This combination can be used for two to three weeks following an episode of liver stagnation, heat and dampness.

As tinctures, dilute 10 drops each of dandelion and burdock plus 1 drop agrimony in 1 ounce distilled water.

Dosage: cats/small dogs: 1 dropperful per day
medium dogs: 2 dropperfuls per day
large dogs: 3 dropperfuls per day

Shou Wu Pian, as listed on page 251, for liver blood deficiency conditions.

LIVER QI STAGNATION

These are nonspecific Western symptoms that in Traditional Chinese Medicine form the pattern discussed on page 255. This condition precedes digestive insults that cause ulcers, food allergies, swellings along the mammary glands or in the groin area, and excessive grooming for no apparent reason.

◆ Acupressure Treatment for Liver Qi Stagnation

General massage along the **Conception Vessel**, which runs along the midline of the chest and abdomen. Begin the light massage in a downward direction from the tip of the rib cage to the pelvis and back again. This facilitates the movement of blood and qi.

Liver (LIV) 3. Known as "Great Pouring," this is the liver source point and facilitates the flow of qi and blood through the liver.
Location and technique: See page 241.

OR

Liver (LIV) 2. Known as the "Walk Between," this point facilitates the flow of qi and the clearing of heat. If the animal is angry, not merely agitated, or if there is vomiting of food, and the animal is very sensitive to touch around the rib cage, this may be the point to use in place of **Liver 3**.
Location and technique: See page 156.

Gall Bladder (GB) 41. Known as "Near Tears on the Foot," this point is used for swellings along the mammary gland or scrotal areas. It spreads and drains the qi and blood of the liver and gall bladder channels. It is a good point to use for the cat who continually grooms the abdomen or inside of the legs for no apparent reason. For this purpose, it can be used in combination with **Liver 2.**

Location: See page 157. Hold the point for 15 seconds.

HEPATIC LIPIDOSIS

◆ Acupressure

Choose points from liver qi stagnation page 262. If there is jaundice, choose points from the hepatitis section, page 259.

◆ Seizures

Seizures will be violent and frequent. The animal will be of an excessive constitution. Treatment is aimed at relieving the wind, clearing the heat and unblocking the channels.

◆ Acupressure Treatment for Seizures

Gall Bladder (GB) 20. Known as "Wind Pond," this point relieves wind, calms the spirit and clears heat from the gall bladder.

Location and technique: See page 152.

Governing Vessel (GV) 20. Known as the "Meeting of 100 Points," this point calms the spirit, balances the yang of the body and sedates seizures.

Location and technique: See page 241.

Liver (LIV) 2. Known as the "Walk Between," this point clears heat from the liver and unblocks qi stagnation.

Location and technique: See page 156.

Heart (HT) 7. Known as "Spirit's Door," this point calms the spirit and opens the channels, to unblock stagnation.

Location: See page 229. Hold the point for 15 seconds.

◆ Nutritional Supplements for All Liver Conditions

Enzyme combinations to break down proteins and fats may be useful.

Vitamin B 12. This vitamin is stored in the liver. It is essential for blood cell production with iron and hemoglobin which carry the oxygen. It is useful in anemias. Use in conjunction with vitamin B complex.

Vitamin B Complex, at the 30 mg level.

Vitamin C, as sodium ascorbate. If the individual can tolerate vitamin C, it is extremely helpful in restoring cellular function to the liver, as well as providing antioxidant action.

> cats/small dogs: 250 mg, twice daily
> larger dogs: 1,500 mg, twice daily, with diarrhea as the limiting factor.

Bioflavonoids and Quercitin, for food allergies, at the 10 mg level.

Chlorophyll, ⅓ human dose.

Lecithin Granules, to clear arteries of build up of toxins.

> cats/small dogs: 1 teaspoon, once or twice daily
> medium/large dogs: 1 tablespoon, once or twice daily

Acidophilus and **Pro-biotics,** to repopulate the intestine with healthy flora. Use one third the human dosage.

Coenzyme Q 10. This enzyme aids in oxydation and clearing toxins.

> cats/small dogs: 10 mg
> medium/large dogs: 50 mg

Trace Minerals and **Microalgae.** These help in mineral storage necessary for liver function. Because the liver stores copper, it is subject to deficiency when the liver malfunctions. It is very helpful in anemias.

Vitamin E, in low levels as an antioxidant. Since the liver needs bile to break down fat-soluble vitamins, overloading of A, E or K will tax the liver.

> cats/small dogs: 50 IU daily
> medium/large dogs: up to 200 IU daily

◆ Dietary Recommendations

Diet is of utmost importance in maintaining a healthy liver. Above all, it is important to feed your animal friend in small portions, three times daily to decrease the stress on the liver.

Cooling foods are essential when heat is present. However, if only cooling foods are used, they can further stagnate the qi. Therefore, it is necessary to use neutral meats and grain proteins with vegetables of all thermal types.

The liver is sensitive to meat proteins which are broken down into amino acids. When broken down, ammonia is formed as a by-product. It is the liver's job to rid the toxic ammonia from the body. If the liver is weak, it has a hard time doing this, so meat proteins should come from easily digestible foods and given in small amounts.

Protein sources should be from hard-boiled egg and non-oily fish, such as cod. If meat is used, rabbit is useful because it has yin qualities, and speeds up the metabolism to encourage the qi to move. (Personal communication P. Pitchford) Small amounts of white meat chicken may be added for its qi tonification and qi moving ability. Protein, however, should be minimal: approximately 15% for dogs to 20% for cats.

The only exception to this is the cat with hepatic lipidosis. According to Western research,[14] high protein foods can be used to increase energy.

Grains should include whole wheat (as bread, or flakes), millet, and thoroughly cooked brown or white rice. If whole grains are too difficult to break down, white flour pasta can be used.

Vegetables should include grated beet, spinach, chard and kale. Small amounts of squash can be added if no bile is being vomited. Broccoli and cabbage are helpful in clearing the liver.

Endnotes

1. Balch, James F,. MD and Phyllis A. Balch, CNC. *Prescription for Nutritional Healing.* (Garden City Park, NY: Avery Publishing Group, Inc., 1990), 140.

2. *Random House Dictionary, Unabridged Edition,* (New York: Random House, 1967), 1330.

3, 4, 8. O'Conner, John and Dan Bensky, ed. trans. *Acupuncture A Comprehensive Text.* (Seattle, WA: Eastland Press, 1981), 263, 280, 178.

5. Fratkin, Jake. *Chinese Herbal Patent Formulas.* (Boulder, CO: Shya Publications, 1986), 182.

6, 10, 11. Holmes, Peter. *The Energetics of Western Herbs, Vol. I.* (Boulder, CO: Artemis Press, 1989), 370, 159, 156.

7. Wiseman, Nigel, Andrew Ellis, Paul Zmiewski. *Fundamentals of Chinese Medicine.* (Brookline, MA: Paradigm Publications, 1985), 232.

9. Naeser, Margaret A., PhD. *Outline Guide to Chinese Herbal Patent Medicines in Pill Form.* Boston, MA: (Boston Chinese Medicine, 1990), 214.

12. Moore, Michael. *Medicinal Plants of the Mountain West.* (Santa Fe, NM: Museum of New Mexico Press, 1979), 117.

13, 14. Tennant, B. *Compendium of Continuing Education for Practitioners.* Pract. Ve. 14(8)1054-1068, 1993.

CHAPTER SIXTEEN

The Spleen/Pancreas and Stomach: The Earth Element

Either directly or indirectly, the earth produces food for all of us who live on it. For plants to grow and thrive in the earth, they need sun and water. If there is not enough sun, the plants grow slowly and are weak. If there is too much sun, the soil becomes parched and devoid of nutrients and the plants wither. If there is not enough water, the plants can't mature and flourish. If there is too much water, and the land becomes flooded, the soil turns to mud. Most plants are not happy in mud. They rot and die. Therefore, balance between the elements and climate is needed to keep the soil productive.

The earth element of the body is like the earth of our planet. The earth or soil provides an environment for seeds to take root and grow into plants. It also provides nutrients and moisture to nourish these plants, which in turn, nourish the animals who eat them. It is able to do this because it receives the remains of dying plants and animals and transforms these remains into nutrition for the next generation of life. So we see that the earth element's job is to transform and distribute whatever is consumed as food into useable nutrients, energy and finally, flesh. The Chinese call this **nutritive qi.**[1]

Just as the soil needs water and warmth in order to perform this transformation process, the body also requires just the right balance of these elements. If there is not enough internal fire to fuel the digestive process, the body becomes easily fatigued and the flesh weakens or accumulates. If there is not enough moisture to nurture the digestion, food isn't absorbed properly, leaving the individual tired and thin. When the earth element is out of balance, vomiting, diarrhea or exhaustion can occur.

The spleen and stomach are of the earth element. For the purposes of simplicity and clarity, I have chosen to call the spleen the **spleen/pancreas** because its functions related to digestion are more easily understood. The earth element is the central core of the body. In the Five Element System, it gets its sun-fire from its mother, the **heart** and **small intestine**. It keeps the floods away by controlling the water element of the **kidney**. The actions of the spleen/pancreas and stomach are kept in check by the wood element of the **liver** and **gall bladder**. Because of their combined digestive functions, they all work closely together. If there is no harmony, burping, flatulence, poor food assimilation and abdominal discomfort may occur.

When I think of a spleen/pancreas-type individual, I think, sweet, sunny, quietly vivacious, perfect weight, patient and calm. They are not often the leaders. Instead, they mother, nurture, support and direct everything around them. They like to feel in control with everything in its proper place. When they are out of balance, they worry and lose or gain weight. This results in a sinking sensation that can lead to hernias, prolapses of different organs and seepage of blood out of their vessels, eventually leading to uncontrolled bleeding. In light of this, the spleen/pancreas is said to govern the blood along with the qi.

According to the circadian clock, the stomach is most active during normal breakfast times, the hours of 7:00 a.m. to 9:00 a.m. The spleen/pancreas is most active later in the morning, between 9:00 a.m. to 11:00 a.m. Animals who like to stay in bed or who are not hungry in the morning may be showing signs of an earth element imbalance. Like the soil, the spleen/pancreas is most sensitive to humidity and dampness, while its partner the stomach is most sensitive to dryness.

QI PROBLEMS: FATIGUE, APPETITE AND LOOSE STOOLS

Marshmallow is a year-and-a-half old, very sweet-natured Orange Tabby cat. She loves to lie in anyone's lap, and even lets the kids pet her and turn her over on her back for her belly to be rubbed. She was a pudgy kitten who had several bouts of diarrhea. As an adult she passes gas when her belly is rubbed, but it makes her feel better. Her stools are runny or soft. Sometimes, the pasty mess sticks to the fur under her tail. It doesn't smell terribly bad but it has bits of undigested food in it. Her humans have tried several types of food to elminate the diarrhea, but the stool stays soft. No longer pudgy, Marshmallow now looks rather pear-shaped, with a slightly hanging belly that sways as she walks. She's not very interested in food, and would rather be petted and loved than eat. She gets her pleasure from making her human family happy. Lately, Marshmallow seems to have lost some of her desire to play and seems to feel the cold more. She's very tired after she moves her bowels or eats and, in fact, she goes immediately after eating. These functions seem to wipe her out.

Despite the different foods and gentle coaxing, Marshmallow *seems* to have a picky appetite. What her people don't understand is that she's not really being picky. Actually, most foods make her feel queasy. She becomes bloated after eating and is very uncomfortable. Interestingly, it's better if she eats later in the day or at night. It seems worse if it's raining. All that water! But her humans don't understand this yet. Whenever she eats she worries that either she will make her humans unhappy or that she'll make herself nauseous.

Marshmallow is the picture of **deficient spleen qi and warming**. The hallmarks of deficient qi are appetite loss, sluggish digestion, gas or burping, worry, fatigue and loose stools or chronic diarrhea. If there is also a lack of internal warming or "coldness," there may also be frequent stools or needing to pass stool soon after eating. Because of incomplete digestion and absorption, bits of food still appear in the stool. If an individual tends to be cold, this quality makes the digestion worse, causing sluggishness and congestion. Excess moisture accumulates along with the food, and nothing moves. The liver is the main organ in the body that tends to stagnate. When stagnation occurs in the digestive tract, the liver and spleen/pancreas become unbalanced. When this happens, an animal may groom excessively along the belly and legs especially after eating. They may be rubbing their stomachs to stimulate digestion or trying to move the accumulations of food and gas along in the intestines. They may even want *you* to rub their stomachs to help the process.

The spleen/pancreas has to extract the nutrients from food and turn them into energy that makes muscle and flesh. When it malfunctions, fatigue, weakness, hanging muscles and weight loss can occur.

If we were to look at Marshmallow's tongue, it might look slightly flabby, wide and very moist. It is probabaly pale in color because proper food assimilation is necessary to make the blood in order to turn the tongue pink.

THE STOMACH

The stomach is the physical organ that receives the food passed through the mouth and down the esophogus. It is the first stage digestive vat which churns up the food and eventually sends it downwards to the small intestine.

The first function the stomach performs is to send some digestive juices upwards toward the mouth to stimulate the saliva. Additionally, in Traditional Chinese Medicine, the stomach is said to make the tongue coating as a by-product of its fermentation fluids. A healthy tongue coating is thin, slightly moist and white with the taste buds standing up.

If there is not enough moisture in the food we eat, or if there are other conditions which predispose the body to dryness, the tongue coating will appear dry. If the condition worsens, the tongue coating may be used up, leaving bald spots on the tongue.

If there is too much moisture from the food we eat, or if the spleen qi warming is weak, the tongue fur becomes overly moist and white. It can become slimy or greasy as the condition worsens.

The stomach is very sensitive to dryness. This usually occurs from a problem originating with the kidneys or lungs which moisten the entire body. Living in an overly dry climate can also add to a dryness tendency. Dryness eventually results in yin deficiency, making the individual thirsty, usually for small, frequent drinks.

If the dryness is severe enough, it can cause a relative internal heat. This is called **false fire** and arises when the body cannot produce enough fluid to cool itself. The animal might have dry, red gums and bad breath with a sickly sweet odor.

Heat in the stomach can also come from an excess heat or **true fire** origin. This situation arises when an individual is predisposed to "run hot." He is usually assertive, likes to eat quickly and boss everyone around. This excess heat weakens the spleen/pancreas and allows the liver to attack it, causing stagnation of the circulation. When fluid stagnates in the digestive tract, it creates a sticky phlegm which heats up causing pain and burning in the stomach. Stomach heat makes an animal voraciously hungry and thirsty. He wants to eat everything in sight, including your furniture! Ulcers in the mouth, stomach and intestine can develop. The animal is extremely thirsty and will drink huge quantities of water to put the fire out. The breath is terrible, like very dirty socks.

WEIGHT AND WORRY

The emotion related to the spleen/pancreas and stomach is worry. Many animals appear to have a worried look on their faces such as a furrowed brow. An animal may be worried about staying alone, or be afraid of being abandoned. They always try to please their people.

Some animals become social eaters, eating only when their people are around to touch them or keep them company. This may lead to weight loss because the animal is worried when the person is not there. He may get so wound up that when he finally eats, he vomits. Some animals, like people, eat more when they are anxious and can gain weight when under stress.

VOMITING

In Traditional Chinese Medicine vomiting is known as **rebellious qi.** It is called this because when the food hits the stomach, instead of being transported downward, the stomach rebels and pushes it back up. A cat or dog eats and the food goes down, but it comes back up shortly thereafter, usually covered with a little bit of water or mucous and is often eaten again.

Some animals vomit water. Here the imbalance is from a backup of excess moisture with weak and cold spleen qi. If the spin cycle of your washing machine isn't working properly, your clothes will become water logged. In the same way, an animal with weak digestive qi can become "water logged" when the moisture in the digestive tract isn't moving properly. This may be worsened when the animal eats cold foods. This includes coldness in food qualities as well as temperature. Vegetables and grains tend to be more cooling than meat proteins. Raw vegetables, such as spinach, chard and broccoli are especially cooling in nature. Grains such as millet and wheat are cooling, as is tofu which also produces moisture. Foods directly from the refrigerator are cool or cold. If your animal has an internal cold from weak spleen or stomach warming, warm up her dinner so she won't vomit when cold foods enter the stomach.

Animals with these conditions may not appear to be uncomfortable. Unlike the violent vomiting of food, phlegm or bile that occurs with liver heat, vomiting from weak stomach qi and warming is more annoying than painful. In deficient conditions of vomiting in general, the stomach feels better with pressure. This is different from an excess or stagnant condition where the liver is more involved. Here, the animal does not like to be touched or feel pressure.

WEIGHT LOSS

Of course, if food cannot be digested properly over a long period of time, this does become a problem. Pain from soreness and chronic weight loss can ensue. This is a very deep problem and usually affects other organs, especially the kidney. The kidney is responsible for the underlying qi and essence of the body that an individual is born with and that is drawn upon during life. It is known as **kidney jing** and it aids and directs the spleen/pancreas in gathering the nutritive qi. Fatigue, thirst, a desire to eat more because of lack of absorption, weight loss and anemia are the results. An extreme example is diabetes, inflammatory bowel disorder or inflammatory bowel disease of the small intestine.

DIABETES

Diabetes is known as a thirsting and wasting disease. During the eighth century in China, if diabetes was suspected, the patient was asked to urinate on a stone outside the clinic. The doctors then waited for the ants to congregate. The ants were attracted to the sugar in the urine. Control of the disease was monitored by repeated "urinalyses on the rock." This was an ingenious test, especially since no urine testing sticks were available for over a thousand years!

In Western terms, diabetes is a disease of the pancreas where a shortage of insulin forces sugar to remain in the blood stream and not enter the cells. Since sugar molecules, called glucose, are necessary to fuel all of our bodily processes, without this fuel, the body breaks down its own muscles for energy. Weight loss and a myriad of problems ensue, including poor circulation, toxic buildup, glaucoma and kidney failure.

In Traditional Chinese Medicine, diabetes is a deficiency disease of the qi and fluids of all the compartments of the body. This makes the individual susceptible to syndromes of dryness and heat, involving the liver, lung, kidney and spleen/pancreas. Great thirst to put out the internal fire, along with lack of absorption leads to fluids being copiously excreted.[2]

Aside from heredity, factors that contribute to diabetes include an aggressive or assertive nature, and/or an individual who overeats rich, fatty foods, such as most commerical dry pet foods. These traits overwork the spleen/pancreas, stomach and liver. Lack of exercise causes stagnation of the liver and qi. Also, stress-induced eating, worrying, fear and anger will all affect the digestion because excessive stress wears down the kidney. Any chronic illness that causes heat to enter the lungs can lead to thirst and the beginning of an escalating problem. Eventually, all these factors upset the precarious balance that the body is trying to preserve.

TREATMENT OF SPLEEN / PANCREAS AND STOMACH IMBALANCES

The goal is to invigorate, warm and regulate the qi. Although animals don't always tell us why they are not eating, we may assume there is nausea, discomfort, a full feeling or low energy. Invigorating the qi will help these problems.

- ◆ **Acupressure of Spleen Qi and Warming Problems: Fatigue, Depressed Appetite, Sluggish Digestion, Gas and Burping**

Stomach (ST) 36. Known as "Three Mile Run," this is the major qi strengthening point in the body. It gives energy to the stomach, spleen, musculature and stamina.
   Location: See page 219. Use a small circular motion for 10 to 15 seconds.

Pericardium (PC) 6. Known as the "Inner Gate," this point calms nausea as well as the sprit. It helps to regulate the qi.[3]
   Location: See page 241. Hold the point for 10 to 15 seconds.

Conception Vessel (CV) 12. Known as "Middle Cavity," this is the alarm point of the stomach. It will help to invigorate the appetite, transporting and transforming processes of the stomach and spleen/pancreas.
   Location: See page 229. Stroke the point in a circular direction.

- ◆ **Herbal Treatment**

Alfalfa.[4] This herb contains eight digestive enzymes, along with trace minerals. It tonifies the spleen/pancreas and stomach.
   Dosage, as powder: cats/small dogs: ¼ teaspoon, daily
      medium dogs: ½ teaspoon, daily
      large dogs: ¾ teaspoon, daily

Shen Qi Da Bu Wan.[5] This is a basic qi tonic to strengthen the spleen. It contains the qi tonics of astragalus and codonopsis. It helps in fatigue, appetite, and sluggish digestion.

Dosage: cats/small dogs: 1 pill, twice daily

medium dogs: 2 pills, twice daily

large dogs: 3 pills, twice daily

Central Qi Tea.[6] This is a qi tonic for the spleen and stomach. It also helps to regulate digestion with the liver. It is good for fatigue, a depressed appetite, bloating, gas and coldness. Qi tonics are neutral or warming in nature. This formula contains the qi tonics of astragalus, codonopsis, licorice, atractylodes, ginger and Chinese dates; the blood tonic of tang kuei; the qi regulators of citrus and cimicifuga; and the liver-clearing herb bupleurum.

Dosage: cat/small dog: 1 to 2 pills, once or twice daily

medium dog: 2 to 4 pills, once or twice daily

large dog: 6 pills, once or twice daily

◆ Dietary Recommendations[7]

The spleen likes warm and sweet foods. Basmati white rice cooked thoroughly, or oatmeal is helpful. Potatoes are warming and help the underlying moisture and qi. Chicken, lean beef, lamb, herring, mackeral and sardines are good protein sources. Vegetables such as green beans, squash, carrots and turnips should be steamed to make them easier to digest.

For dogs, use 50 to 60% grains, 25% protein, and 15 to 25% vegetables. If necessary, omit the vegetables until the animal is eating normally. **For cats**, use 60% protein and 40% grain.

◆ Nutritional Supplements

Papaya Enzymes, to help in digestion. Use ¼ to ½ the human dosage.

Powdered Ginger: ⅛ to ½ teaspoon per meal to warm the stomach and invigorate the qi.

Nutritional Yeast Flakes, high in B vitamins. Their rich taste encourages eating.

Seaweed, helps to stimulate the thyroid gland which increases the metabolism. An increased metabolism encourages the appetite. Use ⅛ to ¼ teaspoon, with loose stool being the limiting factor.

Acidophilus preparations with mixed flora. Use one third to one half the human dose to regulate elimination and digestion.

"DIGESTION IS OFF" COMPLAINTS: LIVER AND SPLEEN / PANCREAS DISHARMONIES, FOOD ACCUMULATIONS AND STAGNATION

Treatment is aimed at balancing the liver and spleen, and regulating the qi.

◆ Acupressure

Urinary Bladder (BL) 18. Known as "Liver's Hollow," this is the association point of the liver and is used to balance the organ.
Location: See page 249. Hold the point for 15 seconds.

Urinary Bladder (BL) 20. Known as "Spleen Hollow," this is the association point of the spleen/pancreas and is used to balance the organ.
Location: See page 204. Hold the point for 10 to 15 seconds.

Conception Vessel (CV) 12. Known as "Middle Cavity," this is the alarm point of the stomach. It is good for regulating the qi and strengthening the stomach.
Location and technique: See page 229.

◆ Herbal Treatment

Hsiao Yao Wan.[8] This is the classic formula for harmonizing the spleen/pancreas, stomach and liver. It helps in food stagnation, irritability and non-specific digestive upsets. It contains the blood tonics of peony and tang kuei; the qi tonics of ginger and licorice, and hoelen and atractylodes, which also move moisture; ginger and licorice along with bupleurum to clear the liver and mentha leaf to regulate qi.

Dosage: cats/small dogs: 1 to 2 pills

medium dogs: 3 to 4 pills

large dogs: 6 pills

Use once daily for one week. If no response, increase to twice daily.

Agrimony.[9] This Western herb releases stagnant qi from the liver. It is useful in situations of abdominal discomfort, bloating with pain upon touch and depressed appetite.

Dosage, as tincture: Add 1 to 4 drops to the drinking water, depending on the size of the animal. Use up to one week.

Chamomile. This Western herb soothes the stomach and relieves constrained liver qi. To make tea steep 1 teaspoon in 1 cup boiled water.

Dosage: cats/small dogs: 1 teaspoon, twice daily with food

medium dogs: 2 teaspoons, twice daily with food

large dogs: 3 teaspoons, twice daily with food

◆ Acupressure Treatment for Weight Loss

General massage of the abdomen in circular sweeps help stimulate the digestive tract and increase appetite.

To the points listed for depressed appetite and spleen qi, page 274, add points to strengthen the blood and yin fluids of the body.

Spleen (SP) 6. This point, known as "Three Yin Junction," stimulates the spleen and the other blood forming organs of the liver and kidney. The blood is the mother of qi. Therefore, to strengthen the blood, we must strengthen the qi.

Location: See page 153. Hold the point for 1 minute.

◆ Herbal Treatment

Alfalfa. This herb contains eight digestive enzymes, along with trace minerals. It tonifies the spleen/pancreas and stomach. See page 274 for dosage.

Women's Precious Pills.[10] This is a blood and qi tonic formula helpful in chronic weak situations. It contains the qi tonics of codonopsis, hoelen, atractylodes and licorice; the blood regulator of ligusticum and the blood tonics of tang kuei, rehmannia and peony.

Dosage is as for Central Qi Tea, see page 275.

Ginseng and Royal Jelly. Ginseng is one of the best qi tonics. It helps tonify the organs, as well as lift the spirits. Royal jelly has excellent nutritive value and helps the essence.

Dosage: cat/small dogs: ¼ vial, daily
medium dogs: ½ vial, daily
large dogs: 1 vial, daily

EXCESSIVE APPETITE AND EATING STRANGE THINGS

Because this is a symptom of excessive stomach fire usually associated with the liver and gall bladder, treatment is aimed at cooling the heat and bringing these organs back into harmony with each other.

Conception Vessel (CV) 14. Known as "Great Palace," this is the alarm point of the heart and what I consider the heartburn point. It helps to clear fire from the stomach.

Location: See page 204. Hold the point.

Stomach (ST) 44. Known as "Inner Court," this point cools and drains heat from the stomach and regulates the qi.[11] It is useful with mouth sores, bad breath and stomach pain.

Location: See page 176. Lightly grasp at the web between the toes for 10 seconds.

Gall Bladder (GB) 41. Known as "Near Tears on the Foot," this point drains heat from the liver and gall bladder, allowing the spleen/pancreas and stomach to rebalance.

Location: See page 157. Hold the point for 10 seconds.

Urinary Bladder (BL) 20. Known as "Spleen Hollow," this is the association point of the spleen/ pancreas and is used to balance the organ.

Location: See page 204. Hold the point or use a small back and forth motion.

◆ Herbal Treatment

Dandelion + Burdock + Wood Betony. These Western herbs clear dampness, and cool heat in the liver and digestive tract.
Use 10 drops each of the tinctures in 1 ounce of distilled water.
 Dosage: cats/small dogs: 1 dropperful, three times daily
  medium/large dogs: 2 to 3 dropperfuls, twice daily

Chamomile. See page 277.

◆ Dietary Recommendations

Cooling and neutral grains and vegetables should be used to cool the liver, including thoroughly cooked brown rice, millet or barley, grated beet and celery. Small amounts of white meat chicken or rabbit can be used to strengthen the spleen.

VOMITING FOOD AND MOTION SICKNESS

This is a condition of rebellious qi. The goal of treatment is to strengthen the qi and regulate its direction.

◆ Acupressure Treatment

See listings for Spleen Qi Problems, page 274.

◆ Herbal Treatment

Make ginger tea by steeping 2 thin slices, fresh ginger root in 1 cup boiled water for 5 minutes. Cool completely and give to your animal friend one half hour before travelling.

Dosage: cats/small dogs: 1 to 2 dropperfuls
medium/large dogs: ⅓ cup

VOMITING WATER

The goal is to strengthen the warming of the spleen/pancreas and kidney, whose deficiency has caused the imbalance.

◆ Acupressure Treatment for Vomiting Water

Conception Vessel (CV) 12. Known as "Middle Cavity," this is the alarm point of the stomach.
Location and technique: See page 229.

Stomach (ST) 36. Known as "Three Mile Run," this point is used to strengthen the qi and to promote the downward movement of stomach qi to help quel vomiting.
Location and technique: See page 219.

Urinary Bladder (BL) 23. Known as "Kidney's Hollow'" this is the association point of the kidney and is used to balance the organ.
Location: See page 189. Hold the point.

Governing Vessel at the Lumbo Sacral Junction. Various books call this point "Baihui" in animals, or "Hundred Meetings." The point is on the midline of the back, just in front of the pelvis at the end of the lumbar spine. The point strengthens the yang of the body. Use finger tip pressure to hold the point for 15 seconds, or you can use a back and forth motion.

◆ Herbal Treatment

Wild Bergamot.[12] This Western herb is pungent, bitter and sweet and can be used either to warm or cool. It is excellent for stomach disorders of any kind and regulates the qi. As tincture, dilute 5 to 10 drops to 1 ounce distilled water.

> **Dosage:** cats/small dogs: 1 dropperful, twice daily
> medium dogs: 2 dropperfuls, twice daily
> large dogs: 3 dropperfuls, twice daily

Chamomile.[13] This Western herb regulates the qi and calms the stomach. It is its drying potential that is useful here. Dosage is as for bergamot above. Equal parts can be mixed together to help in digestion.

Cardamom. The essential oil from the fruit of this herb is used or its fruits are crushed. Cardamom has pungent, regulating and warming properties. It restores spleen qi.

> **Dosage:** Mix 3 drops of the essential oil in 1 tablespoon olive oil. Use 3 to 5 drops of diluted oil per meal or, use powdered herb at ⅛ teaspoon for cats/small dogs, to ½ teaspoon for medium and large dogs.

Fennel.[14] The root of this Western herb is warming, drying and pungent. It regulates and warms the spleen. As tincture, dilute 5 to 10 drops to 1 ounce distilled water.

> **Dosage:** cats/small dogs: 1 dropperful, twice daily
> medium dogs: 2 dropperfuls, twice daily
> large dogs: 3 dropperfuls, twice daily

◆ Dietary Recommendations

Avoid foods that create dampness such as tofu, millet, dairy products, raw vegetables and clams and cooling foods such as wheat and avocado. Warming foods such as chicken, lamb, venison and lean beef are good for this condition, as are white rice and oats. Cooked carrots and squash are excellent vegetables for warming the spleen, as is ginger.

DIARRHEA WITH MILD ODOR, PASTY STOOLS

Treatment is aimed at strengthening the qi and warming the spleen/pancreas and stomach. Treatment includes strengthening the colon, as this is the child of the earth element in the Five Element Creation Cycle.

◆ Acupressure

Spleen (SP) 6. Known as the "Three Yin Junction," this point strengthens the spleen and is especially good for pasty, loose stools.
Location and technique: See page 153.

Stomach (ST) 36. Known as the "Three Mile Run," this point tonifies the qi of the body.
Location and technique: See page 219.

Stomach (ST) 25. Known as "Heaven's Axis," this is the alarm point of the large intestine, and is useful for all types of diarrhea.
Location: On the abdomen approximately ½ inch on either side of the umbilicus. The animal will be tender in that area. Hold the points.

◆ Herb Treatment and Dietary Recommendations

Use the herbs and dietary recommendations listed for **Spleen Qi and Warming Problems,** pages 274–75, as this is a transforming process.

DIABETES

By the time diabetes is diagnosed, your animal friend will be under the care of the veterinarian. Even if the animal is on daily insulin, acupressure and dietary supplementation are helpful to restore balance to the individual. Herbs can be used, but require the supervision of a trained herbalist as they may alter insulin dosages.

Treatment is aimed at clearing the heat of the stomach and tonifying the spleen qi and kidney essence.

◆ Acupressure Treatment for Diabetes

If the animal is weak, choose one point to work on each day, or treat every few days to two weeks. If the animal seems very fatigued after a session, choose fewer points to work on during your next session and hold them for less time.

Spleen (SP) 6. Known as the "Three Yin Junction," this point tonifies the yin and blood of the body.
Location and technique: See page 153.

Urinary Bladder (BL) 13. Known as "Lung's Hollow," this is the association point of the lung and is used to balance and clear heat from the organ. It is especially useful to curb the raging thirst experienced by diabetic animals.
Location: See page 173. Use a short back and forth motion.

Conception Vessel (CV) 12. Known as "Middle Cavity," this is the alarm point for the stomach. It helps in digestive processing and in balancing the organ.
Location and technique: See page 229.

Urinary Bladder (BL) 23. Known as "Kidney's Hollow" this is the association point of the kidney, used to balance this organ.
Location and technique: See page 189.

Stomach (ST) 36. Known as the "Three Mile Run," this point strengthens the qi and the hind legs which tend to weaken with diabetes.
Location and technique: See page 219.

◆ Nutritional Supplements

It has been shown that **brewer's yeast** grown in a chromium enriched medium aids in normal glucose or sugar metabolism. Other factors helping in glucose metabolism are **niacin, zinc, manganese, vitamin B 1, raw liver** and **pancreas concentrates.**[15] Many natural food stores carry supplements under the heading of aids for glucose metabolism.

Dosage: cats/small dogs: one third the human dose

medium/large dogs: one half up to the entire human dose

Enzymes, especially from papaya extracts.

Vitamin C is helpful in oxidation and in eliminating toxins. Can be used as sodium ascorbate if diarrhea is not present. Dosage ranges from 250 mg to 1000 mg, twice daily, with diarrhea as the limiting factor.

Fatty Acid Supplement which includes the omega 3 oils. Flax seed, olive oil and sesame oils are good choices.

Dosage: cats/small dogs: ½ teaspoon

medium dogs: 1 teaspoon

large dogs: 1 to ½ teaspoon

Vitamin A.[16] 1,000 to 2,000 mg for cats and small dogs; up to 4,000 mg for larger dogs.

Chlorophyll.[17] Helps the absorption of minerals and increases nutrient absorption in general. Chlorophyll is green, the color associated with the liver.

Dosage: cats/small dogs: one third the human dose

medium/large dogs: one half the human dose

◆ Dietary Recommendations

These are based on the specific signs that an individual patient is exhibiting. If the basic signs are vomiting food, vomiting water, bloating and diarrhea without odor or straining, a diet that supports the spleen qi and warming is recommended. These signs are usually exhibited by diabetics early on. An extensive discussion of the foods useful in diabetes can be found in Dr. Paul Pitchford's book, *Healing With Whole Foods.*

If yin and jing deficiency signs are most prevalent, with extreme thirst, weight loss, vomiting and/or voracious appetite, foods that are more cooling and moistening should be chosen. (See Chapter Seven, page 98.)

If your animal is not on insulin, small, frequent meals won't overburden his somewhat fragile system. Four meals per day is optimal.

Whole grains that are high in fiber are recommended. Fiber slows down the food as it travels through the digestive tract allowing for greater absorption time. Be sure to cook brown rice thoroughly to soften the hulls and provide optimum moisture. Other useful grains are oat bran, oats, whole wheat and millet. Vegetables that help the spleen qi and yin such as string beans, squash, mushrooms, asparagus, and avocado are good choices. Legumes such as lentils, aduki beans and kidney beans are excellent sources of protein and can be mixed with meat protein for both dogs and cats.

The best meat for diabetes when there is stomach heat and jing essence loss manifesting as a great thirst and voracious appetite with weight loss, is pork. If you skim the fat from ground pork cooked in water, even diabetic cats seem to tolerate it. Muscle meat helps restore jing essence and provide substance. Making stews with trimmed pork is helpful. Remember to skim off the fat. Pork is the coolest of the muscle meats. Rabbit might be another choice, as this has yin and yang tendencies. Sardines are also a good choice if your animal is not vomiting, because it is rich in the omega 3 oils which help in the metabolism of glucose.

THE SPLEEN GOVERNS THE BLOOD

It is said in Traditional Chinese Medicine that the spleen/pancreas "governs the blood." The heart is the prince of circulating the blood, the liver is the general of smoothly directing the blood, and the spleen is the governor of the blood, keeping it within the vessels.[18] Malfunctions of governing the blood result in hemorrhage or seepage from the vessels.

By bleeding I mean oozing such as a nose bleed, blood in the stool that oozes into the rectum, blood in the urine without pain, or easy bruising. Dogs with immune disorders that involve clotting problems fit this category. They can have small hemorrhages on the abdomen or on the gums, appearing as red or red/purple blotches. Dogs with tendencies toward ear hematomas or blood blisters in the ear flap are showing signs of weakened spleen/pancreas.

Anemia is a problem with the ability of the spleen/pancreas to transform food into blood and qi. The spleen/pancreas, kidney and liver all contribute to making the blood. A deficiency in any of these organs can lead to anemia.

Treatment of these bleeding disorders is aimed at restoring and strengthening the spleen qi and blood in general.

◆ Acupressure Treatment for Bleeding Disorders

Spleen (SP) 6. Known as the "Three Yin Junction," this point strengthens the spleen, kidney and liver which are the three blood building organs of the body.
Location and technique: See page 153.

Spleen (SP) 10. Known as the "Sea of Blood," this point harmonizes the nutritive qi of the spleen which helps govern the blood. It is used along with **Spleen 6** in skin rashes which itch. It can also be used to nurture the blood in general.
Location: On the inside of the hind leg, above the knee, on the border of the large muscle belly on the inside of the thigh, known as the vastus medialis. Use a circular motion on the point.

Stomach (ST) 36. Known as "Three Mile Run," this point strengthens the qi of the body.
Location and technique: See page 219.

Urinary Bladder (BL) 23. Known as "Kidney's Hollow," this is the association point of the kidney. It is useful in tonifying the blood, especially in the lower part of the body. Because the spleen controls the kidney in the Five Element Control Cycle, strengthening the kidney indirectly balances the spleen.
Location and technique: See page 189.

◆ Herbal Treatment

Shen Qi Da Bu Wan, as listed on pages 274–75.

Kwei Bi Wan.[19] This is a qi and blood tonic formula used to strengthen the spleen, heart and circulation. It is useful in bleeding due to low platelet counts, as well as in conditions of fatigue and anemia. It contains the spleen qi tonics of codonopsis, hoelen, atractylodes, astragalus and licorice; the blood tonics of tang kuei and euphoria longan fruit; and the heart-calming herbs ziziphus and polygala.

> cats/small dogs: 1 to 2 pills, twice daily
> medium dogs: 3 to 4 pills, twice daily
> large dogs: 6 pills, twice daily

◆ Nutritional Supplements

Vitamin C, as sodium ascorbate, at low doses due to poor spleen qi which makes an individual prone to loose stools.

> cats/small dogs: 100 mg daily
> medium/large dogs: 500 mg daily

Vitamin E, as an antioxidant and to tonify blood vessel walls.

> cats/small dogs: 25 to 50 IU daily
> medium/large dogs: 200 IU daily

Trace Minerals, as kelp powder and seaweeds, sprinkled over food. Use ⅛ to ½ teaspoon daily, depending on the size of the animal.

Alfalfa, for its calcium content:

> cats/small dogs: ¼ teaspoon daily
> medium/large dogs: 1 teaspoon daily

Nutritional yeast flakes, for B vitamin:

> cats/small dogs: ½ teaspooon daily
> medium/large dogs: 1 teaspoon daily

Apple Cider Vinegar. Add ½ teaspoon to 1 tablespoon to 2 cups of drinking water, depending on the size of the animal. Vinegar is an old home remedy to control bleeding.

◆ **Dietary Recommendations**

Choose foods that are warming and help weak spleen qi from those listed on page 275. Kale is an excellent vegetable to help the blood clot and it is one of the only green vegetables that is warming in nature.

Endnotes

1. Dr. Kuan Hin. *Chinese Massage and Acupressure.* (New York: Bergh Publishing Inc., 1991), 79.

2. Flaws, Bob and Honora Wolfe. *Prince Wen Hui's Cook.* (Brookline, MA: Paradigm Publications, 1983), 44–46.

3, 11. O'Conner, John and Dan Bensky, trans. ed. *Acupuncture, A Comprehensive Text.* (Seattle, WA: Eastland Press, 1981), 249, 275.

4, 13, 14. Holmes, Peter. *The Energetics of Western Herbs, Vol. I & II.* (Boulder, CO: Artemis Press, 1989), 370, 462, 292.

5, 6, 19. Naeser, Margaret, A., PhD. *Outline Guide to Chinese Herbal Patent Medicines in Pill Form.* (Boston, MA: Boston Chinese Medicine, 1990), 286, 268, 272.

7. Pitchford, Paul. *Healing with Whole Foods.* (Berkeley, CA: North Atlantic Press, 1993); Henry C. Lu. *Chinese System of Food Cures.* (New York: Sterling Publishing Co., Inc., 1986); Bob Flaws. *Prince Wen Hui's Cook.* (Brookline, MA: Paradigm Publications, 1989).

8, 10. Fratkin, Jake. *Chinese Herbal Patent Formulas.* (Boulder, CO: Shya Publications, 1986), 157,178.

9, 12. Wood, Matthew and Tismal Crow. Herb Lectures, Batesville, IN, 1994.

15. Mertz, W. Effects and Metabolism of Glucose Tolerance Factors. *Nutritional Review*, 33, #5, May 1975, 129–135; Rubenstein, A.H., and N.W. Levin, "Manganese Induced Hypoglycemia," *Lancet,* December 1963, 1348–51.

16. Balch, James F., MD, Phyllis A. Balch, CNC. *Prescriptions for Nutritional Healing.* (Garden City Park, NY: Avery Publishing Group, 1990), 155.

17. Pitchford, Paul. *Healing with Whole Foods.* (Berkeley, CA: North Atlantic Press, 1993).

18. Kaptchuk, Ted., OMD. *The Web That Has No Weaver.* (New York: Congdon & Weed, 1983), 222.

*The Kidneys and Urinary Bladder:
The Water Element*

The jing gives birth to the yin and yang of the body. Because the kidney is the storehouse of the jing, the kidney acts like the roots of a tree carrying water and nutrients into the body and filtering toxins out. It aids the lungs in extracting moisture from the air and the spleen/pancreas in extracting moisture from food.

The kidneys help the body develop and mature. In Traditional Chinese Medicine, it is the kidney that gives us our skeletal framework and is said to rule the bones.

Once our bones are formed, they undergo constant remodelling throughout life. The kidney directs the bone marrow and the outer layer of bone called the cortex. When the jing is weak at birth, an animal can be the runt of the litter. He may have malformed bones such as an elbow that doesn't fuse or hips that develop dysplasia. An animal with weak kidney jing may be destined to develop dental problems, arthritis or osteoporosis in the back and limbs as he ages.

In addition to guiding and filtering fluids, the kidneys are known for "warming the loins." The loins are between the ribs and the pelvis and are associated with reproduction. This warming aspect is known as the **kidney yang**.

The kidneys direct the flow of water through the body at a cellular level, maintaining the fluid we need for existence and filtering out the toxins through the urinary bladder. The kidneys with the urinary bladder form the

water element of the body. To maintain the proper balance of water flow, adequate kidney yin and kidney yang must be present. If there is not enough kidney yin, the body shrivels up like a prune. If there is not enough kidney yang, the body swells like an over-ripe watermelon.

THE WATER ELEMENT ASSOCIATIONS

In Traditional Chinese Medicine, the water element of the kidney and urinary bladder is related to the direction north, and the season of winter.

Many animals get sick during the winter or in cold weather. They catch colds or develop bladder infections. Bladder infections may develop because the animal doesn't want to go outside to urinate when it's cold and wet, so he holds it in too long, irritating the bladder lining. Because the kidney is the root of the qi, it influences how the immune system responds to insult. In fact, it is said that a strong kidney leads to a strong immune system.

The flavor related to the kidneys is **salty**. It is said that if you eat too much salt, you weaken the kidneys. Most commercial dry pet foods are very salty which is partly why animals like them so much.

The odor of imbalance in the kidneys is **putrid**. Those of you who have been close to a person or an animal in kidney failure will recognize this odor of decaying matter.

The sound of the kidney is **groaning** and animals with arthritis may groan when getting up or down.

According to the circadian clock, the urinary bladder is most active from 3:00 p.m. to 5:00 p.m. and the kidney is most active from 5:00 p.m. to 7:00 p.m. Problems at these times of the day may relate to a water element imbalance.

The sense organ affiliated with the kidney is the **ear**. Animals with kidney problems often develop sensitivity to noise. They may hide out in closets and under beds to keep out of the way of external influences.

The emotion associated with the kidney is **fear**. Fear wears down the lubrication of the body. Think of "sweating bullets," or holding your breath with fear. Think of running and panting when you are frightened, or "wetting your pants" out of fear. Fear is related to the kidney and the water element.

THE KIDNEY YIN:
HOW TO KEEP COOL, CALM,
COLLECTED AND MOIST

Coming from the **jing essence**, the kidneys control the underlying yin fluids of the body. Yin fluids support life by moistening, calming and cooling. The yin of the kidney is responsible for the tools and tissue to process urine. When the yin is deficient, the body becomes dry, agitated and easily overheated. When the yin is completely gone, the kidneys no longer function, and death follows.

◆ Moisturizing

The kidney yin helps keep our saliva wet, our stool moist, our sweat glands working and our urine forming in the bladder. This means that symptoms of a dry mouth leading to thirst, dry stool leading to constipation, or dry skin leading to dandruff are signs of **kidney yin deficiency**. Because the lungs feed the kidney in the Five Element System, a dry kidney can borrow moisture from the lungs, creating a dry cough. If there is lack of fluid to fill the bladder, the overly concentrated urine can scald and irritate the system, and the animal will strain or have scant and blood-tinged urine.

In the Five Element Control System, the earth element of the spleen/pancreas and stomach keep the kidney under control. If the kidney yin is weak, the stomach can overpower the kidney, creating dryness, heat and vomiting of food or bile. If left untreated, ulcers may form.

The kidney yin also keeps the blood strong, because blood is made up of cells and yin fluid plasma. The three organs in the body responsible for blood production are the kidney, spleen/pancreas and liver. When there is a problem with not enough red or white blood cells, the kidney is involved. This also means that abnormal blood cells related to autoimmune diseases or blood cancer involve the kidneys.

◆ The Cooling System

Through its water regulation, the kidneys act like air conditioning to moderate body temperature and prevent overheating. Thermal regulation is also governed by the triple heater, which works with the kidneys to adjust internal body temperatures. An individual who heats up easily is having problems with the yin cooling system of the body. An animal who pants as soon as the temperature goes above 65 degrees F. or one who constantly seeks shade, is calling attention to the kidneys. Overheating can also cause hot, itchy skin which turns dry and red.

◆ The Calming System

Moisture keeps the organs properly bathed. If fluid levels are down, the organs become tight and constricted. If the mind or spirit is yin deficient, an individual can become agitated, restless and fearful. In Traditional Chinese Medicine, the spirit, feelings of well-being and balanced behavior are governed by the shen, which is ruled by the heart and pericardium.

The heart and pericardium are kept under control by the kidneys. So if they are weak, unbalanced shen can cause undue fear, timidity, hiding or bad dreams.

◆ A Case of Dwindling Yin

Jody is a three-year old mixed breed dog who was brought to see me because her skin was always itchy. She was a California dog who got regular exercise and was fed a natural, hypoallergenic diet. Despite this, Jody continued to itch.

Jody enjoyed jogging with her human in the cool early evenings. But Jody had become embarrassed because she had to keep stopping to scratch. This annoying problem had begun the previous fall, and it was assumed that she had fleas. But the itching continued even as the weather turned colder. California was in the midst of a drought and just like the land, Jody's skin was very dry, flaky and rough. When she scratched, it turned red. Jody's ears were hot to the touch as well, and her mouth was very dry.

Since puppyhood Jody had been very skittish around other dogs. This may have been due to the fact she was the runt of the litter, and her bigger, stronger brothers stepped on her to get at their mother's milk. Once she bolted into the street to get away from a truck that backfired. Luckily, the on-coming car skidded to a stop without hitting her. Now Jody cowers when she sees or hears big trucks.

More recently, her owner reports that Jody becomes nervous as evening approaches. She hates the dark and reacts as though she sees scary creatures behind every piece of furniture and around every corner.

When I examined Jody, she was very sensitive to my touch and her head and paw pads felt hot. The pads looked dry and the skin between them was slightly red. She was a friendly dog, but I knew I had to approach her gently as she might snap at me or try to run away. When I felt her pulse, on the in-side of the hind leg, it was very rapid and threadlike. Jody appeared to be ter-rified and was panting hard. I could see that her tongue was dark red, with very little saliva or coating.

When I questioned her human, she told me that Jody had had a mild bladder infection at the end of the summer. There were no crystals, very little blood and very concentrated, scant urine. The amount of urine seemed odd, since Jody drank large quantities of water.

Jody was showing signs of a deficient kidney yin. A young dog, who had been the runt of her litter, indicated an inherited weak kidney jing that couldn't nourish the yin.

Her external environment was abnormally dry due to the drought, caus-ing the dry air she breathed to deprive the lungs of moisture. The dry dog food she ate failed to supply the spleen or stomach with fluids for digestion. When the yin stores become low enough, it creates a relative or *false* heat inside the body, which does not allow the individual to cool herself. So she overheats. After a summer heat spell, the insufficient internal fluid was further stressed, leading to the bladder infection of scant urine which irritated the bladder.

Although Jody recovered from the bladder infection with the aid of an-

• Thirst

• Dry mouth

• Constipation

• Vomiting of food

• Dry cough

• Dry, hot skin

• Easy overheating

tibiotics, she was left with a dryness that continued to affect her skin. This made her itchy, dry and red. In humans, false fire causes facial flushing and the soles of the feet and the palms of the hands to become hot and red. Jody experienced this as dry, red, sensitive paws, and a head that was hot and sensitive to the touch.

The yin deficiency also affected her disposition, leading to increased fears and insecurities. The red tongue and small, rapid pulse were further indications of this because there wasn't enough fluid to keep the tongue pink and moist, nor enough fluid to fill the arteries.

Left untreated, Jody might have developed more bladder infections, and, eventually, a kidney problem.

◆ Treatment

Treatment of kidney yin deficiency is aimed at restoring the moisture in the kidneys or related organs in the Five Element System. Early treatment strengthens the kidneys and helps prevent kidney failure later.

◆ Acupressure

Treatment can be done as frequently as necessary to strengthen the organs, depending upon the severity of the symptoms.

Kidney (KI) 3. Known as "Great Creek," this point is used to strengthen kidney yin and regulate its energy. It is useful in thirst, low-back pain and weakness, urinary tract infections with scant urine, dry cough, constipation, dry, itchy, hot skin, heat and noise intolerance.

Location: See page 187. Hold the point for 30 seconds.

Spleen (SP) 6. Known as the "Three Yin Junction," this point strengthens the yin and blood of the spleen, kidney and liver. It is useful in thirst, constipation, dry, itchy, hot skin, anemia, insecurity, heat and noise intolerance.

Location: See page 153. Hold the point, or rub in a short up and down motion in the space between the Achilles tendon and the bone.

Conception Vessel (CV) 12. Known as "Middle Cavity," this is the alarm point of the stomach. It is useful in thirst, vomiting, constipation, digestion and weight loss.

Location: See page 229. Hold the point for 10 to 15 seconds.

Urinary Bladder (BL) 23. Known as "Kidney's Hollow," this is the association point of the kidney and is used to balance the organ.

Location: See page 189. Hold the point.

◆ Herbal Treatment

Liu Wei Di Huang Wan.[1] This is the classic kidney yin formula that also helps strengthen the blood and yin of the liver and the spleen. It is useful in thirst, constipation, low-back pain, hot, itchy feet, face and skin, weight loss, insecurity and agitation. It contains rehmannia to nourish the yin and the blood, cornus to nourish the kidney and liver yin, dioscorea for helping qi, hoelen to promote urination, alisma to clear false fire and moutan to clear heat in general.

> **Dosage:** cats/small dogs: 1 to 2 pills, twice daily
> medium dogs: 3 to 4 pills, twice daily
> large dogs: 6 pills, twice daily

Chamomile. This Western herb cools and calms the stomach and is useful in conditions affecting the stomach and the kidney resulting in vomiting of food or bile. Make a strong tea by steeping ½ to 1 teaspoon flowers in 1 cup boiled water for 30 minutes.

> **Dosage:** cats/small dogs: 10 drops, once or twice daily
> medium dogs: 20 drops, once or twice daily
> large dogs: 30 drops, twice daily

Alfalfa. This Western herb is a tonic for the blood, yin and qi. It is useful for dry skin, general dryness, hyperacidity of the stomach and early ulcers. Use as a powdered herb or food supplement.

Dosage: cats/small dogs: ¼ teaspoon, once or twice daily

medium dogs: ½ teaspoon, once or twice daily

large dogs: ⅔ to ¾ teaspoon, once or twice daily

◆ Nutritional Supplements

Vitamin C, as sodium ascorbate. If there is ulceration in the stomach or a tendency to vomit, this vitamin may not be tolerated well. Diarrhea is the limiting factor.

cats/small dogs: 125 mg, twice daily

medium/large dogs: up to 500 mg, twice daily

Vitamin B Complex: in 30 to 50 mg, depending on the size of the animal.

Vitamin E: cats/small dogs: 50 IU cats, every other day

medium/large dogs: 100 to 400 IU daily

Enzymes from papaya to aid in digestion, at ⅓ to ½ the human dosage.

Trace Minerals, as kelp or other seaweed powder.

cats/small dogs: ⅛ teaspoon

medium/large dogs: ½ teaspoon

Corn Oil, cold pressed: cats/small dogs: 2 to 3 teaspoons, daily

medium dogs: 2 tablespoons, daily

large dogs: 3 tablespoons, daily

If muscle spasms develop, add a potassium supplement, such as **Potassium Chloride.**

cats/small dogs: ⅙ teaspoon, daily

medium dogs: ⅛ teaspoon, daily

large dogs: ¼ teaspoon, daily

◆ Dietary Recommendations

Because kidney yin deficiency causes dryness and heat from lack of fluids, foods that cool and moisten are useful. These foods are also calming to the individual. Yin foods are usually vegetables and grains, with meat protein being more warming, but providing yin substance. Choose from grains such as whole wheat, millet, polenta, and brown rice. Peas are associated with the kidney, as well as other legumes, so choose from lentils, aduki beans, kidney beans or peas. Vegetables such as sweet potatoes, spinach, asparagus, beets and celery are helpful. For animal protein, choose from rabbit or pork, eggs, lowfat dairy products, and fish such as mackerel, sardine, clam, or cod. Avoid very warming foods such as shrimp, salmon, chicken, or lamb.

THE KIDNEY YANG AND THE LOIN FIRE

As part of the kidney jing, the kidney is guardian of the deep yang or fire of the body. This deep fire resides in the loins and is known as the **ming men** or **life's fire gate**. The ming men fuels an individual's reproductive abilities, libido, and general qi or "go get 'em" attitude.

As Westerners, it is sometimes difficult to comprehend that there is a "yang" function to any organ. We see an organ for its physical self. It looks a certain way and performs certain functions. In TCM, however, the roles of the organs according to the meridians and the functional relationships between the organ systems are more complicated and interrelated. The yang is warming and activating, and very closely related to the qi. The yang of the kidney helps to warm the inner parts of the body. It is the organ system most active during the winter, and acts as the body's thermoregulater. Just as it is the kidney yin's job to cool us, it is the kidney yang's job to warm us.

If the kidney yang is deficient, it allows coldness to seep into the core of the body right to the bones. This results in sluggish movement and digestion, with excess water buildup.

◆ The Role of Kidney Yang in Warming the Body

In order to warm the body, the kidney water needs to be heated or "steamed." The life's fire gate accomplishes this by generating fire below the waist and steaming it upwards, creating a mist. As the steam rises upward toward the chest, through the abdomen, it helps to stimulate the digestive juices of the stomach and spleen/pancreas and the qi of the lungs.

If the mist doesn't reach the lungs because it lacks heat to generate it, the water can get trapped in the chest or the abdomen causing congested, moist breathing. When the mist turns back to cold water in the abdomen, it can cause vomiting of water, abdominal bloating, diarrhea and pain. The animal will not be thirsty, because there is already too much water in its system. It will feel cold all the time and want to be covered or near a heating source.

Overall sluggishness will also affect the activity of the entire body, including the bones. The bones of the low back and lower extremities are exceptionally vulnerable to a weak kidney yang. If the yang of the kidney is not active, the fluid in the bone marrow and around the joints can become stagnant, leaving only some areas lubricated. Where there is stagnation, there can be pain and areas of unnatural calcification. Disc problems, arthritis and bone spurs may develop.

The lack of kidney yang fire will decrease sexual desire in both females and males. In males, it may lead to problematic ejaculations, lack of sperm, or lack of interest. In females, it may lead to slowly cycling ovaries, lack of interest or problems in becoming pregnant. In the female reproductive system, it is the kidney and spleen/pancreas that initiate the heat cycle, readying the tissue and hormones to work properly. If the kidney yang is weak, the cycle will never reach the readiness stage.

Hormones in general, including those from the adrenal glands and thyroid are affected by the kidney yang and the triple heater. (See Chapter Twenty-one, page 381.)

A lack of kidney yang may also lead to urine dribbling and incontinence which worsens in rainy, cold weather and at the night. Because of the lack of kidney yang, the urinary tract in general is cold. This makes the animal unable to concentrate his urine adequately, causing him to urinate frequently.

◆ Sex and a Disc

Fernando is a five-year old male Dachsund, a prize-winning show dog who has sired many champion sons and daughters. When Fernando was brought to see me he was in severe back pain. His human was concerned that Fernando might have ruptured a disc. Fernando had had a disc problem the previous winter. He just moved the wrong way, and suddenly, it was difficult for him to walk. Rest, muscle relaxants and steroids got him through the incident. An x-ray showed a "calcified disc" lesion in the middle of his back.

After recovering from the initial injury, Fernando walked stiffly. His back seemed okay, but the lower part of his body lacked suppleness. Fernando lost interest in his female cohorts, possibly because he was afraid of hurting his back again. In any event, he began losing his desire to sire. In fact, he had lost interest in many things like eating and playing. He felt cold a lot of the time and preferred lying in the sun whenever possible. Sometimes when he urinated, only a small stream came out, not much more than a dribble, and sometimes he had to get up at night to urinate. This had never happened before the back injury.

On a very humid day, Fernando was obliged to service a young Dachsund. He was just beginning to mount her when suddenly he made the wrong move. He stopped and didn't want to move again. Finally, not being able to hold the position on his hind legs, he gingerly moved away and lay down. Horrified, his human rushed him to the vet.

X-rays were inconclusive and he was put on steroids to decrease the inflammation. When I examined Fernando, two days later, there was inflammation and tightness over the lower lumbar area. His whole back was contracted

• Cold intolerance

• Frequent, night-
time urination

• Lost libido

• Hormonal
imbalances

• Arthritis

• Joint stiffness

• Disc problems

with pain. His feet felt cool. His tongue was pale and the pulse in the hind legs was slow and deep. I could hear his belly gurgling, and his human told me that he had had loose stool that morning.

Clearly Fernando had a problem with weak kidney yang. Because he was being used as a stud, it is possible that the kidney fires were doused by too much sexual activity. This can happen in humans, but I had not seen it in a dog before.

The weakness in the kidney yang affected the spine leading to stagnation, inflammation and finally the disc problem. After the disc injury, the kidney yang continued to dwindle and stagnate. This led to other kidney yang signs such as coldness, loss of appetite and libido and weak urination. When there is a warming deficiency, the pulse lacks the fire to beat strongly. The tongue of such an individual may appear pale with a white coating. It will be very moist and even have some bubbles around the gums, indicating a lack of steaming ability of the kidney.

Fernando received acupuncture and herbs to clear the stagnation and decrease the inflammation. We also devised a massage plan to regulate the kidney yang with the hope that further injuries would be prevented.

◆ Treatment of Kidney Yang Disorders

Treatment is aimed at warming the kidneys and preventing possible kidney failure, as both the kidney yin and yang are involved in the later stages of kidney disorders.

◆ Acupressure

Governing Vessel (GV) 4. Known as "Life's Fire Gate," this point warms the kidney yang and activates circulation along the spine. It is useful in weakness of the hind end, stiffness in the lower limbs, dribbling urine and incontinence due to kidney yang deficiency.

Location: See page 162. Use small back and forth motion on the point.

Urinary Bladder (BL) 23. Known as "Kidney's Hollow," this is the association point of the kidney and is used to balance the organ. It can be used for warming the kidney, incontinence, bladder straining with small, frequent amounts of urine and weakness and stiffness in the back and hind legs.

Location and technique: See page 189.

Conception Vessel (CV) 4. Known as "Hinge at the Source," this point stabilizes the kidneys, regulates the qi and restores the yang of the kidney. It is useful in incontinence, weak urine stream, diarrhea, infertility, loss of libido, loss of sperm, and irregular ovarian cycling.

Location and technique: See page 250. In male dogs, the penis needs to be moved sideways off the midline to treat this point.

General massage along the conception vessel meridian below the umbilicus to the pelvis is also helpful. Use upward strokes from the pelvic bone to the umbilicus, to direct the flow of yang and qi upward.

Stomach (ST) 36. Known as "Three Mile Run," this point tonifies the qi especially in the lower portion of the body. The qi helps the yang and is useful in digestive disorders, abdominal bloating and coldness.

Location: See page 219. Use circular motion for 15 seconds.

◆ Herbal Treatment

Moxa. Moxibustion is the technique of burning an herb called mugwort, or artemesia vulgaris, near muscles, joints or specific acupoints. It is packaged either dried and loose, or rolled into long, cigar-like rolls. The roll usually has two paper coverings on it. The outer layer is peeled away about one inch from the top of the stick, exposing the underlayer. Light an end, like a cigar, and blow on it until it glows. Once lighted, practice on yourself by holding the moxa roll close to, but not touching, the skin on your free hand. Feel the intensity of the heat. This heat stick, held near an acupoint, treats the point with warmth. To extinguish the moxa roll, bury the lighted tip in soil, or use aluminum foil at the end of the roll. Moxa helps to warm and activate the circulation and relieve pain.

The technique I use on animals is to hold the lit roll in one hand. Then I place my other hand on the animal in the area to be treated. I move the stick above the animal's fur *and* the tips of my fingers. This way, I can keep track of how hot the area becomes and so prevent singeing the animal's fur. I usually treat the point by warming it with moxa for 10 to 15 seconds. Animals who are cold usually like this treatment. Some don't and because each animal is an individual, discontinue treatment if your animal friend seems afraid or uncomfortable. And of course, be careful not to burn the skin or singe the fur.

Moxa is especially good for stiffness that is worse in the cold. Treatment can be done along both sides of the spine, on the Bladder meridian, or on the Conception Vessel meridian to warm the abdomen.

The following points respond well to moxa treatment: **Stomach 36**, **Spleen 6**, and **Governing Vessel 4**, along with the **Bladder** and **Conception Vessel** meridians.

Golden Book Tea.[2] This forumula uses the kidney yin formula of Liu Wei Di Huang Wan with the added herbs of cinnamon and processed, nontoxic aconite to warm the kidney. It is useful in sexual dysfunctions such as decreased desire and infertility, also frequent, copious urination that becomes worse in the cold and at night, low back pain and weak hind legs, abdominal distension and asthma that worsens in cold weather.

Dosage is as listed for Liu Wei Di Huang Wan, see page 296.

Wild Carrot.[3] The head, flowers and upper parts are used for urinary problems, while the root helps restore the sexual organs, particularly in cases of infertility and decreased libido. This herb should not be given to pregnant animals because it will cause an increase in uterine contractions.

Use tincture, mixing 5 to 10 drops in 1 ounce water.

Dosage: cats/small dogs: 1 dropperful, once or twice daily
medium dogs: 2 dropperfuls, once or twice daily
large dogs: 3 dropperfuls, once or twice daily

For disc problems, see Chapter Nineteen, pages 345–49.

For digestive disturbances, in early kidney yang and spleen yang problems, see Chapter Sixteen, pages 268–70, 274–76, 280–82.

◆ Nutritional Supplements

Because this is a cold condition, vitamins C and B may increase the tendency to coldness and loose stool. Use lower doses than listed for the yin deficient conditions on page 297.

◆ Dietary Recommendations

Warming and neutral foods to help nourish the spleen/pancreas will help in balancing and warming the kidney yang. Choose grains such as white basmati rice, brown rice, oats, barley and corn. Choose vegetables such as carrots, squash, kale and string beans. For animal protein, choose from chicken, salmon, liver, lamb, venison and rabbit.

CHRONIC RENAL OR KIDNEY FAILURE

This is a condition where much of the kidney substance and function have been damaged. The yin, yang and blood of the kidney are all affected. This condition is life threatening. Your animal friend's symptoms may include the yin signs of extreme thirst, constipation, overheating, weakness, weight loss, pacing and a red, dry tongue. Yang signs may include frequent urination, diarrhea, fatigue, vomiting and coldness. Anemia or low white blood cells are symptoms of blood deficiency of the kidney, liver and spleen.

When the patient no longer drinks or urinates, the situation is critical because the kidneys have shut down and toxins are building up, poisoning the body. Your animal friend *must* be under the care of a veterinarian.

Chronic kidney failure usually affects older animals between the ages of 12 and 20 years in cats, and 8 to 14 years in dogs. However, there are groups of younger animals, such as certain lines of Himilayan and Siamese cats, who are born with damaged kidneys. These cats may show the signs of kidney failure as early as their first year. This is a function of deficient kidney jing.

While your animal is under veterinary care, you may be administering fluids at home to help keep the kidneys working. In addition to fluid therapy and in some cases, antibiotic thereapy, acupressure and herbs can be an invaluable adjunct to treatment.

◆ Acupressure Treatment for Chronic Renal or Kidney Failure

There are special points to use which regulate the balance between the kidneys, the spleen and the lungs. This treatment was developed in Korea and is known as the "Four Needle Technique." It utilizes the Five Element System of balancing the Control and Creation Cycles. Because the spleen/pancreas controls the kidneys, during renal failure, the spleen is out of control. It must be rebalanced by sedating certain points. The lungs support the kidneys, and points are chosen to strengthen the lungs so that, in turn, the kidneys are strengthened.

◆ Four Needle Korean Technique

Spleen (SP) 3. Known as "Most White," this point is traditionally used for constipation or diarrhea and abdominal distension. It is also the source point of the spleen meridian.

Location: Although there is disagreement as to precisely where this point is located on cats and dogs, I find it on the lower portion of the inside of the hind paw, midway between the ankle and the toes. Because animals do not have "big toes" like humans, the beginnings of the liver and spleen meridians run very close together. Use a downward brushing motion along the inside of the hind paw.

Kidney (KI) 3. Known as "Great Creek," this is the source point for the kidney, used for thirst, overheating and vomiting.

Location: See page 187. Hold this point.

Lung (LU) 8. Known as "Across the Ditch," this point is used for bronchitis, asthma and breathing problems. It will also help decrease thirst and it is a strengthening point for the lung fluid.

Location: On the underside of wrist of the front leg. Flex the wrist. The point is on the wrist crease at the inside margin of the long bone, the radius. Use a small circular motion.

Kidney (KI) 7. Known as "Returning Column," this point strengthens the relationship between the lungs and the kidney, thereby strengthening the kidney. It is used for abdominal distension, bladder infections, back pain, weak legs and excess heat because it regulates the kidney qi.

Location: On the inside of the hind leg, on the border of the Achilles tendon, just below where the muscle bellies end and the tendon begins. Hold the point.

These 4 points are usually used together as the sole treatment, twice weekly, to strengthen the kidneys. After eight sessions, other points can be chosen from those listed for both kidney yin and yang, see pages 295, 301.

KIDNEY DISEASE WITH VOMITING

Conception Vessel (CV) 12.

Location and technique: See page 229.

Stomach (ST) 36.

Location and technique: See page 219.

Urinary Bladder (BL) 20.

Location and technique: See page 204.

♦ **Appetite Stimulants**

Stomach (ST) 36.
> *Location and technique:* See page 219.

Kidney (KI) 3.
> *Location and technique:* See page 187.

Conception Vessel (CV) 12.
> *Location and technique:* See page 229.

♦ **Herbal Treatment**

Herbs are helpful to restore blood flow, promote urination, decrease toxins, lower blood pressure and replenish potassium which is lost when the kidneys are overworked. If the animal is vomiting, you may not be able to administer the herbs until the vomiting is under control. Herbs are chosen according to the most prevalent symptoms. If there is no vomiting, the basic kidney formula Liu Wei Di Huang Wan can be started. See page 296 for dosage.

Variations of this formula such as **Chih Pai Di Huang Wan,**[4] can be used if there is extreme thirst, insomnia, high blood pressure, hot skin including the paws, and nervous irritability. This formula adds the herbs anemarrhena and phellodendron which clear false fire.

♦ **Nutritional Supplements**

Enzymes that aid digestion may be helpful for absorption of nutrients.

Co-Q 10, which aids in oxygenation, is helpful for energy, breathing, lowering blood pressure and eliminating toxins.
> cats/small dogs: 10 mg
> larger dogs: 50 mg

Cod Liver Oil supplies vitamin A and D which are necessary to help bone remodelling.

Care needs to be taken with **Vitamin E** as it may increase blood pressure. Choose from the nutritional supplements listed for kidney yin deficiency, see page 297.

◆ Dietary Recommendations

Western dietary guidlines include restriction of protein and phosphorus. Traditional Chinese Medicine looks at food qualities rather than protein, mineral or calorie intake. Foods that moisten and cool are used for kidney yin problems as listed above. Foods that warm or neutralize are used to help digestion.

The following are some recommendations that may be used as diets to supplement the veterinary formulas, or to be used on their own.

◆ Renal Diets for Dogs

Defatted ground pork or white meat chicken cooked in broth plus 1
    hard-boiled egg: 10 to 15%
Kidney beans or lentils (cooked volume): 10%
½ mashed banana
Thoroughly cooked white/basmati or brown rice, barley, or millet: 65%
Yams, string beans, squash, asparagus 10 to 15%
Steamed vegetables seem easier to digest for the renal deficient
    patient.
Corn Oil: 1½ tablespoons, daily

◆ Renal Diet for Cats

White meat chicken, chicken gizzard plus 2 hard-boiled eggs with
    a touch of clam juice or chicken broth: 20%
Kidney beans, mashed: 10%
Well-cooked white/basmati rice, polenta, barley: 60%
String beans, squash, asparagus, kale: 10%

If a veterinary prescription diet is used, it is possible to entice the animal into eating by adding hard-boiled egg moistened with clam juice, cooked sweet potatoes or yams, asparagus and the water it is steamed in, which promotes urination. If all else fails, feed the animal what he *will* eat. Once he is eating, try to cut the diet with one third cream of rice or cream of barley cereal. This aids digestion.

THE URINARY BLADDER AND ITS PIPES

The urinary bladder collects urine from the kidney through a tube called the **ureter**. The bladder acts as a balloon to hold the urine until it is voided through the exit pipe called the **urethra**. When irritation, inflammation or infection occurs in the urinary system, there is usually pain, a constant urge to urinate, or an inability to urinate.

The urge to urinate usually coincides with voiding small amounts of urine frequently. Blood and/or micro-organsims may be present in the urine sample. When something is blocking the path of the urine as it exits through the urethra, such as sand, gravel, or tumor, the urge is there, but the urine cannot escape. Those of you who have had male cats who suffered from what is called FUS (Feline Urinary Syndrome) can attest to the life-threatening situation that occurs when the urine backs up into the body and the nitrogen toxins cannot be expelled, causing uremic poisoning. Those of you who have suffered from bladder infections personally, will have sympathy for your animal friend who is constantly squatting in the litter box or asking to go out. The animal doesn't know what to do with herself because the urge to go is constant but there is no relief. She cannot find a comfortable position because there *is* no comfortable position for her.

CYSTITIS EAST AND WEST

Western medicine sees bladder infections as being caused by either bacteria or diets that create crystals in the urine which inflame the bladder lining. The condition is almost always treated with antibiotics, and if the inflammation is severe, cortisone is also used. The diet is usually changed to a prescription type diet, creating thirst and promoting urine formation. Many animals respond favorably to this course of treatment, with only occasional bouts of urinary flareups, which are once again treated with medication.

In Traditional Chinese Medicine, problems with the urinary bladder usually fall under the categories of **heat** or **damp heat.** Whether pathogens are present or not, it is the underlying constitution of the individual which has made the animal vulnerable to bladder weakness.

Heat, or inflammatory conditions, usually arise from a dryness or lack of moisture stemming from a kidney yin deficiency previously discussed. Kidney yin deficiency leads to a lack of urine production, because not enough fluid is being manufactured within the body. Since the kidney and bladder are supposed to control the heart and small intestine in the Five Element Control Cycle, when the kidney is weak, these fire organs create more heat in the body. The scanty urine that is formed is highly concentrated and hot, causing burning on the inside of the bladder wall or in the lining of the urethra as it leaves the bladder. This can make the animal wince or cry out either when passing the urine or just afterwards. Cats may run to try to get away from the pain, or scratch furiously in the litter box in an attempt to distract themselves. Due to their extreme discomfort, they may be irritable and intolerant of their housemates. If the yin is sufficiently low, some blood may be present in the urine.

Traditional Chinese Medicine treats these conditions by changing the diet to cooling or yin nurturing foods as well as with herbs that clear fire, restore the yin and restore the calming quality of the heart.

Damp heat situations are more severe than heat situations. In addition to the kidney and heart meridians, when dampness enters the picture, the spleen and the liver are also involved. A heat condition results from a fluid or yin deficiency. Damp heat conditions usually arise from a kidney yang deficiency that affects the spleen. As a result, the spleen cannot process the moisture from food and the tissues become water-logged, causing a feeling of heaviness and bloating. Moisture tends to sink to the lower part of the body, creating stagnation in the bladder area.

When there is stagnation, the liver becomes involved and pockets of cold *and* heat can develop because the movement of the fluid is blocked. Pain and the frequent urge to urinate usually results. If the heat becomes severe, there will be blood in the urine and it will be foul smelling or turbid. When the urine is retained for long periods of time because of the stagnation or because the animal doesn't want to experience the pain of passing it, crystals can develop. Crystal, stone and sand formation are considered stagnant damp heat situations by TCM.

Gravel and stones cause further inflammation, and if they block the urethra, the urine becomes backed up. In situations of damp heat, there is usually diarrhea, possibly with mucous or blood. The tongue is very moist, almost swollen, with teeth imprints along its side edges.

◆ Treatment

Treatment is aimed at clearing the heat, drying the dampness and breaking up the stagnation. Patients are kept on dietary and herbal regimens for long periods of time, first treating the bladder and then the weakened underlying organs.

◆ Acupressure for Heat Situations

Urinary Bladder (BL) 40. Known as "Commission the Middle," this point drains heat from the lower part of the body, helps to decrease inflammation in the bladder and colon and helps relieve pain in the lower back.

Location: See page 250. Hold the point or use small circular motions.

Liver (LIV) 2. Known as "The Walk Between," this point drains liver heat and breaks up stagnation. It allows for the smooth flow of qi and blood and is helpful in bladder pain, penis and urethral pain, scanty urine and abdominal distension.

Location: See page 156. Brush in a downwards direction for 10 seconds.

Urinary Bladder (BL) 23. Known as "Kidney's Hollow," this is the association point of the kidney and balances this organ, giving moisture to the urinary bladder to relieve pain and dryness.

Location and technique: See page 189.

Conception Vessel (CV) 3. Known as "Middle Peak," this is the alarm point of the urinary bladder, useful in acute situations of inflammation.

Location: On the midline of the lower abdomen. Draw an imaginary line from the umbilicus to the pelvic bone. CV 3 is located four fifths of the way down from the umbilicus.[5] Since this is difficult to pinpoint, I suggest doing a gentle, circular massage of the lower half of the abdominal midline.

Once the acute flareup has subsided, continue acupressure to strengthen the kidney and spleen, using such points as:

Kidney (KI) 3.

Location and technique: See page 187.

Conception Vessel (CV) 3.

Location and technique: See above.

Urinary Bladder (BL) 20.

Location and technique: See page 204.

Urinary Bladder (BL) 28. Known as "Bladder's Hollow," this is the association point for the urinary bladder and will balance the organ. It is useful in all problems concerning the bladder, swelling of the genitals, scanty urine, diarrhea or constipation (because of the colon's physical proximity to the bladder) and pain in the low back and over the sacrum.

Location: Over the sacrum. There are four depressions that you can feel, two on either side of the midline. The points are in the second set of depressions. Use short, back and forth movements over the points.

◆ Herbal Treatment

Chih Pai Di Huang Wan. This is a variation of Liu Wei Di Huang Wan listed on page 296, for kidney yin deficiency. This formula adds the herbs anamarrhena and phellodendron to clear false fire signs.

Dao Chi Pian.[6] This is a heat-clearing formula that corrects the heat spilling over from the heart to the small intestine, to the urinary bladder, causing scant, painful, burning urination. It contains the heat-clearing herbs of raw rehmannia, akebia, gardenia, talc and rhubarb and the qi-protective herbs of licorice and hoelen.

This formula comes in a large honey pill. Divide this pill as follows:

Dosage: cats/small dogs: ¼ pill, twice daily
medium dogs: ½ pill, twice daily
large dogs: ¾ to 1 pill, twice daily

Since this is a heat-clearing formula which can damage the qi if taken over a long period of time, use for 1 week.

A Western herbal combination of 3 to 5 drops each of the following tinctures diluted in 1 ounce distilled water can be used. Give 1 to 3 dropperfuls, depending upon the size of the animal, 3 times a day:

Marshmallow Leaves + Bearberry + Cornsilk

The marshmallow coats the bladder lining, the corn silk is a yin tonic and mild diuretic, and the bearberry clears heat and promotes urination.

DAMP HEAT IN THE BLADDER

This causes much straining, blood, mucous, crystals and pain.

◆ Acupressure Treatment

Liver (LIV) 8. Known as "Crooked Spring," this point relieves damp heat in the bladder and relaxes the muscles. It is useful in painful urination, distension and pain of the genitals and abdominal distension.

Location: Behind the stifle (knee), just above the inner margin of the crease formed when the leg is flexed at the knee. Hold the point.

Conception Vessel (CV) 4. Known as "Hinge at the Source," this point stabilizes the kidneys and regulates the qi and the yang. It is useful in painful urination with blood, the constant urge to urinate, diarrhea and abdominal pain.

Location: See page 250. Use a circular motion or a general massage of the lower abdominal midline.

Kidney (KI) 7. Known as "Returning Column," this point clears damp heat from the kidneys and bladder. It is helpful in urinary tract infections with blood and straining and in treating low back pain.

Location and technique: See page 306.

Urinary Bladder (BL) 23. Known as "Kidney's Hollow," this is the association point of the kidneys and is used to rebalance them. Also used for blood in the urine, excessive thirst and fever.

Location and technique: See page 189.

AFTER THE ACUTE SITUATION

The most important aspect of treatment is to keep the qi and blood moving to prevent stagnation. I recommend massage down the spine, in the depressions between the rib spaces and at the ends of the vertebrae. Begin between the shoulder blades and end at the base of the tail. Either light, back and forth motions or small circular motions from the spine outward are beneficial. Additionally, massage the inside of the hind legs just above the ankle in the depression between the Achilles tendon and bone. Massage the entire area, using an up and down motion. In this hollow lies **Kidney 3**, **Spleen 6**, **Kidney** 7 and **Liver 5** (at the very top of the space). These points help keep the meridians flowing and balanced.

◆ Herbal Treatment

Lung Tan Xie Gan Pill (Gentiana Combination).[7] This formula drains damp heat from the lower part of the body, and can be used in acute situations of cystitis, urethritis, prostatitis, vaginitis and pelvic disorders. It contains gardenia, gentiana and scutellaria to clear damp heat; bupleurum to relieve liver qi stagnation; tang kuei and rehmannia to strengthen the blood and yin; and alisma, akebia and plantaginis to promote urination and clear heat.

> **Dosage:** cats/small dogs: 1 tablet, three times daily
> medium dogs: 2 to 3 tablets, three times daily
> large dogs: 4 tablets, three times daily

A Western herb combination of the following tinctures, dissolved in 1 ounce distilled water and given 1 to 3 dropperfuls, three times daily, depending upon the size of the animal:

> **Plantain** – 6 drops
> **Agrimony** – 2 drops
> **Cleavers** – 4 drops

◆ Nutritional Supplements

Cranberry Juice Concentrate:
> cats/small dogs: ¼ human dosage
> large dogs: human dosage

Vitamin E. An antioxidant and ant-inflammatory:
> cats/small dogs: 50 IU, daily
> medium dogs: 200 IU, daily
> large dogs: 400 IU, daily

Vitamin C, as sodium ascorbate or ascorbic acid, with diarrhea as the limiting factor.

> cats/small dogs: 125 mg, twice daily
> medium dogs: 250 mg, twice daily
> large dogs: 500 mg, twice daily

Co Enzyme Q 10: cats/small dogs: 10 mg daily
> larger dogs: 50 mg daily

Vitamin B complex, from a non-yeast source, as the depletion of intestinal flora may make the animal susceptible to yeast infections. Give 10 to 30 mg daily, depending on the size of the animal.

◆ Dietary Recommendations

Individual patients may require slightly different diets because several organ systems are usually involved with bladder problems. In any heat situation, avoid shrimp, salmon, trout and venison, as these foods increase the heat. I had a case where a cat was doing well for three months until one night he ate shrimp which created blood in the urine.

Barley is a good grain for dryness in the urinary bladder and kidneys. Asparagus and celery are also helpful. Ground pork (boiled and with the fat skimmed off), rabbit, egg and beef are the safest animal proteins.

In damp heat situations, avoid foods that create dampness such as tofu, milk products, and processed wheat. Instead, use brown rice or corn. Add well-cooked aduki beans, potatoes cooked with the skins left on, and winter squash.[8] In damp heat situations where the spleen/pancreas is involved, steamed rather than raw vegetables seem to be better tolerated by most animals. Dogs can be fed less meat protein, which helps decrease the dampness, and more whole grains and vegetables. Cats, however, do not fare as well with very little meat protein. The best meats to choose from are beef, rabbit and small amounts of chicken. For animals who are prone to damp heat situations, turkey may increase the dampness, so avoid this food.

CHRONIC URINARY CRYSTALS, SAND AND STONES

The forming of crystals is a combination of heat, dampness and stagnation. Stagnation is the key word here, because in order for a stone to form, it needs time to stay in one place. An individual will develop this problem when there are imbalances between the spleen/pancreas, liver and kidneys. TCM treatment is aimed at relieving the damp heat and the stagnation. Follow the guidelines listed for damp heat situations on pages 313–16. In addition to the acupressure points recommended, treat:

Spleen (SP) 9. Known as "Yin Tomb Spring," this point transforms damp stagnation. It is helpful in both retention of urine or incontinence, abdominal distension and stone formation.

Location: See page 194. Hold the point.

◆ Herbal Treatment

Some herbs have been shown in the literature[9] to break up and in some cases, dissolve stones and sand crystals. In my practice, long-term acupuncture and acupressure treatment seem the best method.

For triple phosphate crystals: cleavers, red clover, eyebright and horsetail.

For uric acid crystals: wild carrot, pipissewa (wintergreen), celery root, cornsilk and gravel root.

For long-term use, up to two months, choose one to three herbs, and use 1 to 3 drops each in 1 ounce of distilled water. Use the dilution once daily. If diarrhea occurs, stop the herb.

Triple phosphate crystals are the most common type of sand found in cats with chronic cystitis. The crystals form in urine with a basic pH. Therefore, it is important to acidify the urine as much as possible. This can be done with cranberry juice concentrate and vitamin C. Vitamin C should be given as rose hips, at 500 mg twice daily, as long as there is no diarrhea. It will be necessary to decrease the dosage if diarrhea develops.

◆ Dietary Recommendations

Avoid feeding shellfish, although small amounts of fresh cod are allowable. Most of the diet should consist of rabbit, chicken and chicken gizzards. Garlic is good to add to the food, as it contains a natural sulfa-type antibiotic as well as an antistagnation factor. The herbs listed on page 317, for triple phosphates can be given once a day for up to two months. If diarrhea or increased thirst arises, discontinue the herbs. What is important to remember is that stone formation is just a symptom of an imbalance between the kidneys, heart, liver and spleen, and that this imbalance needs to be addressed.

FREQUENT URINATION AND INCONTINENCE

This problem has become very common as our animal friends live longer. It is also more prevalent in dogs than cats, and also in females. The tendency seems to have a relationship to the sex hormones which nurture the urogenital tract.

In Traditional Chinese Medicine, frequent urination, uncontrollable urination and incontinence usually stem from a weakness in the kidney yang and the kidney qi. Incontinence and frequent urination are also a function of the qi in general governed by the spleen, because it is said that the spleen keeps the organs and their contents in the correct places. As an individual ages, it is a natural process for the qi to become depleted.

In kidney yang deficiencies, it is necessary to warm the body, using moxa, acupressure and herbs as listed on pages 301–04, in the section on kidney yang deficiency.

In other cases, herbs that are astringent in action are helpful in keeping urine in its correct place.

◆ Astringent Herbs

Lotus Seed.[10] This Western herb has an astringent, sweet and neutral quality. It is useful for incontinence and insomnia.

Dosage, as a powdered herb: cats/small dogs: ¼ teaspoon, daily

medium dogs: ¼ teaspoon, daily

large dogs: ½ teaspoon, daily

Schizandra.[11] This Chinese herb has all five flavors and affects all the meridians, especially those of the kidneys and the heart. It is helpful to balance between these organs for incontinence and irratic behavior. **Dosage** is as a powdered herb, as for lotus seed above.

Bearberry.[12] Acts as an astringent and restorer of kidney function. Use 3 drops of the tincture in ½ ounce of water and give 1 to 2 dropperfuls once a day.

Endnotes

1, 4. Fratkin, Jake. *Chinese Herbal Patent Formulas.* (Boulder, CO: Shya Publications, 1986), 208, 204.

2, 6, 7. Naeser, Margaret, PhD. *Outline Guide to Chinese Herbal Patent Medicines in Pill Form.* (Boston, MA: Boston Chinese Medicine, 1990), 299, 187, 169.

3. Wood, Matthew. Herb Lecture, Indiana, 1995.

5. Yann-Ching Hwang, DVM. *Problems in Veterinary Medicine, Veterinary Acupuncture*, A. Schoen, ed. (Philadelphia, PA: J.B. Lippincott Co., Vol. 4, No. 2, March 1992), 31.

8. Pitchford, Paul. *Healing with Whole Foods.* (Berkeley, CA: North Atlantic Press, 1993), 509, 319.

9. Holmes, Peter. *The Energetics of Western Herbs, Vol. II.* (Boulder, CO: Artemis Press, 1989), 793.

10, 11. Tierra, Michael, CA, ND. *Planetary Herbology.* (Santa Fe, NM: Lotus Press, 1988), 343, 346.

12. Hoffman, David, BSc, MNIMH. *An Elder's Herbal.* (Rochester, VT: Healing Arts Press, 1993), 121.

The Large Intestine: The Metal Element

The large intestine is the last organ where nutrients are absorbed before elimination. A healthy large intestine passes formed stools with ease. An unhealthy large intestine has problems with dryness, heat, misplaced moisture and stagnation. In Traditional Chinese Medicine, the **large intestine** is paired with the **lungs** to form the **metal element**.

Although the large intestine, or colon, resides in the lower body, it's meridian is found in the upper body, in close association with its partner, the lung.

The large intestine meridian begins on the second toe and runs upward between the web of the dewclaw, ending at the nostrils and serving the sinus. There is an internal branch that travels to the colon.

As part of the metal element, the large intestine is particularly sensitive to dryness. If there is an imbalance, it moves between the metal element and the surrounding elements of **earth (spleen/pancreas and stomach), water (kidney) and wood (liver and gall bladder).** As the pendulum swings between two extremes, constipation or diarrhea can occur.

The large intestine is most active between 5:00 a.m. and 7:00 a.m. Those of you who need to walk your dog at these early hours can attest to this.

DIARRHEA AND COLITIS

An individual can have diarrhea from an acute infection or toxic buildup, or from a malfunctioning colon, spleen/pancreas, stomach, liver or kidney.

In the **acute situation** of infections, parasites or toxins, the diarrhea that results is usually sudden and foul smelling. There may be blood or mucous involved if the pathogen has overpowered the individual. The animal won't want to be touched around the abdomen. Depending upon the constitution of the individual and whether he tends to be warm or cool, the invasion of the pathogen may cause vomiting and fever with the diarrhea, as in the hot individual, or depression, and phlegmy, watery stools in the cold individual[1] who feels better on a heating pad.

If the situation is severe, with much fluid being lost, professional veterinary care should be sought. Dehydration can occur very quickly and cause serious complications. In the **chronic situation,** diarrhea or loose stool can be caused by a weak spleen/pancreas that is unable to assimilate the nutrients from food. The proteins, carbohydrates, fats and vitamins cannot be extracted properly. In such cases, the large intestine may try to extract the nutrients, but it ends up eliminating stool that is watery and full of undigested food particles. The stool does not have a bad odor, nor is there pain with passing it, but the animal may seem tired and clingy after elimination.

◆ Acupressure for Diarrhea and Colitis – Acute Situations

Large Intestine (LI) 11. Known as "Crooked Pool," this point is used to relieve heat, clear pain, inflammation and dampness, and to expel pathogen invasion in an acute situation.

Location and technique: See page 156.

Large Intestine (LI) 4. Known as "Adjoining Valleys," this is the source point for the large intestine. It is used to disperse an acute infection and stimulate the immune system.

Location: See page 152. Gently pinch or massage in the web between the first and second toes. If your animal objects, then hold the point with one finger at the web. If the dewclaw has been removed, hold the area where the "nub" remains under the skin.

Spleen (SP) 6. Known as the "Three Yin Junction," this point clears heat, strengthens the qi of the spleen/pancreas and adds moisture if fluid has been lost due to the diarrhea.

Location and technique: See page 153.

◆ Herbal Treatment

Herbs for acute situations can be used for three to five days. If the condition worsens, if the animal becomes dehydrated, or if there is no response after this period of time, veterinary care should be sought.

Marshmallow Root and Leaves.[2] This Western herb with its soft fur on the leaves and moistening root, cools and hydrates the mucosa, as well as stimulates immune response. It is useful if there is bloody, mucousy, stool with much painful straining.

    Dosage, as tincture: mix 20 drops to 1 ounce water.

        cat/small dogs: 1 dropperful, three times daily

        medium dogs: 2 dropperfuls, three times daily

        large dogs: 3 dropperfuls, three times daily

Plantain.[3] This Western herb pulls toxins and inflammation from the mucosa and decreases pain. It clears dampness and heat and activates the immune system. It can also be given to animals experiencing the frequent, sudden need to have a bowel movement with pain, mucous and blood. This herb is useful in the most severe cases. It is best used as a strong tea from crushed leaves, made fresh daily. Dry leaves can be used if fresh is not available.

    Dosage: Use 1 teaspoon per cup of boiling water. Cool and strain.

        cat/small dogs: 1 dropperful, three times daily

        medium dogs: 3 dropperfuls, three times daily

        large dog: 4 dropperfuls, three times daily

    As tincture, use as marshmallow above.

Golden Seal. This antibiotic type Western herb can be used for acute dysentery. It is similar to the Chinese herb coptis, which is used to clear damp heat. Golden seal should not be used over a long period of time, no more than ten days, and only if needed that long. Do not use with pregnant animals.

Dosage, as powdered herb in capsule:

> cat/small dog: #3 or #2, capsule, three times daily
>
> medium dog: #0 capsule, three times daily
>
> large dog: #00 capsule, three times daily

As tincture, use as marshmallow on page 322. If salivation occurs, use 10 drops to 1 ounce water.

If the animal is cold, thirstless, weak and depressed, these are the signs that a cold pathogen is causing the diarrhea. Here the diarrhea is watery, foul smelling and without blood. Use 3 to 5 drops each of the following tinctures in 1 ounce distilled water. Use 1 to 3 dropperfuls, three times daily.

Patchouli[4] + **Magnolia Bark** + **Fennel.** Patchouli helps to expel infection, while fennel and magnolia dry dampness from the spleen and relieve pain. Use ¼ teaspoon of each powdered herb in 1 cup boiling water. Steep and give 1 to 3 dropperfuls three times per day.

Pill Curing.[5] This patent herb is useful in food poisoning, pain, vomiting and diarrhea. The pathogen is cold or hot. It includes herbs to regulate the stomach and relieve dampness in the spleen/pancreas.

> **Dosage:** cats/small dogs: ⅓ vial, twice daily
>
> medium dog: ½ vial, twice daily
>
> large dog: ¾ vial, twice daily

Hollywood is a semi-wild cat who prefers to live outside especially during the winter. Her long fur keeps her warm, but during wet winter storms, she has pasty stools or bouts of diarrhea with undigested food. She likes her tummy rubbed while she lies on her back or to lie on a hard surface, belly down. Hollywood has a deficient condition affecting the spleen/pancreas and kidney. During the wet cold weather, which is particularly hard on the spleen and the kidney, these imbalances are stressed until, finally, diarrhea occurs.

Animals with deficient conditions feel better with pressure and rubbing and the support of hard surfaces. Many cats who have this type of imbalance over a long period of time can become thin and very finicky about what they will eat. With this cold and wet imbalance, they usually have a hanging belly and a tongue coating that is thick and white. The tongue itself appears wide with teeth imprints on the sides.

The most painful type of diarrhea involves the liver and spleen/pancreas. When the spleen/pancreas has been weakened, it can be overpowered by the liver in the Five Element Control Cycle. Liver disturbances cause stagnation of digestion and circulation. With stagnation, pockets of heat and cold can form. If the colon is the target organ, pain, bloating and a heavy, stuck, damp feeling with diarrhea may result. In Western medicine we call this **colitis** or **inflammatory bowel syndrome.** If it is severe enough, blood and ulcers form on the lining of the intestines.

Heat, cold, stagnation and dampness cause pain and straining during elimination. The animal will have a bowel movement and then keep trying, even though there is nothing left. Some cats will actually cry out in pain. Dogs will often just run and squat. They are plagued by the frequent, sudden need to have a bowel movement, which may send them whimpering and scratching at the door to be let out.

When the colon is involved, you can be sure that other parts of the digestive system are also involved. As I often tell my clients, the beginning of the tract and the end of the tract are linked. Diarrhea can depress the appetite and the spirit too, so you may notice that your animal friend appears moody or depressed. Burping or excessive passing of gas are also indicators of intestinal disturbances.

◆ Dietary Recommendations

During acute bouts of diarrhea, stop *all* dry and solid foods. Use broths made from miso or chicken or rice. I recommend rice porridge, called congee. It can be made easily by cooking white rice at 4 parts water to 1 part rice for several hours, until the rice particles fall apart. It is very easy to digest. Alternatively, boiled potatoes are soothing and anti-inflammatory for the colon. Avoid raw foods as these may be difficult to digest while the animal is having diarrhea. Fluid replacers such as human baby products for diarrhea can be used for rehydrating and iron replacement. Use half the baby dose for cats and the full dose for dogs. After two days of broth, small amounts of solid food can be given. It is best to stick with a bland diet of boiled white rice or potato and small amounts of cooked chicken or eggs. Adding enzymes and acidophilus can be helpful. Slowly reintroduce your animal friend's normal food. Dry foods are the hardest to digest and they also create a lot of heat in the body. These should be reintroduced last and only when the animal is no longer experiencing any pain or diarrhea symptoms.

CHRONIC WATERY DIARRHEA, PASTY STOOL WITH FOOD PARTICLES

Treatment is aimed at strengthening and warming the spleen/pancreas so that proper transformation and assimilation of food takes place.

◆ Acupressure

Spleen (SP) 6. Known as the "Three Yin Junction," this point strengthens the spleen/pancreas.

Location and technique: See page 153.

Conception Vessel (CV) 8. Known as the "Middle of the Navel," this point is used to strengthen the yang and the transforming properties of the spleen/pancreas. It can be used for both acute flareups and chronic diarrhea.

Location: On the abdominal midline at the umbilicus. Technique is to use small circular motions, or to hold the point.

Stomach (ST) 36. Known as "Three Mile Run," this point strengthens the stomach, the qi and transforming properties of the spleen/pancreas and stomach.

Location and technique: See page 219.

◆ **Herbal Treatment**

Cinnamon Bark, Elecampane, Ginger Root, Sage, Chamomile: These herbs can be used individually or in combination to strengthen the qi and warm the spleen/pancreas. Use ½ teaspoon powdered herb to 1 cup boiled water. Steep 20 minutes and strain. Use 1 to 3 dropperfuls, depending on the size of the animal and the severity of the symptoms, twice daily with food.

White Oak Bark.[6] This Western herb is used as an astringent for strengthening the muscle tone and surface of the intestine. Use ½ teaspoon to 1 cup boiled water, and use as described above.

PAINFUL CHRONIC DIARRHEA WITH BLOOD, MUCOUS AND STRAINING

Treatment is aimed at clearing the heat, drying the dampness and breaking up the stagnation of the large intestine, liver and spleen/pancreas.

◆ **Acupressure**

Liver (LIV) 2. Known as "Walk Between," this point clears heat and dampness from the liver as well as breaks up stagnation, allowing the qi to move more freely.

Location: See page 156. Rub the inside of the paw in a downward direction to sedate liver heat.

Spleen (SP) 6. Known as the "Three Yin Junction," this point will strengthen the spleen to withstand the liver imbalance and harmonize the two. It also helps regulate heat and dampness.

Location and technique: See page 153.

Stomach (ST) 25. Known as "Heaven's Axis," this is the alarm point of the large intestine, clearing heat and relieving pain and diarrhea.

Location and technique: See page 282.

Urinary Bladder (BL) 25. Known as "Large Intestine's Hollow," this is the association point of the large intestine. It is useful in balancing the organ and helping to alleviate painful bowel movements.

Location: On either side of the midline, in the depression between the fourth and fifth lumbar vertebrae. Hold the point.

◆ Herbal Treatment

Plantain. See page 324.

Agrimony.[7] This herb clears heat, dampness and inflammation. Its target organ is the liver, where it helps to break up stagnant qi. Animals who are tense and irritable and don't like to be touched will respond well to this herb. It can be mixed with plantain to clear damp heat. Only small amounts of this tincture are needed: usually 1 drop to ½ ounce of water. **Dosage** is 1 dropper of the dilution, three times daily, for up to one week.

Golden Rod.[8] This Western herb relieves damp heat in the intestine. It is good for painful defecation with blood, mucous and odor. Use with equal parts of chamomile to relieve stagnation. Boil alcohol off, as described on page 78.

   Dosage, as tincture: dilute 10 drops to 1 ounce water.
         cat/small dogs: 1 dropperful, twice daily
         medium dogs: 2 dropperfuls, twice daily
         large dogs: 3 dropperfuls, twice daily

Slippery Elm.[9] This Western herb is cooling and soothing to the mucous membranes. Use as powder mixed in a small amount of food. Or, mix with warm water, stir and give it immediately to your animal because it will become too sticky if left to stand.

> **Dosage:** cat/small dogs: ¼ teaspoon, three times daily
> medium dogs: ½ to ⅔ teaspoon, three times daily
> large dogs: ¾ to 1 teaspoon, three times daily

◆ Dietary Recommendations

It is difficult to recommend diets as this condition is complex and involves the liver and spleen/pancreas and stomach as well as the large intestine. Because there can be different underlying causes, one combination is not appropriate for all cases. You may need to experiment with different mixtures to find the diet that is just right for your animal friend. You will need to determine whether there is more heat, or more stagnation or more dampness. Remember that your animal friend's personality and constitution type will help you to assess her condition. The animal who is hot, thirsty, stout, stubborn, aggressive or moody, suffers from heat conditions and liver involvment. His tongue is red with a yellow coating. Foods that cool and soothe are most important. These include non-oily fish, millet, potatoes, well-cooked brown rice, raw or lightly steamed vegetables for dogs, non-oily fish such as cod or defatted ground pork for cats.

The animal who is spare, sweet-tempered and thin, has a red tongue without a coating and is thirsty for small amounts of water, is showing signs of heat from an underlying fluid deficiency. Foods that moisten and break up stagnation such as turkey or rabbit are useful.

If the animal is flabby, thirstless, hesitant or overly eager to please, dampness and a spleen constitution predominate. Her tongue is heavy and wet. Overheating is unusual, but frequent eliminations with straining are common. Foods that dry the excess dampness and support the spleen are helpful.

White meat chicken, lean beef, white rice, corn and high-fiber foods are drying. Avoid dairy and raw vegetables as these create more dampness.

If stagnation is the most prominent problem, the animal will appear bloated and fatigued after eating. This condition usually occurs with other components of heat, cold or damp. Avoid dairy foods. Turkey and rabbit may help because these foods are warm or neutral and increase fluid and yang movement to aid in breaking up stagnation.

◆ Nutritional Supplements

Because of poor digestive absorption, digestive supplements such as acidophilus and pancreatic enzymes may be tried in small amounts. Be watchful, because in some cases, *any* supplement can cause more diarrhea.

CONSTIPATION

Constipation is usually a problem of **dryness, qi, heat** or **stagnation**. A deficiency of fluid from blood or yin which causes dryness in the colon usually comes from an imbalance in the lungs, liver, or stomach. Because there are not enough fluids to offset the heat generated from within the body, a deficiency type heat or fire develops. Animals with this condition are thirsty and often have dry, dandruffy skin. Lack of fluids from yin or blood causes constipation with hard, dry, crumbly stools. If the mucosa of the large intestine becomes irritated from friction as the stool moves through, there may be bleeding as well.

Weak qi from the spleen/pancreas and stomach causes sluggish digestion, fatigue and no desire to try to pass stool.

Pekoe is a rather highly strung Pomeranian. As a puppy, Pekoe would run around frantically and then collapse with exhaustion. His appetite was irratic; he liked to eat at dinner time, but often skipped breakfast because he preferred to go out to play. As he grew older, his energy level began to diminish and his appetite became finicky. He was constantly thirsty, but he only drank a few sips at a time. His digestion became extremely sluggish and although it embarrassed him, he burped a lot. As his energy and appetite dwindled, his bowel movements became smaller and less regular. The act of elimination so exhausted Pekoe that he often gave up, which caused severe constipation. I determined that he was having a qi problem, originating in the spleen/pancreas. His nervousness hindered the qi and made digestion difficult. Since the qi is used to feed the muscles, including those of the colon, weakness can lead to poor muscle strength. The resulting lack of energy usually indicates a qi deficiency.

Some animals develop constipation due to an overactive liver which causes excess heat to be produced in the body. This is *true* heat, usually stemming from eating too much yang type or fatty, rich foods or from being constantly angry or frustrated. Excess liver heat can eventually find its way to the colon and cause constipation. An excessive type individual who is robust and pushy both in attitude and body is prone to this situation. He is thirsty for great gulps of water, inhales his food and is ready to eat again as soon as he has finished.

With constipation caused by stagnation, the moisture might be present, but it has become stuck in pockets in the colon. When waste remains stuck in one place for a while, heat develops that can evaporate the colon's normal moisture. This is part of a liver condition that involves the spleen/pancreas and large intestine. Stagnation is associated with pain and discomfort during elimination. While the qi-deficient animal might spend long periods without any desire to go, the animal with stagnation has the frequent urge to try.

◆ Acupressure Treatment of Constipation from Dryness and Deficiency Heat

Stomach (ST) 25. Known as "Heaven's Axis," this is the alarm point of the large intestine and is used to balance and activate the organ.

Location: See page 282. Use a small circular motion directly on the point.

Spleen (SP) 6. Known as the "Three Yin Junction," this point moistens the yin of the body.

Location and technique: See page 153.

Stomach (ST) 36. Known as "Three Mile Run," this point strengthens the qi and blood of the body.

Location and technique: See page 219.

Lung (LU) 7. Known as "Broken Sequence," this point is the meeting place of the lung with the conception vessel. The conception vessel regulates the yin and moisture. The lung is the partner of the large intestine and will share its fluid if the colon becomes depleted. Increasing fluid via the lung helps the large intestine.

Location and technique: See page 173.

◆ Herbal Treatment

Licorice. The root of this Western and Chinese herb is both sweet and moistening. It stimulates the spleen and the qi of the body. Avoid it if your animal is hypertensive.

    Dosage, as tincture: mix 10 drops in 1 ounce water.

        cat/small dogs: 1 dropperful daily

        medium dog: 2 dropperfuls daily

        large dog: 3 dropperfuls daily

Chickweed.[10] This yin herb moistens and coats the large intestine. It is helpful when dryness with deficiency heat causes symptoms such as thirst and dry, crumbly stool. Make a tea using ½ teaspoon to 1 cup water.

    Dosage: cats/small dogs: 1 tablespoon daily

        medium/large dogs: 2 to 3 tablespoons daily

Marshmallow. Its mucosa restoring properties help in constipation, as well as diarrhea.

    Dosage: See page 324.

    Because of their dampening qualities, these herbs may cause sluggishness in some animals. If this occurs, add 2 drops of **lavender** or **wild bergamot** tincture to enhance the circulation.

◆ Dietary Recommendations

With dry, crumbly stool, avoid or limit feeding dry foods as these will only intensify the problem. Also avoid meats high in fats which will create internal heat that uses up internal fluids. Goat's milk and yogurt is sometimes helpful. Oat or wheat bran moistened with olive oil and honey is an old standby to feed on a daily basis.

Use cooling and moistening foods. Whole grains like well-cooked spelt (whole berry),[11] brown rice and millet are good sources of both fiber and moisture. Steamed or baked sweet potatoes will furnish moisture to the intestines, as will yellow squashes. Well-cooked lima bean, peas and lentils are useful, especially for dogs. Raw and steamed vegetables to choose from include spinach, carrots and broccoli. Neutral proteins that stengthen the qi and blood such as lean beef, soft-boiled eggs, and fish such as cod or clams are helpful. Psyllium and flax seeds are good for moistening. Husks are high in fiber, create bulk and cause thirst. However, if there is too much dryness, bulk products may only irritate the situation.

◆ Nutritional Supplements

Acidophilus: ¼ to ½ the human dosage

Icelandic Moss: ½ teaspoon to 1 teaspoon daily. These herbs help restore minerals and intestinal flora.

CONSTIPATION FROM EXCESS LIVER HEAT AND STAGNATION

Treatment is aimed at cooling the liver to decrease the heat, and to promote intestinal and qi flow.

♦ Acupressure

Triple Heater (TH) 6. Known as "Branch Ditch," this point spreads the qi, relieving stagnation and encouraging movement through the intestines. It is used with **Kidney (KI) 6.**[12]

Location: On the front aspect of the forearm. Divide the forearm into four sections, beginning at the wrist and ending at the elbow. Triple Heater 6 is located approximately one quarter of the way up from the wrist, toward the inside of the arm. Because there is only a small depression that may be difficult to find, use a sweeping motion and massage the front of the leg from just above the wrist to one third of the way up the arm to include point.

Kidney (KI) 6. Known as "Shining Sea," this point cools heat and enhances moisture.

Location: On the inside of the hind foot, just below the ankle bone, in the depression below the ankle prominence. Hold the point.

Urinary Bladder (BL) 25. Known as "Large Intestine's Hollow," this is the association point of the large intestine and is used to balance this organ in cases of either constipation or diarrhea.

Location and technique: See page 327.

Liver (LIV) 2. Known as "Walk Between," this point relieves heat and breaks up stagnation.

Location and technique: See page 156.

♦ Herbal Treatment

Herbs to cool the liver and to break up stagnation are used to help this type of constipation. Avoid tinctures containing alcohol or boil off the alcohol, as described on page 78. Alcohol can upset the liver even more. Use equal parts of:

Barberry Root + Dandelion Root + Anise

Barberry and dandelion strengthen the intestinal lining and help stimulate bile flow from the liver. The anise acts as a relaxant and increases flow of energy through the intestine.

> **Dosage:** cats/small dogs: ¼ teaspoon, once or twice daily
> medium dogs: ½ teaspoon, once or twice daily
> large dogs: ¾ teaspoon, once or twice daily

Aloe Juice or **Powder.**[13] This cooling herb helps alleviate heat and stagnation affecting the liver. The powdered root can be used as a short term, medium strength laxative, especially if blood is present. This herb is very bitter and needs to be encapsulated or mixed with apple juice to help temper the flavor. Do not give the powder to pregnant animals. The juice can be used to moisten the intestine.

> **Dosage** as powder:
> cat/small dog: #3 capsule, twice daily for up to 2 days
> medium dog: # 0 capsule, twice daily for up to 2 days
> large dog: #00 capsule, twice daily for up to 2 days
> Juice: ¼ to ¾ teaspoons daily, depending upon size of animal.

◆ Dietary Recommendations

When constipation is caused by excess heat and stagnation from the liver, diet choices should be cooling and neutral. Avoid red meat, shrimp and poultry. Non-oily fish, defatted pork, small amounts of rabbit, egg, soy or other beans may be used. More vegetables and grains are suitable to this type of constipation. Cats can be given whole grains for some of their protein needs, but not all. Lower animal protein in the range of 25 to 30% is adequate. Grains such as well-cooked brown rice, millet and spelt are helpful. For dogs, use a mostly vegetarian diet, including cabbage, sweet potatoes, white potatoes, spinach, asparagus, cucumbers and carrots.[14]

Bran from oats or wheat is helpful. Moisten the bran with a small amount of olive oil or sesame oil and form into a ball. The olive oil helps clear the liver.

cats/small dogs: ½ teaspoon twice daily
medium/large dogs: 1 teaspoon twice daily

LIFESTYLE AND CONSTIPATION

Many of the animals who live with us depend upon our coming home to let them out or to walk them in order to have a bowel movement. With cats and dogs, regular exercise and stimulation facilitates intestinal motion. Many clients tell me that although they let the dog out into the back yard to do her business, she doesn't go until she's out on a walk. Maybe it's the stimulation of walking, the company, or the excitement of being outside—whatever it is, make sure that the dog has ample time to go. Daily walks will help to keep her regular and keep you *both* healthy.

In the case of indoor cats who use a litter box, two scenarios may develop that hinder proper bowel movement. The first is a dirty litter box. Cats will hold it in for excessive periods of time rather than use a full litter box. The other deterrent is a litter box located in a busy place in the house, or in a place where the cat is afraid to pass other housemates. Remember that emotional distress can create stagnation. So please put the box in a place that is comfortable for your cat. She will be happier and healthier for it.

Feeding on a regular basis at fixed times is necessary for proper digestion in general. Sudden changes in diet and erratic feeding times can lead to a poorly functioning disgestive tract and a miserable animal companion.

Endnotes

1. Kaptchuk, Ted, J., OMD. *The Web That Has No Weaver.* (New York: Congdon & Weed, 1983), 291.

2. Jones, Feather. *Turtle Island Herbs.* (Boulder, CO: Southwest Lectures, 1991), 1994.

3, 6, 7. Wood, Matthew and Tismal Crow. Herb Lectures, Batesville, Indiana, 1994.

4, 13. Tierra, Michael, CA, ND. *Planetary Herbology.* (Santa Fe, NM: Lotus Press, 1988), 251, 170.

5. Naeser, Margaret, PhD. *Outline Guide to Chinese Herbal Patent Medicines in Pill Form.* (Boston, MA: Boston Chinese Medicine, 1990), 68.

8, 10. Holmes, Peter. *The Energetics of Western Herbs, Vol. I.* (Boulder, CO: Artemis Press, 1989), 140, 393.

9. Hoffmann, David, BSc, MNIMH. *An Elders' Herbal.* (Rochester, VT: Healing Arts Press, 1993), 245.

11, 14. Pitchford, Paul. *Healing with Whole Foods.* (Berkeley, CA: North Atlantic Books, 1993), 441, 346, 498.

12. O'Conner, John and Dan Bensky, trans. ed. *Acupuncture, A Comprehensive Text.* (Seattle, WA: Eastland Press, 1981), 236.

CHAPTER
NINETEEN

The Bones and Muscles

The bones form the skeleton which is the underlying structure of the body. The exterior surface of bones is made up of a very thin silica, calcium and phosphorus matrix, known as the cortex. On the inside, bones house the blood-rich marrow. The ends of the long bones of the limbs have cushions made of cartilage. Cartilage is less dense than bone, but has much of the same character. Along the spine, cartilage-type structures called discs separate and cushion the vertebrae, giving the backbone resiliency and flexibility. Ligaments are the fibrous strands that join bone to bone. Tendons are the fibrous end parts of muscles that attach to the bones.

A joint is the hinge-like meeting place between two bones that provides a smooth and lubricated surface for rotating or moving sideways, up or down. Joints include bone, cartilage, ligaments and sometimes tendons.

In Traditional Chinese Medicine, it is said that the kidneys rule the bones. As we saw in Chapter Seventeen, the inherited kidney jing creates the blueprint for the entire bony structure of the body before birth. Environmental factors and diet affect the way the bones develop. The liver and gall bladder rule the tendons and ligaments around the bones.

The spleen/pancreas regulates the muscles. Therefore, in TCM healthy bones, joints and muscles require properly functioning kidneys, liver and spleen.

ARTHRITIS

When the bones comprising a joint form an incorrect angle, the normal gliding action is replaced by friction. Stress develops at the bone ends and the joint surfaces become rough and irregular. The resulting irritation and inflammation is called arthritis. Once arthritis inflammation occurs on a regular basis, it can wear down parts of the bone. The body responds by adding on more bits of bone, but not necessarily in the right places. These spurs or rough surfaces create more pain, resulting in limping or muscle tension.

Because this bone remodelling process is continual, most arthritis syndromes are progressive. Because of its chronic nature and inflammatory effects, arthritis is considered an immune disorder.

In Traditional Chinese Medicine, arthritis is called **bi syndrome**. Bi syndrome is an obstruction in the circulation leading to pain. It is related to the environmental factors of wind, cold and damp.[1] These factors enter the muscle layer of an individual who is susceptible due to various pre-existing imbalances. The muscles become tense, pulling on the joints and creating stagnation of the blood flow. The longer the stagnation is allowed to exist, the greater the pain and damage to underlying bones.

There are several forms of bi syndrome. One type comes on suddenly and goes from joint to joint like the wind. This continual "travelling" sometimes makes it hard to locate exactly which joint is painful to the animal. Other forms become worse in damp or cold weather. The most advanced form includes aspects of all of the above, leading to extra bone formation or spurs, stagnation, severe pain and drastic curtailment of movment. In TCM, this is known as **bony bi**. In Western medicine, this condition is called **degenerative joint disease** and is the most prevalent form of arthritis in animals.

BONY BI SYNDROME:
HIP DYSPLASIA AND ARTHRITIS

Hip dysplasia is a form of bony bi. A severe form of arthritis, it is a genetic bone malformation. The hips lie in the pelvic sockets at a certain angle. If the angle is too wide, narrow or shallow, areas of stress develop on the hip joint. Imagine a ball sitting in a bowl. If the ball fits exactly into the bowl, it rolls smoothly. However, if the ball and bowl don't match exactly in shape, the ball winds up sitting partly inside and partly outside of its holder. It is not free to move around because it gets caught on the edges. The hip joint is exactly like this. A perfect fit allows perfect rotation. Because hip dysplasia is hereditary, Traditional Chinese Medicine considers it to be a condition of deficient kidney jing.

Signs of hip dysplasia in young animals include stiffness, reluctance to jump, resistance to being touched around the hind quarters or irritability. Some animals may not show signs of hip dysplasia until later in life, but the hereditary factor is still at work. However, in many cases, regular exercise and a good nutritional program can help put off or lessen the severity of the painful symptoms.

Dysplasia usually affects the hips, but can also affect the elbows. Since all joints are effectively connected to each other, when one joint is out of alignment, it throws the next one off down the line. If one area is painful, the animal will shift his weight to a nearby or opposite area to avoid the pain. This puts further stresses on the body. Thus, when the hip hurts, it is not uncommon for low back or knee problems to develop.

◆ Treatment

Treatment of bi syndrome is aimed at relieving pain by breaking up the stagnation, stimulating the blood circulation, dispelling the wind and pain from the muscles, warming the internal cold and drying the dampness. This approach also helps to normalize the bone remodelling and hinder further deterioration. I encourage regular exercise, except during severely painful episodes. Walking and controlled running are best, building up the animal's stamina gradually.

Because the organs involved in healthy bones, muscles, tendons and ligaments are the kidneys/urinary bladder, spleen/pancreas and liver/gall bladder, acupoints along these meridians are included in treatment. Depending upon the most prevalent symptoms, points are chosen to rebalance the organs according to the dominant factor. For example, points along the spleen/pancreas are used in arthritis that is worse in damp conditions, causing stiffness and muscle sogginess. Points along the liver and kidney meridians are used to clear stagnation and to alleviate pain in all forms of arthritis. Points along the kidney or bladder meridian warm the body and are used in arthritis that becomes worse in the cold. Points along the gall bladder meridian dispel wind and muscle pain in arthritis that moves from joint to joint or that comes on suddenly. Additionally, there are general joint pain points that can be used no matter what area is involved.

There are two sets of acupoints: One set addresses the underlying problems, and one addresses the local area.

◆ Acupressure Treatment for Arthritis

Since stagnation is the most dominant component in arthritis, keeping the circulation stimulated is paramount to relieving pain and decreasing the progressive nature of this condition. As discussed in Chapter Eight, massage along the spine and limbs is helpful in nurturing the circulation and relieving stagnation.

Choose several from the following general points:

Urinary Bladder (BL) 60. Known as "Kunlun Mountains," this is known as the "aspirin point."[2] It disperses wind and relaxes the muscles. It can be used for neck, back, hind or front leg pain and/or stiffness.

Location: On the outside of the hind leg, in the depression at the base of the Achilles tendon, midway between the tendon and the ankle bone. The easiest technique is to grasp both sides of the skin in the area in front of the tendon (this feels like two pieces of skin rubbing together). Rub up and down. You will be treating BL 60 on the outside of the leg and **Kidney 3** on the inside of the leg.

Liver (LIV) 3. Known as "Great Pouring," this point breaks up stagnation, encouraging circulation along the liver meridian. It is useful in lower back pain, pain of the hips, knees and ankles.

Location: See page 241. Hold the point or use a light, upward brushing motion to stimulate the liver circulation.

Urinary Bladder (BL) 40. Known as "Commission the Middle," this point relieves heat and inflammation in the lower part of the body. It is good for low back pain, sciatica, and pain in the hips, knees or ankles. It also helps to strengthen the hind legs.

Location and technique: See page 250.

Urinary Bladder (BL) 23. Known as "Kidney's Hollow," this is the association point of the kidneys. It helps to balance the organ, strengthen the bones, relieve pain in the low back and knees. It warms the body and alleviates dampness.

Location and technique: See page 189.

Gall Bladder (GB) 34. Known as "Yang Tomb Spring," this point strengthens the tendons and ligaments of the body. It is also useful for a weak back end, numbness or paralysis in the limbs and arthritis that is worse in damp weather.

Location and technique: See page 249.

Spleen (SP) 9. Known as "Yin Tomb Spring," this point clears dampness from the body. It is useful for arthritis that worsens in damp weather, as well as arthritis of the knee and lower leg. Because there is an excess of dampness, the individual feels heavy and moves sluggishly. This point helps to clear stagnation along the spleen channel.

Location and technique: See page 194.

Stomach (ST) 36. Known as "Three Mile Run," this point strengthens the qi of the body, which in turn, strengthens the immune system, the bones, and builds stamina. It is useful in all arthritis situations where there is weakness.

Location and technique: See page 219.

The following local points may be very sensitive to the arthritic animal. Be gentle when you hold a point or massage your animal friend. If there is too much pain, she may object politely or not so politely. If there is too much pain, stick to general points until stagnation is cleared. Local points are followed by selected general points to complete the treatment.

◆ Hip Joint

Gall Bladder (GB) 29 & 30. Known as "Stationary Seam,"and "Encircling Leap," these points are in front of and behind the hip joint. They are used for back pain, hip dysplasia/arthritis and paralysis of the leg. They are also good for sciatica.

Location: Find the hip joint by having the animal lie on her side, then flex the leg by picking it up at the foot. The hip joint can be seen as the place where the top of the leg joins the pelvis. There is normally a lot of muscle surrounding the hip joint, so keep flexing the leg until you can locate the hip joint. If the animal is in pain, try locating the hip on a pain-free animal first. Once the hip joint is located, the points lie in depressions in front of and behind the hip socket. Hold the points or use small circular motions.

Add general points: **Gall Bladder 34,** page 249 + **Liver 3,** page 241 + **Urinary Bladder 60,** page 340 + **Urinary Bladder 23,** page 189.

Or **Gall Bladder 34,** page 249 + **Urinary Bladder 40,** page 250 + **Stomach 36,** page 219.
Massaging the sacrum will also help to loosen the muscles of the hind leg.

◆ Knee (Stifle)

"Eyes of the Knee." Located on both sides of the knee cap, these points form the dimples of the knee. Gentle holding of the points is helpful.

Add general points: **Urinary Bladder 23,** page 189 + **Gall Bladder 30,** above + **Gall Bladder 34,** page 249 + **Urinary Bladder 60,** page 340 + **Urinary Bladder 40,** page 250.

◆ Ankle (Tarsus)

Gall Bladder (GB) 40. Known as "Mound of Ruins," this point clears stagnation, moves the liver qi and blood, and is useful in ankle swellings and pain.

Location: On the front of the hind paw, between the fourth and fifth foot bones, just beneath the large ankle bone called the lateral malleolus. Hold the point.

Add general points: **Liver 3,** page 241 + **Gall Bladder 34,** page 249 + **Urinary Bladder 60,** page 340 + **Stomach 36,** page 219.

◆ Shoulder (Scapula)

Find the shoulder by lifting the front leg and bringing it forward. The point of the shoulder is at chest level. The shoulder bone or scapula, lies flat against the side of the rib cage and has a central elevated ridge. At the bottom of the ridge is a protuberance called the acromion. The acromion is what you can feel at the end of the shoulder. The joint is below this, sitting on top of the long bone of the arm, the humerus. With its muscles and tendons the joint forms three depressions. These are the acupressure points of the shoulder.

Large Intestine (LI) 15. Known as "Shoulder Bone," this point is used to clear dampness, stagnation and pain from the shoulder.

Location: This is the most forward facing of the three shoulder points. It lies between the the acromion and the major tendon of the upper arm (biceps) and the head of the humerus. Hold the point, or use a small circular motion.

Triple Heater (TH) 14. Known as "Shoulder Seam," this point is used for shoulder pain.

Location: The second of the points, it lies at the shoulder joint, just behind the major tendon, in the depression just behind the acromion. Hold the point.

Small Intestine (SI) 10. Known as "Scapula's Hollow," this point is used for pain in the shoulder joint, short-stepping and paralysis of the upper limb.

Location: The third of the points, lies behind the shoulder joint, in the dimple of the big muscle mass of the deltoid (over the supraspinatus). Hold the point.

Large Intestine (LI) 11. Known as "Crooked Pool," this point strengthens the forelimbs and alleviates heat and dampness from them.

Location: See page 156. Hold the point or use a small circular motion.

Add general points: **Urinary Bladder 60,** page 340 + **Gall Bladder 34,** page 249.

Shoulder pain causes tightness between the shoulder blades. The animal will usually carry the painful shoulder higher than the other one. This tenses the entire upper back. Massage beween the shoulder blades and down the neck is very helpful.

◆ Elbow

This is the major weight-bearing joint of the front limb. There is relatively little muscle surrounding this joint. General massage around the elbow is helpful. Use the fingers and palm of your hand and gently encircle the front inside area of the elbow. Use a sweeping motion from the inside toward the outside and around the back of the elbow. Do this 8 times.

Large Intestine (LI) 4. Known as "Adjoining Valleys," this point is the master point for the head and upper body. It disperses wind muscle pain and clears stagnation.

Location and technique: See page 152.

Add general points: **Urinary Bladder 60,** page 340 + **Gall Bladder 34,** page 249.

◆ Wrist (Carpus)

General massage around the wrist, beginning on the inside and working all around is effective. You can also use a gentle upward and downward motion.

Small Intestine (SI) 3. Known as "Back Creek," this point is good for acute situations such as sprains or other trauma. It relaxes the muscles and calms the spirit.

Location: On the outside aspect of the front paw, in the depression in the fifth paw bone, just above where the bone joins the toes.

Add points: **Large Intestine 4**, page 152 + **Large Intestine 11**, page 156 + **Urinary Bladder 60**, page 340 + **Gall Bladder 34**, page 249.

◆ Back Arthritis and Muscle Spasms

If your animal sustains a back injury, he should be checked out by a veterinarian without delay. There may be potential disc problems or trauma that requires professional medical care. If your animal friend has been diagnosed with arthritis of the spine with spondylosis, this is a chronic condition for which Western medicine has little to offer except anti-inflammatory medications. In addition to the recommendations of your veterinarian, acupressure can be helpful. General massage in small circular motions or gentle back and forth motion can be used along the muscles on either side of the spine. If the animal's condition is worse in cold weather, **moxa** can be used to warm the muscles (see Chapter Seventeen, pages 302–03.) After you've lit the moxa, place your free hand on the animal's spine and move it concurrently with the other hand. Slowly, guide the moxa over the back muscle, holding it just off the fingertips to monitor temperature and make sure you don't singe your friend's fur. Moxa will reduce muscle spasms and general back pain that become worse in cold weather. Daily massage is helpful in stimulating the circulation.

In addition to working on the spine, use **Gall Bladder 30**, page 342, which relaxes the spine, **Gall Bladder 20**, page 152 (at the nape of the neck), to relax the upper back, **Liver 3**, page 241, **Urinary Bladder 40**, page 250, **Stomach 36**, page 219 or **Gall Bladder 34**, page 249.

DISC PROBLEMS

The discs are the soft, spongy material that act as cushions between the vertebrae. If they become injured and bulge and swell, they can put pressure on the spinal cord, causing pain, numbness and even paralysis. In Traditional Chinese Medicine, disc problems arise from weakened kidney yang which cannot warm and move the circulation properly. This influences the spleen/pancreas and liver, which leads to increased dampness and stagnation, affecting the muscles, tendons and ultimately the bones. With these predispositions, a sudden movement may compromise the back, causing pain, tearing or swelling of a spinal disc.

Disc injuries are medical emergencies. Professional care should be sought immediately. A veterinarian trained in acupuncture can make medical decisions as to whether acupuncture, Western drugs or surgery is appropriate.

Once a disc has been injured, healed and calcified, the disc itself and surrounding areas stay vulnerable to injury and stress. The scene is set for the chronic disc problem. It is natural to want to protect the area by favoring it or using it as little as possible. However, this only causes further stagnation. To avoid compounding these problems, the circulation should be invigorated. General massage along the spine to keep it flexible, along with the following points to strengthen the bones and the qi are helpful.

◆ Acupressure Treatment of Chronic Disc Problems

General gentle back massage +

Urinary Bladder (BL) 11. Known as "Big Shuttle," this point is considered the "influential bone point," which aids in bone remodelling. It is useful in arthritis, back pain and paralysis of the limbs.

Location: On both sides of the spine, just in front of the shoulder blades, at the level of the first rib.

Add general points: **Gall Bladder 34,** page 249 + **Urinary Bladder 60,** page 340 + **Urinary Bladder 23,** page 189 + **Liver 3,** page 241 + **Stomach 36,** page 219.

◆ Herbal Treatment

Liu Wei Di Huang Wan and **Sexoton Pills** or **Golden Book Tea.** These are tonics that nourish the kidneys and help to strengthen weak and stiff backs and lower legs. They are for deficiency of the blood and yin fluid of the kidney and liver, which is the underlying problem with most arthritis cases. Weakness, wobbliness, swaying in the low back area, heat over the spine and hip areas, as well as thirst are strong indications for Liu Wei Di Huang Wan. Weakness, wobbliness, swaying and coolness over the spine and hip areas are strong indications for golden book tea. Dosage and herb ingredients are listed in Chapter Seventeen, page 296.

Du Huo Jisheng Wan.[3] This formula helps in arthritis that worsens in cold and damp weather. It is useful for pain, stiffness, sciatica, and weakness in the hind legs. It is a very warming formula, so if the animal is showing signs of heat such as excess thirst, excessive panting or seems to become easily overheated, this formula should not be used. It contains eucommia to strengthen kidney yang; rehmannia and tang kuei to strengthen kidney yin and blood; codonopsis, ginger, cinnamon bark and licorice to strengthen qi; and du huo, loranthus and hoelen to dispel dampness, wind, muscle pain and decrease stagnation.

>   **Dosage:** cats/small dogs: 1 to 2 pills, once or twice daily
>   medium dogs: 4 pills, twice daily
>   large dogs: 6 pills, twice daily

The following alternative Western herb combination can be used if the animal is in obvious pain and you can feel heat around the joints. It includes plants that contain salicylic acid which is what aspirin is derived from. The plant extracts do not ordinarily cause the same bleeding problems that aspirin does, but care should be taken nonetheless. Signs of depression, blood in the stool, or red or purple skin blotches may be signs of internal bleeding. If these occur, stop administering the herb and see your veterinarian.

Other indications of heat and inflammation may be panting, thirst and restlessness. The joints may feel so hot that the skin above the joint gets a "hot spot" skin eruption.

Meadowsweet + Willow Bark + Nettles + Cayenne + Lavender
Mix 5 drops meadowsweet, 5 drops willow bark, 5 drops nettles and 1 to 2 drops each of cayenne and lavender tinctures to 1 ounce distilled water.
  Dosage: cats/small dogs: ½ to 1 dropperful, once or twice daily
       medium dogs: 1 to 2 dropperfuls, twice daily
       large dogs: 2 to 3 dropperfuls, twice daily

Meadowsweet.[4] This Western herb contains aspirin-like salicylic acid, and relieves inflammation, dampness and heat.

Willow Bark.[5] This Western herb contains aspirin-like salicylic acid, along with tannins, and relieves inflammation, dampness and heat.

Nettles.[6] This Western herb is nutritive and clears inflammation, dampness and heat. Along with vitamins C and B-carotene and lecithin, nettles acts as a diuretic, clearing toxins through the kidneys.

Cayenne. This is a very warm pungent herb that will help break up the stagnation and disperse the other herbs.

Lavender. This is an herb that has both warming and cooling capabilities. It is used to break up stagnation and relieve pain.

Yucca. This Western herb has a cooling quality and is helpful where the joints appear swollen and hot to the touch.
  Dosage, as powdered herb: cats/small dogs: ⅛ to ¼ teaspoon per day
       medium dogs: ¼ to ½ teaspoon per day
       large dogs: ⅔ to ¾ teaspoon per day

Alfalfa. This is a nutritional herb, helpful to the kidney in general. Alfalfa is high in calcium to support bone remodelling. It contains several enzymes and vitamins.

Dosage: cats/small dogs: ½ teaspoon per day
medium dogs: 1 teaspoon per day
large dogs: 2 teaspoons per day

Chin Koo Tieh Shang Wan.[7] This is known in Chinese as the "hit pill" for acute injuries, bruising, swelling and other inflammation. It is used to speed the healing time in trauma, fractures, sprains and strains. Its major ingredient is pseudoginseng which invigorates the circulation and removes toxins and debris from the blood in the affected areas as a fresh blood supply is brought in. This breaks up the stagnation which causes pain and swelling. For short-term use, this herb combination is helpful for up to two weeks following an injury.

Dosage: cats/small dogs: 1 pill, twice a day
medium dogs: 3 pills, twice a day
large dogs: 5 pills, twice a day

◆ Nutritional Supplements

Nutritional supplements and diet are probably the most significant aids in helping bone and muscle problems.

ANTIOXIDANTS AND FREE RADICALS

Western nutritional research has discovered that an unstable oxygen molecule in the body, known as O_3, can cause significant cellular damage. These unstable molecules are known as "free radicals." They are by-products of the body's enzyme reactions which are liberated during the toxic clean-up process.

Toxins enter the body via pesticides and preservatives, pollution in the air or water or viruses and bacteria. When we are exposed to toxic pollution, an over-abundance of free radicals attach to healthy or vulnerable cells. This causes irregularities in the cell walls. If an individual is predisposed to digestive problems the free radicals may attach to mucous membranes lining the various organs of the digestive tract, causing excess mucous, pain and ulcers. If an individual is predisposed to bone problems, these free radicals use the joint surfaces as targets for binding.

Imagine a smooth joint surface, glistening and slick. When free radicals begin attaching to the cells of the joint surface, it becomes eroded and rough. In response to the pain, the body may begin to lay down calcium to fill in the gaps caused by the erosion. Unfortunately, this worsens the condition, causing pain, swelling, bone irregularities and deformities.

Antioxidants bind with free radicals to stop this reaction. Antioxidants circulate and attach to the free oxygen radicals *before* they can bind to the surface of healthy cells.

◆ Sources of Antioxidants

Vitamin A, as cod liver oil or alone:
> cats/small dogs: 2,000 IU daily
> medium dogs: 5,000 IU daily
> large dogs: 10,000 mg daily

Because vitamin A is stored in the liver, if there is a history of hepatitis, liver swelling or cirrhosis, these doses may not be well tolerated and toxicity may develop. Cut the dose in half and use every other day.

Vitamin C, as sodium ascorbate. Use as high a dose as possible with diarrhea being the limiting factor, up to 5,000 mg per day.

Vitamin E. In some animals this vitamin can cause high blood pressure. Usual safe dosage: cats/small dogs: 50 IU daily
> medium dogs: 200 IU daily
> large dogs: 400 IU daily

Enhancing vitamin E with **selenium** is helpful: 10 to 50 mcg daily

Super Oxide Dismutase. This enzyme is helpful in free radical scavenging. Various products are available through holistic veterinarians and natural food stores.

Microalgae/Chlorophyll counters inflammation and helps to restore the connective tissue around the joints.[8] Some animals are sensitive to this supplement and develop diarrhea so, try very small amounts at first.

Kelp Powder, for mineral support:

> cats/small dogs: ⅛ teaspoon daily
> medium dogs: ¼ to ½ teaspoon daily
> large dogs: ¾ teaspoon daily

Nutritional Yeast Flakes, for vitamin B support and trace minerals:

> cats/small dogs: ¼ teaspoon daily
> medium dogs: ½ teaspoon daily
> large dogs: 1 teaspoon daily

Lecithin Granules, to keep the liver circulating the blood freely.

> cats/small dogs: ½ teaspoon daily
> medium dogs: 1 teaspoon daily
> large dogs: 1 tablespoon daily

Essential Fatty Acids, including omega 3 oils. Found in fish oils from salmon, mackeral and sardines, omega 3 fatty acids help to clean the arteries and break up stagnant circulation resulting from an overworked liver.

> cats/small dogs: ¼ human dosage
> medium dogs: ½ human dosage
> large dogs: ⅔ human dosage

Available through veterinary sources and natural food stores.

The preceeding supplements are optimal once bone and joint degeneration set in. They also help prevent the development of arthritis. Add one at a time, so that if there is digestive or behavioral upset, you will be able to determine the culprit and reduce the dosage or eliminate it entirely. I recommend adding a new supplement every three days. Cats are much more finicky than dogs about taking supplements. Of prime importance are the vitamins C and E, so if nothing else, try to get your feline friend to take these.

◆ Dietary Recommendations

Because arthritis is a complex condition involving several organ systems, diets must be highly individualized. I will give you some guidelines, but experience with your animal will be the best teacher. Don't be afraid to experiment—seeing your companion's health improve as a result of your efforts is well worth the occasional frustration of the trial-and-error process.

Good bone formation needs a balance between calcium, phosphorus, silica and magnesium. Once arthritis has begun, the body has difficulty with calcium metabolism. Meats are generally low in calcium and higher in phosphorus. Grains are higher in calcium and lower in phosphorus. Vegetables have trace minerals that are needed for proper bone formation.

Red meats are also high in saturated fats and cholesterol which clog the circulation and lead to liver stagnation. Red meats also contain arachidonic acid, an amino acid which can generate an inflammatory response in the body.[9]

Dairy products can create problems of dampness in the digestive tract and cause sluggishness. As with red meat, dairy is a primary source of an amino acid that causes an inflammatory response in the body by generating prostaglandins and leukotrienes. An excellent discussion of diets and arthritis appears in Paul Pitchford's Book, *Healing with Whole Foods*.

Animal Protein. Keep red meat and animal fat to a minimum. Small amounts are important in thin and weak individuals because they help build muscle tissue and blood. Rabbit is a good choice because its properties can strengthen deficient kidney jing. Poultry and fish are better protein sources in cases of arthritis. In Chinese food therapy, most poultry is considered warming, so it is especially useful in arthritis conditions that are worse in cold, damp weather. If your animal tends to pant or overheat easily, fish may be a better choice, or vegetable and grain proteins. Follow the guidelines listed in Chapter Seven on body types and food qualities, pages 87–90. As each individual is different, you may need to try different foods and see which suits your particular animal friend best.

Grains. If the animal's condition is worse in cold weather, choose warming or neutral grains such as oats, rice, corn, rye or quinoa. If the animal pants excessively and shows signs of irritability or frustration such as pacing, choose cooler grains like millet and barley. Wheat is also a cooling grain, but many individuals have a sensitivity to wheat which comes from an imbalance in the immune system. Because arthritis is part of an immune imbalance stemming from a weakened kidney, wheat may not be the best choice.

Legumes. Adding small amounts of lentils, peas, black beans, aduki or kidney beans is beneficial in cases where dampness and heat affect the body. Beans act as diuretics and coolers and pull excess moisture from swollen joints. Soybeans are moistening and create dampness so use these with care in animals already laden with dampness. Since beans are high in calcium, they are helpful in bone remodelling. If your animal friend is weak and thin, legumes may tax the digestion too much and should be limited.

Vegetables. These are useful for mineral content, as well as B vitamins. Some vegetables, such as beets are higher in oxalic acid which can inhibit calcium metabolism. Asparagus, celery, parsley and broccoli are good in damp conditions. Cabbage, carrots, parsnips and kale are good for arthritis that is worse in the cold, or for those animals having cold extremities.[10] Parsnips also contain silicon which fosters bone remodelling. Garlic and onions are useful in promoting circulation, but if the animal tends to have red, itchy eyes, keep them to a minimum.

ARTHRITIS AND THE YOUNG DOG

Since this is primarily a kidney jing problem, the arthritic animal may seem weaker and thinner than her siblings. If this is the case, choose herbs and foods that strengthen the deficiencies. Foods should include small amounts of red meats to bolster the jing. Rabbit and chicken are good choices. Turkey may be too moistening for the animal with watery stools or sluggish digestion. The best grains would be very well cooked brown rice or oats. If she tends to overheat, mix rice with millet. If the young animal appears robust and excessive, but her x-rays show early hip dysplasia, stick with more vegetarian choices, avoiding red meat and using combinations of poultry, fish, and legumes.

ARTHRITIS AND THE OLDER DOG

As your animal grows older, she will become deficient in kidney and liver blood and spleen qi. Thin and weaker animals need extra nourishment. Choose herbs and foods that supplement these deficiencies. Small amounts of red meat and rabbit, as well as hard-boiled eggs are helpful. Grains such as rice, oats and barley will help strengthen both the digestion and the kidney. Protein from animal products should be limited to 15 to 20% of the diet. Limit legumes, as these may be hard to digest. Grains should be cooked thoroughly and vegetables steamed. If diarrhea is a problem, cut out or minimize the vegetables until the diarrhea is under control. If constipation is the problem, increase the vegetables and add yams or sweet potatoes.

ARTHRITIS AND THE OLDER CAT

Because cats need more animal proteins than dogs, limit animal protein in the diet to a lesser extent. Use poultry, rabbit and small amounts of fish. If your cat is also anemic, small amounts of chicken liver can be added once a week to fortify the blood and warm the body. Always try to use liver from free-range and pesticide-free animals. Cod liver oil or essential fatty acids from sardines is especially good. Kale, cabbage and yams or sweet potatoes are good for the thinner, older cat. Because cats are such fussy eaters, it may be difficult to get your feline friend to take supplements, or even to eat at all. Don't be discouraged. Keep experimenting with different combinations of foods until you find a diet that is tolerable. Use massage and herbal combinations as much as your cat friend will allow.

Endnotes

1. Lian Q., Ming S. The Nanjing seminars, J Chin Med 1985; 47–50, reported by A. Schoen, ed. *Problems in Veterinary Medicine, Veterinary Acupuncture.* (Philadelphia, PA: J.B. Lippincott Co., Volume 4, No. l, Mar. 1992), 89.

2. Limehouse, John, DVM. International Veterinary Acupuncture Course Notes. Santa Monica, CA, 1989.

3, 7. Fratkin, Jake. *Chinese Herbal Patent Formulas.* (Boulder, CO: Shya Publications, 1986), 110, 127.

4, 6. Hoffmann, David, BSc., MNIMH. *An Elders' Herbal.* (Rochester, VT: Healing Arts Press, 1993), 144.

5. Moore, Michael. *Medicinal Plants of the Mountain West.* (Santa Fe, NM: Museum of New Mexico Press, 1979), 161.

8, 9, 10. Pitchford, Paul. *Healing With Whole Foods.* (Berkeley CA: North Atlantic Press, 1993), 188, 121, 508.

CHAPTER
TWENTY *The Skin*

The skin is like a third lung. It acts as the boundary between the outside environment and the inside of our bodies. As it "breathes," it filters toxins and guards against the ultraviolet rays of the sun, the wind, the rain and the snow. With its vast surface area, the skin is affected most by wind and heat that dry it and by an internal deficiency of fluids that also creates dryness. Healthy skin texture depends on the digestive organs whose absorption of nutrients feeds the body's surface. Just as the land becomes parched and cracked or flooded, the skin too can show evidence of drought, floods and freezing.

DRY, ITCHY SKIN

Itching is said to be brought on by the wind. Think of how a breeze tickles your skin, or of how a gust of wind blusters its way around your face or arms. You can't reach out and touch the air as it encircles your body, yet you feel it just the same. It is this amorphous feeling that gave birth to the concept of wind causing itching. In addition to its drying nature, the wind can create a sensation of tingling, heat or irritation in susceptible individuals.

The susceptible animal is one who has a deficiency of circulating blood or yin fluids, due to heredity, poor diet or environment. The deficient fluids cannot nourish the skin, so it appears unhealthy and dry. If an animal lives in a dry or windy environment, the fluids become further depleted. The liver is associated with the wind and the lungs are associated with dryness of the air in TCM. So, most skin problems will involve the liver blood or the lung fluids. The blood stores of the liver are influenced by the inherited kidney fluids.

Some skin problems are the result of too much internal heat from the liver. Diets that create internal heat or stagnate the circulation such as high-fat red meats, some poultry and certain seafoods, can use up fluids in the body. Emotional situations such as the stress of fighting within a household, the illness of a family member (human or animal), irritability at having to stay indoors, or the boredom of staying home alone without enough physical exercise, can use up fluids in the body. All of these factors can lead to a state of susceptibility toward the wind and itching.

If the lung fluids and liver blood are low, the skin is usually dry and flaky as well as itchy. The coat feels dusty and may be thinning. It may even turn a lighter color, like black or grey hair turning brownish or auburn and light colors becoming grey.

If the blood stores are low, the animal may feel cold all over or have cold feet or ears. This may worsen after the animal has rested, when the liver is said to have smoothed and regulated the blood flow. It might also make the animal scratch more when she gets up in the morning or after a nap. At this stage of blood deficiency, there is not much body odor. However, there may be dryness in the breathing, a dry, cracked nose or muzzle, or some uncharacteristic irritability or stubborness.

The lungs act as part of the immune system along with the underlying kidney jing (see Chapter Twenty-one, page 375). If it is weak, the skin will be vulnerable to infection from bacteria and fungi, including ringworm. Mild ringworm infections cause only hair loss, dryness and itching, without redness or scabs.

GENERAL SKIN TREATMENT TIPS

Treatment of skin problems in Traditional Chinese Medicine is aimed at "extinguishing the wind" that causes the itching by either cooling the body or nourishing the blood.[1] Wind is extinguished by invigorating or unblocking stagnant circulation. Proper grooming with a brush or comb and regular massage are good ways of invigorating the circulation. Skin cells replace themselves every three to four weeks, and it is good to rid the body of these dead, dry skin flakes. Shampooing with soaps can dry the animal further so use shampoos made from oatmeal colloids that soothe dry skin and won't take more of the moisture away. Dogs with dry skin should be bathed at three to four week intervals in the warm season, and at two month intervals in colder weather. Cats with dry skin should be brushed regularly, and only bathed when necessary to make the animal feel more comfortable. Spraying the animal with teas listed in the topical section, page 363, can replace bathing. Herbs and supplements taken internally will ultimately help your animal externally.

All skin treatments include components for calming the spirit because once itching sets in, the animal becomes extremely exasperated. Many practitioners feel that, in large measure, successful treatments focus as much on balancing the emotional causes of itching as on the physical causes. So, in addition to herbs, an appropriate diet, and acupressure, I recommend regular exercise for dogs *and* cats. The latter might include indoor games like chasing string or playing with your cat's favorite catnip mouse. One of my clients told me that she would lock her cat outside the front door. The cat would have to run around to the back of the house, and climb a tree to get in through the back window. Another client who is a dog parent told me that she was able to stop the scratching by running her dog for half an hour without a break. The dog would be so tired, he would forget to scratch. In TCM terms, the stagnation associated with the itchy skin was relieved by the exercise.

◆ Acupressure Treatment of Dry Itchy Skin

Gall Bladder (GB) 20. Known as "Wind Pond," this point helps to extinguish wind from the body. It also calms nervous irritability.
Location and technique: See page 152.

Spleen (SP) 6. Known as the "Three Yin Junction," this point nourishes the blood and fluid of the liver, kidney and spleen/pancreas and brings fluid to the body.
Location and technique: See page 153.

Large Intestine (LI) 4. Known as "Adjoining Valleys," this point is the master point for the head and upper body. It disperses wind and stimulates the immune system. It is good for itching and dryness around the nose and muzzle.

Location: See page 152. Gently grasp the web. If the animal has had the dewclaw removed, hold the point on top of the "nub" of the dewclaw.

Lung (LU) 7. Known as "Broken Sequence," this point disperses wind and regulates the moisture of the lungs and the body's yin.

Location: See page 173. Use small circular motions on the point and the inside aspect of the wrist.

General body massage will promote the circulation of blood to the surface.

◆ Herbal Treatment

Shou Wu Pian.[2] This single herb extract of polygonum shou wu nourishes the liver and kidney blood. It helps to keep the skin moist and to reverse or stop hair color changes.

> **Dosage:** cats/small dogs: 1 tablet, twice daily
> medium dogs: 2 tablets, twice daily
> large dogs: 3 to 4 tablets, twice daily

Liu Wei Di Huang Wan.[3] This is the classic kidney formula which nourishes the kidney, liver and spleen yin and blood. It contains the yin and blood tonic rehmannia; the astringent herb cornus, that nourishes the fluids of the liver and kidney; the spleen qi tonics dioscorea and hoelen; and the heat-clearing herb of moutan to regulate the liver and kidney.

> **Dosage:** cats/small dogs: 2 pills, once or twice daily
> medium dogs: 4 pills, once or twice daily
> large dogs: 6 pills, once or twice daily

Chamomile + Chickweed + Geranium. This Western herb combination is used to relieve liver wind, smooth the circulation and moisten the yin of the body. Use internally as a tea or in the glycerine tinctures, or externally as a spray.

As tea, use ½ teaspoon of each herb to 1 pint water. Let stand 10 minutes.
Dosage, internally: cats/small dogs: 1 tablespoon, 1 to 3 times daily
medium/large dogs: 2 ounces 1 to 3 times daily.
As tincture: 5 drops of each to 1 ounce distilled water. Use 1 to 3 drop-perfuls, 1 to 3 times daily, depending upon the size of the animal.

◆ Externally

Baths or sprays made from cooled black, green, chamomile or chickweed teas are helpful in alleviating itching and in soothing and nourishing the skin. Teas or lotions made with calendula flowers also moisten the skin.

SCABS AND SMELLS

As the intensity of the internal dryness increases, more heat develops within the body. The liver, lung and kidney fluid and blood stores have diminished significantly, and a relative internal heat or inflammation, called false fire, surfaces. The animal becomes more restless and hot to the touch and persists in continual intense biting, licking and scratching that produces dry, red rashes, bloody scabs or small red bumps. As the heat increases the animal exudes a distinctly "doggy" smell. This stronger odor is an indication of the body's inability to moisten and bathe its internal parts in healthy fluids. As her internal heat increases, so will her thirst, restlessness and irritability. She may seek relief from this heat on a cool tile floor or in the shade. Along with increased panting (in dogs), the tongue will be dark pink or red. But because there are not enough fluids, it will appear dry and have little coating.

The scabby skin eruptions are not only caused by the animal's condition of dryness but can also be a result of an overactive, rather than undernourished liver. If the liver is compromised by toxins from too much rich food or excessive anger, it responds by becoming stagnant or hot (see Chapter Fifteen, page 252). The scabs are the liver's way of expressing these insults, and so the animal continues scratching frantically. The greater the internal heat, the worse the smell.

The animal's moodiness and irritability will be more forceful and intense than in the dry deficient condition. When there is more liver heat from toxic buildup, the tongue itself is red with a yellowish coating. It is important to distinguish between the two conditions, because in dry, deficient conditions foods and herbs that build the blood and cool the individual should be used. If there is a lot of liver heat built up, the heat needs to be cleared before anything else will help.

In Western terms, all these dry skin conditions are classified as allergic dermatitis, flea allergies, food allergies, or fungal or bacterial infections. In TCM they are all phases along a continuum of imbalances created when the blood stores are used up either from an underlying deficiency or an overheating from toxins.

◆ Treatment

Treatment is aimed at cooling the heat that rises to the surface, clearing the wind that causes the itching and strengthening the yin to balance the original condition. Because of the intensity and duration of the situation, it may be a slow process to rebalance all the organs involved.

◆ Acupressure

Gall Bladder (GB) 20. Known as "Wind Pond," this point is used to clear the wind and calm the animal.

Location and technique: See page 152.

Large Intestine (LI) 11. Known as "Crooked Pool," this point clears heat from the upper part of the body, and strengthens the immune system. It can be used with **LI 4**, page 152. It is useful when there is scratching with redness, a rash or scabs, especially in the upper body from either deficiency situations or toxic infection.

Location: See page 156. Hold the point or use small, circular motions.

Liver (LIV) 2. Known as "Walk Between," this point clears heat from the liver channel and helps to spread the qi and blood. It is used for the animal who is hot, irritable, thirsty and who has areas of skin eruptions either around the neck, the groin or the lower back and legs.

Location and technique: See page 156. Use in conjunction with **Large Intestine 11**, page 156.

Spleen (SP) 6. Known as the "Three Yin Junction," this point is used to strengthen and balance the yin and blood.

Location and technique: See page 153.

As the heat dissipates from the body, the skin will feel cooler and the scabs will begin to disappear. The itching will eventually subside, but the skin may still appear to be dry. As these heat signs clear, follow the acupressure points listed for dryness above.

◆ Herbal Treatment

Lien Chiao Pai Tu Pien.[4] This formula is used for excess heat when itching, scabs, restlessness, thirst and a strong, "doggy" odor is present. It is also good for hives and the acute onset of skin problems with swollen glands from toxic buildup. These heat-clearing herbs can damage the qi if taken over a long period of time, so I recommend usage for no more than two weeks. If diarrhea develops, stop the herb. It contains forsythia, lonicera, dictamnus, rhubarb and gardenia to clear heat; scutellaria to clear heat and dampness; siler and cicada to expel wind and heat; and red peony to invigorate the blood and relieve pain from swelling. Do not use if the animal is pregnant.

Dosage: cats/small dogs: ½ tablet, twice daily
medium dogs: 1 tablet, twice daily
large dogs: 2 tablets, twice daily

Margarite Acne Pills.[5] This formula clears internal heat created by the yin and blood deficiencies which cause liver stagnation and heat patterns. It is useful if the animal is hot and losing fur over his whole body, scratching constantly and has red bumps or small scabs, has a noticeable odor, a dry mouth and eyes, and a reddish tongue with little coating. It contains margarita pearl and rehmannia to nourish the yin and blood; lonicera, scrophularia, adenophora, phellodendron and rhubarb to clear the heat.

Calendula + Burdock + Lavender
This Western herb combination clears the lymph system, drains liver toxins, moistens the body in general and invigorates the circulation.

Calendula.[6] This Western herb is used for cooling and nourishing the skin. It is used for wind heat conditions and wind heat with dampness. It clears lymph channels and helps to relieve itching.

Burdock.[7] Used for chronic skin eruptions from internal heat with itching, it dispels wind and heat and softens the skin. The Chinese know this herb as arctium, and tend to use the fruit. Western practitioners use the entire plant including the root.

Lavender. The essential oil released from this plant activates the circulation, cools the surface of the body and clears toxins.

Make 1 pint of tea out of dried herbs using ½ teaspoon of each herb and steep for 20 minutes. Of the tea use 1 teaspoon to tablespoon for a cat or small dog, up to 3 tablespoons for medium to large dogs, twice daily. If excessive urination occurs, decrease dosage by half.

◆ Topicals

Make teas from selfheal, calendula flower and chickweed. Allow to cool, then decant into a spray bottle or sponge on the affected areas. Wild bergamot can be added to relieve stagnation of circulation. Aloe vera gel can also be used to cool the skin and relieve itching. Bathing your animal friend in oatmeal colloid shampoos or aloe vera-based shampoos can be helpful, as are tea rinses after bathing.

◆ Dietary Recommendations

For dry, flaky skin and for dry, hot conditions, neutral and cooling foods are best. If the animal has a dry skin condition, dry food should be minimized, as most dry foods are high in fat and the drying process itself removes moisture. Animal proteins that are cooling or neutral include eggs, defatted ground pork, clams, cod or white fish, rabbit and lean beef. Grains include millet, whole wheat, and barley. Corn and brown rice are neutral, while white rice is slightly warmer. Potatoes are neutral, but have many yin qualities, such as being juicy because they are roots grown under ground in both cold and warm climates.[8] Vegetables that are cooling are spinach, broccoli, celery, mushrooms, mung beans and pumpkin. Neutral vegetables are carrots and string beans.

ITCHING, OOZING AND ODOR

Does your animal friend smell like old gym socks? Does he leave blood or sticky stains on his bedding or your couch? Does he have yellowish-brown, thick, flaky scabs? These are indications that your animal friend is suffering from wind damp heat with the additional component of the spleen/pancreas as part of the problem.

In the Five Element System, the liver controls the spleen/pancreas and the spleen/pancreas controls the kidney. The kidneys keep the liver moist while the lungs help keep the kidneys moist.

With itchy, oozing skin eruptions such as skin ulcers, thick, moist scabs, intense itching, and musty odor, four out of the five organ systems are involved: the kidney, liver, spleen/pancreas and lungs. Western medicine treats these conditions with cortisone and antibiotics. Things are so complex at this point, it's hard to know where to begin. Fortunately, the organs themselves are not yet compromised. Instead, they are pushing all their imbalances to the surface where they can be identified and treated.

Other examples of damp heat and wind on the skin are chronic staph infections, pimples, blisters, rashes that are dull red or purplish, eruptions with pus, fungal infections, psoriasis and eczema.

You and your animal friend are both miserable by now. She wants to be consoled and petted, but you are a bit hesitant because it's not pleasant to do so. The appetite swings between voracious and nonexistent. The spleen/pancreas is responsible for making qi and blood from food and if the spleen is compromised the digestion will be off, causing bloating, gas or vomiting. This makes the animal not want to eat because she feels so unwell afterwards. Later, she becomes very hungry but she doesn't feel satisfied because her body is unable to absorb the nutrients from her food. This makes the animal lethargic.

◆ Treatment

Treatment is aimed at activating the blood to eliminate stagnation, clearing the heat, drying the dampness and alleviating the wind. After treating the skin, attention should be given, to rebalancing and harmonizing the liver and spleen.

◆ Acupressure

Governing Vessel (GV) 14. Known as "Big Vertebra," this point clears wind and increases the yang to decrease stagnation. It also calms the mind, so that the animal will not be as frantic and irritable.

Location: See page 166. Use a mild back and forth fingertip motion.

Large Intestine (LI) 11. Known as "Crooked Pool," this point is used to clear heat and wind.

Location and technique: See page 156.

Urinary Bladder (BL) 40. Known as "Commission the Middle," this point relieves heat from the lower body and increases circulation to the hind legs.

Location: See page 250. Hold the point or a use gentle circular motion.

Spleen (SP) 6. Known as "Three Yin Junction," this point regulates moisture in the body. It is good for all scabby eruptions with and without oozing moisture. It is good for hives that are purplish when used along with **Spleen 10,** below.

Location and technique: See page 153.

Spleen (SP) 10. Known as the "Sea of Blood," this point harmonizes and nourishes the blood and the qi. It also cools heat and is good for hives and hot, scabby eruptions. Use with **Spleen 6,** above.

Location: On the inside of the thigh, above the knee, at the bulge of the large muscle, the vastus medialis. Because it is difficult to explain its exact location, circular massage on the inside of the thigh near the knee should include the point.

◆ Herbal Treatment

Lung Tan Xie Gan Pill.[9] This combination clears the gall bladder and liver and is useful in moist eruptions and hives. It contains gentiana, gardenia, plantago, alisma and scutellaria to clear heat and dampness; bupleurum to clear the liver; clematis to relieve wind itching; tang kuei and rehmannia to nourish blood and yin; and licorice for qi support.

> **Dosage:** cats/small dogs: 1 to 2 pills, twice daily
> medium dogs: 3 pills, twice daily
> large dogs: 4 pills, twice daily

Yellow Dock + Red Root + Chamomile
This Western herb combination will cool and clear the liver, relieve wind itching, drain the lymphatics and dampness, soothe the spirit and help spleen qi.

Yellow Dock.[10] Used for skin eruptions, especially around the neck, and rashes caused by internal liver heat.

Red Root.[10] Used to drain lymph in the lower part of the body, to help clear dampness and to relieve heat and stagnation.

Chamomile. Along with its antiseptic, heat and damp-clearing abilities, chamomile will relax tension and calm the spirit which helps to stop the itching. Mix 5 drops of each tincture in 1 ounce of distilled water.

Dosage: cats/small dogs: 1 dropperful, two to three times daily
medium dogs: 2 dropperfuls, two to three times daily
large dogs: 3 dropperfuls, two to three times daily

Thuja occidentalis.[11] This is good for ringworm and fungal infections that are flaky and itchy, moist and red in the center and dry around the round edges. It is also good for prickly heat rashes. Use for up to two weeks. If irritable urination develops, discontinue the herb. Dilute 10 to 15 drops to 1 ounce distilled water.

Dosage: cats/small dogs: 1 dropperful, once or twice daily
medium dogs: 2 dropperfuls, once or twice daily
large dogs: 3 dropperfuls, once or twice daily

◆ Topicals

Grindelia squarrosa.[12] Make a tea out of the fresh plant, cool thoroughly and use as a wash on itchy, scaly eruptions. It is especially good for poison oak or poison ivy.

Plantain.[13] Use fresh or dried leaves to make a tea, cool thoroughly and use as a wash. It draws out toxins and decreases inflammation.

Calendula. Make a tea out of the tincture or flowers using 30 drops to 1 cup boiled water. Cool thoroughly and sponge on affected areas.

Golden Seal. Use powdered root and sprinkle onto moist oozing sores, or make a paste with water and paint on affected areas.

Witch Hazel. Dilute 40 drops of the tincture in 1 pint of water, decant into a spray bottle and spray on affected areas.

◆ Dietary Recommendations

Because the spleen, as well as the liver, lung and kidney are involved in damp wind heat conditions, cooling foods are used only in small amounts, because they create more problems with dampness and the spleen/pancreas. When there is dampness, there is a tendency for things to sink, stagnate and cause diarrhea or bloating. Mix one quarter cooling foods (listed on page 98) with foods that are neutral and warming to help restore the functioning of the spleen to circulate the blood and lymph.

For animal protein, choose beef, rabbit, and chicken. Overall, use less animal protein as this may create excess internal heat. Small amounts of mackeral are helpful because it dries dampness and helps the spleen.[12] Avoid or limit turkey, shrimp and other shellfish, salmon, eggs, and dairy products as these foods may create more heat or dampness. Grains should be rice, corn or oats. Vegetables may include carrots, squash, kale and broccoli.

HOT SPOTS

Hot spots are areas of stagnant heat that rise to the surface of the body. They are usually moist, but can sometimes be dry. They pop up quite suddenly, sending the animal into a frenzy of chewing or licking. The smell assaults your nose almost immediately. Under the fur, you will find a scab surrounded by a yellowish, gooey mess. The area is so tender that the animal sometimes refuses to let you look at it or treat it topically. Sometimes there is no pus, but instead, a bloody type of ulcer.

Gooey, weepy hot spots are caused by damp wind heat. Hot spots that appear inflamed, ulcerated and bloody are caused by wind heat.

Notice where the hot spot comes up, then try to identify the associated meridian or joint. Hot spots usually appear where the body is weak and the circulation is stuck. Hot spots along the front legs may correspond to pain in the neck region, while those on the hind legs may refer to hip or low-back pain. These points will correspond to the meridians serving the areas. In this way you can trace their possible origins. Hot spots on the left side of the lower body may refer to pain in the colon. Those on the right side may indicate pain in the small intestine. In many cases, they are areas where the animal already has pain, such as around the hips, ankles, knees, elbows or wrists. Treat the hot spot, but then look for the underlying cause and try to treat it.

◆ Acupressure Treatment for Hot Spots

Treatment is aimed at clearing the heat and dampness, extinguishing the wind that is causing the itching and encouraging the circulation. Acupressure behind the ears at **Gall Bladder 20,** page 152, or in front of the shoulders at **Governing Vessel 14,** page 166, along with **Large Intestine 11** at the elbows, page 156, and **Urinary Bladder 40** behind the knees, page 250, will usually assist in temporarily relieving the heat and pain so that you can get to the area of the hot spot to treat it.

◆ Herbal Treatment

Gently clip the hair away from the area, exposing the "spot." Because it is so tender, it is sometimes easiest to spray or sprinkle something on the area, rather than to apply a salve or lotion directly. Use sprays made from teas of plantain and black, green or chamomile, cooled to room temperature. Do this as many times as the animal will allow so that the area can be cleaned with the solutions. If the animal will let you, compress the area with this solution. Follow with a mixture of powdered herbs placed in a salt shaker so that you can sprinkle it on to the area as a covering. Use powdered echinacea or golden seal mixed with a little powdered basil or thyme which will help to disperse the stagnation and cool the heat and dampness. If the hot spot is dry, use aloe vera gel with a drop of tea tree oil or lavender oil mixed into it. There are also commerical preparations containing this combination available in natural food stores. As the hot spot heals, you can use the solutions of plantain and calendula to soak and soothe the affected areas.

You can also use the juice of cucumbers to cool hot spots, and then lemon water made from a sliced lemon soaked in a pint of water or black tea.

◆ Dietary Recommendations

Refer to Chapter Seven, pages 95–98, 115, to choose foods that cool and clear the heat. Add very thoroughly cooked brown rice or steamed potato to the diet to clear toxins and cool the heat. Cooked mung beans will cool the system[13] and cabbage helps the circulation.

Topical and dietary treatment is usually enough to clear most hot spots. However, if the spot is stubborn, consult your veterinarian.

WOUNDS, BLEEDING AND BITES

Traditional Chinese Medicine uses herbs that *activate* blood in order to *stop* bleeding. A famous prescription that was used in the Viet Nam War to stop bleeding from gunshot wounds is a form of pseudoginseng root, the patent herb **Yunnan Pai Yao**.[14] It is used for both internal and external bleeding. I find it helpful in tongue lacerations where the animal is bleeding profusely out of the mouth from having bitten into a sharp object, usually while scavenging for food.

Yunnan Pai Yao comes in small vials of powder, along with a tiny red pill at the top of each bottle. The powder can be sprinkled directly on a wound. At first, the wound will appear to bleed more, but the blood is brighter red. This is the invigorating aspect of the herb that brings new blood to the area. Wait a few minutes and sprinkle again. Soon the bleeding will begin to decrease and eventually stop. For more severe bleeding, use this herb internally on your way to the veterinarian.

> **Dosage:** cats/small dogs: #1 capsule (⅛ teaspoon)
> medium/large dogs: #00 capsule (½ teaspoon)

It is very bitter tasting, so try to encapsulate the powder unless you are using it for tongue lacerations.

Yarrow.[15] Use the flowering tops internally as a strong tea and externally as a poultice for deep cuts. It is also good for blood blisters that begin to gush, or ear hematomas that continuously fill the ear flap. Use externally as a compress. As tea, use 1 to 3 dropperfuls, three times daily, depending upon the size of the animal. Energetically it works similarly to a blood activator and astringent.

Nettles.[16] Used for nose bleeds. Make a strong tea, cool thoroughly and use a dropper to insert into the nose. Use internally, 1 to 3 droppers every 2 hours for three doses. Then follow directions for strengthening the blood, as nosebleeds are usually a consequence of underlying spleen, liver and kidney problems.

Oak Bark and Leaves.[17] The bark is useful for intestinal bleeding, and cuts and abrasions. It contains tannins that help with clotting and disinfection. For insect bites, chew the fresh leaves to release the enzymes, and place on the bite wound.

Plantain. For insect bites or bite wounds, use either the fresh chewed leaves or the dried plant soaked in hot water. Use it as a wash or a poultice by placing the moistened herb in a gauze pad and compressing the affected area.

ABSCESS AND BITE WOUNDS

Clean the wound area with hydrogen peroxide, which will bring oxygen into the area. Compress with plantain tea 3 to 4 times daily for two to three days. This draws out the toxins, and helps to keep the wound open. Internally, use echinacea or usnea[18] tinctures, at 15 drops to 1 ounce distilled water. These can be given at a dosage of 1 to 3 droppers three times daily. Usnea acts like penicillin.

During the early phases of bite wounds, do not use golden seal or calendula topically because these tend to heal the tissues too quickly. Abcesses form from bite wounds that are deep with the top skin healing over before the underlying tissue. This closes the wound to oxygen, and bacteria builds up creating a pocket of infection.

Once infection has set in, it is imperative to bring it to a head and re-open it to release the toxins. If you cannot get to the veterinarian, use warm salt water or Epsom salt compresses 4 to 5 times daily to help open the pocket. Internally, use echinacea, usnea or yarrow in the amounts as indicated above. Abscesses that cause fever and toxic buildup can become emergency situations, especially if the location of the wound is near the head. So if the situation worsens take the animal to a veterinarian.

Once the abscess has been opened, soaking and cleaning with calendula solutions and following with calendula ointment will heal the wound.

FLEA PROBLEMS

Many skin problems are associated with "flea allergies." Holistic practitioners believe that an individual animal has to be in a vulnerable or susceptible condition to have a flea allergy.

In Traditional Chinese Medicine, this means that there is usually an underlying blood deficiency of the liver or kidney that allows stagnation, heat and wind to develop. Strengthening the animal using the guidelines above, together with the nutritional supplements listed at the end of this section, will be of great help in alleviating the allergic reaction. Eating a healthy diet that includes garlic, cabbage, and carrots helps clear and strengthen the liver.

Of course, controlling the flea population is part of the program. My point here is that unless the individual is totally overrun with fleas, a "flea allergy" condition is not just from the parasite. It occurs in animals who have underlying disorders. This is why some flea allergies continue even when there are no fleas around.

I recommend vacuuming regularly along with the use of pyrithrin powders. There are various borax type powders on the market that have also been proven to be effective in controlling fleas. Check with your local holistic veterinarian.

Topically, plant extracts such as cedar, tea tree, eucalyptus, lavender and citronella oils are all helpful in deterring fleas. Mix 10 drops of any of these oils into 1 tablespoon olive oil and add to 1 cup of warm water, shake and spray on your animal friend.

◆ Nutritional Supplements

Vitamin C, as sodium ascorbate:
> cats/small dogs: 250 mg
> medium/large dogs: up to 1500 mg

Divide into two daily doses. Decrease dosage if diarrhea occurs.

Bioflavinoids + Quercitin. Helps to absorb Vitamin C and to decrease allergic symptoms.
> cats/small dogs: ¼ the human dose
> medium/large dogs: ½ human dose

Vitamin B supplement. Either as nutritional yeast flakes if the animal has not been on antibiotics, or in synthetic form.
> cats/small dogs: ¼ human dose
> medium/large dogs: ½ human dose

Vitamin E, as an anti-inflammatory:
> cats/small dogs: 50 IU daily
> medium dogs: 200 IU daily
> large dogs: 400 IU daily

Vitamin A, as cod liver oil: ½ to 1 teaspoon, every other day.

Seaweeds, for trace mineral content:
> cats/small dogs: ¼ teaspoon, daily
> medium/large dogs: 1 teaspoon, daily

Alfalfa for its enzymes, and vitamin content:
> cats/small dogs: ¼ teaspoon, daily
> medium/large dogs: 1 teaspoon, daily

Pancreatic Enzymes, from plant sources such as papaya. These help break down proteins into their amino acids to help digestion and to help minimize the effects of food allergies.

cats/small dogs: ⅛ to ¼ teaspoon per meal
medium/large dogs: ½ to ¾ teaspoon per meal

Co-Q 10. A cellular enzyme that helps relieve allergies:
cats/small dogs: 10 to 20 mg daily
medium/large dogs: up to 50 mg daily

Endnotes:

1. Naeser, Margaret A., PhD. *Outline Guide to Chinese Herbal Patent Medicines in Pill Form.* (Boston MA: Boston Chinese Medicine, 1990), 138.

2, 3, 4, 5, 9, 14. Fratkin, Jake. *Chinese Herbal Patent Formulas.* (Boulder, CO: Shya Publications, 1986), 182, 208, 83, 80, 82, 133.

6, 11, 12, 18. Jones, Feather. *Turtle Island Herbs Professional Guide.* Boulder, CO, 1990.

7, 10, 13, 16. Moore, Michael. *Medicinal Plants of the Mountain West.* (Santa Fe, NM: Museum of New Mexico Press, 1980), 143, 164, 129, 114.

8, 12. Pitchford, Paul. *Healing with Whole Foods.* (Berkeley, CA: North Atlantic Press, 1993), 116.

14. Lu, Henry C. *Chinese System of Food Cures.* (New York: Sterling Publishing Co., Inc., 1986), 14.

15, 17. Wood, Matthew. Herb Lectures, Batesville, IN, 1994.

CHAPTER
TWENTY-ONE

The Immune System and the Glands

The glands of the body regulate internal temperature, digestion, sexual functions, hormones, metabolism and immunity. They act like gears that intermesh with the precision of a very complex machine. If there are any malfunctions or imbalances among them, a cascade of events can occur leading to serious illness.

The glands include the tonsils, salivary glands, thymus, thyroid, adrenals, pituitary, ovaries, prostate, pancreas and lymph nodes. In Traditional Chinese Medicine, the health, balance and regulation of the glands are primarily under the auspices of the kidney yang and the triple heater. The kidney yang is the "fire aspect of the kidney" while the triple heater is one of the fire element meridians. The kidney yang is an offspring of the kidney essence or jing which governs the underlying immune system that is determined from birth (see Chapter Seventeen, page 290). The triple heater acts like middle management of the body, regulating and overseeing the smooth circulation of fluids and qi between the three heaters, or compartments of the body. The three compartments are the chest, the middle abdomen and the lower abdomen (see triple heater meridian, page 18). The triple heater plays a role in regulating the hormones as well as directing the wei qi, which is the first line of the body's immune system. The wei qi circulates just below the surface of the body, holding the environmental excesses of wind, heat, cold, bacteria and viruses at bay. The triple heater is associated with the tonsils.

The lungs and spleen/pancreas assist both the kidney and the triple heater. When there is an imbalance within any of these four organ systems, it invariably affects the liver whose job of smoothing the flow of blood and qi permeates the workings of all the organ systems. This means that the immune system as we know it in Western terms includes all five of the elements in Traditional Chinese Medicine.

Because the immune system affects all of the elements in the body, it is intimately tied to an individual's general vitality or qi. A weakening of the qi immediately impacts the immune system. Because qi is derived from the inherited kidney jing, the food we eat (spleen qi) and the air we breathe (lung qi), susceptibility to illness increases if the qi is weak. As the qi circulates the blood and lymph, it is easy to see that a failing immune system affects the body at a deep level from both an Eastern and Western point of view.

We all know what blood is. But what is lymph? Lymph carries white blood cells and substances that aid digestion and perform the task of toxic cleanup throughout the body. The lymph system has its own vessels that travel very close to regular blood vessels.

The price we all pay for high technology is the high-tech pollution in the water, the soil, the air and our food. Each of these pollutants can adversely affect the immune system and glands, creating a constant challenge to maintain health. In this section, we will look at the thyroid and the lymph system and how they relate to different types of cancer in our animal friends.

THE THYROID

The thyroid gland controls the body's rate of metabolism. It helps control the heart rate, the rate of digestion, mobility and waste removal through the digestive tract, the rate of skin cell turnover, and internal temperature. It sits on both sides of the neck near the larynx, or what in humans is the Adam's apple. Two basic imbalances occur in the thyroid — it either *under*functions, which is known as **hypo**thyroidism, or it *over*functions, which is known as **hyper**thyroidism. Either condition can stem from a malfunction in the kidney yang, spleen/pancreas or triple heater.

A hyperthyroid condition also includes aspects of an overactive and malfunctioning liver.

When food enters the stomach of a **hypothyroid** animal whose metabolism is slower, it may sit in the stomach for several hours until enough digestive juices are present to move it along into the intestinal tract. It creeps along until, finally, it reaches the large intestine. What's left of it remains here longer than it should because the animal's low energy and poor muscle tone can't easily expel it.

This is an entirely different scenario from the one in which food enters the stomach of a **hyperthyroid** animal. Its as if the food is on rollerblades. It passes through the stomach so quickly, there is barely enough time for the hydrochloric acid to get to it. As it sails through the system at top speed, only part of it is digested, absorbed or utilized. When the food skids into the large intestine, much of it is still intact, trailing mucous along with other bits and pieces of undigested food. Unprocessed stool exits the body in a gush as if traveling through the gut in fast forward.

Simply put, hypothyroid is a condition where the kidney yang, known as "Life's Fire Gate," cannot generate enough action to fire up the body. Hyperthyroid, on the other hand, is a condition where your "Life's Fire Gate," operates in overdrive all the time and burns itself up.

◆ Hypothyroid Condition

If the thyroid underfunctions, your animal friend becomes easily fatigued. Her skin dries and flakes and her hair may fall out in clumps. She might have loose, thickened darker skin, especially flabby around the tail base. Most animals with a hypothyroid condition seem to put on weight by just eyeing their food. Because of her lack of "umph," she has a hoarse or weak bark, decreased libido or inability to conceive, constipation and an aversion to cold weather. Since the thyroid sits in the upper body, it is closely related to the lungs and defends the first-line immune system. Western medicine is now linking some malfunctions of the immune system with an underfunctioning thyroid. Hypothyroidism usually occurs in middle-aged animals, but can occur in some younger, pure-bred animals, especially the Golden Retriever, Dachshund and Doberman.

◆ Treatment

Because a hypothyroid condition is considered a deficient and cold condition, treatment is aimed at warming the kidney yang and strengthening the qi and blood. Since the qi and yang are warm and keep the lymph, blood and digestion moving, supporting these aspects helps speed up metabolism and support the thyroid.

For marginally low thyroids, acupressure, herbs and diet may be all that is necessary to kick-start the thyroid. For more serious disorders, your veterinarian will prescribe medication, usually a form of synthetic thyroid. You can supplement this treatment by adding alternative therapies. Remember that just giving the thyroid doesn't really help the underlying condition which is coldness and sluggishness of the kidney, spleen/pancreas and the triple heater.

◆ Acupressure Treatment for Hypothyroid Conditions

Kidney (KI) 7. Known as "Returning Column," this point regulates the kidney yang and qi.

Location and technique: See page 306.

Conception Vessel (CV) 6. Known as the "Sea of Qi," this point strengthens the kidneys, the spleen qi and yang of the body, including the qi of the triple heater.

Location: On the abdominal midline between the umbilicus and the pelvis. If you halve the distance, this point is located about a centimeter above the halfway mark. Without exact anatomical knowledge, it will be difficult for you to locate the point precisely. Massage along the middle third of the midline, between the umbilicus and pelvis, will insure that you have treated the point.

Urinary Bladder (BL) 22. Known as "Triple Burner's Hollow," this is the association point of the triple heater and is used to balance the functions of this meridian.

Location: In the depressions of the muscles on both sides of the spine, between the first and second lumbar vertebrae. Hold the point.

Stomach (ST) 36. Known as "Three Mile Run," this point strengthens the qi of the body which directs the digestion and blood.
Location and technique: See page 219.

Urinary Bladder (BL) 13. Known as "Lung's Hollow," this is the association point of the lung and will help strengthen the upper body.
Location and technique: See page 173.

◆ Herbal Treatment

Alfalfa. With its eight digestive enzymes,[1] this Western herb supports the digestive qi and metabolism of the body.
> **Dosage,** as powder: cats/small dogs: ¼ teaspoon, twice daily
> medium dogs: ½ teaspoon, twice daily
> large dogs: ¾ teaspoon, twice daily

Fennel. This Western herb supports the kidney yang and qi and helps the stomach and spleen yang transform and transport the food in a sluggish and stagnant digestive system. Dilute 10 drops to 1 ounce distilled water.
> **Dosage,** as tincture: cats/small dogs: 1 dropperful daily
> medium dogs: 2 dropperfuls daily
> large dogs: 3 dropperfuls daily

Oats.[2] This is a tonic herb that is warming for the kidney and spleen yang, and helps with blood and qi deficiency.

◆ Nutritional Supplements

Vitamin C in moderate doses, as higher levels may interfere with the thyroid's hormone production.[3]

cats/small dogs: 125 mg, twice daily
medium/large dogs: up to 250 to 500 mg, twice daily

Vitamin B Complex, from a nutritional yeast source to aid in cell metabolism.
cats/small dogs: ½ teaspoon daily
medium/large dogs: up to 2 teaspoons daily

Essential Fatty Acids, for its assistance with the immune system, as a sluggish thyroid keeps your wei qi low to fight off infections.
cats/small dogs: ¼ human dose
medium dogs: ½ human dosage
large dogs: human dose

Kelp Powder or **Irish Moss,** for its iodine and trace mineral content:
cats/small dogs: ½ teaspoon daily
medium/large dogs: up to 1 teaspoon daily

Vitamin E: 50 to 400 IU daily.

Parsley, fresh: up to 2 tablespoons daily.

Microalgae: trace amounts for chlorophyll content to increase cellular metabolism.
cats/small dogs: ⅛ to ¼ teaspoon, daily with food
medium/large dogs: ½ to ¾ teaspoon, daily with food

Cod Liver Oil, as a source of omega-3 fish oils, and preformed **Vitamin A.** Thyroid deficient individuals may not have the capacity to convert beta-carotene to vitamin A.
cats/small dogs: ½ teaspoon daily with food
medium dogs: ¾ teaspoon daily with food
large dogs: 1 to 1½ teaspoons daily with food

◆ **Dietary Recommendations**

Because this is a sluggish, possibly moist and cold condition, foods that are neutral or warming for the spleen and kidney are beneficial. Choose from chicken, chicken liver, lamb, beef, tuna, salmon, herring or mussels among the animal proteins. Brown rice, corn, potatoes, squash, kale and cabbage are neutral or warming. Garlic may be added to increase vitality. Spices such as ginger, saffron, rosemary, cayenne pepper, cinnamon and sweet basil can be used to strengthen the qi and yang. Avoid tofu and millet as these may introduce too much moisture and coolness. Since hypothyroid individuals are usually overweight, small portions of nutritious whole foods are best.

◆ Hyperthyroid Condition

This condition, which effects mostly cats, occurs when there is an underlying excess heat and the thyroid gland gets revved up. It raises the body temperature, the heart rate and the rate of food transit through the intestinal tract. When this occurs, the food has no time to be absorbed and the cat loses weight. There is usually watery diarrhea that has a strong, offensive odor and sometimes there is mucous in the stool. There may also be vomiting if the stomach is being over activated. Your cat may not want to eat at all, or his appetite might become ravenous and unusual in an attempt to fill the void created by poor food absorption.

Jerry is a black and white cat who was once slightly overweight. Last summer during a heat spell, something happened which changed his metabolism. It seemed to coincide with the arrival of a new cat on the block who started to bully him. At first Jerry got angry, but the new cat was a terror and Jerry retreated, feeling anxious and frustrated. Jerry couldn't go to his favorite haunts because he was afraid that the new cat would appear and fight him. This made Jerry's heart race in anxiety and fear.

Since the summer, Jerry's racing heart rate has become much worse. His heart beats so hard, his person can feel it pounding through the chest wall. It has made Jerry overly sensitive about being picked up, and he no longer enjoys sitting on his person's lap. He is anxious and uncomfortable all the time now. He no longer sits in the sun because he gets too hot. Sitting outside on the fence in the open air with the wind on his face is the most tolerable. If he has to be inside, Jerry prefers a dark closet or the cool tile floor of the bathroom. Although he is restless, he is often too weak to move around.

Emotional upsets that generate internal fire, especially anger or fear, can trigger a complex set of circumstances that affect the thyroid. A precariously balanced thyroid may also be vulnerable to very hot environments or very rich, fatty foods. Hyperthyroidism is a serious advanced condition, whose detailed explanation is beyond the scope of this book. Suffice it to say that so much internal heat is generated that the heart and liver overpower the rest of the organs so that the animal cannot function normally. It is a life threatening situation and requires professional veterinary care. Holistic veterinarians do have alternatives to offer or add to traditional Western treatments.

◆ Dietary Recommendations

Choose neutral foods such as beef, cod, eggs, chicken gizzards, brown rice, polenta, string beans, aduki beans, lentils, kidney beans, potatoes or yams. Cooling foods can be used especially if the cat is agitated and irritable. These include barley, millet, whole wheat bread, clams, celery and spinach. Avoid high-fat diets, as fats are difficult for the body to break down. Proportions should be 40% animal protein source, 50% grain and 10% vegetables. Remember that with this condition the cat is often so voracious, he will probably eat anything, so try to give him foods that can be easily digested and readily absorbed. Include pancreatic enzymes which aid digestion. If crunchiness is desired, use rice cakes with millet broken into moist food. If the cat won't eat fresh foods, try the rice cakes crumbled into canned food.

THE LYMPH SYSTEM AND CANCER

In Traditional Chinese Medicine, the lymph is part of the yin fluids and is guided by all the meridians, especially by the spleen/pancreas. The lymph drains into and through its own storage houses called lymph nodes. When the body is confronted with infections or toxins, the lymph system circulates cells to fight the invading pathogens. The lymph system also filters our body's toxic waste.

There are lymph nodes in each region of the body and these are served by the meridians that serve that particular area. Lymph nodes congregate in the neck and throat, and swell up during ear, tooth or throat infections. The meridians that serve this region include the stomach, large and small intestine and triple heater. The next set is under the arm in the axillary region. These are under the influence of the liver, gall bladder, stomach and spleen. Lymph nodes are also found in the chest, around the wind pipe, bronchi and lungs. These are under the guidance of the lungs and the kidney yang. The next major set of lymph nodes are found in the abdomen which drain the intestines. The meridians involved here are the spleen, stomach, liver and kidney yang. The lymph nodes in the groin area are drained by the liver and spleen/pancreas meridians, while those behind the knee are serviced mostly by the kidney.

An animal who tends to get sick often has a weakened immune system. Frequent colds, sinusitis, asthma or bronchitis all weaken the lung qi. Urinary bladder infections weaken the kidney qi. Digestive flus, vomiting, diarrhea or colitis weaken the spleen/pancreas or stomach qi. Conversely, if any of these organs is already weak, it makes the individual vulnerable to attack by pathogens.

Lymph, like blood, needs regular drainage and constant, even circulation. This requires the healthy functioning of the spleen/pancreas. When the circulation is impeded, stagnation develops. This creates a blockage which acts like a plugged sink drain. When an individual has a chronically swollen gland, it makes the meridians serving that area work harder. Longtime overwork can fatigue the qi and make an individual susceptible to further infections.

Cancer doesn't just happen. It is a progressive form of immune imbalance. An individual's immune system, including the kidney, spleen/pancreas, triple heater, lung and liver channels, have usually been out of balance for a considerable period of time before cancer develops. If cancer develops as a tumor that forms within an organ, there has been a blockage of energy there for some time, affecting the meridan serving that area. The only signs the animal may show are fatigue, chronic digestive or respiratory disorders or a continually swollen gland. Many of our animal friends are good at hiding their imbalances and it takes a trained veterinary investigator or holistic practitioner to locate the problem.

CANCER, TUMORS AND ENTANGLED QI

Chronic problems can cause the qi to flow irregularly. If the qi becomes "entangled," the liver, whose job it is to smoothly circulate the blood and qi, malfunctions. The result is that an energetic or qi blockage turns into a "solid" physical blockage. Qi stagnation progresses to a substance type blockage of "blood" and "phlegm." Phlegm is fluid that heats up from stagnation and becomes sticky and tenacious, like pudding. This sticky substance accumulates in the tissues. The accumulation forms into a lump that can become a tumor. The harder the tumor, the longer and tougher the stagnation and blockage has been present and the harder it is to remove.

In other words, TCM believes that cancerous tumors develop as a result of a long-standing energy blockage that was originally caused by an imbalance along the meridians and between their organs. Since the qi and the blood and fluids of the body are so intimately linked, the more chronic the qi or energy blockage, the greater the chance for the circulation to become stagnant. Stagnant blood creates a tumor.

Problems associated with the blood, like anemia, or high or low white blood cell counts, relate to the organs associated with making and storing the blood, that is, the spleen/pancreas, kidney, and liver. So Traditional Chinese Medicine treats these organs to help with blood problems. Cancer of the blood or lymph nodes, such as leukemia or lymphoma also involve the blood-making and storing organs. The appearance of abnormal cells or a lack of normal cells can be caused by any of these organ systems going awry. Just as tumors develop from a chronic problem of qi stagnation, blood cancers develop from an imbalance within the kidney, spleen/pancreas or liver and how they interact.

◆ Cancer and Stress

One of the biggest health problems of the twentieth century is *stress*. Stress is emotional imbalance. Stress can manifest as anger, frustration or anxiety. These emotions overwork the liver which, when it has been insulted, tends to heat up or stagnate.

Stagnation can create tumors. Heat uses up fluids in the body and affects the blood production and circulation. Because the liver stores the blood, the blood stores may become depleted if the liver is overly taxed.

How can an animal become stressed? Simply by living with humans for one thing. Since an animal provides companionship, relaxation, recreation and love, the human's stress level always affects the animal. Dogs and cats handle their human's stress in different ways. Cats are like emotional sponges. Those of you who live with cats know that whenever you are upset, your feline friend will try to curl up in your lap to make you feel better by absorbing your distress. Dogs will try to break up an argument or distract us from our unhappy feelings by asking us to pet them or inviting us to play.

Other forms of stress may arise in a multiple animal household where personalities clash, shared litter boxes become dirty, or access to the outdoors to eliminate is denied. Your work schedule may keep your dog inside for long hours, crossing her legs so as not to have an accident in the house. Lack of adequate exercise can frustrate the athletic or hyperactive animal, and sheer boredom can make the sofa cushions start to look very tempting to the normally well-behaved animal.

◆ Directing a Healthy Immune System

We all want to keep our immune systems and those of our animals healthy. Acupressure, massage, regular exercise, good diet and nutritional supplements help. Daily massage with your animal can alert you to any unusual lumps or bumps. Massage at the diagnostic points indicated in Chapter Five, on the Traditional Chinese Exam, page 44, can detect an early sensitivity associated with a meridian or organ system. Massage along with exercise also helps decrease the tendency toward stagnation and keep the blood and lymph moving smoothly. The freer the circulation, the less chance there is for the body to form lumps, bumps and swellings.

Of course, whenever you find any unusual lumps or swellings on your animal friend, particularly if accompanied by any changes in her behavior, eating habits, elimination habits or drastic change in weight, always consult your veterinarian immediately. It really is true that an ounce of prevention is worth a pound of cure, and early detection of serious problems is the next best thing.

◆ Acupressure for Immune Support and Stress-Related Disorders

Research has shown that certain acupoints increase white and red blood cell production and stimulate the immune response which clear toxins from the body. Acupuncture does this by causing the body to set up a chain of events that release such substances as hormones, neurotransmitters, ion exchanges, antibodies, antihistamines and interferon.[4] These cell transmitters ease the movement of the pathogens or abnormal cells across the cell walls into the blood and lymph system to be removed from the body.

The acupoints that enhance the operations of the immune system are:[4]
Large Intestine (LI) 4 Known as "Adjoining Valleys," this point stimulates the immune response by increasing white blood cell production and activity to clear toxins. It increases interferon production which is helpful in fighting viral infections.[4] It can be used during an acute outbreak, to lower fever and, preventatively, to keep the lymph system functioning and support the wei qi.
Location: See page 152.

Large Intestine (LI)11. Known as "Crooked Pool," this point can be used to increase white blood cell production and to clear toxins, as with **Large Intestine 4**. It is also good for reducing fevers.
Location: See page 156.

Stomach (ST) 36. Known as "Three Mile Run," this point strengthens the qi in the entire body, fostering the wei qi, stimulating white blood cell production[5] and helping the spleen and stomach.
Location: See page 219.

Spleen (SP) 6. Known as the "Three Yin Junction," this point helps the fluid and blood of the body. The three yins of the leg are the meridians of the kidney, spleen/pancreas and liver. Since the blood is the mother of the qi, it helps strengthen blood movement and qi. It is especially useful in illness with diarrhea, vomiting and weight loss.
Location: See page 153.

Pericardium (PC) 6. Known as "The Inner Gate," this point increases white blood cell production,[5] especially when used with **Stomach 36.** It is useful in problems with anxiety and nausea, especially following chemotherapy.
Location: See page 241.

Conception Vessel (CV) 12. Known as "Middle Cavity," this is the alarm point of the stomach which balances and strengthens the qi derived from food. It enhances the immune response, especially with problems in the stomach and upper gastrointestinal tract. It also helps drain regional lymph nodes.
Location: See page 229.

Governing Vessel (GV) 14. Known as "Big Vertebra," this point stimulates the circulation of white blood cells to help clear toxins. It also reduces fever and is especially useful in acute infections.
Location: See page 166.

Kidney (KI) 3. Known as "Great Creek," this is the source point of the kidney and so is in direct communication with the kidney which regulates the immune system. This point is good for anemia, leukemia, bone marrow problems and dehydration.
Location: See page 187.

Urinary Bladder (BL) 23. Known as "Kidney's Hollow," this is the association point of the kidney and stimulates the immune response. It is used just like **Kidney 3**, page 387.

Location: See page 189.

Important note on the technique to use: The technique to use for all of the above points is to hold the point or to use small circular motion for no more than 15 seconds. Choose three points at a time, according to the needs of the animal. If the animal is very weak, just treat one point at a time. The animal can receive treatment once or twice daily for short periods of time.

Points are chosen during an active infection, to help fight the infection, and between infections to help strengthen the immune system and the individual in general. For example, **Large Intestine 11** and **Governing Vessel 14** might be chosen during an outbreak of a cold with fever, while **Stomach 36** and **Large Intestine 4** might be chosen to strengthen after the incident.

AFTER CHEMOTHERAPY OR RADIATION

If your animal has undergone chemotherapy or radiation treatments, he will be in a depleted state. These therapies may have saved his life, but they play havoc with the immune and digestive systems. It is important to remember that although the cancer has been reduced or even eliminated, the underlying cause may not have been addressed. When I see animals who have had their spleens removed from hemangiosarcomas, the imbalance between the spleen/pancreas and liver or kidney is still present, even though the spleen is absent. If the imbalance goes untreated, cancer in another organ may develop.

Acupressure and herbs can be helpful during your animal's convalescent period. Choose from the points listed above, including **Pericardium 6** for nausea and as an appetite stimulant, **Conception Vessel 12** for vomiting, gas, depressed appetite and stomach pain, **Spleen 6** for diarrhea or bloating and **Stomach 36** for general energy strengthening.

Herbs which help the immune system are broken down into two main groups. The first clears infection, while the second strengthens or tonifies the immune system and the organs that serve it.

The infection fighting herbs are considered heat clearing in TCM terms. They are used during an active infection, with or without fever. In some cases, they can be used in smaller doses between infections to help prevent infections from recurring. Some of the herbs have antiviral as well as antibacterial properties.

The tonic herbs are used to help bolster or nourish the individual. They can be used after bouts of infection, after surgery, chemotherapy, radiation treatment or with chronic wasting problems that leave an individual weak or thin. The tonic herbs strengthen the qi, the blood and the yin fluids.

◆ Heat-Clearing Herbs Used for Fighting Infection

Echinacea purpurea and Angustifolia.[6] This Western herb stimulates the immune response to fight infection. It is good for mouth sores, swollen glands, tonsillitis, upper respiratory infections, bite wounds and viral infections. In humans, it has been found that it's effectiveness is dose-related, and higher doses are needed during acute infections, as compared to preventative use. During active infection, mix 25 to 30 drops in 1 ounce distilled water.

Dosage: 1 to 3 dropperfuls, two to three times daily, depending upon the size of the animal and the intensity of the symptoms. Duration of treatment is from 10 to 14 days for acute infections. It can be used for up to one month for chronic infections at this dosage, then lower to preventative dosages.

For prevention between infections, in the face of exposure to other animals with infections, or to stimulate the immune response, dilute 10 drops to 1 ounce distilled water.

Dosage: cats /small dogs: 1 to 2 dropperfuls, once or twice daily
               medium/large dogs: 2 to 3 dropperfuls, once or twice daily

Calendula.[7] This Western herb cleans the lymphatic system. It is good for acute and chronic infections, with and without lymph node swelling. It has bitter, sweet, salty and pungent qualities[8] which means that it has an affinity for spleen, kidney, lung and heart meridians. It works especially hard at strengthening the spleen/pancreas and balancing it with the liver. Calendula helps to heal lacerations and tissue wounds, especially in those patients with weakened or tired immune systems.

Mix 15 drops to 1 ounce distilled water

Dosage: 1 to 3 dropperfuls, two to three times daily, depending upon the size of the animal or severity of the problem.

Golden Seal.[9] This Western herb clears heat and dampness. It acts like an antibiotic and helps to curtail excessive bleeding. Use for up to two weeks only, as it can damage the flora of the colon over longer periods of time. It is especially helpful for dysentary type disorders, anal gland abscesses and fissures, as well as reproductive disorders.

Dosage, as powder: cats/small dogs: # 3 capsule, 2 to 3 times daily
medium dogs: # 1 capsule, 2 to 3 times daily
large dogs: # 00 capsule, 2 to 3 times daily

Inmortal.[10] This Western herb is known in the Spanish and native cultures of New Mexico for lung problems, including chronic bronchitis and asthma. It will help drain lymph nodes in both the upper body and those affecting the respiratory system.

Dosage: In humans, it is recommended to boil ½ teaspoon of the root in water, but animals won't tolerate the bitter taste. Try the tincture at 5 to 10 drops to 1 ounce distilled water, dosing at 1 to 3 dropperfuls once to twice daily, depending upon the size of the animal or severity of the problem.

Dandelion and Burdock Roots.[11] Both of these herbs help to clear liver circulation and toxins. It is helpful with fluid buildup in the chest and abdomen. These are mild herbs and are usually tolerated by most animals.

Mix 8 drops of each to 1 ounce distilled water. Use 1 to 3 droppers twice daily, depending upon the size of the animal.

Red Root.[12] Red root clears toxins and drains lymph nodes in the lower body. It is useful in prostate, uterine, and vaginal areas, as well as for engorged swollen inguinal lymph nodes. It also helps to relieve spleen swelling.

Mix 10 drops of tincture to 1 ounce of distilled water. Use 1 to 3 dropperfuls twice daily, depending upon the size of the animal. Use for up to one month.

Milk Thistle.[13] This herb helps to restore liver and gall bladder function. It is particularly helpful after bouts of lipidosis, hepatitis and toxins accumulated through fever. Milk thistle also strengthens the blood cell wall, so is recommended for ulcers and healing tissues in the body in general. Milk thistle can therefore be used as both an infection fighter and a tonifying herb.

Mix 10 drops tincture to 1 ounce distilled water, using 1 to 3 droppers twice daily, depending upon the size of the animal.

◆ Herbs to Strengthen the Individual and Enhance Immunity

Astragalus.[14] This Chinese herb has become reknowned in the West for helping to treat cancer. Astragalus contains flavones, which help circulation and blood production. Because it enhances circulation, it helps prevent stagnation which can cause tumors to form. Astragalus also contains polysaccharides which helps to inhibit tumor formation. It has been shown to increase strength, stamina and digestion after chemotherapy and radiation treatment, and to increase survival rates in cancer patients after these treatments.

In TCM terms, astragalus is a qi tonic. It is good for food absorption, normalizing urination and blood production. Use twice daily.

Dosage, as powder: cats/small dogs: #2 capsule (⅛ to ¼ teaspoon)
medium dogs: #0 capsule
large dogs: #00 capsule

American or Siberian Ginseng. These are the "cooler" ginsengs, rather than the "warmer" Korean Red Ginseng. Ginseng is a qi tonic which helps to build stamina and strength and is good for general health and stress reduction. It may be a good idea to give it to your animals if you leave them at home or in a kennel while you are on vacation. It is considered an "adaptogen"[15] helping to normalize blood pressure, fluid balance, and to strengthen heart and body muscle. It is also useful in diabetes to stabilize thirst and appetite.

> **Dosage** as for astragalus, page 391.

Shen Qi Da Bu Wan.[16] This Chinese patent herb contains two qi tonics: astragalus and codonopsis. It helps to stimulate appetite and decrease thirst. It is especially good for FeLV or FIV cats.

> **Dosage:** cats/small dogs: 1 to 2 pills, twice daily
> medium dogs: 3 pills, twice daily
> large dogs: 5 pills, twice daily

Liu Wei Di Huang Wan. This is the classic kidney formula, useful to restore blood and energy of the kidney and spleen/pancreas. See ingredients and dosage in Chapter Seventeen, page 296.

Women's Precious Pills.[17] Also known as "Eight Treasure Tea," this is a blood and qi tonic used for weight loss and general debility. It contains the blood tonics of tang kuei, rehmannia, peony; the blood activator, ligusticum; and the qi tonics of codonopsis, hoelen, atractylodes and licorice.

> **Dosage:** cats/small dogs: 2 pills, twice daily
> medium dogs: 4 pills, twice daily
> large dogs: 6 pills, twice daily

AUTOIMMUNE DISEASE

Autoimmune disease occurs when an animal's immune system goes awry, mistaking it's own healthy cells for pathogens of some kind. In the confusion, the immune system begins to attack and destroy the body's own cells. The end result is tissue breakdown, inflammation and pain and eventually, greater vulnerability to other opportunistic pathogens.

In some cases anemia develops, because the cells the body sees as toxic are really its own red blood cells. An example of such an immune mediated problem in the blood is *thrombocytopenia*, which develops in purebred dogs such as Weimaraners, Dobermans and Standard Poodles. Breakdown of the red blood cells cause hemorrhage and anemia. Autoimmune problems can also act as arthritis that comes on suddenly, causing swelling and sometimes travelling from joint to joint as in systemic *lupus erythematosis*.

In each case, the problem occurs where your animal is most vulnerable. So, in Traditional Chinese Medicine, if the blood is being attacked, the underlying responsible organs are the kidney, spleen/pancreas and liver. If the joints are being attacked, the weakness probably lies within the liver and kidney. If the skin is under attack and ulcers form, the kidney, lung and spleen/pancreas are out of balance.

For treatment, choose from the general immune acupressure points listed earlier in this chapter and locate the primary symptoms in Chapters Fifteen, Sixteen and Seventeen.

FELINE LEUKEMIA VIRUS (FeLV) AND FELINE INFECTIOUS VIRUS (FIV)

Both the Feline Leukemia Virus and its newer companion, the Feline Infectious Virus, can devastate a cat's immune system. In both cases, as with any infectious illness, the individual animal must be susceptible or vulnerable in order to get sick. Many animals are exposed to these viruses but their immune systems are able to fight them off. This means that those who succumb are already in a weakened condition, either through stress, poor nutrition or inherited factors of weak kidney jing or lung qi.

Once an animal becomes infected, if she withstands the initial, acute onset of the disease, she is left with an impaired immune system that may not be able to combat other infections. Therefore, it is important to strengthen the immune system on an ongoing basis.

During or between acute bouts, acupressure points to modulate the immune system, as listed on pages 386–88, are helpful adjuncts to any treatment schedule. The acupressure points listed for encouraging the production of white blood cells, such as **Stomach 36**, page 219, **and Pericardium 6**, page 241, are especially useful during the periods of time between outbreaks of fevers. Points such as **Large Intestine 11**, page 156, and **Governing Vessel 14**, page 166, are useful in reducing fevers. Fevers act to heat up the body in an attempt to overpower the virus and eliminate it. Long-standing fevers, however, indicate that the individual is not strong enough to get rid of the virus, but keeps trying.

Points such as **Spleen 6**, page 153, **Liver 3**, page 241, **Large Intestine 4**, page 152, **Kidney 3**, page 187, and **Stomach 36**, page 219, help to restore blood, yin and qi to the body. Many animals live long, normal lives as carriers of the virus once the immune system adjusts.

◆ Nutritional Supplements for the Immune System

Recently, more Western practitioners are looking into vitamins, minerals and antioxidants to fight cancer. This is probably due to the fact that two out of five humans have developed, or will develop cancer during the 90s.[18] In our animal population, cancer is also on the rise. Since I began practicing in 1978, the number of cancer cases I see has grown astronomically.

It is much easier to use vitamins and nutritional supplements, along with a good diet as a *preventative* measure, before the immune system comes under attack. Once the immune system is out of balance, supplementation becomes an essential adjunct to life.

Antioxidants are substances that help clear toxins from the body at the cellular and blood levels. They are intracellular, such as superoxide dismutase or extracellular, such as vitamins C and E. (See arthritis in Chapter Nineteen, pages 349–51.)

Vitamin C, as sodium ascorbate. Doses are as high as possible with diarrhea being the limiting factor.

> cats/small dogs: 500 mg, twice daily
> medium dogs: 1,000 mg, twice daily
> large dogs: 2,000 mg, twice daily

Bioflavonoids with Quercitin. These help in the absorption of vitamin C, and reduce allergic reactions. They are especially useful in respiratory problems including allergic asthma and bronchitis.

> ⅓ to ¾ recommended human dose

Vitamin E with Selenium. Vitamin E acts as an anti-inflammatory, decreasing swelling in the joints and musculoskeletal system, as well as softening and moistening the skin. Selenium helps with absorption and increases the effectiveness of the E. Use once daily.

> cats/small dogs: 50 IU E, with 5 to 10 mcg selenium
> medium dogs: 100 to 200 IU E, with 20 to 25 mcg selenium
> large dogs: 400 IU E, with 50 mcg selenium

Vitamin A with mixed carotenes, including Beta-Carotene. This vitamin is especially good for the respiratory mucosa, helping in sinusitis and lung problems. Since it is a fat-soluble vitamin, over-dosage can be a problem if there is an unhealthy liver.

> cats/small dogs: 2,000 mg daily
> medium dogs: 5,000 mg daily
> large dogs: 10,000 mg daily

Vitamin A along with omega 3 rich oils can be found in cod liver oil which is a good alternative to synthetic vitamin A.

Microalgae. Algae in general is highly nutritious, containing large amounts of chlorophyll which decrease bacteria and clear toxins from the body.[19] Cats seem especially sensitive to the algae, causing digestive upsets in some, including diarrhea or depressed appetite.

Dosage for cats and dogs can be quite minimal and still produce positive effects, from as low as ¹⁄₁₆ to ⅛ teaspoon, or just "a pinch" in the food.

Vitamin B Complex, including B₁₂. This can be from nutritional yeast flakes if the animal is not on antibiotics, or from a non-yeast source if antibiotics have been used.

> cats/small dogs: ¼ human dose
> medium/large dogs: ½ human dose

Kelp Powder or other seaweeds. The trace minerals are essential to cell function, including magnesium which aids in calcium absorption for strong bones.

> cats/small dogs: ⅛ teaspoon daily
> medium/large dogs: ½ teaspoon daily

Acidophilus and Bifidus combinations repopulate the intestines with essential flora. If the intestinal flora is overpopulated with good microbes, there is no room for toxic flora to abound.

> cats/small dogs: ¼ human dose
> medium/large dogs: ½ human dose

Super Oxide Dismutase and other antioxidants such as catalase and peroxidase. These intracellular antioxidants remove toxins from the body that are stored within the cells. They are especially good for helping to clear the liver and joint surfaces.

> Dosage is according to the specific veterinary product.

Essential Fatty Acids. These convert into prostaglandins, known as PGE₁ which activate the immune system and help fight cancer, as well as removing toxins and regulating autoimmune diseases. Available through your veterinarian in appropriate dosages.

New approaches to cancer and immune enhancement are in the forefront of the nutritional supplement industry. Check with your local natural food stores on a regular basis, as well as your holistic veterinarian.

◆ Dietary Recommendations

Diet is probably *the* most important factor in aiding the immune system. Our emphasis on convenience when feeding ourselves and our animal friends may have led to the increase in immune problems, including cancer. Feeding from a bag or a can lacks vitality. When the immune system is weakened it needs fresh foods to restimulate it.

One of the first things to avoid are foods with preservatives such as ethoxyquin and BHA, both shown in European studies to be carcinogenic. If you are feeding only commercial foods, supplement this diet with natural, whole foods. Whole grains are rich and balanced sources of magnesium and phosphorus, as well as fiber. Some practitioners advocate mixing grains that represent each of the Five Elements in order to rebalance the body. Equal amounts of cooked brown rice, corn or polenta, barley, millet, rye flakes and oats, would be a balanced mixture of grains. The corn and rice are sweet and neutral, helping the spleen, stomach, large intestine and heart. The rye is bitter and neutral, drying dampness and serving the heart. The barley and millet are cooling, being salty and sweet, with a downward direction, and serving the kidney and stomach. The oats are warming and sweet, serving the spleen, stomach, heart and general qi. Whole wheat can be added to nourish the liver.

Steamed and raw vegetables are good adjuncts, as they are rich in trace minerals, chlorophyll and have fluid-supporting properties. Vegetables such as carrots, broccoli, beets, kale, greens, cabbage and sweet potatoes are excellent for immune impaired individuals.

Fresh fish, especially sardines, are good sources of essential fatty acids and easily utilized proteins. Meat from free-range animals, not injected with hormones or antibiotics, builds jing essence and muscle mass and supports the qi and blood. Meat is especially important after an animal has undergone chemotherapy or radiation. Broths and soups made with meat and bones are easily digested.

For dogs whose weight is adequate, a more vegetarian diet is helpful with small amounts of meat. Supplementing protein with legumes such as lentils or aduki beans provides fiber and complex vegetable protein. I do not recommend that cats be given vegetarian diets, as they require more meat than dogs. However, reducing the amount of meat somewhat may be beneficial.

For specific organ system involvment, please check the different sections for dietary recommendations. For dietary guidelines in general, check Chapter Seven.

Finally, what is most important is that you give love with every meal and every treatment. Let your animal friend know you care. The intention for healing plays an important role in the process.

Animals give us so much just by being themselves, and ask for so little in return. We expect them to adapt completely to our world, and sometimes they are the worse for it. The very least we can do is give them the best that we can, in both sickness and in health.

Endnotes

1, 2, 8. Holmes, Peter. *The Energetics of Western Herbs, Vol. I & II.* (Boulder, CO: Artemis Press, 1989), 370, 360, 565.

3. Balch, James. F., MD., P. A. Balch. *Prescription for Nutritional Healing.* (Garden City Park, NY: Avery Publishing Group, 1990), 213.

4. Schoen, Allen M., DVM, MS. *Veterinary Acupuncture, Ancient Art to Modern Medicine.* (Goleta, CA: American Veterinary Publishers, 1994), 243–67.

5. Schoen, Allen M., DVM, MS. Lectures, Veterinary Acupuncture Certifcation Course. Atlanta, GA, 1994.

6. Hobbs, C. Echinacea: A Literature Review, *Herbal Gram*, No. 30, Winter, 1994, 38–41.

7. Wood, Matthew. Herb Lectures, Batesville, IN, 1994.

9. Tierra, Michael, CA, ND. *Planetary Herbology.* (Santa Fe, NM: Lotus Press, 1988), 192.

10, 12. Moore, Michael. *Medicinal Herbs of the Mountain West.* (Santa Fe, NM: Museum of New Mexico Press, 1979), 89,140.

11, 13. Jones, Feather. *Turtle Island Herb Practitioner Guide.* Boulder, CO, 1990.

14. Dharmananda, Subhuti, PhD. *Chinese Herbal Therapies for Immune Disorders.* (Portland, OR: Institute for Traditional Medicine & Preventive Health Care, 1988), 28.

15. Leung, Albert Y. *Chinese Herbal Remedies.*(New York: Universe Books, 1984), 77–78.

16. Naeser, Margaret, A., PhD. *Outline Guide to Chinese Herbal Patent Medicines in Pill Form.* (Boston, MA: Boston Chinese Medicine, 1990), 286.

17. Fratkin, Jake. *Chinese Herbal Patent Formulas.* (Boulder, CO: Shya Publications, 1986), 178.

18. *Nutrition Action Newsletter,* January 1995.

19. Pitchford, Paul. *Healing with Whole Foods.* (Berkeley, CA: North Atlantic Books, 1993), 189.

Index

Italic letters refer to plates. **Boldface page numbers** indicate discussions of acupressure point locations.